# Call Center Leadership and Business Management Handbook and Study Guide

*Version 2.1*

**Brad Cleveland and Debbie Harne**
**Editors**

*Part of ICMI's Handbook/Study Guide Series*

Published by:
Call Center Press
A Division of ICMI, Inc.
Post Office Box 6177
Annapolis, Maryland 21401 USA

Notice of Liability
This handbook/study guide is designed to provide information in regard to the subject matter covered. The purpose of this publication is to educate. While every precaution has been taken in the preparation of this handbook/study guide, neither the authors nor Call Center Press (a division of ICMI, Inc.) shall have any liability or responsibility to any person or entity with respect to any loss or damage caused, or alleged to be caused, directly or indirectly by the information contained in the publication. If you do not wish to be bound by this, you may return this book to the publisher for a full refund.


Printed in the United States of America
ISBN 0-9709507-7-2

# Call Center
# Leadership and Business Management Handbook and Study Guide

*Version 2.1*

**Brad Cleveland and Debbie Harne**
**Editors**

*Part of ICMI's Handbook/Study Guide Series*

Call Center Press
*A Division of ICMI, Inc.*

## Acknowledgements

The publications in this series are the result of a lot of hard work on the part of many people. **We would like** to thank the following individuals for their contributions:

Gerry Barber
Jean Bave-Kerwin
Michael Blair
Lori Bocklund
Henry Dortmans
Mike Dunne
Rebecca Gibson
John Goodman
Cindy Grimm
Linda Harden
Susan Hash
Cheryl Helm
Ellen Herndon
Ted Hopton
Betty Layfield
Jill Leigh
Greg Levin
Don McCain
Teresa Metzler
Jay Minnucci
Tim Montgomery
Rose Polchin
Paul Pope
Laurie Solomon
Wanda Sitzer

Without their hard work, dedication and talents, this project would not have been possible!

Brad Cleveland and Debbie Harne
Editors

To Sophia, may the little things in life continue to bring you joy.

Debbie Harne

To Kirsten, thank you for your unfailing love and support.
And to Grace Elizabeth Cleveland (born August 2002); Grace means God's love, and you truly are!

Brad Cleveland

# Call Center
# Leadership and Business Management Handbook and Study Guide

*Version 2.1*

**Brad Cleveland and Debbie Harne**
**Editors**

*Part of ICMI's Handbook/Study Guide Series*

## Contents

# Section 1

# *Introduction*

Thank you for purchasing this publication – we hope it provides you with solid information that helps you advance your organization and your career! Although designed to stand alone, it is one of an integrated, four-part series, which includes:

- Call Center People Management Handbook and Study Guide
- Call Center Operations Management Handbook and Study Guide
- Call Center Customer Relationship Management Handbook and Study Guide
- Call Center Leadership and Business Management Handbook and Study Guide

The series was originally developed to prepare call center professionals for CIAC Certification assessments (and it follows the CIAC competency model and format, providing 100 percent coverage of CIAC competencies for both strategic and operational levels). However, many people have told us they are using the guides for internal training programs, team meetings and general reference. Content is sliced into digestible servings of information that lend themselves to these uses.

If you have received training from ICMI in the past, you will see some familiar diagrams and explanations. We have compiled information from ICMI courses, books and *Call Center Management Review* to develop an effective resource. We encourage you to be creative so you get the most out of this material.

However you plan to use the series, we hope it will also serve as an introduction (or re-introduction) to Incoming Calls Management Institute (ICMI) and the many content areas in which we can provide training and consulting services. We've included a summary of ICMI's products and services, but be sure to visit www.incoming.com for the latest offerings.

If we can assist you in any way, please let us know. We welcome your comments, feedback and questions, so let us know how we can help you.

Best wishes,

Brad Cleveland
President and CEO
ICMI, Inc.
bradc@incoming.com

Debbie Harne
Director, Educational Services
ICMI, Inc.
debbieh@incoming.com

Section 2

# *If You Are Pursuing Certification*

If you are pursuing CIAC certification, congratulations on your decision to increase your skills and knowledge in the area of Leadership and Business Management. As you prepare for CIAC assessments, you will learn valuable information to help you succeed in your profession.

We have worked hard to provide you with a handbook/study guide that is clear, concise and complete. Since each of us has a different set of past experiences and training, there will be some topics that you know well and others with which you may be unfamiliar. This guide is intended to meet a variety of needs by providing summary review information, as well as reference lists for further study. We encourage you to use it in whatever way works best for you. (Please remember that all material is either owned and copyrighted to ICMI or has been used with permission and noted as such; any reproduction of this material by any means is strictly prohibited.)

The remainder of this section includes the following:



## ICMI's Role with the Call Center Industry Advisory Council (CIAC)

Incoming Calls Management Institute (ICMI) is an independent think tank and membership organization that specializes in call center management research, education, publications and consulting. While ICMI co-founded the CIAC in 1997, the CIAC is now a nonprofit organization consisting of an elected body to represent the industry in certification matters. ICMI is independent of the CIAC and does not control the quality or administration of the CIAC certification process.

## CIAC Certification Options – Strategic vs. Operational

The CIAC certification assessments are delivered at both the operational and strategic levels:

- Managers with tactical, day-to-day operational responsibilities will generally choose to take the operational level exams, and are certified with the CIAC Certified Operations Manager (CCOM) designation. The operational role competencies are also applicable to individuals pursuing certification as a CIAC Certified Management Apprentice (CCMA).
- Managers with higher-level, strategic responsibilities will generally choose to take the strategic level exams, and are certified with the CIAC Certified Strategic Leader (CCSL) designation. The strategic role competencies are also applicable to individuals pursuing certification as a CIAC Certified Management Consultant (CCMC).

This handbook/study guide is designed to prepare you for either the operational (CCOM or CCMA) or strategic (CCSL or CCMC) level of certification. If you are pursuing operational level certification, you can skip over the topics labeled strategic. If you are pursuing strategic level certification, you will need to be knowledgeable in all areas of the study guide. For each certification level, we have included an outline of the competencies and the contents of this guide. The strategic outline begins on page 5; the operational outline begins on page 9.

Note: In many call centers, the line between what is strategic and what is operational is becoming increasingly blurry as distinctions between job roles fade. In short, we encourage managers in operational roles to also acquire an understanding of strategic issues.

## How to Get the Most From Your Handbook/Study Guide

To get the most out of this guide, we'd like to explain how it works. In the pages that follow, you will find the CIAC Leadership and Business Management competency outlines, as well as information on ICMI services. We hope these assist you in understanding CIAC certification and the ways in which ICMI can support you in achieving your certification goals.

The CIAC Leadership and Business Management competency outlines provide the competencies and where they are covered in this study guide. We have carefully structured each section to cover the required material in the most logical manner. The material is presented in a building-block fashion for review purposes, and does not always flow in the same order as the competency model.

Sections three through seven include the content for the assessment. Each section is divided into topics that are organized as follows:

- Subject
- Key Points
- Explanation
- Exercise (in the back of each section)
- References for further study (in the back of each section)

This structure is designed to give you the flexibility to spend as much or as little time studying each topic as you require. The boxes on the top right of each topic are available for you to perform a self-assessment. Read through the key points to determine if your understanding of the material is:

[1] unfamiliar territory, more time is needed here
[2] pretty good, but worth reviewing
[3] excellent

You can then review your self-assessment to focus your study time in the areas that need it the most. To complete a self-assessment of all topics at once, see page 11 of this introduction.

We've provided article reprints and other materials including a comprehensive glossary in sections eight and nine. Each section provides references for further study. These are intended to give you more detailed information on areas that you may have limited knowledge. We hope you'll continue to use this material for ongoing self-development.

The goals of the *Call Center Leadership and Business Management Handbook and Study Guide* are:

- Increase learners' knowledge and skills regarding leadership and business management in call centers
- Prepare candidates to pass the CIAC certification knowledge assessment for Module Four, Leadership and Business Management

The learning objectives of the *Call Center Leadership and Business Management Handbook and Study Guide* include the ability of the learner to:

1. Recognize, identify, discuss, and/or list key leadership and business management concepts, principles, and processes related to:
   - Strategy and valuation
   - Leadership and communication
   - The call center business environment
   - Business management principles and practices
   - Financial principles and practices
2. Apply key leadership and business management concepts, principles, and processes to call center situations

## Assessment Information

CIAC certification exams assess knowledge, skills and abilities in each competency domain. Candidates demonstrate role-specific knowledge and skills, and the application of these on the job through an objective assessment and work products.

This guide is intended to prepare you for the objective assessment. The objective assessment is composed entirely of multiple-choice questions. Some questions simply involve selecting from a list of possibilities to determine the correct answer, to the stated question. Other questions may require you to select the choice that is not true or the exception, select the choice that is the best or least correct answer, or select all of the correct answers from a list of choices. Multiple-choice questions also are included that require the interpretation of tables, charts or scenarios to determine the correct answer.

Your handbook/study guide includes exercises in many different formats, such as fill in the blank, multiple choice, and matching, with the answers to the exercises included in Section 10. These exercises are intended to help you determine your readiness to take the CIAC exam.

The specific questions on the CIAC assessments have been developed and validated by a diverse team of industry professionals. As an independent organization, ICMI provides educational services for the assessments, but is not responsible for the quality of the test questions.

For more information:

- See the CIAC Certification Handbook in Section 11
- See www.ciac-cert.org
- See www.incoming.com

# The CIAC Leadership and Business Management Competency Outline – Strategic Level

This document maps the content of this study guide with CIAC leadership and business management competencies. In order to produce a study guide that is easy to use and understand, we have presented the contents of each section in building-block fashion. Therefore, contents may be presented in a different order than in the competency list. We have taken care to ensure that all content is covered in each section, so that you can be confident in your preparation for the test at the strategic level.

This guide covers requirements for certification at both the strategic and operational levels. If you are studying for certification at the strategic level, you will need to be knowledgeable in all areas of the guide. The "Strategic" designation of some topics within each content section of the guide indicates that managers pursuing certification at the operational level do not need to be familiar with this material.

| Study Guide Contents | Leadership and Business Management Competencies – Strategic Level |
|---|---|
| | **A. Apply Leadership Practices, Principles, Values, and Vision** |
| Strategy and Valuation<br>Section 3 | 1. Collaborate with staff to establish the center's vision and mission<br>• Create a shared vision resulting in employee commitment and loyalty<br>• Align day-to-day activities with the center's vision and mission |
| Leadership and Communication<br>Section 4 | • Communicate the center's vision, mission, and role to internal and external audiences<br>• Model the organization's core values, principles, and philosophies<br>• Determine community relations initiatives and implement appropriate programs and activities |
| Strategy and Valuation<br>Section 3 | 2. Develop and execute a strategy to accomplish the center's mission and support organizational objectives<br>3. Align the center's objectives with organizational and customer objectives<br>4. Position and promote the center as value-added to the organization<br>• Identify how the center adds value to the organization<br>• Develop and implement a plan that communicates the center's value proposition |
| Leadership and Communication<br>Section 4 | 5. Act as a conduit for information flow from customers and employees to senior management |

| Study Guide Contents | Leadership and Business Management Competencies – Strategic Level |
|---|---|
| | **B. Apply Business Management Practices and Principles** |
| Business Management Principles and Practices<br>Section 6 | 1. Develop and execute a business strategy for the center<br>• Create and implement a strategic business plan<br>• Translate organizational objectives into goals for the center<br>• Create and implement an annual operating plan<br>• Translate center goals into project plans<br>• Manage a project plan to ensure a successful outcome |
| The Call Center Business Environment<br>Section 5 | 2. Acquire knowledge of the industry, business drivers and trends, competitors, and applicable regulatory requirements of customers<br>• Furnish market research and intelligence to the organization |
| Leadership and Communication<br>Section 4 | 3. Develop and implement a plan to communicate center initiatives |
| Business Management Principles and Practices<br>Section 6 | 4. Develop and apply a methodology to improve operational results |
| | **C. Demonstrate Knowledge of the Contact Center Business Environment** |
| The Call Center Business Environment<br>Section 5 | 1. Describe the role of the center<br>2. Identify and adhere to applicable regulations<br>3. Proactively respond to applicable regulatory requirements<br>4. Demonstrate an understanding of contact center terminology |
| | **D. Apply Financial Practices and Principles** |
| Financial Principles and Practices<br>Section 7 | 1. Identify and leverage risk-and-opportunity tradeoffs<br>2. Develop an annual operating budget for the center<br>• Negotiate approval of a call center budget<br>• Manage a budget in accordance with variance reports<br>3. Demonstrate working knowledge of key financial concepts:<br>• Buy versus lease<br>• Depreciation schedules of fixed assets<br>• Profit center versus cost center |

| Study Guide Contents | Leadership and Business Management Competencies – Strategic Level |
|---|---|
| Financial Principles and Practices<br>Section 7 *(continued)* | • Return on Assets (ROA); Return on Sales (ROS); Net Present Value (NPV); Internal Rate of Return (IRR); Return on Investment (ROI); and Cost/Benefit Analysis (Ratio)<br>4. Interpret the organization's financial statements |
| | **E. Establish and Manage Contractual Relationships** |
| Business Management Principles and Practices<br>Section 6 | 1. Establish contractual criteria<br>• Negotiate contracts that are mutually beneficial<br>2. Establish and manage a contractual relationship<br>• Assess the quality of a contractual relationship<br>• Utilize data to manage a contractual relationship<br>3. Identify issues that need to be escalated and the proper channel(s) for escalation |

# The CIAC Leadership and Business Management Competency Outline – Operational Level

This document maps the content of this study guide with CIAC leadership and business management competencies at the operational level. In order to produce a study guide that is easy to use and understand, we have presented the contents of each section in building-block fashion. Therefore, contents may be presented in a different order than in the competency list. We have taken care to ensure that all content is covered in each section, so that you can be confident in your preparation for the test.

This guide covers requirements for certification at both the strategic and operational levels. If you are studying for certification at the operational level, you will need to be knowledgeable in the areas of the guide that are NOT designated as "Strategic."

| **Study Guide Contents** | **Leadership and Business Management Competencies – Operational Level** |
|---|---|
| | **A. Apply Leadership Practices, Principles, Values, and Vision** |
| Strategy and Valuation<br>Section 3 | 1. Align day-to-day activities with the center's vision and mission |
| Leadership and Communication<br>Section 4 | 2. Communicate the center's vision, mission, and role to internal audiences<br>• Model the organization's core values, principles, and philosophies<br>• Identify community relations initiatives and implement supporting programs and activities |
| Strategy and Valuation<br>Section 3 | 3. Execute a strategy to accomplish the center's mission and support organizational objectives<br>4. Promote the center as value-added to the organization<br>• Identify how the center adds value to the organization |
| Leadership and Communication<br>Section 4 | • Implement a plan that communicates the center's value proposition<br>5. Act as a conduit for information flow from customers and employees to senior management |
| | **B. Apply Business Management Practices and Principles** |
| Business Management Principles and Practices<br>Section 6 | 1. Implement a strategic business plan<br>• Develop and implement an annual operating plan<br>• Translate the center's goals into project plans<br>• Manage a project plan to ensure timely delivery of outcomes |

| Study Guide Contents | Leadership and Business Management Competencies – Operational Level |
|---|---|
| The Call Center Business Environment<br>Section 5 | 2. Compile market research and competitive intelligence |
| Leadership and Communication<br>Section 4 | 3. Develop and implement a plan to communicate center initiatives |
| Business Management Principles and Practices<br>Section 6 | 4. Apply a methodology to improve operational results |
| | **C. Demonstrate Knowledge of the Contact Center Business Environment** |
| The Call Center Business Environment<br>Section 5 | 1. Describe the role of the center<br>2. Identify and adhere to applicable regulations<br>3. Proactively respond to applicable regulatory requirements<br>4. Demonstrate an understanding of contact center terminology |
| | **D. Apply Financial Practices and Principles** |
| Financial Principles and Practices<br>Section 7 | 1. Develop an annual operating budget for the center<br>• Negotiate budget approval<br>• Manage a budget in accordance with variance reports<br>2. Demonstrate working knowledge of key financial concepts:<br>• Buy versus lease<br>• Depreciation schedules of fixed assets<br>• Profit center versus cost center<br>• Return on Assets (ROA); Return on Sales (ROS); Net Present Value (NPV); Internal Rate of Return (IRR); Return on Investment (ROI); and Cost/Benefit Analysis (Ratio)<br>3. Interpret the organization's financial statements |
| | **E. Establish and Manage Contractual Relationships** |
| Business Management Principles and Practices<br>Section 6 | 1. Establish and manage a contractual relationship<br>• Assess the quality of a contractual relationship<br>• Utilize data to manage a contractual relationship<br>2. Identify issues that need to be escalated and the proper channel(s) for escalation |

## Pre/Post Self-Assessment for Call Center Leadership and Business Management Study Guide

The purpose of this self-assessment tool is to provide you with an opportunity to identify areas where you are confident in your knowledge and experience, and areas where you may need to do some additional study or receive additional training.

First, go through the pre-assessment and circle your perceived level of knowledge for each area. As you study the guide, focus on the areas where you are not satisfied with your current knowledge level.

Following your study, conduct a post-assessment. For each area, note the shift in your ratings. Place a check (√) by the content areas you in which want to pursue more in-depth training. ICMI offers training and further resources on most of these topics. For further information, on ICMI's Leadership and Business Management training, see page 17.

Use the following scale to indicate your level of knowledge in the areas described.

1 = Unfamiliar territory, more time is needed here

2 = Pretty good, but worth reviewing

3 = Excellent

| | Pre-Assessment | | | | Post Assessment | | | | √ Training |
|---|---|---|---|---|---|---|---|---|---|
| **Strategy and Valuation, Section 3** | | | | | | | | | |
| **Vision, Mission and Strategy** | | | | | | | | | |
| 1. Definition of Values, Vision and Mission | 1 | 2 | 3 | | 1 | 2 | 3 | | |
| 2. Identifying Core Values | 1 | 2 | 3 | | 1 | 2 | 3 | | |
| 3. Creating a Shared Vision [Strategic] | 1 | 2 | 3 | | 1 | 2 | 3 | | |
| 4. Developing a Mission Statement [Strategic] | 1 | 2 | 3 | | 1 | 2 | 3 | | |
| 5. Definition and Application of Strategy | 1 | 2 | 3 | | 1 | 2 | 3 | | |
| 6. The Role of the Customer Access Strategy | 1 | 2 | 3 | | 1 | 2 | 3 | | |
| 7. Creating an Effective Strategic Development Process [Strategic] | 1 | 2 | 3 | | 1 | 2 | 3 | | |
| 8. Aligning Tactical Activities with Values, Vision and Mission | 1 | 2 | 3 | | 1 | 2 | 3 | | |
| **The Call Center's Contribution to Value** | | | | | | | | | |
| 9. Defining the Call Center's Value Proposition | 1 | 2 | 3 | | 1 | 2 | 3 | | |
| 10. The Call Center's Contribution to Unit Strategies | 1 | 2 | 3 | | 1 | 2 | 3 | | |
| 11. The Call Center's Contribution to Customer Satisfaction and Loyalty | 1 | 2 | 3 | | 1 | 2 | 3 | | |
| 12. The Call Center's Contribution to Quality and Innovation | 1 | 2 | 3 | | 1 | 2 | 3 | | |
| 13. The Call Center's Contribution to Marketing | 1 | 2 | 3 | | 1 | 2 | 3 | | |

| | Pre- Assessment | | | | Post Assessment | | | | √ Training |
|---|---|---|---|---|---|---|---|---|---|
| 14. The Call Center's Contribution to Products and Services | 1 | 2 | 3 | | 1 | 2 | 3 | | |
| 15. The Call Center's Role in Efficient Service Delivery | 1 | 2 | 3 | | 1 | 2 | 3 | | |
| 16. The Call Center's Role in Self-Service Usage and System Design | 1 | 2 | 3 | | 1 | 2 | 3 | | |
| 17. The Call Center's Contribution to Revenue/Sales | 1 | 2 | 3 | | 1 | 2 | 3 | | |
| **Leadership and Communication, Section 4** | | | | | | | | | |
| **Call Center Leadership** | | | | | | | | | |
| 1. Qualities and Characteristics of Effective Leaders | 1 | 2 | 3 | | 1 | 2 | 3 | | |
| 2. The Distinction Between Leadership and Management | 1 | 2 | 3 | | 1 | 2 | 3 | | |
| 3. Leadership Challenges in Call Centers | 1 | 2 | 3 | | 1 | 2 | 3 | | |
| 4. Modeling Values and Maintaining Integrity | 1 | 2 | 3 | | 1 | 2 | 3 | | |
| 5. Developing Strong Community Relations | 1 | 2 | 3 | | 1 | 2 | 3 | | |
| **Call Center Communications** | | | | | | | | | |
| 6. Principles of Effective Communication | 1 | 2 | 3 | | 1 | 2 | 3 | | |
| 7. Creating a Communication Plan for Internal Audiences | 1 | 2 | 3 | | 1 | 2 | 3 | | |
| 8. Creating a Communication Plan for External Audiences | 1 | 2 | 3 | | 1 | 2 | 3 | | |
| 9. Principles of Effective Reporting | 1 | 2 | 3 | | 1 | 2 | 3 | | |
| **The Call Center Business Environment, Section 5** | | | | | | | | | |
| **The Call Center's Unique Environment** | | | | | | | | | |
| 1. Understanding and Applying Call Center Terminology | 1 | 2 | 3 | | 1 | 2 | 3 | | |
| 2. Unique Operational Dynamics | 1 | 2 | 3 | | 1 | 2 | 3 | | |
| **The Call Center's Emerging Role** | | | | | | | | | |
| 3. Characteristics of the Call Center's Emerging Role | 1 | 2 | 3 | | 1 | 2 | 3 | | |
| 4. Strategies and Actions to Support the Call Center's Emerging Role | 1 | 2 | 3 | | 1 | 2 | 3 | | |
| 5. The Impact of E-commerce on the Call Center | 1 | 2 | 3 | | 1 | 2 | 3 | | |
| **Understanding Market Forces** | | | | | | | | | |
| 6. Principles of Conducting an Environmental Scan | 1 | 2 | 3 | | 1 | 2 | 3 | | |
| 7. Key Principles of Market Research | 1 | 2 | 3 | | 1 | 2 | 3 | | |
| 8. Identifying External Factors Impacting Strategy and Operations | 1 | 2 | 3 | | 1 | 2 | 3 | | |

| | Pre-Assessment | | | | Post Assessment | | | | √ Training |
|---|---|---|---|---|---|---|---|---|---|
| **The Legal and Regulatory Environment** | | | | | | | | | |
| 9. Major Legal Requirements Impacting the Call Center - US | 1 | 2 | 3 | | 1 | 2 | 3 | | |
| 10. Major Regulatory Requirements Impacting the Call Center - US | 1 | 2 | 3 | | 1 | 2 | 3 | | |
| 11. Major Legal and Regulatory Requirements Impacting the Call Center – Canada | 1 | 2 | 3 | | 1 | 2 | 3 | | |
| 12. Tracking and Adhering to Legal and Regulatory Requirements | 1 | 2 | 3 | | 1 | 2 | 3 | | |
| **Business Management Principles and Practices, Section 6** | | | | | | | | | |
| **Developing Business Plans** | | | | | | | | | |
| 1. Definitions of Strategic Business Plan and Related Terms | 1 | 2 | 3 | | 1 | 2 | 3 | | |
| 2. Developing an Effective Strategic Business Plan [Strategic] | 1 | 2 | 3 | | 1 | 2 | 3 | | |
| 3. Components of an Annual Operating Plan | 1 | 2 | 3 | | 1 | 2 | 3 | | |
| 4. Managing and Controlling Project Plans | 1 | 2 | 3 | | 1 | 2 | 3 | | |
| **Improving Operational Results** | | | | | | | | | |
| 5. Identifying Methods for Improving Operational Results | 1 | 2 | 3 | | 1 | 2 | 3 | | |
| 6. Quantitative and Qualitative Analysis | 1 | 2 | 3 | | 1 | 2 | 3 | | |
| 7. Quality Control Tools and Techniques | 1 | 2 | 3 | | 1 | 2 | 3 | | |
| 8. Benchmarking | 1 | 2 | 3 | | 1 | 2 | 3 | | |
| 9. Innovation Principles and Methodologies | 1 | 2 | 3 | | 1 | 2 | 3 | | |
| 10. Identifying and Overcoming Obstacles to Performance Improvement | 1 | 2 | 3 | | 1 | 2 | 3 | | |
| **Managing Contractual Relationships** | | | | | | | | | |
| 11. Identifying Outsourcing Opportunities | 1 | 2 | 3 | | 1 | 2 | 3 | | |
| 12. Components of Effective Contractual Agreements | 1 | 2 | 3 | | 1 | 2 | 3 | | |
| 13. Legal Issues Surrounding Contractual Relationships | 1 | 2 | 3 | | 1 | 2 | 3 | | |
| 14. Qualifying Vendors and Writing the Request for Proposal | 1 | 2 | 3 | | 1 | 2 | 3 | | |
| 15. Principles of Effective Negotiation | 1 | 2 | 3 | | 1 | 2 | 3 | | |
| 16. Developing Service Level Agreements | 1 | 2 | 3 | | 1 | 2 | 3 | | |
| 19. Maintaining Effective Outsourcing Partnerships | 1 | 2 | 3 | | 1 | 2 | 3 | | |

| | Pre-Assessment | | | | Post Assessment | | | | √ Training |
|---|---|---|---|---|---|---|---|---|---|
| **Financial Principles and Practices, Section 7** | | | | | | | | | |
| **Understanding Risk and Opportunity Tradeoffs** | | | | | | | | | |
| 1. Identifying Key Risk/Opportunity Tradeoffs | 1 | 2 | 3 | | 1 | 2 | 3 | | |
| 2. Applying the Principles of the Technology Adoption Lifecycle | 1 | 2 | 3 | | 1 | 2 | 3 | | |
| **Developing an Annual Operating Budget** | | | | | | | | | |
| 3. Principles of Developing an Effective Annual Operating Budget | 1 | 2 | 3 | | 1 | 2 | 3 | | |
| 4. Key Steps to Developing and Obtaining Approval for an Annual Operating Budget | 1 | 2 | 3 | | 1 | 2 | 3 | | |
| 5. Utilizing Variance Reports | 1 | 2 | 3 | | 1 | 2 | 3 | | |
| **Understanding Financial Concepts** | | | | | | | | | |
| 6. Definitions of Key Financial Concepts | 1 | 2 | 3 | | 1 | 2 | 3 | | |
| 7. Using Capital Budgeting Methods | 1 | 2 | 3 | | 1 | 2 | 3 | | |
| 8. Buy vs. Lease Considerations | 1 | 2 | 3 | | 1 | 2 | 3 | | |
| 9. Understanding and Using Depreciation Schedules | 1 | 2 | 3 | | 1 | 2 | 3 | | |
| 10. Definitions of Profit and Cost Centers | 1 | 2 | 3 | | 1 | 2 | 3 | | |
| **Interpreting Financial Statements** | | | | | | | | | |
| 11. Interpreting and Using Key Financial Statements | 1 | 2 | 3 | | 1 | 2 | 3 | | |

## Frequently Asked Questions

### What is CIAC certification?

The Call Center Industry Advisory Council (CIAC) is a nonprofit and independent organization established and funded to develop competencies and provide industry-standard certification for call center managers. Successful completion of CIAC certification means formal recognition of the individual's mastery of specified competencies and commitment to staying abreast of new developments in the profession.

CIAC Certification requires successful completion of the CIAC certification assessment process. There are four modules; each has its own test:

- People Management
- Operations Management
- Customer Relationship Management
- Leadership and Business Management

Tests are provided at regularly scheduled times and locations. See www.ciac-cert.org for a complete listing.

### Why does ICMI support CIAC certification?

In recent years, a number of call center vendors have promoted their own versions of certification programs. Some of these programs have since come and gone, but ICMI has maintained from the beginning that there can be no valid certification program without a broadly-representative and recognized body overseeing the process. The CIAC is a nonprofit organization established by the industry to develop, administer and govern professional certification for the call center profession. It has broad support from end-users, consultants and suppliers, and will likely remain in favor with the industry as long as it remains unbiased, representative, open and tuned in to industry needs.

### Are certain training classes required?

No. The CIAC does not provide educational services, but is instead committed to an "open-systems" approach whereby managers can acquire required competence through the combination of on-the-job experience, training courses and published materials they choose. This ensures that call center professionals are free to choose the best training programs and publications available as they build their knowledge and skills. And it enables experienced managers to avoid the expense and time involved in the prescribed training classes that are often necessary in other programs.

### Do these handbooks/study guides replace ICMI seminars?

That depends on your objectives. The handbook/study guide series is designed to cover CIAC certification competencies. Each guide covers a significant range of material in a review fashion but does not replace the need for job experiences nor the formal training other ICMI courses provide. However, through a step-by-step review process, the guides enable managers with sufficient experiences or management training to identify areas that require further study, and they provide the essential information needed to fill in any gaps.

**How else can ICMI help?**

ICMI has developed innovative review courses and self-study resources for those who want an efficient review of the content areas addressed by CIAC competencies. In addition, ICMI's full range of call center management training and publications support specific content areas included in the CIAC competencies. See information on additional ICMI services, next page.

**Where can I find more information?**

- See the CIAC Certification Handbook in Section 11
- See www.ciac-cert.org
- See www.incoming.com

## Additional ICMI Services

If you have chosen to pursue certification through the CIAC, ICMI is the authoritative source for the information and training you need for success. The CIAC is a nonprofit organization that administers certification but, by design, does not provide certification training. That enables you to choose the training alternatives you need and prefer.

That's where ICMI comes in. ICMI offers many choices, including:

### Handbook/Study Guide Series

The ICMI handbook/study guide series, which this book is part of, includes four publications:

- *Call Center People Management Handbook and Study Guide*
- *Call Center Operations Management Handbook and Study Guide*
- *Call Center Customer Relationship Management Handbook and Study Guide*
- *Call Center Leadership and Business Management Handbook and Study Guide*

These guides provide a 100 percent comprehensive review of each module along with self-study tools to ensure you are prepared.

### Foundational Seminars

ICMI's powerful instructor-led seminars are designed to provide a practical working knowledge of core call center management disciplines. As over 50,000 ICMI alumni from around the world will attest, these two-day courses offer an unmatched combination of content, support materials, expert facilitation and interaction. Current offerings include:

- *Essential Skills and Knowledge for Effective Incoming Call Center Management*
- *Results-Oriented Monitoring and Coaching for Improved Call Center Performance*
- *Understanding and Applying Today's Call Center Technologies*
- *Effective Leadership and Strategy for Senior Call Center Managers*
- *Workforce Management: The Basics and Beyond*

### Web-Based or In-Person Study Courses

Perhaps you'd like to combine the power of self-study with personal guidance from call center experts. ICMI's CIAC study courses enable your entire management team to successfully prepare for certification. Through expert facilitation and focused study, your team will prepare for the assessment, and acquire the skills and knowledge you need to advance your call center's services. These courses can be delivered in traditional classroom style or, for organizations with geographically dispersed centers, over the Internet. Public seminars (Web-based and in-person) are also available. ICMI's handbook/study guide series is included with these courses.

### Combination

Those who need preparation only in specific content areas can choose from ICMI's full range of Web seminars, books, papers, studies and other services. Consistency, quality and usability are trademarks of these services.

For more information, or help with planning your approach, contact us at icmi@incoming.com or 410-267-0700.

# Section 3

# *Strategy and Valuation*

# Section 3: Strategy and Valuation



## Contents

## 1. Definition of Values, Vision and Mission

Ready? | 1 | 2 | 3 |



### Key Points

- Effective organizations understand and communicate their fundamental essence and reason for being: they know who they are and what they are about.
- An organization's core values must be stable, not shifting as conditions change. They describe the principles the organization turns to when making its most critical decisions.
- The vision statement describes a future state of the organization in vivid, compelling terms that inspire all involved to strive to achieve it. The organization's vision is a snapshot of the future.
- The mission clarifies the organization's purpose. The mission statement declares why the organization exists and, therefore, what it strives to do in every transaction and decision it makes.

### Explanation

Effective organizations understand and communicate their fundamental essence and reason for being: they know who they are and what they are about. Effective call centers must do the same, while aligning themselves with the larger organization. The three basic tools organizations use to define themselves are well known to experienced managers: statements describing core values, vision and mission. Each of these is discussed, in turn, in the next three sections.

Together, these three statements comprise the foundation upon which organizational strategy is built. In the best of organizations, the core values, vision and mission serve to unify the many individuals who must work separately, but together in purpose, to make the organization succeed. In call centers – where so many agents interact with so many customers – core values, vision and mission guide agents in handling the daily unanticipated situations they encounter, enabling their individual decisions and responses to align with the organization's principles.

**Core Values**

An organization's core values must be stable, not shifting as conditions change. They describe the principles the organization turns to when making its most critical decisions. They are not just moral imperatives, however. They describe simply and concisely how individuals are expected to approach any situation.

**Vision**

The organization's vision is a powerful tool for change. The vision statement describes a future state of the organization in vivid, compelling terms that inspire all involved to achieve it. The organization's vision is a snapshot of the future. Vision is at the heart of great leadership because it allows leaders to communicate persuasively where the organization desires to go, and motivates everyone to work toward the same end.

**Mission**

While the core values describe principles upon which the organization acts and the vision communicates where the organization wants to be, the mission clarifies the organization's purpose. The mission statement declares why the organization exists and, therefore, what it strives to do in every transaction and decision it makes. The mission should be understood by everyone in the organization and should be practiced daily.

**All Together**

Core values, vision and mission are simply three interrelated components of defining and describing an organization's essence. Instead of charts, numbers and graphs, carefully crafted words convey who and what the organization is. Together, the core values, vision and mission tell a story about the organization, and human beings respond intuitively to good stories, grasping their meaning and identifying with them almost effortlessly. The hard work, of course, is in writing the story well.

## 2. Identifying Core Values

Ready? | 1 | 2 | 3 |



### Key Points

- **Not all organizations have inspiring core values:**
  - **Some that espouse lofty values do not, in fact, practice them.**
  - **Others have not explicitly defined their core values and are unaware that their actions implicitly define them every day.**
  - **Other organizations confuse core values with management trends and attempt to revise their values in response to changes in the business environment.**
- **How call centers conduct themselves goes a long way toward defining, in customers' eyes, what the values of the organization truly are.**

### Explanation

The core values of great organizations have become legendary. Nordstrom's "service to the customer above all else" has guided the company for 100 years. Disney's belief that it should promote "wholesome American values" is at the core of their historical success. But the act of writing and proclaiming core values is insignificant compared to the importance of "living" the core values. In fact, the famous "HP Way" set of core values defined by David Packard was understood and practiced at Hewlett-Packard for many years before it was written down and codified.

Some examples of core values include:

- Being a pioneer, not following others
- Encouraging individual ability and creativity
- Attention to consistency and detail
- Opportunity based on merit
- Honesty and integrity
- Excellence in reputation
- Service to the customer above all else

The core values of an organization should describe its culture. Core values are not descriptions of how to get things done, or what will be offered to customers. Core values describe the motivation and guiding principles behind the decisions employees make on a daily basis.

Not all organizations have inspiring core values. Some that espouse lofty values do not, in fact, practice them. In such conditions, so-called core values produce cynicism instead of motivation throughout the organization. Others have not defined their core values, and so are unaware – and perhaps would be ashamed – of what their actions indicate that they actually hold as values. Other organizations confuse core values with management trends and attempt to revise their values in response to changes in the business environment. Many dangers await ships that sail without a steady compass.

Core values are descriptive, but they can be changed. The first step toward change is honest recognition of reality, and that requires describing the core values that the organization actually upholds in practice. When managers do not like what they see in the mirror, they need to develop plans to implement change.

**Core Values of the Call Center**

It should go without saying that the core values of the call center must be aligned with those of the organization. It is futile for the call center to create core values if the organization does not subscribe to them. Call center core values should be an extension of those of the larger organization.

Because of the call center's vital role as the front line or "face" of the organization in customer interactions, call center staff are key to the success or failure of the organization in "living" its values every day. In practice, how call centers conduct themselves goes a long way toward defining, in customers' eyes, what the values of the organization truly are.

**Branding and Core Values**

Core values are a key component of branding. A brand publicly describes what an organization says it is, while the values it holds and practices define who the organization actually is. When brand and core values match up and reinforce each other, the organization's image is successfully portrayed. When brand and values conflict, it creates confusion and doubt for employees and customers alike.

### Identifying Core Values

To identify the core values of your own organization, push with relentless honesty to define what values are truly central. If you articulate more than five or six, chances are that you are confusing core values (which do not change) with operating practices, business strategies, or cultural norms (which should be open to change). Remember, the values must stand the test of time. After you've drafted a preliminary list of the core values, ask about each one. If the circumstances changed and penalized us for holding this core value, would we still keep it? If you can't honestly answer yes, then the value is not core and should be dropped from consideration.

Excerpt from "Building Your Company's Vision" by James C. Collins and Jerry I. Porras, *Harvard Business Review*, Sept-Oct 1996.

## 3. Creating a Shared Vision [Strategic]

Ready? | 1 | 2 | 3 |

### Key Points

- **The call center's vision should be based on its value contribution to the organization.**
- **An effective call center vision both communicates and inspires. Vision is at the heart of great leadership.**
- **Envisioning the future is an inherently creative process that must combine knowledge of the organization and its environment with intuition and risk-taking.**
- **An inspiring vision must be communicated both widely and deeply. The vision should be woven into the fabric of the organization's culture and understood, adopted and absorbed by all.**

### Explanation

Vision is at the heart of great leadership because it allows leaders to communicate persuasively where the organization desires to go, and motivates everyone to work toward the same end. The quality of an organization's vision is, therefore, a direct reflection of its leadership team.

#### Developing an Effective Call Center Vision

Obviously, the call center's vision must be aligned with the larger organization's vision. But being aligned does not necessarily mean being the same. The call center's vision should be unique to the call center, but complementary to the overall organizational vision.

There are many ways to envision the role of the call center in organizations. The call center's vision should be based on its value contribution to the organization, including:

- **Contribution to unit strategies:** By providing customer feedback and data from interactions that help other departments meet their objectives.
- **Improved customer satisfaction and loyalty:** By enabling customers to reach the services they need and to effectively interact with the organization when and as they wish.

- **Improved quality and innovation:** By capturing a constant stream of information from customer contacts, pinpointing quality problems early and acquiring customer input that leads to significant product and service innovations.
- **Highly focused marketing:** By tracking buying trends, capturing customer feedback, analyzing demographic information, and establishing permission-based marketing campaigns.
- **Improved products and services:** By providing input directly from customers that can lead to products and services that better meet their needs.
- **More efficient delivery of services:** By helping customers understand and use the access channels and self-service alternatives available to them.
- **Improved self-service usage and system design:** By assisting customers with self-service systems and providing customer input that can create more intuitive, comprehensive self-service solutions.
- **Additional revenue/sales:** By enabling customers to reach human representatives as they wish before and during checkout, and providing upselling and cross-selling opportunities along the way.

(See Defining the Call Center's Value Proposition, this section.)

An effective call center vision both communicates and inspires. The challenge is to use words to communicate an image in the mind: a picture of the call center in the future. The image must be readily understood and easily remembered by everyone associated with the organization, both inside and outside of the call center. Equally important, the vision should be compelling. It should be vivid, conveying passion and emotion that will inspire and motivate individuals to make it real.

## Principles to Creating a Shared Vision and Ensuring Buy-In

There is no one recipe for creating a shared vision, just as there is no "right" vision for an organization. Envisioning the future is an inherently creative process that must combine knowledge of the organization and its environment with intuition and risk-taking. Remember that a vision is not a forecast that will be evaluated by how accurate it was. A vision statement inspires people to make something real that is only imagined.

The vision should receive buy-in from everyone in the organization, from front-line employees to top-level executives. The principles for creating a shared vision, though they may vary in application, include:

- **Envision the future:** Pick a point in the distant future and imagine what you wish the organization would be like then.
- **Encourage collaboration:** Involve many people from all levels in the organization, both to learn from them and to foster their ownership of the process.
- **Enable dialogue:** Listen, question, brainstorm, and encourage open and honest feedback.
- **Foster ownership and buy-in:** Organizational buy-in comes from participation in creating the vision and from the power of the vision itself.
- **Communicate widely and deeply:** The vision should be woven into the fabric of the organization's culture and understood, adopted and absorbed by all.
- **Live the vision:** Refer to the vision when making large and small decisions, reinforce it with every staff interaction and build it into every customer relationship.
- **Celebrate accomplishments:** Even celebrating smaller accomplishments can help reinforce vision and the direction of the organization.

Imagining the future can and should be exciting and invigorating. Involvement in this process is a natural way to develop commitment to it. But the quality of the vision that results will be the ultimate determinant of success. Participation alone will not be enough if the end result is disappointing.

## 4. Developing a Mission Statement [Strategic]

Ready? | 1 | 2 | 3 |



### Key Points

- Mission statements are created through iterative group processes of discovery and creative thinking. It takes time, patience and skill to question, listen, probe, brainstorm, synthesize, revise and build understanding and consensus.
- A mission statement answers questions that begin with "why."
- Pitfalls to avoid when developing mission statements include:
  - Trying to say too much
  - Sounding pompous
  - Practicing self-delusion
  - Not digging deeply enough
  - Not stretching far enough
  - Stating the obvious
  - Confusing vision with mission

### Explanation

While the core values describe principles upon which the organization acts, and the vision communicates where the organization wants to be, the mission clarifies the organization's purpose. The mission declares why the organization exists and, therefore, what it strives to do in every transaction and decision it makes.

Great mission statements convey striking insight in just a few words. They should elicit an "aha!" from the reader, instantly make sense and inspire commitment. They should make employees proud of their work by placing it in a positive light. Merck has included their mission statement on their Web site, www.merck.com:

> The mission of Merck is to provide society with superior products and services – innovations and solutions that improve the quality of life and satisfy customer needs – to provide employees with meaningful work and advancement opportunities, and [to provide] investors with a superior rate of return.

### Developing a Mission Statement

The process used to create mission statements is similar to the process for developing statements of core values and vision. (See Creating a Shared Vision, this section.) It is an iterative group process of discovery and creative thinking. It takes time, patience and skill to question, listen, probe, brainstorm, synthesize, revise and build understanding and consensus. Many organizations will find the services of a trained and experienced facilitator invaluable, particularly one with no connection to the organization's internal politics.

A mission statement answers questions that begin with "why," so the starting point for creating a mission statement is to ask and attempt to answer questions about why the organization does what it does and is what it is. The process is one of introspection, and it will take time and wisdom to do it well.

### Pitfalls to Avoid

Mission statements may be powerful and memorable, but not all meet this standard. Some of Scott Adams' most memorable Dilbert cartoons skillfully parody the vague and fluffy prose that characterizes ineffective mission statements. There are many ways to go astray with mission statements, including:

- **Trying to say too much:** A mission statement should be concise. It's a statement, not an essay or even a paragraph. Boil the words down.
- **Sounding pompous:** A mission statement is, indeed, a defining description of the organization, full of importance and significance. But it must inspire, so arrogance should be avoided.
- **Practicing self-delusion:** The mission statement must resonate with the reality of what the organization really is. Pretending to be something that you are not by calling it your mission will simply produce cynicism.
- **Not digging deeply enough:** Don't describe the products you sell or the markets you serve. Ask why your organization does what it does. Products and markets may change over time, but your mission should be long-lasting.
- **Not stretching far enough:** It is tempting to describe the current state as the "purpose" of the organization. Dare to imagine what the organization could be.
- **Stating the obvious:** If what you come up with is abundantly apparent, go back to the drawing board. Don't waste words or your staff's time

simply for the sake of having a mission statement. If it doesn't capture the essence of your organization's purpose or is not motivating, it's not an effective mission statement.

- **Confusing vision with mission:** Ensure that everyone understands the difference between the vision statement and the mission statement. Explain that the vision statement is a snapshot of the future, while the mission clarifies the organization's purpose – the "why" behind what is done.

## 5. Definition and Application of Strategy

Ready? | 1 | 2 | 3 |



### Key Points

- **Strategy is the overall approach for accomplishing the organization's mission.**
- **Strategy must be developed on two general levels:**
  - **The organization's overarching strategy**
  - **Business unit strategies**
- **Business unit strategies must work together to support the organization's overall strategy, vision and mission.**

### Explanation

Before purchasing technology, before recruiting, hiring and training, before establishing organizational structure, the organization must develop a vision of where it wants to go. This vision will serve as a compass and reality check to ensure that all ensuing decisions and activities are in alignment with the organization's desired direction. Strategy follows vision. (See discussions of values, vision and mission, this section.)

However, without effective strategy, even the most compelling visions will go nowhere. Strategy provides the overall framework for how the organization will turn the vision into reality. It creates tangible advantages that result in a whole greater than the sum of its parts. It provides the mechanism through which daily activities and priorities are established.

We refer to strategy generally as the overall approach or framework for accomplishing the organization's objectives. It is distinct from vision, but is guided by it. For example, in the early 1960s, President John F. Kennedy articulated the vision of putting an American on the moon and returning him safely to earth, sometime before the end of the decade. The strategy for accomplishing that vision included the development of the National Aeronautics and Space Administration (NASA). The plans, resources and initiatives created by NASA became the means through which the vision was accomplished.

Just as vision must drive the development of strategy, strategy in turn shapes tactics. Tactics are the steps, procedures, tasks and decisions necessary to further strategy. Research and development, recruiting practices, training programs, cooperative agreements and many other activities made up the tactics that supported NASA and the overall strategy necessary for reaching the moon.

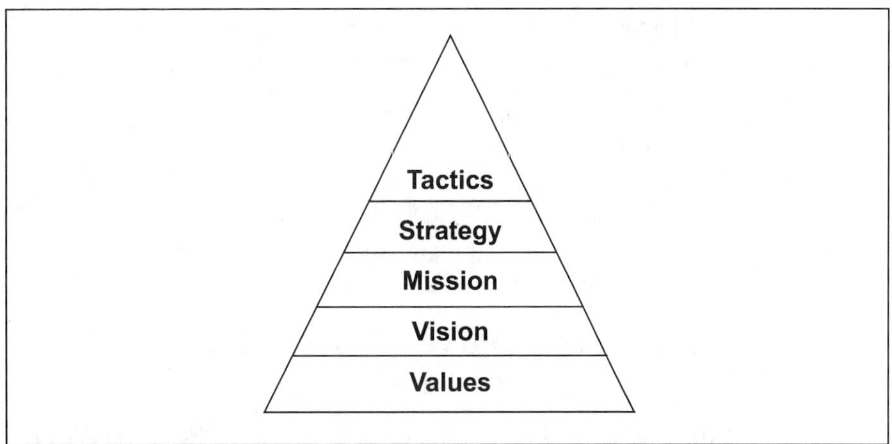


**Strategic Objectives**

An organization's overall strategic objectives often include:

- Increase sales or margins on sales
- Increase profitability
- Introduce new products or services
- Increase customer retention
- Improve customer satisfaction
- Advance into new customer markets or geographic areas
- Reduce costs
- Increase productivity

To meet these objectives, strategy must be developed on two general levels. The first level, consisting of the organization's overarching strategy, must be supported by the second level that consists of compatible strategies in individual business units and functional areas of the organization. Major corporate strategies include:

- **Cost leadership:** To achieve a competitive advantage through policies, practices, procedures and actions that enable the organization to be the low-cost provider.
- **Product leadership:** To achieve a competitive advantage through superior products and services.

- **Differentiation:** Distinguishing the organization by creating product and service offerings that are perceived by the market as unique.
- **Focus:** Targeting defined customer groups, product lines or geographic markets in order to better serve those segments.
- **Brand leadership:** Building your organization's reputation and popularity to gain the largest market share.
- **Defender:** Focusing on protecting and sustaining market share.
- **Prospector:** Pursuing growth and market share through competition, innovation and speed to market.

(Corporate strategies are covered in more detail in ICMI's *Call Center People Management Handbook and Study Guide.*)

There is much interplay and overlap between these general classifications. (Note: "Sticking to Core Competencies," which means cutting back operations to activities on which the organizations' reputation was built, can be considered an additional strategy.) Further, a wide variety of analysts and scholars have presented alternative frameworks. For example, in *Strategy Safari*, Bruce Ahlstrand, Joseph Lampel and Henry Mintzberg categorize strategy formation into 10 overall schools of thought, ranging from a visionary process to a process of transformation – each with different frameworks and outcomes. Whatever the framework or labels, effective strategy provides the overall means to accomplish the organization's vision and objectives.

**Business Unit Strategies**

Business unit (or department/functional area) strategies make up the second level of strategy. For example, marketing strategy may include customer segmentation initiatives that enable the organization to reach and serve specific target markets. Product development strategy may encompass design and production capabilities to best serve those segments. Call center strategy – which is embodied in the customer access strategy – defines the means by which customers interact with the organization, and shapes access channels, services provided, agent group structure, etc. (See The Role of the Customer Access Strategy, this section.)

Business unit strategies must work together to support the organization's overall strategy. The call center can and must help business units and the organization as a whole achieve primary strategic objectives.

## 6. The Role of the Customer Access Strategy

Ready? | 1 | 2 | 3 |



### Key Points

- **A customer access strategy is a framework – a set of standards, guidelines and processes – defining the means by which customers are connected with resources capable of delivering the desired information and services.**
- **An effective customer access strategy includes the following components:**
  - **Customer segmentation**
  - **Major contact types**
  - **Access channels**
  - **Service level and response time objectives**
  - **Hours of operation**
  - **Routing methodology**
  - **Person and technology resources required by contact**
  - **Knowledge bases**
  - **Tracking and integration**
- **While corporate strategy must ultimately define the customer access strategy, the customer access strategy can influence broader corporate strategy.**

### Explanation

In recent years, call centers have been in the midst of enormous strategic developments. The convergence of Internet, telecommunications and computer technologies is creating vast new types of services and multiplying the connections among customers, organizations, suppliers, industry interest groups and government. Today's customers are informed and connected, and organizations must transition sales and customer service delivery systems to serve them better – or run the risk of dissatisfying, disillusioning or driving them away.

Consequently, there is enormous pressure in call centers to be accessible, personalize service, give customers choice, handle increasingly complex transactions, lower costs, integrate with organizationwide initiatives and

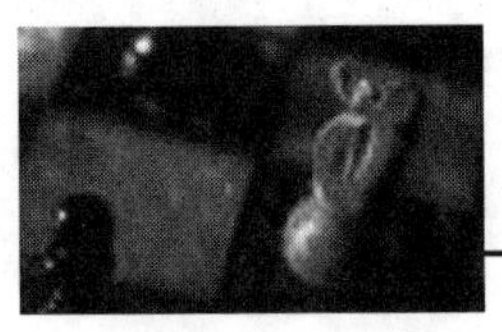

contribute tangible strategic value to the organization.

Developing effective strategy is a signature characteristic of organizations that meet these challenges. In the call center environment, strategy is primarily embodied in the customer access strategy, which is a framework – a set of standards, guidelines and processes – defining the means by which customers are connected with resources capable of delivering the desired information and services.

The need for a cohesive customer access strategy is driven by a number of interrelated factors:

- Traffic across all access channels (e.g., telephone, text-chat, email, etc.) is growing.
- Customer expectations are evolving rapidly, and customers are increasingly savvy and well informed.
- Services are becoming more complicated from both the customer's and organization's perspective.
- With many technology "owners" across the organization, ensuring a common customer focus is essential.
- Being "easy to do business with" is a primary driver of customer satisfaction.

As with general corporate strategy, a customer access strategy can take many different forms. However, the most sustainable customer access strategies include the following components:

- **Customer segmentation:** How customers and prospective customers are segmented, e.g., by geography, purchasing behavior, demographics, volume of business and unique requirements. Customer segmentation generally comes from the organization's marketing strategy and is a direct reflection of how customers are defined.
- **Major contact types:** This identifies the reasons for interaction between the organization and customers. General categories include placing orders, changing orders, checking account status and resolving problems. Each type of interaction should be analyzed for opportunities to build customer value and enhance customer satisfaction and loyalty.
- **Access channels:** Access channels include telephone, Web, fax, email, IVR, kiosk, handhelds, face-to-face service and postal mail, as well as corresponding telephone numbers, Web URLs, email addresses, fax

numbers and postal addresses. The organization may choose to open different access channels to different customer segments.

- **Service level and response time objectives:** This part of strategy definition essentially determines how fast the organization intends to respond to customer contacts. Different objectives may be appropriate for different customer segments.
- **Hours of operation:** The days and hours the call center will be open for business. This, too, can vary for different customer segments.
- **Routing methodology:** How, by customer, type of contact and access channel, each contact will be routed and distributed. Call routing may vary by type of customer if the call center establishes agent groups for unique customer segments. Call routing may also apply to outbound contacts, e.g., specifying the agent group or system through which contacts will be made to customers.
- **Person and technology resources required by contact:** The resources, including people, technologies and databases, required to provide callers with the information and assistance they need, and to provide the organization with the information it requires to track and manage customers and services. This aspect of strategy also guides hiring, training, technology deployment, database development and many other aspects of operations.
- **Knowledge bases:** The information systems used to capture, store and process information on customers, products and services.
- **Tracking and integration:** The methods and systems required to capture information on each customer interaction and define how that data will be used to strengthen customer profiles, identify trends and improve products and services. This is an essential component of strategy and defines how data will be used to focus marketing campaigns, build customer-specific products and services, and provide customer services geared toward customer needs and wants.

The customer access strategy is not something that can be developed in a vacuum; it must be developed within the context of broader corporate strategy. However, while corporate strategy must ultimately define the customer access strategy, the customer access strategy can influence broader corporate strategy. For example, 24x7 call center services have enabled some insurance companies to differentiate their services from competitors who only provide in-person service. Similarly, call center and Web-based sales and services have enabled some computer companies to become low-cost providers vs. those who sell through distributors.

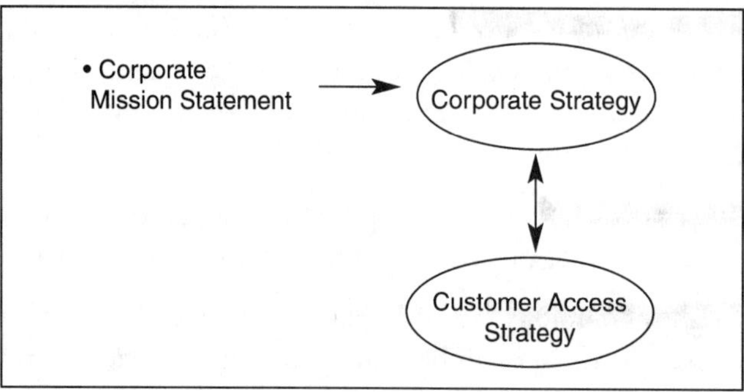


Developing a sound customer access strategy requires leadership, persistence, and cross-functional collaboration. But when approached with the right commitment and buy-in, a customer access strategy is a powerful tool for unleashing the potential and value of customer contact. It guides decisions related to all aspects of operations, including people, processes and technologies. And it provides a framework for ongoing developments.

Note: Because an effective customer access strategy is the blueprint for all call center activities, it is presented in each of ICMI's other study guides, including:

- *Call Center People Management Handbook and Study Guide*
- *Call Center Operations Management Handbook and Study Guide*
- *Call Center Customer Relationship Management Handbook and Study Guide*

## 7. Creating an Effective Strategic Development Process [Strategic]

Ready? | 1 | 2 | 3 |



### Key Points

- Without a system or approach for ongoing development, strategy quickly becomes out-of-date and ineffectual.
- A sound strategic development process consists of seven essential steps:
  - Create a connected vision
  - Shape the supporting strategy
  - Build skills, knowledge and leaders
  - Implement connected plans and processes
  - Apply enabling technologies
  - Make the required investments
  - Unleash innovative quality
- The key to effective strategic development is to see each step as part of a continuum.

### Explanation

The customer access strategy is an essential aspect of developing a cohesive, effective customer contact environment. But developing an effective customer access strategy is no easy task – and is not a once-and-done activity. Because the customer access strategy touches virtually every traditional business unit, it requires an immense amount of collaboration, cooperation and leadership. And, as each of the processes is interrelated, changes to one will impact all others. In short, developing strategy is an ongoing process. Without a system or approach for ongoing development, strategy quickly becomes out-of-date and ineffectual. The tactics chosen to carry out a strategy must be achievable and adequately funded or the strategy simply will not work.

A sound strategic development process must consider seven essential components, including vision, strategy, people, processes, technologies, funding and innovation. Together, they can be viewed as interrelated steps in an overall strategic development process.

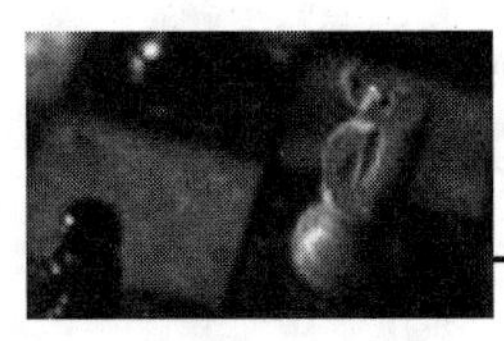

ICMI
Incoming Calls Management Institute
Advancing the Call Center Profession Worldwide

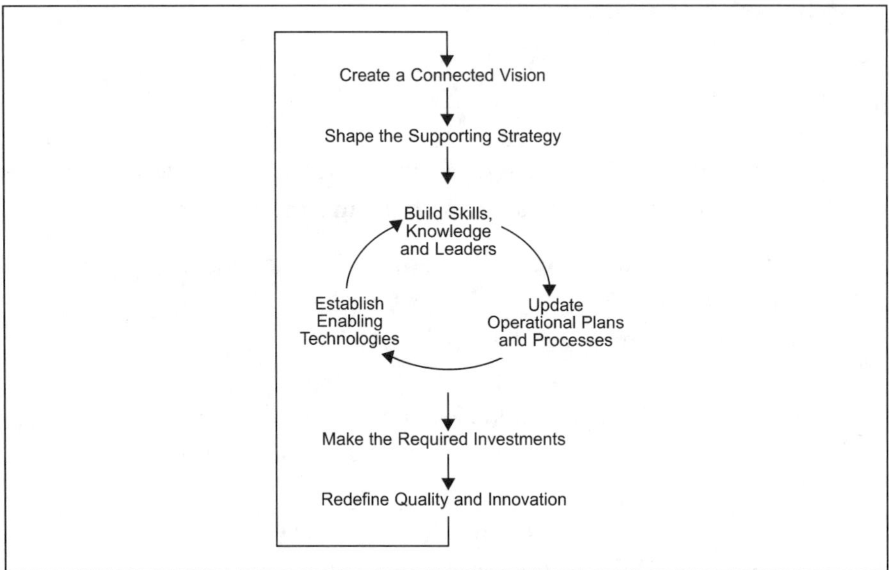
Create a Connected Vision
Shape the Supporting Strategy
Build Skills, Knowledge and Leaders
Update Operational Plans and Processes
Establish Enabling Technologies
Make the Required Investments
Redefine Quality and Innovation

This process is simple, effective and enduring. As a framework, it provides focus to your efforts to keep strategy current, along with an approach for tying the pieces together.

### 1. Create a Connected Vision

Vision comes first. Vision is the creative ability to see beyond current circumstances to what could be. Vision remains the undisputed motivation behind any human change or action. We refer to a "connected" vision because it must be appropriate for today's fast-changing, interconnected organizations and economy.

Key questions often serve as a useful catalyst in this effort. For example, how do your customers define great service? What sort of organizational structure best supports the integration of e-commerce and traditional telephony services? How can the call center help the organization understand customers better? How can the call center's vision and purpose be better communicated? (See Creating a Shared Vision, this section.)

### 2. Shape the Supporting Strategy

It is within this context that the customer access strategy is created and/or refined. The customer access strategy is a mechanism for turning vision into operational reality and will serve as a framework for developing the steps that follow. (See The Role of the Customer Access Strategy, this section.)

### 3. Build Skills, Knowledge and Leaders

This initially involves developing a "map" of current versus required competencies for every key requirement (position) in the call center and identifying areas where you may be vulnerable, i.e., where only a few key people possess important management or technical know-how. Other important aspects of this step involve developing appropriate hiring and training plans; implementing a systematic process for recognizing and cultivating management and leadership competencies; instilling an understanding of queuing dynamics and unique call center planning and management implications into the culture; establishing appropriate performance standards; and defining and developing attractive career and skill path alternatives. (These subjects are covered in detail in ICMI's *Call Center People Management Handbook and Study Guide.*)

### 4. Implement Connected Plans and Processes

This refers specifically to putting the planning and management processes in place necessary to support the customer access strategy. In today's environment, this usually involves forecasting, scheduling and real-time management across all channels of contact; simulating "what-if" scenarios given increasingly complex routing and distribution requirements; redefining agent group structure to move towards a true multimedia queuing environment; and improving collaboration and planning across the organization. (These subjects are covered in detail in ICMI's *Call Center Operations Management Handbook and Study Guide.*)

### 5. Apply Enabling Technologies

The obvious focus of this step is to specify the technology infrastructure required to turn vision into reality. To do this, the technology migration plan should be aligned with the customer access strategy. The customer access strategy will keep call center technology focused on overall business transformation, as opposed to simply meeting one operational need. Using the customer access strategy as a guide is particularly important since both technology and call center operational processes continue to evolve.

An equally important aspect of this process is to address the "technology conundrum," consisting of three important questions:

1. **Should you buy now or buy later?** If you buy now, you begin conquering the learning curve early and will enjoy the benefits sooner. However, if you buy later, the technology will be cheaper, faster and better,

and other organizations will have worked out the kinks. Once you decide to buy now, the question becomes, "Should we buy, build or lease?" This question should be answered by looking at expertise of existing staff, integration issues with existing technologies, costs, how quickly the new capability is needed, and the future needs of the call center.

**2. Is the capability a sea change or diversion?** For example, widespread video capabilities in call centers have, thus far, proved to be elusive while e-commerce services are quickly and fundamentally changing the customer service environment. New technologies are particularly risky because an incorrect answer to this question can have enormous consequences.

**3. Who's in charge of specification and implementation decisions?** Important considerations of this question include determining if current staff have the appropriate background to deploy the technology, and what time and resources are required for successful implementation.

These questions should be reviewed and addressed as part of this step, and they should be considered in the context of the other steps. (Technologies are covered in detail in ICMI's *Call Center Operations Management Handbook and Study Guide.*)

### 6. Make the Required Investments

Here's where vision, strategy and many lofty ambitions and plans can run into cold reality. For that reason, some say this step should occur much sooner in the process. But we disagree. Why have a call center – or, for that matter, why have an organization – if budgetary allocations predetermine possibilities? No one would choose to spend money in any of these areas unless there is a reasonable return for both customers and the organization. And therein is the reality: you don't even know what the possibilities are without going through the previous steps. Yes, return on investment (ROI) analysis, staff budgeting and capital planning play an important role in good management. And in the end, it's all semantics anyway because no step, including budgeting, is inseparable from any other. But as a matter of principle, the budget should not short circuit vision and strategy before new possibilities get a chance to make their case. (See Principles of Developing an Effective Annual Operating Budget, Section 7.)

### 7. Unleash Innovative Quality

When it comes to quality, three prevailing questions can help guide thinking and decisions:

1. What are customer expectations?
2. Are you meeting them?
3. Are you using the fewest possible resources to do so?

Typical customer expectations include:

- Be accessible
- Treat me courteously
- Be responsive to what I need and want
- Do what I ask promptly
- Provide well-trained and informed employees
- Tell me what to expect
- Meet your commitments, keep your promises
- Do it right the first time
- Be socially responsible and ethical
- Follow up

Quality has never consisted only of the attributes of a product or service; it must always be aligned with customers' needs, wants and expectations, and the organization's ability to deliver on them efficiently. The invention and application of toll-free services, ACD capabilities, Internet-based services, speech recognition – the list can go on – have all raised expectations to new levels. (For a complete discussion on customer expectations, see ICMI's *Call Center Customer Relationship Management Handbook and Study Guide.)*

### A Continuum

As customer expectations change and factors impacting strategy and operations evolve, you will need to redefine your vision – which takes you back to the beginning of the process. (See Identifying External Factors Impacting Strategy and Operations, Section 5.) Business analyst and former *Wall Street Journal* editor Thomas Petzinger, Jr. proclaimed that "strategy, once an event, is now a continuous process." The key to effective strategic development is to see each step as part of a continuum.

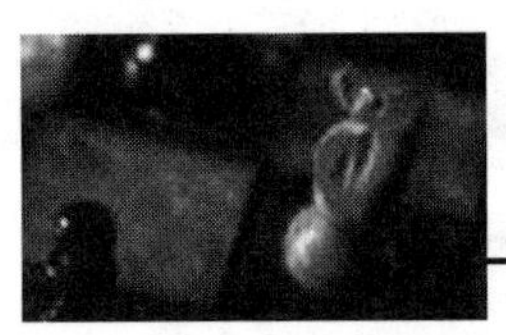

## 8. Aligning Tactical Activities with Values, Vision, and Mission

Ready? | 1 | 2 | 3 |

### Key Points

- **Today's customer contact environment is in a constant state of change. Without a logical approach for ongoing development, plans quickly become out-of-date and ineffectual – even if the organization has the right vision and supporting strategy.**
- **The strategic development process also serves as a useful framework for aligning tactical activities with values, vision and mission. The framework provides a step-by-step structure for considering implications and ensuring alignment.**
- **For major developments, a cross-functional development team that includes representation from the call center and from across the organization can ensure that decisions and developments are in sync.**

### Explanation

Today's customer contact environment is in a constant state of change. Management activities have multiplied, and the interrelated nature of decisions requires constant coordination and systemic thinking. Customer requirements, workflows, business rules, screen designs, scripts, Web pages, menus, reports and much more are all changing. Without a system or approach for ongoing development, plans quickly become out-of-date and ineffectual – even if the organization has the right vision and supporting strategy.

Conveniently, the strategic development process is not only an effective tool for developing strategies, but also serves as a useful framework for aligning tactical activities with values and mission. (See Creating an Effective Strategic Development Process, this section.)

As an alignment tool, this process provides a logical structure for thinking through implications of changes and developments. Consider the example of adding email and text-chat support to Web-based services. The framework provides a step-by-step structure for considering implications and ensuring alignment. For example:

- **Vision:** Email and text-chat open up additional contact channels, furthering the organization's vision of giving customers choice and adding value to Web-based interactions.

- **Strategy:** Email and text-chat affect contact types, agent group structure, customer communications and other components of the customer access strategy.
- **People:** Employee selection criteria will need to evolve to find agents proficient in real-time, written communication. Training and education programs will need to reflect the new type of work, and performance standards will evolve.
- **Processes:** Forecasting and scheduling processes will need to reflect new work types and patterns, as well as the overall workload. Reporting and communication will also have to evolve to reflect new types of work and workload patterns.
- **Technologies:** The agent desktop, along with routing tools and programming, will need to be updated.
- **Budgets:** Funding requirements will be impacted by each of the proceeding steps/developments.
- **Quality and innovation:** New considerations include coaching and monitoring for the new channels of contact, customer surveys across these channels, the ability to capture and leverage customer input, and integration with other contact channels.

In short, each step highlights issues and decisions that must be viewed in terms of their impact on each other and on overall results and direction. The seven components of the process provide a logical framework for identifying alignment requirements.

**Major Projects**

For major projects, essential steps in ensuring that tactical developments align with values and vision include:

1. Build a cross-functional development team that includes representation from the call center, information technology (IT), human resources (HR), marketing, training, finance and other key areas to direct strategic initiatives and ensure necessary decisions and developments are coordinated.

2. Ensure that the team is using the strategic development process framework as an alignment tool.

3. Ensure major developments are approved and supported by the cross-functional team.

4. Avoid bureaucracy and red tape. Ensure the collaborative team has an orientation toward supporting and furthering sensible developments. The team should meet often enough to minimize delay in considering and addressing initiatives.

5. Publish guidelines that help managers think through the impact of developments on people, processes and technologies. For example, a simple checklist of questions can help facilitate project proposals that consider overall impact.

Alignment is a work in progress. Surveys show that up to 65 percent of customer relationship management initiatives fail to live up to expectations. Major technology projects suffer similar odds. In many cases, the root causes of failure are due to insufficient efforts to align people, processes and technologies with the objectives. But with the right framework, along with the time and commitment required, aligning tactical activities with vision, values and strategy will ensure that the organization is moving in the right direction, as efficiently as possible.

### The Balanced Scorecard Approach

As companies around the world transform themselves for competition that is based on information, their ability to exploit intangible assets has become far more decisive than their ability to invest in and manage physical assets. Several years ago, in recognition of this change, we introduced a concept we called the balanced scorecard. The balanced scorecard supplemented traditional financial measures with criteria that measured performance from three additional perspectives – those of customer, internal business processes, and learning and growth. It therefore enabled companies to track financial results while simultaneously monitoring progress in building the capabilities and acquiring the intangible assets they would need for future growth. The scorecard wasn't a replacement for financial measures; it was their complement.

Recently, we have seen some companies move beyond our early vision for the scorecard to discover its value as the cornerstone of a new strategic management system. Used this way, the scorecard addresses a serious deficiency in traditional management systems: their inability to link a company's long-term strategy with its short-term actions.

Most companies' operational and management control systems are built around financial measures and targets, which bear little relation to the company's progress in achieving long-term strategic objectives. Thus the emphasis most companies place on short-term financial measures leaves a gap between the development of a strategy and its implementation.

Managers using the balanced scorecard do not have to rely on short-term financial measures as the sole indicators of the company's performance. The scorecard lets them introduce four management processes that, separately and in combination, contribute to linking long-term strategic objectives with short-term actions.

The first process – translating the vision – helps managers build a consensus around the organization's vision and strategy.

The second process – communication and linking – lets managers communicate their strategy up and down the organization and link it to departmental and individual objectives.

The third process – business planning – enables companies to integrate their business and financial plans.

The fourth process – feedback and learning – gives companies the capacity for what we call strategic learning.

Excerpt from "Using the Balanced Scorecard as a Strategic Management System" by Robert S. Kaplan and David P. Norton, *Harvard Business Review*, January-February 1996.

# 9. Defining the Call Center's Value Proposition

Ready? | 1 | 2 | 3 |



## Key Points

- **The call center's value proposition, or set of specific benefits it provides to the organization and customers, affects budgeting, strategy, technology, management, interdepartmental cooperation and personnel assignments in the call center.**
- **There are many viable call center value propositions, but most comprise contributions to one or more of the following:**
  - **Unit strategies**
  - **Customer satisfaction and loyalty**
  - **Quality and innovation**
  - **Marketing**
  - **Products and services**
  - **Efficient service delivery**
  - **Self-service usage and system design**
  - **Revenue/sales**

## Explanation

Defining the call center's value proposition, or the set of specific benefits it provides to the organization and customers, has wide-reaching implications. Organizational perception of call center value affects budget allocations, strategic objectives and direction, technology resources, management authority and autonomy, levels of interdepartmental cooperation and even the quality and commitment of personnel assigned to the call center.

The value proposition is a key component of organizational strategy. For call centers, there are many examples of different value propositions, but most comprise one or more of the following alternatives, each of which is explained in detail later in the handbook/study guide:

- Unit strategies
- Customer satisfaction and loyalty
- Quality and innovation
- Marketing

- Products and services
- Efficient service delivery
- Self-service usage and system design
- Revenue/sales

Call center managers need to be aware of all the benefits a call center can provide, and then they need to establish which sets of benefits best fit their call center's role in their organization. This is a dynamic process that must consider the call center's emerging role. (See Strategies and Actions to Support the Call Center's Emerging Role, Section 5.)

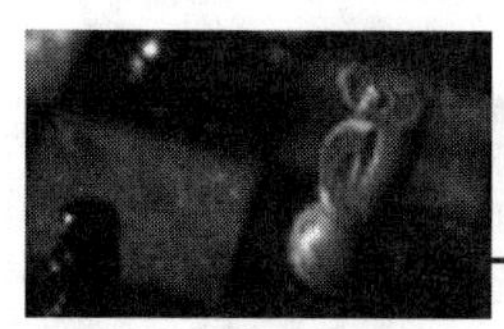

# 10. The Call Center's Contribution to Unit Strategies

**Ready?** | 1 | 2 | 3 |

## Key Points

- **Call center managers should actively seek out the key people in other departments to share the benefits of the call center to their business units.**
- **Key considerations when contributing to unit strategies throughout the organization include:**
  - **Ensure that disseminating information is a priority in your call center**
  - **Don't get overwhelmed**
  - **Don't get caught up in perfectionism**
  - **Footnote assumptions and unknowns**
  - **Ensure information is absolutely truthful**
  - **Build teams and continually improve processes for capturing and analyzing value-added information**

## Explanation

As the primary customer touch point, the call center provides the entire organization with much of its customer intelligence. The call center collects data from daily contact handling and is often the place where customer surveys are administered. This information allows every business unit to make strategic decisions about how their actions impact customers. Therefore, the call center must take responsibility for providing the appropriate data to each department in a timely manner. This is one of the most effective ways for other departments to realize the strategic value of the call center.

### Share the Benefits

Call center managers should actively seek out the key people in other departments to share the benefits of the call center to their business units. This information is often communicated most effectively through in-person meetings that focus on how the call center can work with the department to accomplish the most for the organization.

When determining and communicating the benefits to each department, consider these tips:

- Study the organization's annual report
- Acquire and review departmental mission statements and published objectives
- Build a small, capable team to work with you on supporting unit strategies
- Ask each unit director two powerful questions:
    1. What keeps you up at night (what challenges do you face in your area)?
    2. What gets you excited (what opportunities do you have)?

The following table lists important benefits to various business units.

| Business Unit | The Call Center Provides These Benefits... |
|---|---|
| Marketing | • Supports segmentation/branding<br>• Provides detailed customer demographics<br>• Tracks trends (purchases, customer service and support issues, etc.) and response rates<br>• Enables permission-based marketing<br>• Enables targeted marketing<br>• Provides customer surveys and feedback |
| Financial | • Contributes to the control of overall costs<br>• Contributes to shareholder value through strategic value contributions<br>• Is essential in establishing budgetary strategy and priorities<br>• Serves as an early warning system (positive and negative)<br>• Contributes to successful mergers and acquisitions |
| HR/Training | • Contributes to recruiting and hiring<br>• Contributes to skill and career path development<br>• Contributes to coaching and mentoring<br>• Helps foster a learning organization<br>• Contributes to legal compliance |
| Manufacturing/ Operations | • Pinpoints quality and/or production problems<br>• Provides input on products' and services' usability and clarity<br>• Contributes to clear manuals and procedures<br>• Highlights distribution problems and opportunities<br>• Facilitates communication related to capacity or production problems |

*(continued, next page)*

| Business Unit | The Call Center Provides These Benefits... |
|---|---|
| Research & Development (R&D)/Design | • Provides information on competitive direction and trends<br>• Highlights product compatibility issues and opportunities<br>• Provides customer feedback on usability<br>• Differentiates between "features" and "benefits" from the customer's perspective<br>• Identifies product and service differentiation opportunities |
| IT/Telecom | • Provides the essential human bridge between diverse processes and systems<br>• Furthers organizationwide infrastructure development<br>• Is a key driver in IT/Telecom investments<br>• Furthers self-service usage and system design<br>• Provides a concentrated technology learning ground |
| Legal | • Enables consistent and accurate customer communications and policies<br>• Serves as an early warning system of quality problems<br>• Identifies and addresses impending customer problems<br>• Provides a rapid response to news/media<br>• Contributes to internal communication<br>• Serves as a training ground for legal compliance and policies |

Key considerations when contributing to unit strategies throughout the organization include:

- **Ensure that disseminating information is a priority in your call center:** If the call center is not delivering this information in a timely, easily understood manner, then it is not leveraging its strategic potential. In fact, it is hampering the organization's ability to strategically position itself for the future.

- **Don't get overwhelmed:** When it comes down to it, there is an infinite amount of information that you could provide to each business unit in your organization. Instead of focusing on the volume of data, work with each department to determine what information will have the most impact.

- **Don't get caught up in perfectionism:** Spending too much time tweaking reports can lead to frustration and unnecessary delays. Begin this process with the assumption that reports will be refined as the relationship continues.

- **Footnote assumptions and unknowns:** Ensure that everyone involved understands where the data came from and what considerations are present. Strategic decisions based on misinterpreted reports can be worse than if there were no reports at all.

- **Ensure information is absolutely truthful:** Altering the data to make a case or sway opinions will ultimately damage the call center's integrity.
- **Build teams and continually improve processes for capturing and analyzing value added information:** Individuals with the knowledge and abilities to uncover better ways to communicate and analyze data contribute enormously to better decisions.

(See Creating a Communication Plan for Internal Audiences, Section 4.)

Section 3

## 11. The Call Center's Contribution to Customer Satisfaction and Loyalty

Ready? | 1 | 2 | 3 |

### Key Points

- The basic formula for maximizing customer satisfaction and loyalty is to do the job right the first time and effectively manage customer contacts, including the feedback loop to product/service improvement.
- Research has shown that, if an organization has an effective customer service system in place, many of those customers who have questions or experience problems can be retained.
- The impact of the call center's contribution to customer satisfaction and loyalty is not limited to, but includes:
  - Positive word-of-mouth
  - Repeat purchases
  - Cross-sell and upsell opportunities
  - Increased market share
  - Enhanced feedback

### Explanation

The call center plays a key role in maximizing customer satisfaction and loyalty. As shown in the following graphic, the basic formula for maximizing customer satisfaction and loyalty is to do the job right the first time and effectively manage customer contacts, including the feedback loop to product/service improvement.

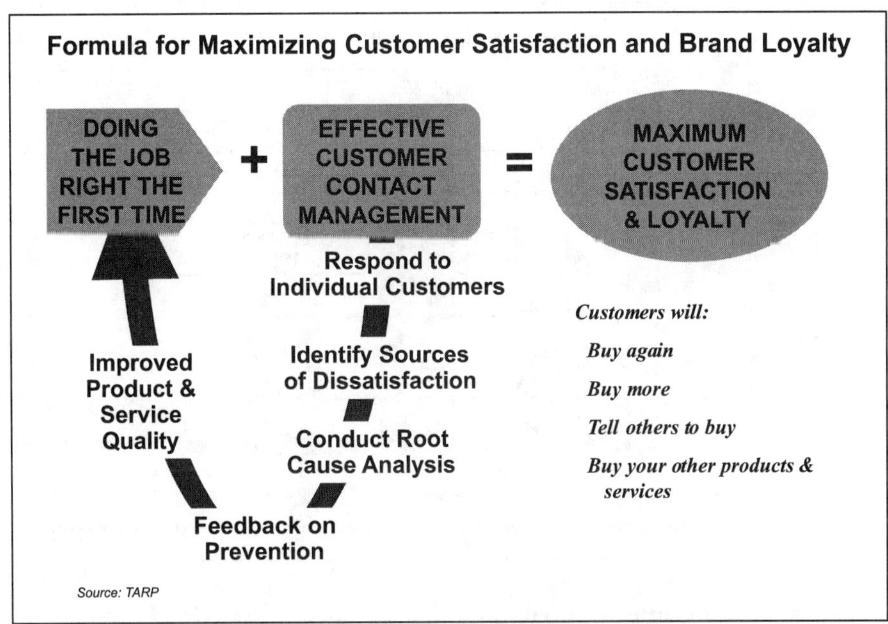
Formula for Maximizing Customer Satisfaction and Brand Loyalty
DOING THE JOB RIGHT THE FIRST TIME
+
EFFECTIVE CUSTOMER CONTACT MANAGEMENT
=
MAXIMUM CUSTOMER SATISFACTION & LOYALTY
Respond to Individual Customers
Identify Sources of Dissatisfaction
Conduct Root Cause Analysis
Feedback on Prevention
Improved Product & Service Quality
Customers will:
Buy again
Buy more
Tell others to buy
Buy your other products & services
Source: TARP

Doing the job right the first time requires effective product/service development, including design, manufacturing processes, product/service delivery and sales practices. This will ensure that, in most cases, customer needs and expectations are met.

However, no product or service completely meets customer needs and expectations 100 percent of the time. Customers do experience problems and they do have questions. Thus, an organization needs to have an effective system in place to handle these issues when they arise. This is the customer service component of the customer satisfaction formula and is a primary role of the call center.

### How Effective Customer Service Increases Loyalty

Research has shown that, if an organization has an effective customer service system in place, many of those customers who have questions or experience problems can be retained. As the following chart illustrates, satisfied complainants can be nearly as, or even more loyal than, customers who did not experience a problem. This phenomenon is a direct result of the more personal relationship that the customer now has with the organization due to the contact experience.

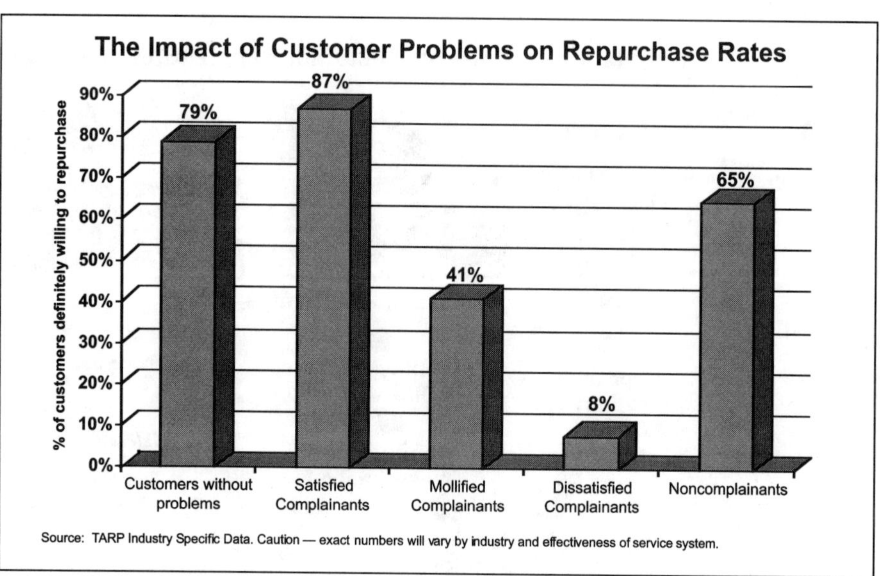


### Call Center Contributors to Customer Satisfaction

Key drivers of customer satisfaction that are within the call center's control include:

- **Accessibility:** TARP has found that accessibility, as measured by service level and response time, can be a significant customer dissatisfier if it is outside the customer's expectations. However, as long as the call center provides a service level within the customer's expectations, answering the call faster doesn't significantly contribute to higher customer satisfaction.
- **Resolution on first contact:** TARP has found in hundreds of studies that "resolution on first contact" is nearly always a key driver of customer satisfaction. Increasing the percentage of contacts that are resolved to the customer's satisfaction on the first call will increase customer satisfaction and ensure that the service will be perceived as "hassle free."
- **Follow through on promised action:** A close second to "resolution on first contact" as a key driver of customer satisfaction is "follow through on promised action in the expected timeframe." Agents need to know that an overly optimistic promise to a customer can backfire if the organization is not able to meet that promise. It is better to be conservative with promises, such as shipping times, product replacement timeframes, and order processing times, and delight customers with even better actual results.

- **Knowledge of the agent:** For certain types of call centers, "knowledge of the agent" can also be a key driver of satisfaction. In some industries, contact with an agent is the service provided to the customer. For example, customers rely on the knowledge and experience of agents in technical support centers and information desks to receive their primary deliverable – knowledge. Customers can also experience frustration if they reference marketing promotions or products, for example, which agents are unaware of. It is hard to satisfy customers who are more knowledgeable than the agent who is attempting to help them.



### The Impact

What is the impact of the call center's contribution to customer satisfaction and loyalty? Positive word-of-mouth, repeat purchases, cross-sell and upsell opportunities, increased market share and enhanced feedback are just some of the ways the organization benefits from this call center contribution. For almost every organization, even those in government or nonprofit sectors, customer satisfaction is the ultimate goal and the call center is either increasing or decreasing customer satisfaction contact by contact, based on the quality of service it provides.

(For a thorough discussion of customer satisfaction and loyalty, see ICMI's *Call Center Customer Relationship Management Handbook and Study Guide.*)

## 12. The Call Center's Contribution to Quality and Innovation

Ready? | 1 | 2 | 3 |

### Key Points

- **The call center should act as a consultant to the rest of the organization related to improving product/service quality and innovation.**
- **Integration of call center collected data with the quality decision-making process involves five basic steps:**
  1. **Evaluation of the problem or question severity**
  2. **Extrapolation to the marketplace**
  3. **Estimation of the market impact**
  4. **Comparison to internal measures**
  5. **Determination of the probable cause of the problem**
- **The call center's impact on quality and innovation includes:**
  - **Lower overall costs**
  - **More attractive products and services**
  - **Differentiation opportunities**

### Explanation

Data gathered from customers with problems and questions should be used to improve the quality of goods and services by identifying and correcting the root causes of customer problems and by identifying product/service innovations. The call center is a primary source of data on customer problems related to the product/service quality. Therefore, the call center should act as an internal consultant to the organization, integrating the "voice of the customer" into other business decisions, such as quality improvement and new products and services.

Data collected by the call center on the reason for contact should be combined with quality data for a comprehensive view of product and service quality. Integration of call center data with the quality decision-making process involves five basic steps:

1. **Evaluation of the problem or question severity:** To determine if the problem or question is worth worrying about from a quality resource allocation perspective.

2. **Extrapolation to the marketplace:** To estimate from the number of contacts the actual number of occurrences of the problem in the marketplace.

3. **Estimation of the market impact:** By estimating the number of customers lost because of the problem experience plus those lost because of negative word-of-mouth.

4. **Comparison to internal measures:** To correlate the impact with internal measures of quality.

5. **Determination of the probable cause of the problem:** By using root cause analysis to pinpoint the source of the problem.



**The Impact**

When the call center's contribution to quality and innovation is leveraged the benefits include:

- **Lower overall costs:** As quality improves, fewer customers will need to call with a problem or question, resulting in lower overall service costs to the organization.
- **More attractive products and services:** Customers will receive more reliable products and services and, as a result, will be more likely to remain loyal to the organization.
- **Differentiation opportunities:** Organizations that deliver high-quality and innovative products and services can differentiate themselves among competitors.

# 13. The Call Center's Contribution to Marketing

Ready? | 1 | 2 | 3 |

## Key Points

- **In addition to providing data on campaign response rates, call centers can capture valuable information on:**
  - **The ability of marketing efforts to appropriately represent the product or service**
  - **Customer profiles, segmentation and value**
  - **Feedback on buying trends and habits**
- **To assist the marketing department in appropriately representing the organization's products and services, the call center should provide actionable feedback. One solution is to use the *Index of Marketing Quality* (IMQ)™ to quantify the percentage of profits lost due to incorrectly set expectations.**

## Explanation

In addition to providing data on campaign response rates, call centers can capture valuable information on:

- The ability of marketing efforts to appropriately represent the product or service
- Customer profiles, segmentation and value
- Feedback on buying trends and habits

### Appropriate Product or Service Representation in Marketing

Much market damage and unnecessary service expense is attributable to the absence of a link between marketing and sales functions on the one hand, and service and customer retention functions on the other. Without such a link, as marketing and sales "make their numbers" for the month, they lack the incentive to worry about the service expense or future customer attrition.

One solution, suggested by TARP, is to create an *Index of Marketing Quality* (IMQ)™ that quantifies the percentage of profits lost due to incorrectly set expectations. The steps to creating this index include:

1. **Determine the service cost:** Multiply the volume of customer contacts

related to incorrectly set expectations by the average cost of handling each of these contacts.

Service cost = volume x average cost per contact

**2. Calculate the expected damage to loyalty:** Multiply the volume of customer contacts due to the mistake by the percentage of customers at risk of defecting due to the mistake – typically determined through a baseline survey. Then, multiply the result by the average customer value.

Expected damage to loyalty = volume x percentage of customers at risk x average customer value

**3. Determine the total cost of incorrectly set expectations:** Add the service cost to the expected damage to loyalty.

Total cost = service cost + expected damage to loyalty

**4. Calculate the percentage of profits lost due to incorrectly set expectations:** Divide the total cost of incorrectly set expectations by the total gross profit from the marketing campaign.

Percentage of profits lost = total cost ÷ total gross profit

The following example illustrates the application of the IMQ.

Scenario: Credit card customers were misled by the literature about the interest rate they would receive.

- The company gets 20,000 calls on interest rates at a cost of $2 per call.
- Interest rate surprises decrease loyalty by 25 percent.
- An average customer is worth $200 annually in gross profit.
- Total gross profit of the marketing campaign was $30 million

Service cost = 20,000 x $2 = $40,000

Expected damage to loyalty = 20,000 x .25 x $200 = $1,000,000

Total cost = $40,000 + $1,000,000 = $1,040,000

Percentage of profits lost = $1,040,000 ÷ $30,000,000 = 3.5%

In this example, the profits are 3.5 percent lower than they would have been if the marketing department communicated more clearly with customers.

It should be noted that the IMQ does not account for the negative word-of-mouth spread by dissatisfied customers, which usually amounts to approximately eight to 10 people per dissatisfied customer. If the marketing department understands the long-term implications of misleading messages, the profitability and success of marketing initiatives are greatly improved.

**Information on Customer Profiles, Segmentation and Value**

Marketing uses customer profile data to segment customers into groups based on their commonalities. The marketing for each customer segment can then be customized to most effectively attract those types of customers. The call center collects much of the information typically used for marketing segmentation, e.g., geography, demographics, and profitability.

The call center also usually houses the information needed to determine customer value. The information about customer value can tell the organization which customer segment provides the most revenue, or if a specific segment doesn't provide enough value to pursue. Marketing can use this information to help determine where to focus its efforts.

The call center should work with marketing to develop a customer segmentation strategy. This strategy should include how to attract each customer segment as well as what call center services should be made available to them. Through effective coordination, the organization will be able to serve customers based on the promises it makes at the time of the sale.

(For a detailed discussion of customer profiling, segmentation and valuation, see ICMI's *Call Center Customer Relationship Management Handbook and Study Guide.*)

**The Impact**

The call center's contribution to marketing will result in:

- **Increased wallet share:** As customer expectations set at the time of the sale are met through the organization's products and services, customer satisfaction and loyalty – and, in turn, wallet share – will increase.
- **More successful marketing messages and focus:** As the call center shares segmentation intelligence, marketing will be equipped to attract those customers that are most valuable to the organization.
- **Improved response:** Response rates will improve as marketing messages are tailored to each customer segment.

## 14. The Call Center's Contribution to Products and Services

Ready? | 1 | 2 | 3 |



### Key Points

- **Call centers can contribute to products and services in three primary ways:**
  - **Communicate customer perceptions of product/service design and quality**
  - **Provide customer education to enhance the use of the product/service**
  - **Become a part of the product/service through value-added service**
- **Two commonly used approaches to customer education are:**
  - **Encourage customers to contact the organization before having a problem**
  - **Make a proactive outbound contact**

### Explanation

Call centers can contribute to products and services in three primary ways:

- **Communicate customer perceptions of product/service design and quality:** Call centers provide a ready source of customer perceptions regarding product/service design and quality. Agents in the call center often talk to many more customers in a year than traditional marketing or quality surveys ever reach. Agents can ask certain follow-up questions that can greatly enhance product and service design. For example, at one packaged-goods manufacturer, the product design department regularly provides key questions for agents to ask; the answers enable the organization to identify opportunities for innovation.
- **Provide customer education to enhance the use of the product/service:** Call centers can provide customer education that can greatly enhance the use of the product/service and decrease customer-caused problems, e.g., unnecessary product returns, product misuse, etc. TARP's research has found that proactively telling the customer about common problems and how to avoid them can greatly increase customer satisfaction and loyalty toward the product. The call center can play an active role in this type of "welcome center" activity.

- **Become a part of the product/service through value-added service:** Call centers can themselves become part of the product/service. Organizations that offer high-quality call center services can use the call center as an added feature in their "sale" of the product/service. General Electric has been quoted as saying they can charge $40 more per refrigerator simply because of the existence of the GE Answer Center. Some health insurance companies compete as much on the quality of their call center support as their premiums.

> **Educate Customers Aggressively**
>
> Customers blame the organization when problems occur, even when the customer contributes to their cause. Therefore it is in the organization's interest to educate the customer. Two commonly used approaches to customer education are to get the customer to call before having a problem or to otherwise proactively provide information.
>
> Armstrong, a floor manufacturer, took the first approach. Armstrong printed a toll-free telephone number on the topside of the floor itself. This highly visible number stimulated the customer to call Armstrong for directions on how to remove it from the floor's surface. During the call, Armstrong personnel were able to educate the customer on how to maintain the floor properly and avoid damaging the finish. The few dollars spent on the educational call prevented maintenance problems that could have cost Armstrong $12,000 in revenue per customer, over the customer's average period of loyalty. Thus, Armstrong was able to use an inexpensive external fix for a problem rather than a more costly internal fix.
>
> The second approach to customer education is through a proactive outbound contact. For example, Vodafone proactively calls customers three weeks after cell phone activation. They both solve operating problems and assure proper expectations about the amount of the first bill, which is often higher than what the consumer expected. In another example, General Motors has compensated their salesforce for providing education to customers on how to use all of the vehicle's options and how to maintain the car. Internal research showed that this session could have a significant impact on customers' long-term satisfaction and loyalty.
>
> Source: TARP, 2002.

### The Impact

The call center's contribution to products and services can impact the organization through:

- **Complementing new product and service development:** Customer data can guide the organization's development of new products and services. These products/services can be tailored to the specific needs of each customer segment.

- **Enhanced sales and market share:** As customers become more satisfied with products and services, they are more likely to purchase again.
- **Differentiating the organization:** If call center services become a value-added part of each sale, the organization can differentiate itself based on its customer service excellence.

## 15. The Call Center's Role in Efficient Service Delivery

Ready? | 1 | 2 | 3 |

### Key Points

- Efficient service delivery is a fundamental role of the call center. The pooling principle lies at the heart of call center effectiveness.
- In addition to pooling agents, call centers also bring together other components that can enable greater levels of efficiency. These components may include:
  - Hiring and other human resources initiatives
  - Training initiatives
  - Network and routing technologies
  - Desktop tools and information systems
  - Workforce management tools and processes
  - Queuing capabilities and real-time management tools and reports
- The call center also contributes to efficiencies in other business units (e.g., by helping manufacturing pinpoint quality problems, helping IT design better self-service systems, enabling research and development to focus on appropriate innovations, and enabling people in other departments to concentrate on other tasks).

### Explanation

Efficient service delivery is a fundamental role of the call center. Call centers enable organizations to pool resources (people, processes and technologies) in order to provide on-demand assistance efficiently and effectively. For many organizations today, this includes handling multiple access channels or operating in a virtual, multi-site environment.

Before implementing a call center, organizations often find that customer contacts are going to various departments or individuals, either through the switchboard or via direct dial into specific areas. All too often, customers receive poor or inconsistent service, and individuals and/or specific departments are burdened with a growing customer contact workload. Routing technologies, customer information systems, desktop tools, workforce management capabilities and other tools that make up the backbone of call center infrastructure are either nonexistent or dispersed and inaccessible.

## Pooling – the Heart of Call Center Effectiveness

The pooling principle lies at the heart of call center effectiveness. The powerful pooling principle states: Any movement in the direction of consolidation of resources will result in improved traffic-carrying efficiency. Conversely, any movement away from consolidation of resources will result in reduced traffic-carrying efficiency.

Put more simply, if you take contacts going to multiple departments and individuals, and send them to a group of pooled agents, the environment becomes measurably more efficient. Or, by extension, if you take several small, specialized agent groups within an existing call center, effectively cross train them and put them into a single group, you'll have a more efficient environment.

| Calls in 1/2 Hour | Service Level | Agents Required | Occupancy | Avg. Calls Per Agent |
|---|---|---|---|---|
| 50 | 80/20 | 9 | 65% | 5.6 |
| 100 | 80/20 | 15 | 78% | 6.7 |
| 500 | 80/20 | 65 | 90% | 7.7 |
| 1000 | 80/20 | 124 | 94% | 8.1 |

Assumption: Calls last an average 3.5 minutes.

As the table illustrates, mathematically, larger groups of pooled agents are more efficient than smaller groups, at the same service level.

A clear trend in recent years is the recognition that different types of callers often have different needs and expectations, and that different agents with a mix of aptitudes and skills are required to provide the necessary knowledge base. Capabilities in the intelligent network and in intelligent ACDs give call centers the means to pool resources, as well as segment and prioritize their customer base. Skills-based routing is a notable example. But it's important to remember that pooling remains the driver behind call center effectiveness.

The pooling principle is a consideration from the highest levels of strategic planning (How many call centers should we have? How should existing call centers be networked?) down to moment-to-moment decisions about overflowing calls between groups, or structuring skills-based routing routines.

## Call Centers Pool More Than Staff

While pooled agents are an important part of call center efficiency, call centers bring together other components that enable greater levels of efficiency, including:

- Hiring and other human resources initiatives, ensuring that the right people with the necessary skills, knowledge and abilities are brought into the call center.
- Training initiatives, which ensure agents receive consistent training on products and services, systems, processes, customer service, and contact handling techniques.
- Network and routing technologies, which deliver the right contacts to the right places at the right times.
- Desktop tools and information systems, which deliver the right information to agents at the right times, boosting first call resolution, and minimizing average handling time. These systems also enable the call center to capture customer history and other essential data.
- Workforce management tools and processes, which optimize the match between required staff and the organization's service level objectives.
- Queuing capabilities and real-time management tools and reports. Since the call center's workload must be handled as it arrives, information on real-time conditions, as well as queuing, routing and overflow capabilities, can ensure that contacts are handled as efficiently as possible.

**Efficiencies Across the Organization**

The call center also contributes to efficiencies in other business units. For example, consider the impact on the organization's workload and efficiency when the call center:

- Helps manufacturing pinpoint quality problems
- Alerts higher-ups to potential legal troubles (e.g., consumer safety issues)
- Helps IT design better self-service systems, based on where and how customers need help when using these systems.
- Enables research and development to zero in on innovations customers are suggesting or requiring
- Enables people in other departments to concentrate on other tasks (versus handling contacts that would otherwise come to their areas)

(These and other contributions are covered in more detail throughout Section 3.)

**Federal Communications Commission Centralizes Call Center Operations**

Located in the heart of the historical battlefield district of Gettysburg, Pennsylvania, the Federal Communications Commission (FCC) has established a state-of-the-art, toll-free telephone customer service center. The FCC National Call Center was conceived and produced by the commission's compliance and information bureau, which administers this innovative and cost-effective public service.

The FCC's new centralized call center responds to a wide range of public inquiries concerning telecommunications issues including, but not limited to, broadcasting, cable, new technologies, cellular, telephone rates and long-distance carriers. When commissioned subject matter experts must be consulted, the caller can be electronically transferred directly from the call center to FCC headquarters in Washington, D.C., at no additional cost to the caller.

According to compliance and information bureau officials, this unique government service is already providing 95 percent of its customers with the information they are seeking and only 5 percent have to be referred to other FCC offices. Further, these officials estimate that, because of these efficiencies in the call center operations, two call center employees saved the equivalent of three work years of other FCC office and bureau personnel. This tremendously cost-effective program is greatly supporting the commission's ongoing commitment to make information available to the public, expeditiously and inexpensively.

Excerpt from Federal Communications Commission video, 1998.

(Note: This example is also used in ICMI's *Call Center Customer Relationship Management Handbook and Study Guide*, in the context of government and nonprofit service-improvement initiatives.)

## 16. The Call Center's Role in Self-Service Usage and System Design

Ready? | 1 | 2 | 3 |

### Key Points

- As the reigning experts in customer service, call center personnel are uniquely positioned to understand and recommend self-service system solutions.
- There are many specific ways for the call center to contribute to self-service system improvements, including:
  - Support self-service systems
  - Educate customers on self-service options
  - Capture caller feedback about self-service systems
  - Collect and analyze data about calls currently handled in the call center
  - Observe agents at work
  - Brainstorm with agents and get them to map process flows
  - Analyze call monitoring data and quality results
  - Integrate self-service systems with call center systems
  - Share expertise and experience

### Explanation

Call centers can play a critical role in self-service systems improvement. As the reigning experts in customer service, call center personnel are uniquely positioned to understand and recommend self-service system solutions. Whether the self-service system is developed within the call center or outside of it, call center management should be included as critical members of the project team.

A prerequisite for positive call center involvement, however, is the establishment of a customer-centric view of "service" across the organization. Self-service systems must be an integrated part of a customer access strategy, with their purpose clearly defined. If self-service systems are perceived primarily as replacements for call center agents, rather than supplemental access channels, then call center personnel will be less than enthusiastic about helping to improve them.

There are many specific ways for the call center to contribute to self-service system improvements, including the following:

- **Support self-service systems:** If there is not live, "real person" help available to explain how to use self-service systems when users get stuck, then organizations risk being perceived as trying to avoid customers by shoving them into low-cost, low-value contact channels. Call center support may take many forms:
- A clearly identified way to escape from an IVR application to reach an agent
- A prominently displayed telephone number on a Web site to call for live help
- Text-chat for instant online help
- Co-browsing technology to make assisting customers easy
- Email addresses for questions, suggestions and complaints for those who prefer that mode

Data should be tracked from all support modes, and analyzed for improvement opportunities; specifically, why do customers seek extra help?

- **Educate customers on self-service options:** In addition to supporting self-service options, call center agents should promote the use of self-service alternatives. Agents should be trained on the advantages of self service so that they can encourage customers to use these options when appropriate.
- **Capture caller feedback about self-service systems:** This is useful for improving them. Analyze complaints, in particular. Those callers who feel strongly enough to tell you about their dissatisfaction are just the tip of the iceberg; in most cases there will be several times as many customers who were dissatisfied but did not bother to tell you.
- **Collect and analyze data about calls currently handled in the call center:** Look for opportunities to provide self-service features that callers will want to use. Improved speed of access or around-the-clock access can both be appealing. Routine inquiries are prime candidates for self-service, as are transactions concerning potentially embarrassing information, where the customer might prefer an automated system (e.g., asking for an extension on a payment deadline).
- **Observe agents at work:** Call center agents know how to serve customers. Watching them at work, and asking them why they do things

the way they do, presents many opportunities for developing and improving self-service systems. In some cases, self-service systems should be modeled after effective agent practices. Look for ways to automate what these professionals do. There are also significant opportunities in identifying inefficient agent processes. In the course of helping agents work more effectively, self-service system ideas may surface.

- **Brainstorm with agents and get them to map process flows:** In addition to observing agents, get them in a room and encourage them to open up, so you can learn what really happens as opposed to what official procedures dictate. This must be done in a risk-free setting, where agents feel no fear of reprimand or retribution for revealing their "secret workarounds," or else the information they provide will not be worth much. The objective is to identify processes that could be automated in a self-service system, not to enforce compliance with organizational policies.
- **Analyze call monitoring data and quality results:** Many call centers capture valuable data as part of the quality monitoring process. If screen capture is used, all the better. Where could accuracy be improved by providing automated access? Check whether agents are referring callers to automated options to encourage customer use. How helpful are agents in assisting callers with using the self-service systems? Customer education is a critical role in building acceptance and usage of self-service systems.
- **Integrate self-service systems with call center systems:** The call center contributes to self-service systems naturally when those systems are the same as or integrated with the systems their agents use. The call center should be involved with self-service systems from development through implementation and all maintenance phases. The call center has a vested interest in ensuring the following:
    - Consistent treatment of callers, regardless of the access channel they select
    - Consistency of information provided, whether live or automated
    - Completeness of contact history across all channels
    - Making it easy for callers to switch channels (switching from self-service to live agent without having to repeat everything already entered in the automated channel; easily switching from live service to self-service, as well)

- **Share expertise and experience:** The call center can be a valuable partner in the development of self-service systems. Call center personnel can:
  - Serve on project teams working on self-service systems
  - Monitor and test the systems
  - Continue their traditional mission of helping customers by creating the best customer service experience possible, and recognizing that this includes self-service options

By keeping the focus on improving ways to service the customer, self-service systems can become part of an overall program of building call center value.



### The Impact

The call center's role in self-service usage and system design positively impacts the organization in the following ways:

- **Heightens customer confidence:** Customers who have access to their information at any time of the day or night will feel more confident in the organization's ability to serve them. Of course, a prerequisite to this confidence is that they receive correct information and have access to help if they need it.
- **Drives down access costs:** It is generally less expensive to service customers via self-service systems than through agent support. Paradoxically, providing agent assistance encourages the usage of self-service systems.
- **Reduces abandoned transactions:** If a customer needs help during a self-service transaction, the live support offered by the call center can make the difference between a purchase and an abandoned transaction.

## 17. The Call Center's Contribution to Revenue/ Sales

Ready? | 1 | 2 | 3 |

### Key Points

- **The essence of the call center's contribution to revenue and sales can be summarized as the maximization of the opportunities presented during customer contacts.**
- **In addition to handling incoming sales contacts and making sales calls, specific ways call centers contribute to revenue and sales include:**
  - **Customer satisfaction**
  - **Customer retention**
  - **Upselling and cross-selling**

### Explanation

Call centers that were designed to handle incoming sales calls make obvious contributions to revenue and sales, but many customer service call centers are now recognized, as well, for their direct and indirect impact on the bottom line. Due in part to the popularity of customer relationship management concepts, call centers formerly regarded as service centers are enjoying upgraded status as valuable partners in the sales process.

The essence of the call center's contribution to revenue and sales can be summarized as the maximization of the opportunities presented during customer contacts, especially customer-initiated contacts, which call centers have been explicitly designed to handle. The different types of opportunities are explained below. Almost every customer contact presents one or more of these opportunities, which are frequently closely related or even overlapping. They will be treated separately here to clarify how each one is part of the call center's contribution to sales and revenue.

- **Customer satisfaction:** The starting point for the call center's contribution to revenue and sales is the reason that many call centers were created: to ensure and improve customer satisfaction. By responding to customers skillfully and pleasantly, answering their questions and solving their problems, call centers are responsible for an important component of customer satisfaction. The impact of satisfied customers upon sales and revenue can be difficult to quantify, but that is no reason to dismiss it. Organizations can acquire valuable insight when they analyze the lifetime value derived from satisfied customers compared to that from dissatisfied customers. Such findings can help call center managers quantify the contribution their operations make to company profits. (See The Call Center's Contribution to Customer Satisfaction and Loyalty, this section.)

- **Customer retention:** As the primary point of contact with customers, call centers play a significant role in customer retention. Research has shown that customer satisfaction is critical to customer retention, which in turn has a positive impact on long-term profits. As illustrated in the graph, studies have illustrated that the longer people continue to be your customers, the more revenue you will realize in return for your initial customer acquisition cost. Keeping customers longer is generally less expensive than acquiring new ones. Customers who call with problems or complaints represent especially fertile retention opportunities for the call center, because research also shows that converting a dissatisfied customer to a satisfied one generally results in above-average loyalty from that customer.

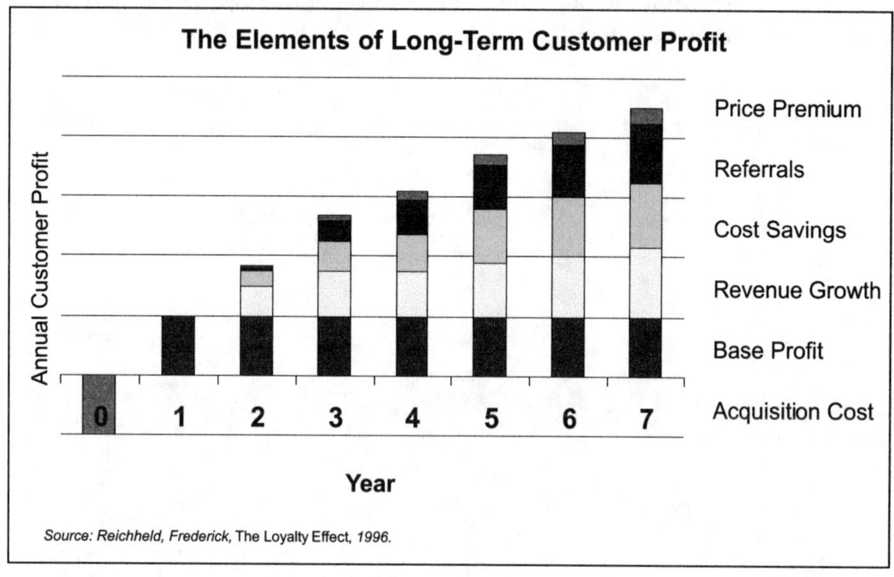


- **Upselling:** Upselling, or offering a current customer a more expensive version of your product or service, is ideally suited to the call center. When upsell offers are targeted to customers who genuinely need the higher-level product/service, both the customer and the organization benefit. Frequently, the best resource the organization has for identifying and acting upon these opportunities is the customer service agent during the course of a customer-initiated phone call. In the course of servicing the customer's needs, an upsell offer can become part of the service provided. In these situations, call centers simply need to ensure adequate tracking systems exist to measure the direct impact their operations have upon sales.

- **Cross-selling:** Cross-selling, or offering a current customer another product, is similar to upselling in its ideal suitability for the call center. Again, the key to effectiveness is making the sales offer a natural part of the customer service interaction. Customer knowledge, a primary component of customer relationship management, is essential to tailor the cross-sell offer to unmet customer needs. Again, sales tracking systems need to be implemented to measure the call center's contribution to increased revenue.

### The Impact

The impact of the call center's contribution on revenue/sales is significant. Sales from the call center increase overall revenue, average revenue per customer and market share.

# Strategy and Valuation

## Exercises

### Definition of Values, Vision and Mission

1. Select the most appropriate answer to each question.

Which of the following clarifies the organization's purpose?

a. Core values

b. Vision

c. Mission

d. Strategy

Which of the following describes a future state of the organization?

a. Core values

b. Vision

c. Mission

d. Strategy

### Identifying Core Values

2. True or false

___T___ Core values are present in every organization since it is actions, not words, that define core values.

**Creating a Shared Vision [Strategic]**

3. Select the most appropriate answer to the question.

Which of the following statements are true?

I. A vision is a forecast of the future that will be evaluated by how accurate it was.

II. The call center's vision should be based on its value contribution to the organization.

III. Envisioning the future is an inherently creative process that must combine knowledge with intuition and risk-taking.

IV. The vision will be successful if the entire organization participates in its development.

a. I and II only

b. III and IV only

c. II and III only

d. I, II and IV only

**Definition and Application of Strategy**

4. Match the following corporate strategies with their definitions. You will use each definition only once.

______Cost leadership

______Defender

______Differentiation

______Focus

______Product leadership

______Prospector

a. Distinguishing the organization by creating unique products and services.

b. Focusing on protecting and sustaining market share.

c. Pursuing market share through competition, innovation and speed to market.

d. Targeting defined customer groups, product lines or geographic markets.

e. Achieving a competitive advantage by being the low-cost provider.

f. Achieving a competitive advantage through superior products and services

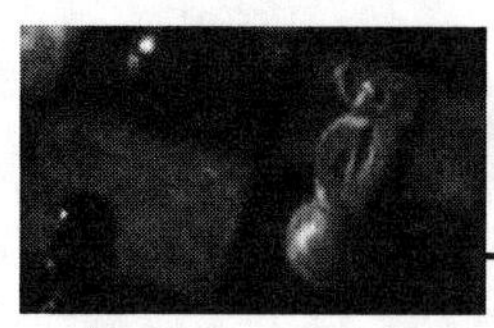

**The Role of the Customer Access Strategy**

5. What are the major components of an effective customer access strategy (in any order)?

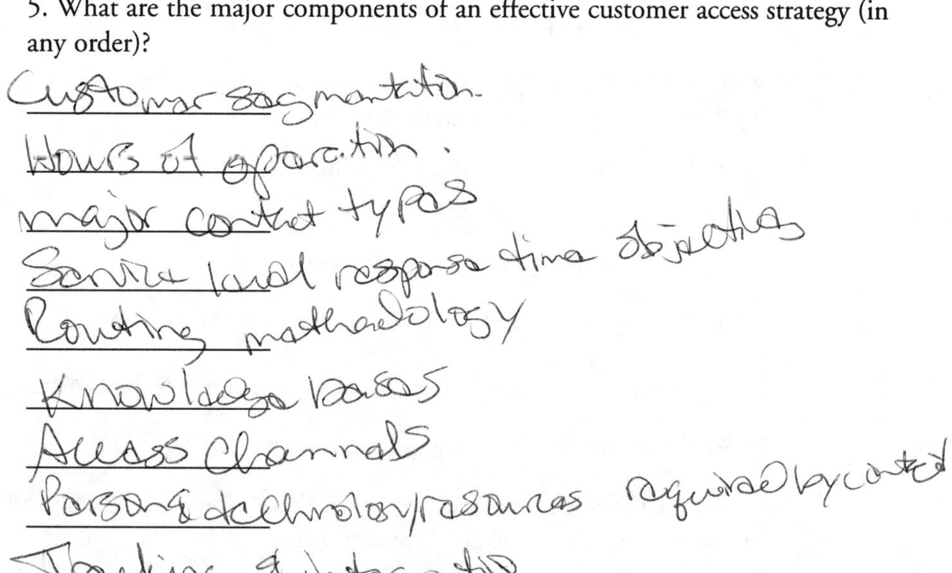

**Creating an Effective Strategic Development Process [Strategic]**

6. Fill in the blanks to complete each step of an effective strategic development process.

a. Create a connected vision

b. Shape the supporting strategy

c. Build skills, knowledge and leaders

d. Implement connected plans and process

e. Apply enabling technologies

f. Make the required investment

g. Unleash innovative quality

**The Call Center's Contribution to Unit Strategies**

7. Select the most appropriate answer to the question.

Which of the following is NOT a key consideration when contributing to unit strategies throughout the organization?

a. Don't get caught up in perfectionism

b. Don't get overwhelmed

c. Ensure this is a priority in your call center

d. Wait for others in the organization to ask for the input they need

**The Call Center's Contribution to Customer Satisfaction and Loyalty**

8. Briefly answer the following question.

Why are satisfied complainants often nearly as, or even more loyal than, customers who did not experience a problem?

**The Call Center's Contribution to Quality and Innovation**

9. Select the most appropriate answer to the question.

What is the correct order for the following five steps of integrating call center collected data with the quality decision-making process?

I. Comparison to internal measures

II. Determination of the probable cause of the problem

III. Estimation of the market impact

IV. Evaluation of the problem or question severity

V. Extrapolation to the marketplace

a. IV, V, III, I, II

b. IV, I, V, III, II

c. III, IV, V, II, I

d. III, IV, I, V, II

## The Call Center's Contribution to Marketing

10. Given the data below, calculate the following:

 a. Service cost = ____________________

 b. Expected damage to loyalty = ____________________

 c. Total cost of incorrectly set expectations = ____________________

 d. Percentage of profits lost due to incorrectly set expectations = ____________________

> Scenario: Credit card customers were misled by the literature about when payments are considered late (thus incurring unexpected interest rate charges).
>
> The company gets 30,000 calls on interest rates at a cost of $3 per call.
>
> Interest rate surprises decrease loyalty by 10 percent.
>
> An average customer is worth $300 annually in gross profit.
>
> Total gross profit of the marketing campaign was $20 million

## The Call Center's Role in Self-Service Usage and System Design

11. True or false

______Customers who have access to their information at any time of the day or night will feel more confident in the organization's ability to serve them.

______It is generally less expensive to service customers via self-service systems than through agent support.

______Providing agent assistance encourages the usage of self-service systems.

**Answers to these exercises are in Section 10.**

Note: These exercises are intended to help you retain the material learned. While not the exact questions as on the CIAC Certification assessment, the material in this handbook/study guide fully addresses the content on which you will be assessed. For a formal practice test, please contact the CIAC directly by visiting www.ciac-cert.org.

# Strategy and Valuation Reference Bibliography

## Related Articles from *Call Center Management Review* (See Section 9)

A Primer on Developing Effective Call Center Strategy (Two Parts)

Mission, Vision and Values in the Call Center

Navigating the Future: A Mission Statement Can Guide Centers through Turbulent Times

The Impact of the Contact Center on Corporate Profits

Dispel the 'Complaint Center' Image: Promote Value Through Visibility

The Impact of Service Delivery on Customer Satisfaction

## For Further Study

### Books/Studies

Mintzberg, Henry, Bruce Ahlstrand and Joseph Lampel. *Strategy Safari : A Guided Tour Through the Wilds of Strategic Management.* Simon & Schuster, 1998.

### Articles

Collins, James C. and Jerry I. Porras. "Building Your Company's Vision." *Harvard Business Review,* Sept-Oct 1996.

Goodman, John. "Don't Fix the Product, Fix the Customer and Marketing." TARP White Paper, www.tarp.com, April 2001.

Goodman, John, Scott Broetzmann and Steve Newman. "Using Complaints for Quality, Service, and Marketing Decisions." TARP White Paper, www.tarp.com, May 2001.

Kaplan, Robert S. and David P. Norton. "Using the Balanced Scorecard as a Strategic Management System." *Harvard Business Review*, January-February 1996.

"Market Damage Model Overview." TARP White Paper, www.tarp.com, 1988, revised 2001.

**Seminars**

*Effective Leadership and Strategy for Senior Call Center Managers* public seminar, presented by Incoming Calls Management Institute.

*Communicating the Value of the Call Center Across the Organization* web seminar, presented by Incoming Calls Management Institute.

## Section 4

# *Leadership and Communication*

# Section 4: Leadership and Communication

## Contents

# 1. Qualities and Characteristics of Effective Leaders

Ready? | 1 | 2 | 3 |

## Key Points

- According to leadership expert Stephen Covey, effective leaders form habits that enable them to:
    - Practice service-orientation
    - Radiate positive energy
    - Believe in other people
    - Lead a balanced life
    - See life as an adventure
- Key areas in which leaders reveal themselves within an organization:
    - Character
    - Relationships
    - Knowledge
    - Intuition
    - Experience
    - Past success
    - Ability
- While there is not a definitive list of the characteristics and qualities of an effective leader, there is one quality that is critical: effectiveness.



## Explanation

Determining the qualities and characteristics of effective leaders can be difficult to grasp definitively. The business world is full of examples of leaders who were lacking in many of the qualities that are listed as essential by leadership experts, and yet, were still considered to be effective leaders.

### Qualities and Characteristics of Effective Leaders

For their own personal development, it can be helpful for individuals to study the qualities and characteristics of proven effective leaders. Leadership expert Stephen Covey cites these traits, or "habits," in his many books, including *Principle-Centered Leadership*. He finds that leaders do not leave these traits at the door of their offices, but develop effective habits that guide their entire lives. Some of the habits he includes are:

- **Practice service-orientation:** Leaders are able to look outside themselves – their desires, ambitions, and goals – to lead others through a sense of responsibility, service and contribution.
- **Radiate positive energy:** Covey describes a charisma that surrounds leaders and brings out the best in others.
- **Believe in other people:** Leaders are able to see others as unique individuals with strengths and weaknesses, and visualize their potential. They understand that everyone does not have the same work ethic, views or needs.
- **Lead a balanced life:** Leaders live sensibly and are able to bring a healthy perspective to each encounter.
- **See life as an adventure:** Relying on strong character, leaders are able to takes risks in new experiences with courage and to enter each new experience with a sense of excitement.

These personality characteristics translate into leadership effectiveness through the way individuals implement them in their business activities. In *The 21 Irrefutable Laws of Leadership*, leadership expert John Maxwell stresses that while individuals may have innate personality characteristics that are in line with common leadership traits, all of the qualities can be learned. He cites seven key areas in which leaders reveal themselves within an organization:

- **Character:** The depth of the leader's integrity inspires trust in others. He or she can be relied on to be truthful, honest, courageous and to stand behind his or her beliefs. A leader acts on his or her convictions and takes the necessary steps to make things right.
- **Relationships:** A leader is able to understand the importance of developing the right kind of relationships with the right kind of people and has the skills to achieve this. He or she understands that these relationships are the key to being able to guide employees toward a vision.
- **Knowledge:** A focus on continuous learning and the acquisition of knowledge is vital to a leader. Without it, he or she won't be able to grasp complex issues or create a vision for the future.
- **Intuition:** Seeing through what Maxwell terms "a leadership lens," leaders rely on instincts and feelings to add another dimension to the facts they use to make decisions. They use this intuition to focus on what is most important.

- **Experience:** While past experiences and challenges do not automatically connote credibility, they do allow the leader to learn from past mistakes and use them to inform future decisions.
- **Past success:** Those asked to follow will consider whether the leader has led others to success in the past.
- **Ability:** If the leader is able to deliver on his or her mission and if followers believe the mission is a valid one, people will acknowledge him or her as their leader.



### Fleshing It Out

What does it take to have the focus required to be a truly effective leader? The keys are priorities [or vision] and concentration. A leader who knows his priorities but lacks concentration knows what to do but never gets it done. If he has concentration, but no priorities, he has excellence without progress. But when he harnesses both, he has the potential to achieve great things.

So the important question is, How should you focus your time and energy? Use these guidelines to help you:

**Focus 70 Percent on Strengths**

Effective leaders who reach their potential spend more time focusing on what they do well than on what they do wrong. Leadership expert Peter Drucker notes, "The great mystery isn't that people do things badly but that they occasionally do a few things well. The only thing that is universal is incompetence. Strength is always specific! Nobody ever commented, for example, that the great violinist Jascha Heifetz probably couldn't play the trumpet very well."

**Focus 25 Percent on New Things**

Growth equals change. If you want to get better, you have to keep changing and improving. That means stepping out into new areas. If you dedicate time to new things related to areas of strength, then you'll grow as a leader.

**Focus 5 Percent on Areas of Weakness**

Nobody can entirely avoid working in areas of weakness. The key is to minimize it as much as possible, and leaders can do it by delegating.

Excerpt from *The 21 Indispensable Qualities of a Leader* by John C. Maxwell, Thomas Nelson Inc., 1999.

## Born Leaders vs. Leadership Development

Though there are some people who seem like they were born to be leaders, leadership ability is not an innate personality characteristic. In *The Effective Executive,* management consultant Peter Drucker writes:

> These practices [of effective leaders] are not "inborn." In forty-five years of work as a consultant with a large number of executives in a wide variety of organizations – large and small; business, government agencies, labor unions, hospitals, universities, community agencies; American, European, Latin American and Japanese – I have not comes across a single "natural": an executive who was born effective. All the effective ones had to learn to be effective. And all of them had to practice effectiveness until it became a habit. But all the ones who worked on making themselves effective executives succeeded in doing so. (p. vii)



**Effectiveness as the Critical Leadership Trait**

While there is not a definitive list of the characteristics and qualities of an effective leader, there is one quality that is critical: effectiveness. Drucker summarizes this point by stating:

> To be effective is the job of the executive. "To effect" and "to execute" are, after all, near synonyms. Whether he works in a business or in a hospital, in a government agency or in a labor union, in a university or in the army, the executive is, first of all expected to get the right things done. And this is simply that he is expected to be effective. (*Executive*, p. 1)

Knowledge, integrity, honesty, intuition and experience are essential resources, but it is effectiveness which converts them into results. And without results, a leader has no enduring value to the organization.

**Different People, Different Needs**

In *Leadership as an Art*, author Max De Pree writes:

> The signs of outstanding leadership appear primarily among the followers. Are the followers reaching their potential? Are they learning? Serving? Do they achieve the required results? Do they change with grace? Manage conflict? (p. 12)

Although leaders need to be very self-aware, effective leaders know that their success depends on the success of others – individuals with a variety of preferences, skills, strengths and weaknesses. Effective leaders realize that there are no cookie-cutter solutions to successfully leading everyone. Instead, they pay close attention to the specific needs of others to discover the best way to inspire each individual to reach his or her potential.

## 2. The Distinction Between Leadership and Management

Ready? | 1 | 2 | 3 |

### Key Points

- **Management is defined by a set of responsibilities needed for the organization to achieve its objectives and goals. Leadership ability is a combination of the skills, knowledge and experience that an individual possesses, which can contribute to his or her effectiveness as a manager.**
- **The ability to simultaneously act as a manager and a leader does not inevitably lead to conflict and, as the role of the call center manager evolves, more managers must also be leaders.**



### Explanation

The distinction between management and leadership has sparked endless discussion in recent years. After all, the time-worn cliché has been that leaders do the right things and managers do things right. But is this true? Can a manager also be a leader? Do organizations need leaders rather than managers? Should all leaders also be able to manage?

The conflict essentially boils down to the definition of the terms used. In *Executive Leadership: A Practical Guide to Managing Complexity*, Stephen Clement and Elliott Jaques write that, often, the term "leadership is endowed with virtue, strength and creativity, whereas management (and administration) are seen as concerned with the mundane, dull and tedious everyday routines of work." (p. 18) From this viewpoint, an individual who is a strong manager will unimaginatively follow the organization's processes and procedures to the letter, but is unlikely to competently function in a strategic, visionary role. Whereas someone who is a good leader will feel comfortable communicating the organization's vision, but will be unlikely to effectively manage its day-to-day operations. Clement and Jaques suggest that organizations should not make this "unrealistic and incorrect separation in defining job roles and responsibilities." (p. 18)

Instead, the following definitions may help to distinguish management and leadership. Management is a set of responsibilities needed for the organization to achieve its objectives and goals. Leadership ability is a combination of the skills, knowledge and experience that an individual possesses, which can contribute to his or her effectiveness as a manager. Leadership inspires others to achieve a common goal, while management guides them in how to reach this goal. (See Qualities and Characteristics of Effective Leaders, this section.)

### Leadership and Management in the Call Center

The ability to simultaneously act as a manager and a leader does not inevitably lead to conflict and, as the role of the call center manager evolves, more managers must also be leaders.

### Management Styles

Although there are many ways to classify management styles, the following two general categories appear in almost every classification:

- **Authoritarian:** Managers with authoritarian styles expect their subordinates to carry out orders similar to a chain-of-command environment. The subordinates are not expected to make decisions, so they bear little responsibility for what they are doing. Decision-making takes less time in authoritarian style management, but it may be very difficult to maintain a motivated workforce. Without the ability to contribute to the decision-making process, most employees will feel devalued and resentful.
- **Participative:** Managers with participative styles encourage their subordinates to participate in decision-making and accept responsibility for their performance. This type of manager is better described as facilitator, coach and collaborator, as opposed to director or overseer. Participative style management focuses on removing obstacles, providing assistance as needed and empowering the workforce. Subordinates of participative managers are more likely to experience intrinsic motivation, e.g., job satisfaction or sense of achievement, which has been proven to be more effective than extrinsic motivation, e.g., pay or incentives.

#### Supervisors as Leaders

As call centers evolve into high-visibility, strategic roles within an organization, a natural spin-off effect is the change in management roles, which are likewise progressing.

A new call center study reveals that the frontline supervisor position also is undergoing an evolution. According to *Best Practices in Call Center Management*, a report conducted and sponsored by ProSci Research and cosponsored by Vanguard Communications Corp., leadership skills have become the No.1 hiring criteria for frontline supervisors, compared with people management and coaching skills in 1999.

The study found this trend "to be consistent with the rapidly changing call center environment and the need for call center supervisors to play an active role as change agents and leaders in the change process."

"The ability to coach agents on how to perform their jobs has taken a back seat to the ability to innovate, think creatively and initiate change," says Jeff Hiatt of ProSci Research. "Call centers are looking for the whole package: leaders, coaches and managers."

Study participants considered the following abilities to be the top three leadership skills necessary for call center supervisors:

- The ability to articulate call center strategies and goals clearly, as well as identify improvement opportunities.
- The ability to motivate agents through personal example, and to lead improvement initiatives.
- The ability to set goals, make decisions and maintain a results orientation.

Excerpt from "Leadership Skills No.1 Criteria for Supervisors, Says Study" by Susan Hash, *Call Center Management Review,* August 2001.

## 3. Leadership Challenges in Call Centers

**Ready?** | 1 | 2 | 3 |



### Key Points

- As call centers are recognized for their strategic role within the organization, call center management will be required to address ongoing leadership challenges in their centers.
- Common leadership challenges in call centers include:
  - Aligning values, vision and mission with the larger organization
  - Leading the right people to do the right things
  - Creating new leaders
  - Communicating the call center vision to internal and external audiences
  - Securing the necessary resources
  - Enabling collaboration with other departments
  - Integrating the right tools and technologies into the environment
  - Staying abreast of industry trends

### Explanation

As call centers are recognized for their strategic role within the organization, call center management will be required to address ongoing leadership challenges in their centers. Leaders work to communicate and facilitate agreement with the organization's values, vision and mission. Their challenges revolve around focusing the efforts of their organization, call center or team in one direction and achieving the defined objectives. Common leadership challenges in call centers include:

- **Aligning values, vision and mission with the larger organization:** Every business unit should be aligned with the organization's values, vision and mission. However, for the call center, this principle gains greater importance since call center agents communicate these organizational principles to customers in the level of service they provide. The leaders in the call center must carefully consider if they are translating organizational principles into a way of delivering service that will positively impact customers. (See Aligning Tactical Activities with Values, Vision and Mission, Section 3.)

- **Leading the right people to do the right things:** With the growing complexity of demands on the call center (e.g., multichannel customer access, increased value contribution and customer relationship management initiatives), call center managers must direct a greater diversity of activities while responding to the ever-changing business environment. The skill requirements for call centers are increasing and managers must focus attention on recruiting, hiring and training practices, as well as employee retention, in order to have the staff in place to accomplish the center's objectives.
- **Creating new leaders:** The large agent pool currently employed in call centers across the country, and around the world, is the next generation of call center leaders. Developing leadership talents in call center employees through empowerment, trust, integrity and responsibility will ensure the call center industry will be able to successfully adopt to changes. More experienced call center managers must mentor junior managers in the art of call center management.
- **Communicating the call center vision to internal and external audiences:** Although many individuals inside and outside of the call center understand the center's role as the hub of communication for the organization, it can be difficult for call center leaders to get the support they need because of a lack of understanding about the call center's unique operating environment. Leaders must diligently educate those inside and outside of the call center on the fundamental principles that drive call center management practices. Only through these educational efforts will others be able to understand the planning and management involved in the call center's accomplishment of its goals and objectives. (See Principles of Effective Communication, this section.)
- **Securing the necessary resources:** Ongoing developments in technologies coupled with evolving customer expectations continue to up the ante – creating new pressures for call centers and outstripping the ability of many organizations to keep up with customer demands. Unfortunately, even as personnel requirements are snowballing, many call centers are having trouble getting the funding and support they need to attract, train and retain required talent. Call center managers must educate executives on the balance between staffing resources and workload so that they can secure the staff they need to meet service levels and satisfy customers. (See Principles of Developing an Effective Annual Operating Budget, Section 7.)
- **Enabling collaboration with other departments:** As call centers have

grown in importance, call center mangers are increasingly working shoulder to shoulder with colleagues in other departments and with upper-level managers to develop strategy and integrated processes. Even ongoing call center processes, such as forecasting, quality monitoring and customer data collection, require input from other departments to be executed effectively. Call center managers must take the initiative in developing cross-functional processes and increased support for the call center. (For discussions on collaboration, see ICMI's *Call Center Customer Relationship Management Handbook and Study Guide.*)

- **Integrating the right tools and technologies into the environment:** Call center leaders today have many choices when it comes to technology. With customer relationship management initiatives and multichannel access demands, call center leaders must sort through the vendor landscape to find those technologies that will best aid the call center's needs. The effective leader must strike the right balance between implementing technology that enables the center to be more effective and frustrating employees with too much change. Technology decisions take time and thoughtful consideration to implement successfully. (For detailed information on technology, see ICMI's *Call Center Operations Management Handbook and Study Guide.*)
- **Staying abreast of industry trends:** In the fast-paced, ever-changing call center industry, it can be difficult for leaders to stay abreast of industry trends. There are ongoing changes in so many areas – technology, terminology, management initiatives, and hiring options, to name a few. In particular, the industry is changing as newer customer access channels mature and the call center's value contribution to the organization becomes more recognized. Electronic and print newsletters, industry conferences and trade publications are obvious ways to keep up with what's happening, but an often overlooked approach is maintaining active discussions with your peers. Time spent learning from what others are experiencing can quickly cut through to what matters the most.

### Difficult Circumstances Test Effective Leadership

When economic conditions are less than favorable, the organization is restructuring, or the organization is shifting strategy, employees need the reassurance and commitment of effective leaders. You cannot wait until the tough times to practice good leadership. It takes time to build a foundation that will withstand rough weather.

### Retaining Staff During a Downsizing

My first key learning experience about retaining staff during a downsizing occurred in the mid-1980s while working at Atari. An announcement was made to employees that our division would be closing in three months. My boss, John Reddoch, who directed a significant portion of the operation was faced with a major challenge – how could the company maintain productivity and results if employees began to leave in droves before the closing? He used an honest, common sense approach that was highly successful. I later used the same approach when faced with similar challenges managing the support organizations at Privada, Myteam.com and JBL. Here are the key elements:

- Be completely honest with your staff. In these types of situations, there is often a lack of specific information filtering down. Do your best to clarify these issues and give as many details as possible.
- Take the time to personally speak to each agent about his or her individual needs. (Do not delegate this responsibility!)
- Offer agents as much assistance and support as possible. I conducted mock interview sessions with interested staff during work hours to help them hone their interviewing skills.
- Communicate on a daily basis, even if nothing has changed. Frequent communication squelches rumors.

Excerpt from "Maintaining Service Loyalty during a Downsizing" by Ivan Temes, *Call Center Management Review*, March 2002.

## 4. Modeling Values and Maintaining Integrity

Ready? | 1 | 2 | 3 |



### Key Points

- The commitment of the organization's leaders to identifying core values and modeling them consistently shapes the culture of the entire organization. It is through this commitment that integrity – the consistent, unwavering dedication to those values – is demonstrated.
- Core values serve as the guiding principles for all organizational actions and decisions. A deliberate process should be followed to link the call center vision and mission with these values. This process includes:
    1. Create a shared vision and mission
    2. Check alignment
    3. Evaluate management style
    4. Communicate and celebrate the vision, mission and values
    5. Model the values

### Explanation

The commitment of the organization's leaders to identifying core values and modeling them consistently shapes the culture of the entire organization. It is through this commitment that integrity – the consistent, unwavering dedication to those values – is demonstrated.

**Instilling Core Values**

Core values serve as the guiding principles for all organizational actions and decisions. A deliberate process should be followed to link the call center vision and mission with the words used to describe the qualities and beliefs that comprise these values.

1. **Create a shared vision and mission:** Develop clear, well-defined vision and mission statements that incorporate the core values of the organization. Then, ensure the vision and mission are understood and internalized at all levels of the organization. (See discussions on values, vision and mission, Section 3.)

2. **Check alignment:** The structure and processes of the organization should serve to reinforce its values. Managers who espouse investment in people as an organizational value, but who do not invest in the equipment and tools for employees to effectively do their jobs, negatively affect the integrity of the organization.

3. **Evaluate management styles:** Management's philosophy and actions should embody the vision and values of the organization. For example, an organization that commits to innovation as a core value, but has managers who respond negatively to new ideas, creates a disconnect between what the organization says and what they do.

4. **Communicate and celebrate the vision, mission and values:** Plan an event to introduce your organization's commitment to employees (and the larger organization, if necessary). Illustrate the connection between the shared vision, mission and value statements and employees' contributions.

5. **Model the values:** Ensure that your words and actions demonstrate the organization's values. Create ways to keep your commitment to these principles visible and alive.

The most eloquent, lofty values will prove hollow if the organization is not willing to provide the structure and support that encourages employees to live these values. Where values do not equal practices, employees and customers will lose trust in the organization, resulting in high employee turnover, low morale, poor teamwork, customer defections and loss of revenue.

### Preventing Practices that Damage the Organization's Integrity

Call center leaders should be alert to actions by their peers or employees that compromise the organization's values. A departure from these values results in a loss of integrity with others in the organization, with customers and with other stakeholders.

Many negative examples abound that illustrate how leaders allowed their own ambition, desire or unwillingness to admit mistakes to cloud their judgment. These missteps have resulted in countless lawsuits and have been the downfall of more than a few organizations. However, there are also positive examples of organizations that have faced difficult circumstances and have chosen to operate with integrity and commitment to their values.

## Classic Case of Doing the Right Thing

In the fall of 1982, McNeil Consumer Products, a subsidiary of Johnson & Johnson, was confronted with a crisis when seven people on Chicago's West Side died mysteriously. Authorities determined that each of the people that died had ingested an Extra-Strength Tylenol capsule laced with cyanide. The news of this incident traveled quickly and was the cause of a massive, nationwide panic. These poisonings made it necessary for Johnson & Johnson to launch a public relations program immediately, in order to save the integrity of both their product and their corporation as a whole.

Phase one of Johnson & Johnson's public relations campaign was executed immediately following the discovery that the deaths in Chicago were caused by Extra-Strength Tylenol capsules. As the plan was constructed, Johnson & Johnson's top management put customer safety first, before they worried about their company's profit and other financial concerns.

The company immediately alerted consumers across the nation, via the media, not to consume any type of Tylenol product. They told consumers not to resume using the product until the extent of the tampering could be determined. Johnson & Johnson, along with stopping the production and advertising of Tylenol, recalled all Tylenol capsules from the market. The recall included approximately 31 million bottles of Tylenol, with a retail value of more than 100 million dollars. (Broom, Center, Cutlip, 381)

This was unusual for a large corporation facing a crisis. In many other similar cases, companies had put themselves first, and ended up doing more damage to their reputations than if they had immediately taken responsibility for the crisis. An example of this was the crisis that hit Source Perrier when traces of benzene were found in their bottled water. Instead of holding themselves accountable for the incident, Source Perrier claimed that the contamination resulted from an isolated incident. They then recalled only a limited number of Perrier bottles in North America. (Broom, Center, Cutlip, 59, 381)

When benzene was found in Perrier bottled water in Europe, an embarrassed Source Perrier had to announce a world-wide recall on the bottled water. Apparently, consumers around the world had been drinking contaminated water for months. Source Perrier was harshly attacked by the media. They were criticized for having little integrity and for disregarding public safety. (Broom, Center Cutlip, 59)

Johnson & Johnson, on the other hand, was praised for their actions by the media for their socially responsible actions. Along with the nationwide alert and the Tylenol recall, Johnson & Johnson established relations with the Chicago Police, the FBI, and the Food and Drug Administration. This way the company could have a part in searching for the person who laced the Tylenol capsules and they could help prevent further tamperings. Johnson & Johnson was given much positive coverage for their handling of this crisis. (Atkinson, 2) (Broom, Center, Cutlip, 381)

An article by Jerry Knight, published in *The Washington Post* on October 11, 1982, said, "Johnson & Johnson has effectively demonstrated how a major business ought to handle a disaster." The article stated that, "This is no Three Mile Island accident in which the company's response did more damage than the original incident." *The Washington Post* cited many incidents where public relations programs at large companies failed in crisis situations. They applauded Johnson & Johnson for being honest with the public.

Excerpt from "The Tylenol Crisis: How Effective Public Relations Saved Johnson & Johnson" by Tamara Kaplan, The Pennsylvania State University. References to Glen Broom, Allen Center, Scott Cutlip's *Effective Public Relations,* 7th edition. Prentice-Hall Inc., 1994, and Rick Atkinson's "The Tylenol Nightmare: How a Corporate Giant Fought Back," *The Kansas City Times,* November 12, 1982.

## 5. Developing Strong Community Relations

Ready? | 1 | 2 | 3 |

### Key Points

- Strong community relations develop and maintain ties between the organization (and the people who work there) and the community (and the citizens who live there).
- Organizations will realize far-reaching benefits in their call centers by looking for opportunities to impact the community. Investing in community relations initiatives allows organizations to:
    - Promote the values of the organization
    - Instill employee pride
    - Build public goodwill and trust
    - Foster learning and education
    - Leverage existing assets
- When developing community relations initiatives, managers should:
    - Determine and agree on the organization's responsibilities and approach to community service
    - Partner with credible community agencies whose visions align with the values of the organization
    - Solicit employee and customer input
    - Provide employees with the opportunity to contribute
    - Determine how initiatives will be communicated with stakeholders

### Explanation

Every organization is an economic and social force that touches the communities in which it resides or does business. Strong community relations develop and maintain ties between the organization (and the people who work there) and the community (and the citizens who live there). Community relations may also extend the resources of the organization beyond the confines of the immediate geographic community to state or national organizations. Organizations often include their responsibilities to the community within their mission statement.

## The Value of Community Relations Initiatives

The benefits of investing time and effort in building strong community relations is more than just a positive public relations move. Organizations will realize far-reaching benefits by looking outside their walls for opportunities to impact the community. Investing in community relations initiatives allows organizations to:

- **Promote the values of the organization:** By modeling desired values and providing opportunities for employees to demonstrate these values, organizations can impact the culture of their organization. Community relations activities can help employees develop responsibility, empowerment and satisfaction through helping others.
- **Instill employee pride:** Most individuals want to associate themselves with an organization in which they feel a sense of identification and pride. Community relations efforts can confirm employees' beliefs that their values align with those of the larger organization.
- **Build public goodwill and trust:** Investing time, resources and money in the community provides organizations with the opportunity to publicize their positive values. This can result in increased customer loyalty when customers feel that, through their association with the organization, they have a stake in the organization's contributions.
- **Foster learning and education:** By partnering with schools or colleges and sponsoring educational opportunities for members of the community through scholarships and grants, the organization realizes an additional benefit: the opportunity to invest in the future workforce of the community.
- **Leverage existing assets:** Initiatives that are related to the organization's core business offer the best opportunity for maximizing impact. The airline America West has implemented a program that encourages employees to donate free flying vouchers for cancer patients traveling to receive medical treatment.

## Types of Community Relations Programs

There are many different ways for an organization to contribute to the community. The range of programs implemented should be aligned with the organization's (and its employees') values. The three major types of programs are:

1. **Community revitalization and the arts:** These programs involve

museums, cultural events, environmental organizations and community renewal projects. For example, an organization may choose to sponsor the building of a house through Habitat for Humanity or allow employees to take time off to volunteer at an environmental conservation agency.

2. **Education:** Partnering with schools and education providers allows the organization to shape the curriculum to address their industry requirements and reach potential future employees. Orkin Pest Control, for instance, underwrites the O. Orkin Insect Zoo at the Smithsonian Institution's Museum of Natural History.

3. **Health and human services:** Developing relationships which impact the health and quality of life for individuals is another alternative. The United Way, National Urban League, and the American Red Cross are examples of agencies to which the organization might choose to contribute time, energy and resources.



### Identifying Community Needs and Implementing Partnerships

The organization should choose agencies and programs that will appeal to customers and employees and that are in alignment with the organization's values. When developing community relations initiatives, managers should:

- **Determine and agree on the organization's responsibilities and approach to community service:** This includes whether the organization wants to focus at the local, national or international levels, or some combination. The approach also depends on the time, money and resources the organization is willing to invest.
- **Partner with credible community agencies whose visions align with the values of the organization:** Careful consideration should be given to the types of programs that are implemented. Relationships with controversial agencies may prompt some employees, customers or members of the community to disassociate themselves with the organization's investment.
- **Solicit employee and customer input:** The most effective relationships are supported across all levels of the organization. Survey employees and customers to determine which programs they would support and find most meaningful.
- **Provide employees with the opportunity to contribute:** Providing time for employees to work on community initiatives can reinforce an organization's commitment to employee development.

- **Determine how initiatives will be communicated with stakeholders:** The organization must strike a balance between overtly advertising its good deeds vs. not communicating adequately the contributions it makes.

**Philanthropy as Public Relations – Tricky Business**

Almost unanimously, the public says it wants information about a company's record on social and environmental responsibility to help decide which companies to buy from, invest in and work for. But philanthropy is a tricky facet of corporate public relations. Good deeds can redound to a company's credit. But they can be overlooked if untrumpeted, making the company a target for unfair criticism, and they can backfire if consumers view the purported philanthropy as profiteering or if the company fails to live up to the good-neighbor image it projects. In short, promoting philanthropy is perilous, and companies can find they're damned if they do and damned if they don't.

These are among the findings of the annual corporate-reputation survey conducted by the Reputation Institute, a New York research group, with the market-research firm Harris Interactive Inc. The survey of 21,630 people was conducted in October. Charles Fombrun, executive director of the Reputation Institute, says that Americans have a general skepticism about corporate philanthropy "because there hasn't been a long tradition of doing good in this country. ... The typical reaction is, 'Hmm, there must be something in it for the company.'"

Consumers and investors are more often than not left in the dark about a company's good works. Of 20 corporate attributes in the Harris/Reputation Institute survey, the question of whether a company supports good causes elicited the largest percentage of "not sure" responses.

Corporate-communications officials are understandably confused about how to publicize their good works given that the public itself is split over the best approach. About half of the respondents to the reputation survey believe advertising and press releases are appropriate, but 40% prefer a less splashy message and recommend using annual reports and corporate Web sites for philanthropic information.

Excerpt from "Perils of Corporate Philanthropy" by Ronald Alsop, *The Wall Street Journal*, January 16, 2002.

## 6. Principles of Effective Communication

Ready? | 1 | 2 | 3 |



### Key Points

- Effective communication creates meaning and direction for people, and is central to a high-value, productive environment.
- Twelve principles of effective communication are present in leading call centers. They include:
    1. Create a positive culture
    2. Ensure that structure and policies support communication
    3. Drive out the "fear"
    4. Commit to keeping people in the know
    5. Develop formal and informal channels of communication
    6. Establish appropriate communication tools
    7. Develop a communication agreement
    8. Eliminate unnecessary bureaucracy
    9. Consistently communicate progress on projects and objectives
    10. Listen actively and regularly
    11. Establish a systematic, collaborative workload planning process
    12. Don't overdo it

### Explanation

In some call centers, you can feel the energy as soon as you walk in the door. It takes many forms: pride of workmanship, enthusiasm, a feeling of community, commitment and the willingness to make the "extra effort." The call center "clicks." Everybody knows what the mission is; everybody is pulling in the same direction. While there are a myriad of factors that go into creating this sort of environment, effective communication plays a central role.

Communication creates meaning and direction for people. Organizations of all types depend on the existence of what Warren Bennis, noted organizational theorist, calls "shared meanings and interpretations of reality," which facilitate coordinated action. When good communication is lacking, the symptoms are predictable: conflicting objectives, unclear values, misunderstandings, lack of coordination, confusion, low morale and people doing the bare minimum required.

Although cultures and communication styles vary, there are 12 notable principles that are consistently present among high-value call centers.

**1. Create a positive culture:** Culture – the inveterate principles or values of the organization – tends to guide behavior and can either support and further, or, as some have learned the hard way, ruin effective communication. Unfortunately, there's no guaranteed formula for creating a supporting culture. But many call center managers agree that shaping the culture of the organization is a primary leadership responsibility. They do not believe that culture should be left to fate. As a result, they spend an inordinate amount of time understanding the organization and the people who are part of it. Part of this understanding comes from gathering information about employee satisfaction and dissatisfaction and communicating it to the upper levels of the organization.

One of the most distinguishable aspects of a positive culture is that the vision and mission are well known and understood. Why does the call center exist? What is it working to achieve? What's in it for employees? What's in it for customers and for the organization? Unfortunately, quite a few people have been through the process of creating vision and mission statements that, for one reason or another, have had little or no impact on actions.

Take steps to ensure employee commitment to the vision. This should include such actions as soliciting input from employees as the vision is being developed, publishing the vision in a place that is easily accessible to all employees, and regularly communicating – and celebrating – with employees as the organization progresses toward realizing the vision. (See discussions of vision and mission, Section 3.)

When employees are distributed geographically, building a positive culture can be particularly challenging. Start by creating opportunities for the people in your distributed group to get to know each other. It's also important to ensure that everyone gets key information at the same time and that all are abreast of major decisions.

**2. Ensure that structure and policies support communication:** The organization's structure defines the alignment of roles and responsibilities for business units, departments and individuals. Organizational design is constantly exerting its forces as it channels communication, shapes protocol and establishes lines of authority. In hierarchical structures, functions can become silos with conflicting objectives or competition for scarce resources. Flatter, more collaborative organizations help foster an environment in which trust and communication flourish.

Policies and procedures can also impact trust and communication. For example, monitoring and coaching programs with a bent toward demerits or discipline (e.g., only catching things that are wrong) tend to create mistrust – mistrust in the approach, the organization and those who are part of the process. But programs that truly contribute to the growth and well being of individuals and the organization help to build trust and encourage communication.

(For more information on organization structures and policies, see ICMI's *Call Center People Management Handbook and Study Guide.*)



**3. Drive out the "fear:"** Creating a high-performance culture in which effective communication thrives also means driving out fear. This was a theme the late W. Edward Deming spoke of passionately, especially in his later years, and is one of his famous "Fourteen Points." Sometimes, however, fear goes unrecognized by managers. For example, if individual performance results are regularly posted for all to see, agents may manipulate their statistics and cheat the system. Essentially, they may be more afraid of reporting accurate statistics than of manipulating reports. That is a symptom of what Deming would have called fear.

Of course, there are those things that people should be fearful of, such as the consequences of being dishonest or irresponsible. But it's the wrong kind of fear, such as the fear of taking reasonable risks or the fear of constructive dissent that effective leaders must work so diligently to abolish. Fear inhibits effective communication.

**4. Commit to keeping people in the know:** Leaders of high-performance organizations are predisposed to keeping their people in the know. They actively share both good news and bad. This minimizes the rumor mill, which hinders effective, accurate communication. It also contributes to an environment of trust.

Peter Senge, who popularized the notion of a learning organization in his widely read book, *The Fifth Discipline* described a place "where people continually expand their capacity to create the results they truly desire, where new and expansive patterns of thinking are nurtured, where collective aspiration is set free, and where people are continually learning how to learn together." (p. 3) Shared information is the fundamental ingredient in organizational learning – and learning both contributes to and is dependent on effective communication.

5. **Develop formal and informal channels of communication:** Effective leaders cultivate both formal and informal channels of communication. The communication formats can include newsletters, meetings, visual displays, electronic mail, voicemail, posters, intranets and informal "hallway meetings." But the mission and values being communicated remain consistent. As Bennis puts it, "leadership...is based on predictability. The truth is that we trust people who are predictable, whose positions are known and who keep at it; leaders who are trusted make themselves known, make their positions clear." (*Leaders*, p. 41)

One of the common formal means of communication between front-line workers and management is employee satisfaction surveys. The best call centers track results and monitor trends to ensure continuous improvement. Survey results are communicated back to employees, and teams are often formed to address specific problems that are identified in the surveys. The progress towards resolving the problem is then tracked and communicated.

6. **Establish appropriate communication tools:** A prerequisite to an environment in which communication thrives is that individuals and teams have compatible and capable communications technologies. Telephone, email, intranet, and collaboration and conferencing tools offer enormous potential if available and compatible across the organization. Further, creating a directory (generally online) of contact numbers and addresses just for the organization gives people the basic information they need to collaborate, and creates symbolism that reinforces the principle that communication is important.

The email communication channel has exploded in recent years and for good reason. Email is an efficient way to communicate the same information to a group of people, it allows all recipients to see the comments and questions of others, and it creates an historical trail that can be referenced in the future. What email does not do, however, is eliminate the need for face-to-face communication. Even in distributed environments, face-to-face meetings should occur when feasible since they go a long way toward building trust.

7. **Develop a communications agreement:** Even with all the technology bells and whistles, good communication may be lacking. Effective communication requires some ground rules that stipulate levels of priority and appropriate responses for:

- Urgent messages requiring immediate response

- Routine messages requiring response within 24 hours or so
- Non-urgent informational messages that require no response

Email messages should have descriptive titles and should be written like a newspaper story with headlines first, the main points second and necessary supporting details last. One-way communication, e.g., email, should not be used to relay negative information to someone, especially related to their performance. An in-person meeting, or a telephone or video conference, will allow the kind of immediate interaction that can prevent a problem from becoming even more serious and emotionally charged.

**8. Eliminate unnecessary bureaucracy:** Peter Drucker, respected management consultant, has insisted that, "So much of what we call management consists of making it difficult for people to work." It's important for the leader to regularly and vigilantly look for ways to scrap (or, at least, minimize) the impact of unnecessary hierarchies and cumbersome bureaucracies. That's easier said than done, but is one of the most important steps you can take to facilitate productive communication. This also involves helping the members of the center accomplish cross-functional tasks by eliminating or minimizing interdepartmental barriers.

**9. Consistently communicate progress on projects and objectives:** Hazy objectives and vaguely defined tasks will destroy productivity and morale. The objectives of teams and individuals – as well as the call center itself – should be as concrete as possible. Projects should have clearly defined milestones, with beginning and ending points.

For projects or long-term objectives, tools such as Gantt charts and flow charts can be useful for identifying resources required, showing the interrelated nature of individual tasks and tracking progress. They give focus to the mission of the workgroup and can help address questions such as: Where are we? How far have we come? What's next? They should be updated and distributed as often as something substantial changes in the ongoing direction and plans. (See Managing and Controlling Project Plans, Section 6.)

**10. Listen actively and regularly:** Listening encourages communication. When leaders listen to those around them, they give others the opportunity to contribute ideas, which creates a sense of ownership. Further, listening encourages diverse perspectives, enables individuals to grow and creates community within the organization. Active listening enables a culture that brings out the best in people.

Listening also benefits leadership directly. There is a common myth that great leaders create compelling visions from an inner source that others don't have. But many studies on the subjects of leadership and strategy have shown the visions of some of history's greatest leaders often came from others. The leaders may have selected the best vision to focus on, shaped it and communicated it to others in a compelling way, but they rarely originated the vision.

**11. Establish a systematic, collaborative workload planning process:** Leading call centers have cultivated a systematic, collaborative approach to call center workload planning. This process generally includes forecasting, staffing, scheduling, budgeting and related activities.

Systematic planning contributes to effective communication in several ways. It creates a body of information that wouldn't otherwise be available, e.g., here's our call load pattern and, therefore, why the schedules are structured as they are. It also forces people to look into the future and see their work in the context of a larger framework. Perhaps most important, formal planning requires communication about values, on issues such as resource allocations, budgeting and workload priorities. (The planning process is covered in detail in ICMI's *Call Center Operations Management Handbook and Study Guide.*)

**12. Don't overdo it:** Experienced leaders are aware of an interesting paradox: too much communicating inhibits effective communication. There is an optimal level of communication beyond which more communication becomes counterproductive. Too many meetings, memos, conferences, email messages and on-the-fly discussions may be symptoms of weaknesses in plans and processes. With better tools, more focused training and appropriate levels of empowerment, the need for excessive communicating can be avoided.

### An Ongoing Process

Call centers need to be comprised of good communicators. After all, communication is the business of call centers. Not only should management staff have the communication skills to manage operations effectively, call center agents need solid communication skills as well.

Studies have shown that, in a face-to-face interaction, 58 percent of communication is through body language, 35 percent through how it was said and a mere seven percent through the content of the message. Without the advantage of body language, call center agents must "connect" with customers, e.g., establish rapport, know when to ask probing questions and "read" between the lines. Call center agents must learn how to minimize miscommunication with customers by taking full advantage of the communication tools at their disposal, such as vocal inflection, tone, rate of speech and, of course, the words they choose.

Effective communication is inseparable from effective leadership. Leaders are only as effective as their ability to communicate. Effective communication results in a shared vision. And, when people are aligned behind a set of compelling values, enthusiasm, commitment and significant productivity tend to follow.

## 7. Creating a Communication Plan for Internal Audiences

**Ready?** | 1 | 2 | 3 |

### Key Points

- **There are important reasons for call center leadership to develop an effective communication plan for internal audiences, including:**
  - **The call center is the first line of communication with customers**
  - **Root-cause resolutions and innovation opportunities must often be implemented in other parts of the organization**
  - **Numerous objectives and processes inherently depend on cross-functional support**
- **Key steps in developing an effective communication plan for internal audiences include:**
  1. **Identify the audience and relevant information to be exchanged**
  2. **Identify the tools that best enable exchange**
  3. **Document required processes**
  4. **Establish liaison roles and cross-functional teams**
  5. **Prepare issue- and action-oriented consulting reports**
  6. **Establish service level agreements (if applicable)**
  7. **Establish collaborative executive education**

### Explanation

Effective communication across the organization is essential to meeting strategic objectives and leveraging the potential of the call center to create strategic value. The reasons to develop a communication plan for internal audiences (others across the organization) can be summarized as follows:

- **The call center is the first line of communication with customers:** In most organizations, the call center interacts with more customers than any other department. As the primary touch point for customer information and interaction, the call center is the ideal consultant to the organization on the "voice of the customer."
- **Root-cause resolutions and innovation opportunities must often be implemented in other parts of the organization:** The call center may be

the repository of customer intelligence, but often the resulting improvements must be implemented in other parts of the organization. For example, the root cause of customer dissatisfaction may involve a process far outside of the call center's control. Similarly, the primary opportunity for a major innovation or quality improvement may lie in another department.

- **Numerous objectives and processes inherently depend on cross-functional support:** Forecasting, quality improvement, career development, budgeting and training are notable examples of issues that require efforts from across the organization.

In short, organizationwide collaboration and communication is essential to the organization's success. It is the call center's responsibility – and imperative – to proactively nurture relationships with others in the organization.

### Creating a Communication Plan

An effective communication plan essentially answers variations of the tried-and-true questions: Who? What? Where? When? Why? Key steps in developing an effective communication plan for internal audiences include:

1. **Identify the audience and relevant information to be exchanged:** The first step in the communication plan is to identify who the audience is and the kinds of information that need to be exchanged. An effective

communication plan identifies both the audience and relevant information to be exchanged. (See The Call Center's Contribution to Unit Strategies, Section 3.)

Communication with other departments must be reciprocal. For example, the marketing department must communicate customer segmentation plans to the call center, but the call center must communicate to marketing how well those segmentation plans are working – along with associated trends and relevant input on how segmentation might best evolve. Similarly, the call center must communicate system improvement opportunities to IT, just as IT must communicate improvement and upgrade opportunities to the call center.

2. **Identify the tools that best enable exchange:** In general, effective internal communication relies on and can benefit from the same technologies many organizations are deploying to achieve knowledge management initiatives. In fact, communication and knowledge management are highly interrelated. Based on the work of consultant Jenny McCune, the following table illustrates the major technological aspects of a knowledge management system.

| Area of focus | Tools |
|---|---|
| Connectivity | • Computer networks<br>• Email<br>• Intranet<br>• Internet |
| Containers (repositories of knowledge) | • Data warehouses, data marts and assorted databases<br>• Document management programs<br>• Electronic directories or "experts," such as corporate yellow pages and expert systems, which compile information in an intelligent database<br>• Large storage cupboards, usually on a corporate intranet |
| Locators (technology for searching and locating information) | • Browsers<br>• Search engines<br>• Knowledge maps (indices that classify information and help users locate the information they need)<br>• Electronic card catalogues (tools to summarize and categorize data)<br>• Push-and-pull Web technology (enables users to request information or organizations to send information on specific topics) |

| Area of focus | Tools |
|---|---|
| Learning vehicles | • Knowledge portals at employees' desktops for easy access to all useful data in the company<br>• E-learning<br>• Web collaboration software<br>• Web seminars |
| Upcoming technology developments | • Filters, browsers and locators based on natural langurage (spoken or written) CTI-enabled solutions that synthensize and interpret infomation from call center systems |

In summary, the objective of this step is to identify and implement tools that facilitate the productive exchange of information. (Knowledge management and related topics are covered in ICMI's *Call Center People Management Handbook and Study Guide.*)

3. **Document required processes:** Documenting required processes is a three-pronged effort that involves:

- Identifying necessary communication processes
- Documenting processes using clear process flows that include action, decision-points, responsibilities and definitions
- Distributing process flows and updates, as necessary

Required processes will be dictated by the type of function-specific information that needs to be communicated. Function-specific information is information that is suited and applicable for specific functional departments. For example, purchasing trends would be of interest to marketing, while budget variance would be of interest to the financial department.

There are three types of function-specific information, including:

- **One-of situations:** Crises, notable cases that require input or exchange with another department, and unusual opportunities.
- **Project-oriented issues:** Cross-functional initiatives such as technology upgrades or customer surveys.
- **Ongoing processes:** Processes that require regular cross-functional input.

The following table provides examples of one-of situations, project-oriented issues and ongoing processes.

| One-of Situations | Project-Oriented Issues | Ongoing Processes |
|---|---|---|
| • Crises<br>• Notable cases<br>• Unusual opportunities (for the customer and/or organization) | • Segmentation strategy<br>• Product design<br>• Financial studies<br>• Customer surveys<br>• Recruiting, hiring, training policies<br>• Technology and facilities upgrades<br>• Employee surveys | • Resource planning and budgeting<br>• Marketing<br>• Quality/innovation<br>• Self-service improvements<br>• "Voice of the customer"<br>• Product updates and support<br>• Staff development |

4. **Establish liaison roles and cross-functional teams:** For many processes, the complexity of interdependency creates the need for a formalized team structure – the cross-functional team – to facilitate effective communication and cooperation. Cross-functional teams can orient groups toward a common set of customer relationship initiatives by:

- Sharing information and tools
- Highlighting the role of the call center and the role of other departments
- Addressing barriers to achieving objectives
- Aligning departmental objectives with overall strategic objectives
- Understanding processes from beginning to end

(For a complete discussion of teams, see ICMI's *Call Center People Management Handbook and Study Guide.*)

5. **Prepare issue- and action-oriented consulting reports:** The most important ingredients in effective reporting are leadership and sound communication principles. Well-managed call centers view call center reporting as an ongoing communication process, not an end result. Presenting data in a clear, concise and actionable format is essential to effective communication. Further, reports must be followed with a forum for discussing and acting on the information; this becomes an opportunity to turn information into sound business decisions. (See Principles of Effective Reporting, this section.)

6. **Establish service level agreements (if applicable):** Effective call center managers focus on getting the call center the support it requires. Traditionally, service level agreements (SLAs) define the performance expectations between a service bureau (also called an outsourcer) and client. Increasingly, however, SLAs are also used to identify and describe requirements between departments or call center units within an organization. (See Developing Service Level Agreements, Section 6.)

7. **Establish collaborative executive education:** A prerequisite to getting good support from managers throughout the organization, especially in the interrelated areas of marketing, finance, information systems and human resources, is that they have a solid understanding of the unique environment in which call centers operate. Progressive call centers work hard to teach call center dynamics to key managers outside the call center, in order to create a clear understanding of how individual tactical decisions and actions link with overall effectiveness. This includes covering the impact of random call arrival, forecasting challenges, occupancy, schedule adherence, service level, quality and the time-sensitive nature of the environment. (See Unique Operational Dynamics, Section 5.)

The reverse is also true: call center executives need a solid understanding of the concerns, challenges and objectives in other areas of the organization. This mutual understanding and education forms a strong foundation for effective communication.

## 8. Creating a Communication Plan for External Audiences

Ready? | 1 | 2 | 3 |

### Key Points

- **Communication can't be confined to internal audiences. The call center has a responsibility to communicate appropriately with external audiences, including customers, investors, suppliers and vendors, outsourcers, resellers and distributors, lawmakers and regulators.**
- **There are two broad categories of information that can be communicated to outsiders:**
  - **Public information**
  - **Sensitive data**
- **An important step in developing a communication plan for external audiences is to identify the most effective media, e.g., Web, print, radio, press releases, intranets and extranets, seminars, targeted reports, and others.**

### Explanation

Communication can't be confined to internal audiences. The call center has a responsibility to communicate appropriately with external audiences, including customers, investors, suppliers and vendors, outsourcers, resellers and distributors, lawmakers and regulators. The benefits that effective communication will create for both the call center and larger organization include:

- Gaining a deeper understanding of the marketplace and the organization's customers for use in product development, marketing, sales and customer service
- Educating customers and investors about processes and technologies that demonstrate the organization's commitment to customer satisfaction and retention
- Providing suppliers and vendors with key information about the organization and its customers' needs, allowing them to, in turn, target products and services more effectively

- Increasing the flow of critical information to resellers and distributors, improving their ability to identify the right markets and satisfy customer needs
- Influencing and educating lawmakers and regulators in areas of customer privacy and confidentiality, fostering an environment that protects both the individual's right to privacy and the organization's desire to personalize services
- Analyzing information that comes from communication, to better align business objectives, processes and tools to best meet the needs of customers



**Two Categories of Information**

Business intelligence takes many forms and the information an organization chooses to share will vary. There are two broad categories of information that can be communicated to outsiders:

- **Public information:** Public relations efforts, annual reports and the organization's Web site provide opportunities for the organization to communicate its chosen position in the market and the justification behind expenditures, investments, policies, products and services. Brand messages and marketing information communicate the organization's priorities and commitment to customer service and customer relationship initiatives.
- **Sensitive data:** The organization may provide specific sensitive information (e.g., trade secrets) to suppliers, distributors, resellers or others so they may cooperate and contribute. In addition, the organization may offer confidential information (via training, reports, corporate intranet, newsletters, etc.) on a "need-to-know basis," detailing relevant customer buying histories, account and personal data, customer segmentations and differentiation strategies.

**Communication Media**

Communication within an organization is relatively easy compared with communication requirements necessary to reach an outside audience. A particularly important step in developing a communication plan for external audiences is to identify the most effective media. The following table outlines common stakeholder categories and the communication methods most used to communicate with them.

| Stakeholders | Communication Methods |
|---|---|
| Customers | • Call center services<br>• Retail sales<br>• Field sales force<br>• Marketing materials (e.g., Web, print, TV, radio)<br>• Public relations and press<br>• Self-service IVR<br>• Web site |
| Investors | • Annual report<br>• Investor briefings<br>• Marketing materials (e.g., Web, print, TV, radio)<br>• Public relations and press<br>• Self-service IVR<br>• Web site |
| Suppliers and vendors | • Employee interaction<br>• Marketing materials (e.g., Web, print, TV, radio)<br>• Seminars for partners<br>• RFIs/RFPs<br>• Targeted reports<br>• Public relations and press<br>• Self-service IVR<br>• Web site, Intranet and/or Extranet |
| Resellers and distributors | • Employee interaction<br>• Marketing materials (e.g., Web, print, TV, radio)<br>• Seminars for partners<br>• Targeted reports<br>• Self-service IVR<br>• Web site, Intranet and/or Extranet |
| Lawmakers and regulators | • Marketing materials (e.g., Web, print, TV, radio)<br>• Public relations and press<br>• Web site<br>• Lobbying |

**Summary of the Process**

Essentially, the process for developing an effective communication plan for external audiences is the same as for internal audiences. (See Creating a Communication Plan for Internal Audiences, this section.)

1. **Identify the audience and relevant information to be exchanged:** The external audience consists of customers, investors, suppliers and vendors, outsourcers, resellers and distributors, lawmakers and regulators. The information is categorized as public and/or sensitive data.

2. **Identify the tools that best enable exchange:** Specific media (e.g., the

Section 4

examples in the table) must be selected according to the audience and information being exchanged.

3. **Document required processes:** As with internal communications, required processes will be dictated by the type of "function-specific" information that needs to be communicated.

4. **Establish liaison roles:** Specific individuals within the organization may be tasked with liaison roles for identified stakeholders.

5. **Prepare issue- and action-oriented reports:** The communication method, via reports, press releases, public announcements, training, or others, must be appropriate for the audience and purpose of the communication.

6. **Establish service level agreements (if applicable):** This step generally applies to contractual relationships, e.g., service bureaus or suppliers.

7. **Establish collaborative executive education:** Although this step is primarily focused on internal audiences, it does have some application with outsiders. For example, the call center may focus on educating customers on self-service options and, in turn, make a concerted effort to learn more about their access preferences and habits.

(This topic is similarly addressed in ICMI's *Call Center Customer Relationship Management Handbook and Study Guide.*)

Section 4

# 9. Principles of Effective Reporting

Ready? | 1 | 2 | 3 |

## Key Points

- **A variety of well-chosen reports is necessary to paint a clear picture of what's going on in a call center. Virtually any measurement by itself can be misleading.**
- **An effective reporting process involves seven steps, including:**
  1. **Determine your objectives**
  2. **Identify supporting information**
  3. **Put information in a user-friendly format**
  4. **Clarify information that could be misleading**
  5. **Annotate exceptions**
  6. **Augment reports with executive education**
  7. **Organize an ongoing forum for discussing and acting on the information**
- **New developments in reporting technologies are creating new opportunities for more closely integrating the call center with other parts of the organization and providing the supporting information upper-level managers need.**

## Explanation

Call center managers have the responsibility of adequately yet succinctly communicating call center activities to senior management and other managers throughout the organization. However, this is quite a feat – after all, there's a lot going on in a call center and summary reports tend to gloss over important information. On the other hand, recipients do not have the time to pore over detailed reports.

Further, the level of activities in most call centers continues to climb. Consider just one facet of reporting call center activity: what happens to callers? Along with telephone contacts, a growing number of transactions involve email, Internet services, voice processing technologies, or some combination of these capabilities. As new ways of providing services are created – and subsequently demanded by customers – it becomes more critical and more involved to measure the service that customers are receiving, and their perceptions of that service. Summarizing and reporting this activity can seem like a monumental task.

Good communication doesn't happen just because detailed information is available. Any call center manager buried in system reports yet struggling to convey basic realities can testify to that fact. Clearly, the process you establish to communicate call center activities is as important as the information itself.



### The Reporting Process

A variety of well-chosen reports is necessary to paint a clear picture of what's going on in a call center. Virtually any measurement by itself can be misleading. Consider the instruments in an aircraft cockpit. By looking at key information together, such as altitude, airspeed, rate of climb or descent, rate of turn, the pilot knows what is happening. But any measurement by itself is of limited use.

The following seven-step framework will help you identify and prepare meaningful reports and ensure that they are understood and utilized.

#### 1. Determine Your Objectives

What are the objectives for the reports? In other words, what should other managers know about the call center or the information it has acquired, and why? To find the answers, assemble a team for a working discussion. A cross-section of managers from across the organization, call center managers, supervisors and agents should be involved. General areas of concern usually include:

- Customer satisfaction and quality measurements
- Workload handled and workload forecast
- Costs and revenues
- Resource utilization (e.g., staffing and scheduling needs)
- Queue reports (e.g., service level, abandonment)
- Access alternatives (e.g., email, IVR, telephone, Web)

From these major categories, key performance measurements will emerge. It's often useful to preface this exercise with a question like, "If we could wave a magic wand, what would we really want to know about our call center?" At this stage, don't be concerned about whether or not you have the reports to support the objectives you identify. Your objectives – not the reports you happen to have – should drive this process. The objectives your team comes up with will be enlightening and will provide much needed direction for the steps that follow.

Part of determining call center objectives is identifying how these objectives are aligned with organizational goals. Making this connection when you report to senior management will help them better understand the call center's strategic impact.

### 2. Identify Supporting Information

List the possible reporting alternatives under each of the objectives you identified in the first step. Include information from the automatic call distributor (ACD), databases (e.g. customer relationship management systems, customer information systems), voice processing system, telecommunications network, workforce management system, email servers, customer surveys, as well as possibilities from other systems and departments.

The challenge now becomes one of selection. Stephanie Winston, author of the popular book, *The Organized Executive,* advises that a report should not simply collect facts, but serve as a judgment tool for management. To pare down the lists, Winston suggests asking a variety of questions: Is the report really necessary? What questions does it answer? Which reports would you dispense with if you had to pay for them? Could several reports be combined? Will you act on the information to affect change?

### 3. Put the Information in a User-Friendly Format

Once you have a list of desired reports, the next step is to compile them into a simple, understandable format. This often means creating graphs of the information. For example, simple line charts can illustrate trends that would otherwise appear as hard-to-decipher numbers. Reports that rely on graphs may take more pages, but a ten-page report consisting primarily of graphs is often quicker to read and easier to comprehend than two pages of detailed numbers in rows and columns.

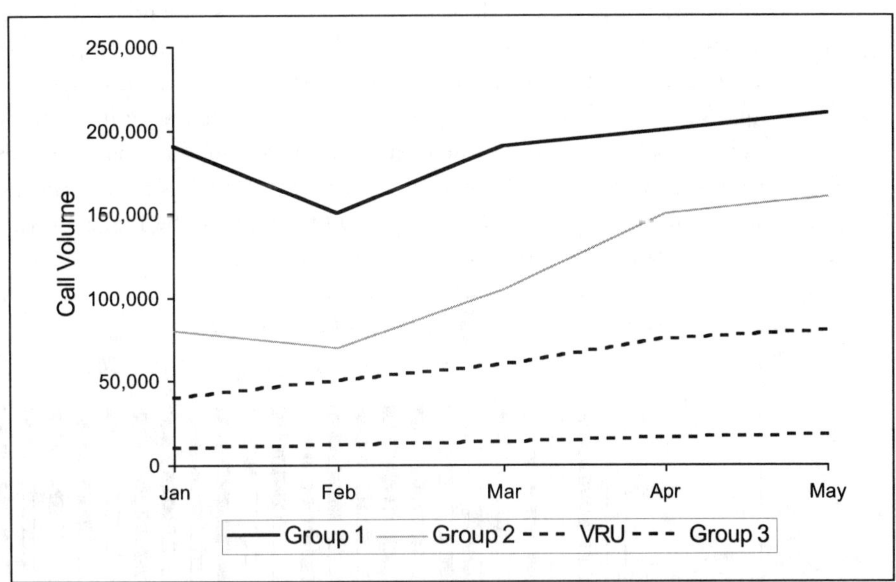

Look for data that should be combined to provide a more complete story. For example, service level should be interpreted with blockage (busy signals) and abandonment. Put these reports together, and use the same general format for headings, periods of time covered and chart types.

### 4. Clarify Information that Could Be Misleading

It's no secret with statistics: you can make many reports tell the story you want them to tell. For example, service level is a particularly challenging activity to report, given the many intervals, customers and agent groups involved. You can prop up service level by generating controlled busy signals, overflowing calls to other groups, or taking messages for later callbacks. Or you can provide overall reports that combine data and conceal problematic intervals. Clearly, simply providing a high-level report on service level can be misleading – the reader needs more information.

Cumulative summary reports are particularly problematic. Many managers produce monthly totals of key information: "Our service level for the month of June was 82 percent in 20 seconds," or, "our average speed of answer for the month was 12 seconds." However, your service level can be lousy every Monday morning, but if you have idle staff at other times, then the average may look just fine. In fact, if you're shooting for averages, there's an inclination to keep people on the phones during slower times – when they could be handling other types of transactions, in training, or working on special projects – so you can make up for lost ground from the times service level significantly dropped.

One way to get around these challenges is to illustrate how often you are hitting a target, versus over or under the objective. For example – again using service level as an illustration – a "100 percent stacked bar chart" will provide a quick view of how often you are meeting the objective by interval. To create this type of chart, specify the number of half-hours each day you were within your target service level range (i.e., 70 percent to 90 percent answer in 20 seconds), the number of half-hours you were above the range, and the number of half-hours you were below the range, for each day.

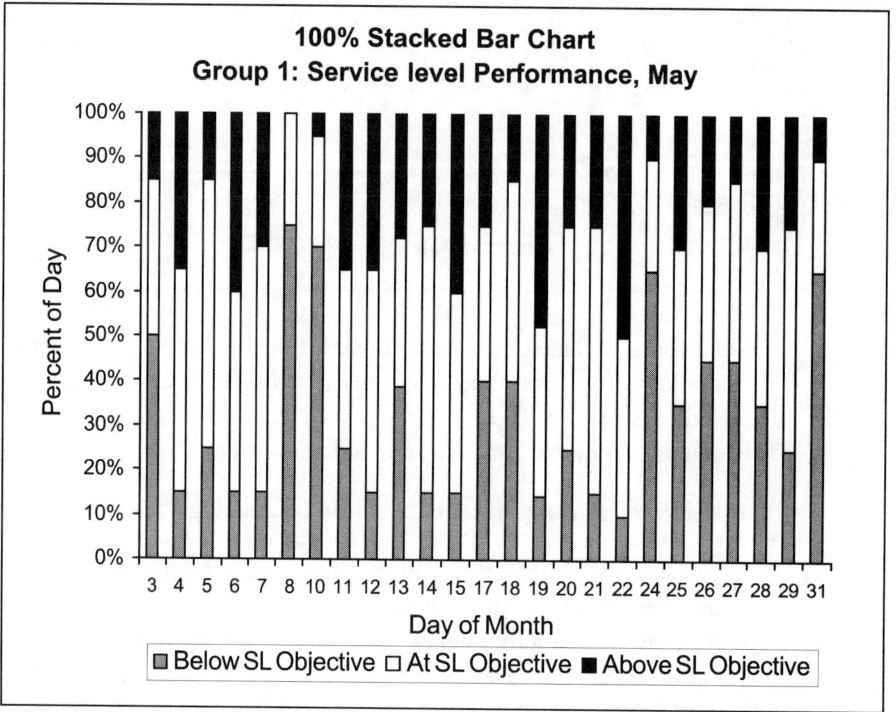


It's usually best to break out reports by agent group. Some managers use weighted averages to combine the reports of multiple groups, small and large alike, into one set of numbers, the rationale being that the service level in small groups should have less impact on the final report than the service level in larger groups. The problem is, your small groups may be important, e.g., platinum level customers, but those results get downplayed.

Resist the temptation to put the call center in an exceptionally good light. If you mask serious resource deficiencies or process problems, the call center is less likely to get the resources and support it needs. That, in turn, will undermine the call center's ability to perform. There's also the related issue of human psychology. When upper-level managers see room for improvement, they tend to feel more assured that they are getting the whole story.

### 5. Annotate Exceptions

There will be points that are clearly out of the norm. Don't leave your audience guessing. Explain deviations – both what happened and why. Why did service level drop and average speed of answer go through the roof in early February? A simple footnote can provide the answer: "February blizzard – call load 40 percent higher than normal."

### 6. Augment Reports with Executive Education

Giving recipients a report to read on what happens on Monday mornings versus bringing them into the call center to observe what happens is the difference between night and day. You need to do both. It is virtually impossible to understand call center reports without spending at least some time in the call center.

This step also involves providing collaborative executive education. Teaching key call center dynamics to managers outside the call center is necessary to create a clear understanding of how cross-functional decisions and actions link with the call center's overall effectiveness. And call center executives need a solid understanding of the concerns, challenges and objectives in other areas of the organization. This mutual understanding forms a strong and essential foundation for effective reporting and communication. (See Creating a Communication Plan for Internal Audiences, this section.)

### 7. Organize an Ongoing Forum for Discussing and Acting on the Information

Information is not passive. Providing managers outside the call center with focused, accurate information on call center activities may bring unwanted attention. On the other hand, it can be a boon to the interest level and support the call center receives. The key, of course, is how the information is used and the management environment that exists.

Effective call center reporting is an ongoing communication process, not an end result. Presenting data in a clear, concise and actionable format is a start. But reports must be followed with a forum for discussing and acting on the information. This becomes the primary opportunity to turn information into sound business decisions and leverage the call center's strategic value.

**New Developments, New Reporting Opportunities**

Unfortunately, the reality today is usually, to varying degrees, a fragmented reporting environment with different reports coming out of different systems. But things are changing and new developments in reporting technologies are creating new opportunities for more closely integrating the call center with other parts of the organization and creating strategic value. Many ACDs, workforce management tools and reporting systems have the capability to export data to a variety of formats, such as relational database programs and spreadsheets. This puts the information into environments that programmers understand. They can then develop custom reports that combine information from various systems.

Further, a key benefit of computer telephony integration (CTI) and customer relationship management capabilities is the means to produce reports that give a rich, integrated view of transactions and customers. In addition to knowing how long calls queue, where they are routed and how long they last, you can analyze other details, such as databases searched, on-screen assistance offered, calculations performed and services provided. These capabilities provide a "three-dimensional" view of activities.

Whatever the progress in reporting, remember to keep your eye on the prize. The purpose of information is to support the strategic objectives of the organization. Ensure that other managers understand the essentials of how the customer contact environment works and the support the call center requires. Utilize a logical, clear process for preparing and relaying information. And remember the principles of effective communication. (See Principles of Effective Communication, this section.) These steps will ensure that your reports are read and understood, and that you are truly "communicating" and not just reporting.

# Leadership and Communication

## Exercises

### Qualities and Characteristics of Effective Leaders

1. True or false

______Effective leaders are born, not made.

______While there is not a definitive list of the characteristics and qualities of an effective leader, there is one quality that is critical: service-orientation.

### The Distinction Between Leadership and Management

2. Complete each statement with either leadership or management.

______________ is a set of responsibilities needed for the organization to achieve its objectives and goals.

______________ is a combination of the skills, knowledge and experience that an individual possesses.

### Modeling Values and Maintaining Integrity

3. Fill in the blanks to complete the process of linking the call center vision and mission with core values.

a. Create a ______________ vision and mission

b. Check ______________

c. Evaluate ______________ style

d. ______________ and ______________ the vision and values

e. ______________ the values

**Principles of Effective Communication**

4. Beside each statement below, indicate whether it is a contributor of communication (with a "c") or an inhibitor of communication (with an "i").

__i__Bureaucracy

__c__Clear vision and mission

__c__Communication ground rules

__c__Communication technologies

__i__Fear

__c__Flat organizational structure

__c__Formal communication channels

__i__Hierarchical organizational structure

__c__Informal communication channels

__c__Listening

__i__Project plans

__c__Sharing both good news and bad

__i__Systematic workload planning

5. True or false

__F__There can never be too much communication.

**Creating a Communication Plan for Internal Audiences**

6. Fill in the blanks to complete key steps in developing an effective communication plan for internal audiences.

a. Identify the audience and relevant issues

b. Identify the tools

c. Document required processes

d. Establish liaison roles and crossfunctional teams

e. Prepare issue- and action-oriented reports

f. Establish service level agreements (if applicable)

g. Establish collaborative executive education.

7. What are three types of function-specific information that call centers communicate to other departments?

~~Service level~~ one of situations

Project oriented issues

Ongoing processes

*(continued, next page)*

## Principles of Effective Reporting

8. Briefly answer the following questions.

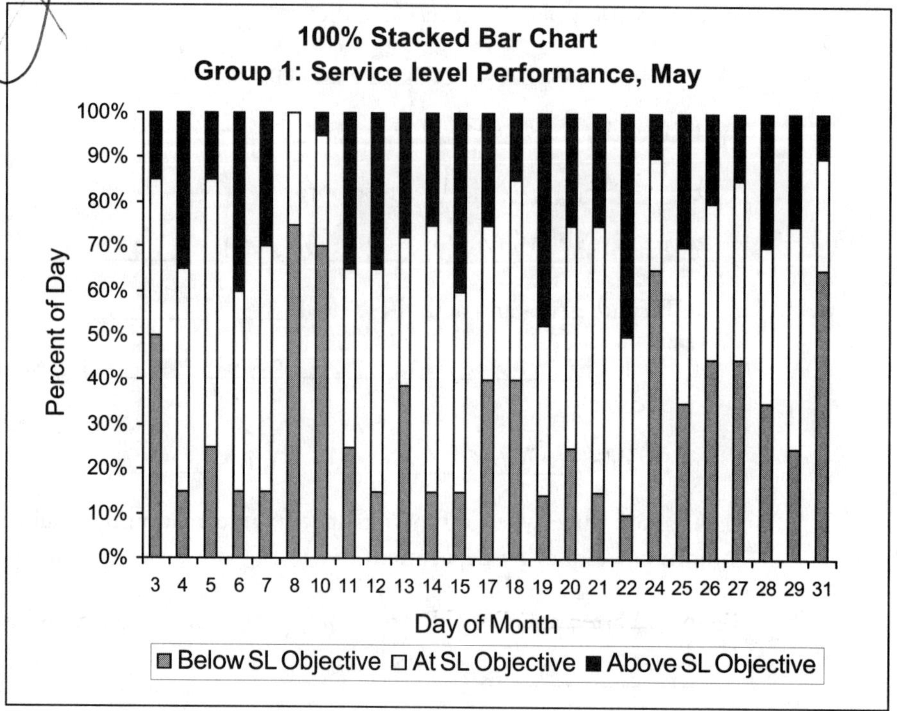


a. Why is the above graph a better representation of service level performance than a graph showing the average service level for each day?

b. Why might it be a bad idea to put the call center in an exceptionally good light?

**Answers to these exercises are in Section 10.**

Note: These exercises are intended to help you retain the material learned. While not the exact questions as on the CIAC Certification assessment, the material in this handbook/study guide fully addresses the content on which you will be assessed. For a formal practice test, please contact the CIAC directly by visiting www.ciac-cert.org.

# Leadership and Communication Reference Bibliography

## Related Articles from *Call Center Management Review* (See Section 9)

Successfully Leading Distributed and 24x7 Teams

Ways Call Center Managers Impede, Ways They Advance Their Careers

Effective Communication: A "Best Practice"

How to Get the Attention of Key Decision Makers

A Process for Reporting Call Center Activity



## For Further Study

### Books/Studies

Bennis, Warren and Burt Nanus. *Leaders: Strategies for Taking Charge.* HarperBusiness, 1997.

Clement, Stephen D. and Elliot Jaques. *Executive Leadership: A Practical Guide to Managing Complexity.* Cason Hall and Company Publishers, 1991.

Covey, Stephen R. *Principle-Centered Leadership.* Summit Books, 1990.

Drucker, Peter F. *The Effective Executive.* HarperBusiness, 1995.

Maxwell, John C. *The 21 Indispensable Qualities of a Leader.* Thomas Nelson Inc., 1999.

Maxwell, John C. *The 21 Irrefutable Laws of Leadership.* Thomas Nelson Publishers, 1998.

Senge, Peter M. *The Fifth Discipline: The Art and Practice of the Learning Organization.* Currency/Doubleday, 1994.

Winston, Stephanie. *The Organized Executive: The Classic Program for Productivity: New Ways to Manage Time, People, and the Digital Office.* Warner Books, 2001.

**Articles**

Alsop, Ronald. "Perils of Corporate Philanthropy." *The Wall Street Journal,* January 16, 2002.

Hash, Susan. "Leadership Skills No.1 Criteria for Supervisors, Says Study." *Call Center Management Review,* August 2001.

Kaplan, Tamara. "The Tylenol Crisis: How Effective Public Relations Saved Johnson & Johnson." *The Pennsylvania State University.*

Temes, Ivan. "Maintaining Service Loyalty during a Downsizing." *Call Center Management Review*, March 2002.

**Seminars**

*Effective Leadership and Strategy for Senior Call Center Managers* public seminar, presented by Incoming Calls Management Institute.

*Communicating the Value of the Call Center Across the Organization* Web seminar, presented by Incoming Calls Management Institute.

## Section 5

# *The Call Center Business Environment*

# Section 5: The Call Center Business Environment

## Contents

# 1. Understanding and Applying Call Center Terminology

Ready? | 1 | 2 | 3 |

## Key Points

- **A sound understanding of call center-specific terminology will enable you to communicate effectively, form reasoned judgments and take appropriate actions. It will also allow you to get the most from educational resources and assistance from peers.**
- **There are a number of challenges associated with call center terminology, including:**
  - **Industry terms vary by country, organization and technology vendor**
  - **Some terms are misleading**
  - **Some terms are used interchangeably when they refer to very different things**
  - **Some terms refer to measures that can be calculated different ways**
  - **Call center terminology continues to evolve**
- **Call center managers should ensure that everyone who interacts with the call center has a common understanding of terms that are used in discussions.**



## Explanation

Like any profession, the call center industry has unique terms and acronyms that describe everything from performance objectives to technology considerations to underlying operational dynamics. A sound understanding of call center-specific terminology will enable you to communicate effectively, form reasoned judgments and take appropriate actions. It will also allow you to get the most from educational resources and assistance from peers.

The glossary included in Section 8 of this study guide will provide you with the specific acronyms, terminology and definitions with which you need to be familiar. However, there are some challenges associated with gaining a common understanding of call center terminology. These include:

- **Industry terms vary by country, organization and technology vendor:** For example, after-call work can also be called wrap-up, wrap, ACW or post call processing. Similarly service level can be referred to as total service factor, telephone service factor or TSF.

- **Some terms are misleading:** For example, the term interactive voice response (IVR) may seem to refer to technology that responds based on speech recognition, but, in practice, the technology more often responds to input from a caller's telephone keypad.
- **Some terms are used interchangeably when they refer to very different things:** A good example of this problem is the confusion over the terms occupancy and adherence to schedule. Occupancy is the percentage of time agents are handling calls during a specified interval (usually a half hour). It is a result of workload volume and service level, and is therefore out of the agent's control. On the other hand, adherence to schedule measures the extent to which an agent follows his or her schedule. Agents have some control over their adherence to schedule as they make decisions throughout the day, e.g., when to come back from breaks, when to go to lunch. Despite the clear differences in these two measures, many people use these terms as if they were synonymous.
- **Some terms refer to measures that can be calculated different ways:** This challenge is best illustrated by looking at what has become the primary performance indicator for call center accessibility – service level. Service level is commonly calculated four different ways, each of which will produce a different result. Call center managers need to understand which formula their system uses and whether this is the most appropriate formula for their center. (For more information on calculating service level, see ICMI's *Call Center Operations Management Handbook and Study Guide.*)
- **Call center terminology continues to evolve:** Currently, there is even debate over the term call center. Call center, contact center, interaction center, customer care center, help desk...the list could go on. While you should stay abreast of these debates within the industry, it's equally important to prevent different terminology from becoming a stumbling block to continuous improvement or effective communication with others.

### The Importance of Educating Others

Call center managers should ensure that everyone who interacts with the call center has a common understanding of terms that are used in discussions. Misunderstandings of terminology can hinder collaboration. Situations where applying proper call center terminology is critical include:

- Developing strategic plans
- Working with internal support groups, e.g., IT or telecommunications
- Forecasting the workload
- Training and orientation
- Union negotiations
- Investigating appropriate technologies
- Developing and approving budgets
- Monitoring and coaching for performance improvement
- Working with external suppliers, e.g., equipment suppliers, outsourcers or telecommunications providers

This item was developed with Henry Dortmans and Mike Dunne of Angus Dortmans Associates Inc.

## 2. Unique Operational Dynamics

Ready? | 1 | 2 | 3 |



### Key Points

- **A prerequisite to managing or supporting a call center effectively is to have a solid understanding of the unique call center environment.**
- **Seven critical issues that demonstrate the uniqueness of the call center environment are:**
  1. **Workload arrives randomly**
  2. **There's a direct link between resources and results**
  3. **Service level and quality work hand-in-hand**
  4. **When service level improves, "productivity" declines**
  5. **You need more staff on schedule than on the phones**
  6. **Staffing and telecommunications budgets must be integrated**
  7. **The demands on call center agents are increasing**

### Explanation

The following section summarizes the unique operational dynamics of the call center environment. These issues need to be understood by call center managers and managers from other parts of the organization. They are covered in detail throughout ICMI's study guide series and are presented here in summary format only.

#### 1. Workload Arrives Randomly

Even with near perfect forecasts, the actual moment-to-moment arrival of contacts is a random phenomenon – the luck of the draw. It is ultimately the result of countless decisions made by callers, based on a myriad of individual habits and motivations. It is simply not possible to plan for handling the workload in a call center the way you would plan work in most other parts of the organization.

There are two important implications to random call arrival. First, base staffing must be calculated by using either a queuing formula that takes random call arrival into account (typically Erlang C) or a computer simulation program that accurately models this phenomenon. Traditional approaches to staff planning, common in other areas of the organization, lead to insufficient staffing in the call center. Unfortunately, it's not just staffing that will be off because staffing impacts the load the network and systems must carry.

Second, performance standards must take random call arrival into account. For example, a standard of "N widgets per day" may make sense in a traditional assembly line setting, but it doesn't work in an environment where the workload comes in randomly and must be handled when it arrives.

**2. There's a Direct Link Between Resources and Results**

The principle of service level (and the related measure, response time) is at the heart of incoming call center management. Without a service level objective, the answers to many important questions would be left to chance. How accessible is the call center? How many staff do you need? How do you compare to the competition? Are you prepared to handle the response to marketing campaigns? How busy are your agents going to be?



The relationship between staff and service level should be demonstrated in the budgeting process. The best call centers first decide on the objectives they want to achieve. They then allocate the resources necessary to support those objectives, through careful calculations and planning. Effective call center managers constantly reinforce the fact that a certain level of resources are required to achieve a specified objective.

**3. Service Level and Quality Work Hand-in-Hand**

On the surface, it appears that service level and quality are at odds. After all, you can have an excellent service level, but agents can still:

- Misunderstand callers' requests
- Enter the wrong information
- Relay the wrong information to callers
- Make callers mad
- Fail to accomplish the primary purpose (sell or service)
- Unnecessarily cause repeat calls
- Miss opportunities to capture valuable feedback

However, it's important to put service level in context. A good service level is an enabler – it means that calls are getting in and answered, so your agents and your callers can get on with things. A poor service level will rob the call center of productivity. As service deteriorates, more and more callers are likely to verbalize their criticisms when their calls are finally answered. Agents spend valuable time apologizing to callers.

At some point, quality begins to suffer, which has a further negative impact on service level. When agents are overworked due to constant congestion in the queue, they become less accurate. Mistakes contribute to repeat calls, unnecessary service calls, escalation of calls and complaints to higher management and callbacks, all of which drive service level down further.

In short, a poor service level tends to be a vicious cycle. There is no such thing as quality versus service level – at least not in the long term. Service level and quality go hand-in-hand.

**4. When Service Level Improves, "Productivity" Declines**

Here's a sobering immutable law, from a productivity aspect: As service level goes up, each agent handles fewer calls. Put another way, as service level goes up, occupancy goes down. The better the service level, the more time your agents will spend waiting for calls to arrive.

Occupancy is the percentage of time during a half hour that agents are actually handling calls. The inverse of occupancy is the time agents spend waiting for inbound calls, plugged in and available.

The relationship between occupancy and service level is often misunderstood. The incorrect logic goes something like, "If agents really dig-in, service level will go up and so will their occupancy." In reality, if occupancy is high, it is because agents are taking one call after another, with little or no wait between calls. Calls are stacked up in queue and service level is low.

When service level gets better, occupancy goes down. Therefore, average calls taken per individual also goes down. Some managers can't stomach this reality – heaven forbid any "unproductive" time. However, the time agents spend waiting for calls is sliced into 12 seconds there, two seconds there, and so on, the result of random call arrival.

Since occupancy depends on the same input as service level, it is influenced by inbound call volume and average handling times. If the number of agents stay the same and the call volume increases, occupancy will increase as well (and service level will decrease).

**5. You Need More Staff on Schedule Than on the Phones**

Many call center managers have, at one time or another, looked at a supervisor monitor or done a count out on the floor and wondered, "Where is everybody?" Some are on break. Some at lunch. Some are absent, or in a team meeting. Some are in the restroom. The possibilities go on and on.

This is one of those "real-world" call center issues. However accurately you predict base staffing needs, you can still miss your service level objective by a long shot because you don't have the staff you expected in the right places at the right times. Schedules need to realistically reflect the many things that can keep agents from actually being at their desks, taking calls.

**6. Staffing and Telecommunications Budgets Must Be Integrated**

Staffing and trunking needs are inextricably associated. The more staff you have handling a given call load, the less the load on the telecommunications network. In other words, staffing affects telecommunications costs. Spending some money on staffing can save a lot more on network services costs. The tradeoff between staff and network costs is direct and reasonably predictable.

Despite the inseparable relationship between staff and trunks, many call centers budget for these costs independently. Staff and trunks are a classic example of the need to look at the "big picture." Knowing this tradeoff will lead to better planning and budgetary decisions.

**7. The Demands on Call Center Agents Are Increasing**

The agent jobs that are emerging are those that add value through problem identification and problem resolution. These jobs are process-oriented, not just task-oriented. Customer are increasingly better informed, more demanding of excellent service and require service through more channels, such as the Internet and email. The transactions that need live assistance will require agents equipped with higher levels of knowledge and better tools than ever.

The trends are clear. Call centers are paying higher salaries, hiring people with more education and giving them more responsibility. The industry needs people with the smarts, training and skills to understand the processes of which they are a part, and to contribute to improvements. People will make the difference in the new generation of call centers.

**Part of a Larger Effort**

The call center is an important part of a much bigger process – the organization. Call center managers who consistently get the best results know that. They take the initiative in coordinating with other departments. They work hard to integrate call center activities with developments in other parts of the organization. They have an incessant focus on strengthening the call center's support of the organization.

An important part of that effort is to ensure that they and other managers both inside and outside the call center have an awareness of the fundamental principles that make call centers unique. That will provide the necessary understanding on which to build.

# 3. Characteristics of the Call Center's Emerging Role

Ready? | 1 | 2 | 3 |

## Key Points

- Call centers today bear little resemblance to the static back-office operations of yesteryear. New technologies, channels of contact, strategies and career opportunities are changing the face of call centers worldwide.
- Among the key facets of today's call center's emerging role are:
  - Multichannel contact management
  - E-support
  - Customer relationship management
  - Expanded hours for customer access
  - Heightened strategic value contribution



## Explanation

Call centers have come a long way from the static back-office operations that once dominated the industry. New technologies, new channels of contact and new customer support strategies, as well as the evolution of passive "operators" into proactive and influential sales and support professionals, have changed – and continue to change – the face of call centers today.

### A Whole New Role

Here's a look at the key facets of the modern call center's emerging role:

- **Multichannel contact management:** While the majority of transactions continue to take place via live phone conversations in most call centers, customers are demanding different customer contact options. These include fax, interactive voice response (IVR), email, Web self-service and real-time Web-based support options such as chat, Web callback and "click-to-talk." Call centers hoping to succeed in the new era need to not only offer, but effectively manage, these various channels. Customers have come to expect choices, quality and consistent service regardless of how they choose to "enter" the organization.
- **E-support:** E-commerce has changed the traditional call center forever. The demand for Web-based customer contact can no longer be ignored by organizations. It's up to the call center manager to ensure that the

right technology, people and processes are in place to turn the center into a high-powered hub for e-support. Customer emails, self-service capabilities and chat sessions are growing exponentially. Organizations that best handle the barrage will be rewarded with unmatched customer loyalty and increased revenue.

- **Customer relationship management:** Customer relationship management – which revolves around treating different customers differently – is no longer considered a trend; it's become a necessary component for any business that cares about customer retention. While customer relationship management requires teamwork and communication throughout the organization, no department has as much impact on its success as the call center. The call center has its finger on the pulse of the customer. It's where key customer data is most easily collected – data that can be used to greatly enhance personalized sales, service and support throughout the organization. With the right tools and strategy in place, call center managers can become customer relationship management champions for the entire organization. (For a complete discussion of customer relationship management, see ICMI's *Call Center Customer Relationship Management Handbook and Study Guide.*)

- **Expanded hours for customer access:** The nine-to-five business model has become a dinosaur in the call center world. Some new numbers – 24x7 – have made their way into the limelight. Customers expect to be able to make purchases and have their questions answered whenever they wish, and many call centers have responded to their desires. Expanded hours of operation, powerful self-service options and dynamic virtual call center environments provide the key to increasing the availability of call center services to customers.

- **Heightened strategic value contribution:** As organizations seek to use call center data and services to increase customer loyalty, the call center's value to the organization has come into focus. Call centers today must communicate their strategic value throughout the organization to get the budget and support they need to help transform the organization to meet customer expectations. The following are generally recognized areas in which call centers add strategic value:

  - **Unit strategies:** With advanced data warehousing and mining capabilities available today, call centers are collecting and analyzing more and more information for other business units, enabling them to make better strategic and operational decisions. (See The Call

Center's Contribution to Unit Strategies, Section 3.)

- **Customer satisfaction and loyalty:** Building customer relationships that enable customer satisfaction and encourage loyalty has become a strategic necessity for organizations today. As most organizations' primary customer touch point, the call center is key in achieving these objectives. (See The Call Center's Contribution to Customer Satisfaction and Loyalty, Section 3.)
- **Quality and innovation:** Many organizations today must differentiate themselves among many competitors and alternative services. Call centers provide the organization with customer data to make innovative improvements that will meet the needs of their most valuable customers. (See The Call Center's Contribution to Quality and Innovation, Section 3.)
- **Marketing:** In addition to its traditional role of supplying marketing with response rate data and feedback, today's call center also carries out marketing strategies, e.g., customer profiling and segmentation. (See The Call Center's Contribution to Marketing, Section 3.)
- **Products and services:** As customer segmentation becomes more advanced in organizations today, the call center provides the customer insight into which products and services will best meet the needs of each customer segment. (See The Call Center's Contribution to Products and Services, Section 3.)
- **Efficient service delivery:** Increasing operational efficiency has long been a primary goal of organizations. However, as customers continue to demand more access alternatives and expanded service availability, the call center becomes that much more vital to the organization's ability to service them effectively and efficiently. (See The Call Center's Role in Efficient Service Delivery, Section 3.)
- **Self-service usage and system design:** With the growth of e-commerce, customers are demanding greater levels of self-service. Call centers provide both the data for determining the best way to offer those services as well as personal support when self-service options become insufficient. (See The Call Center's Role in Self-Service Usage and System Design, Section 3.)
- **Revenue/sales:** For-profit organizations continue to seek ways to increase wallet share of customers. Call centers assist with that objective by providing well-trained agents that have the tools to

upsell and cross-sell effectively. (See The Call Center's Contribution to Revenue/Sales, Section 3.)

**Factors Driving the Emerging Role**

While there are many interrelated factors that drive the call center's emerging role, several key factors include:

- **Global economy:** Goods and services are now accessible worldwide. The Internet, electronic commerce and the opening of borders and trade have created a truly global economy. As organizations seek to service customers regardless of their language or location, the call center's role must evolve to accommodate customers across many timezones and languages.
- **More choice with less time to choose:** In most industries, customers have multiple competitors to choose from, but often have less time to investigate them. Organizations are increasingly depending on customer intelligence to anticipate the needs of customers. The call center has a new responsibility to manage this data and communicate it throughout the organization.
- **Better educated and more demanding consumers:** Today's consumers are empowered with more information than at any other time in history. They know the choices available to them and they demand services that meet their evolving expectations.
- **Technological innovations in customer access alternatives:** The development of new customer access technologies is changing the landscape of many call centers. Although some of these technologies will take time to gain widespread acceptance, customers continue to demand more convenient ways to access organizations.
- **More importance placed on customer retention vs. customer acquisition:** Many studies are emerging that illustrate the value of long-term customers, who are less expensive to sell to and service, and typically buy more over time. The call center manages several key contributors of customer satisfaction, and in turn loyalty, including accessibility, resolution on first contact, follow through on promised action and knowledge of the agent. (For a detailed discussion on contributors of customer satisfaction, see ICMI's *Call Center Customer Relationship Management Handbook and Study Guide.*)

## 4. Strategies and Actions to Support the Call Center's Emerging Role

**Ready?** | 1 | 2 | 3 |

### Key Points

- Actions for managing multichannel contacts include:
  - Offer a full range of contact options as they become feasible
  - Develop appropriate service level and response time objectives
  - Get a handle on the complexity of forecasting and scheduling
  - Address new hiring and training issues
  - Ensure consistency and customer satisfaction across all contact channels
- Actions for providing top-notch e-support include:
  - Implement key e-support technologies
  - Staff the center with qualified "Net reps"
  - Develop appropriate response time objectives
  - Build workflow processes via business rules
  - Implement a formal "e-monitoring" program
  - Measure online customer satisfaction
- Actions for managing customer relationships include:
  - Openly exchange information with other key departments
  - Revamp training and performance measurement practices
  - Align group design with customer segmentation
  - Implement enabling call center tools
- Actions for expanding hours for customer access include:
  - Implement customer-focused self-service tools
  - Expand hours at single-site call centers
  - Create a virtual environment
- Actions for developing the call center's strategic value include:
  - Communicate the value of the call center across the organization
  - Define the benefits the call center provides to each department
  - Educate other departments on the unique call center environment
  - Act as "voice of the customer" consultant

## Explanation

Today's call centers are playing a more strategic role in organizations than ever before. It is important for managers to understand the call center's role, but recognition of its components isn't enough; managers need to put the right strategies, tools, processes and people in place to effectively support the call center's emerging role.

The following is a guide to the practices that managers should consider to ensure success in the new era of customer contact.



### Managing Multichannel Contacts

How multichannel contacts are offered, promoted and managed should be based on the organization's strategic objectives for customer access. The following are essential actions for managing multichannel contacts:

- **Offer a full range of contact options as they become feasible:**
    - Phone (live agent)
    - IVR self-help applications
    - Fax
    - Email
    - Text-chat
    - Web self-services
    - Web call through
    - Web callback
    - Web collaboration

  Which of these contact options should be offered to your customers will depend on your customers' expectations, needs and value. In fact, some customer segments may be given different contact options than other segments, if appropriate. Be cautious, however, in denying any customer segment access to live telephone service. Most customers expect to be able to reach a person when necessary, so you could ultimately hurt customer loyalty.

- **Develop appropriate service level and response time objectives:** Develop reasonable and acceptable service level and response time objectives to provide efficient service across all contact channels.

- **Get a handle on the complexity of forecasting and scheduling:** With the variety of customer contacts flowing into the call center, forecasting the workload and getting the right number of appropriately skilled staff in place to handle that workload is more complicated than ever. While it's a good idea to use modern workforce management technologies to help you, these tools can't work magic. It's important to understand historical data and trends and make intelligent assumptions about the expected workload.

  Understanding the differences of handling each channel is vitally important, especially when there may be little historical data for newer channels. For example, although email contacts do not have to be handled immediately, as telephone contacts do, email contacts typically have higher average handling times than telephone contacts, given the same contact type.

- **Address new hiring and training issues:** New contact types mean new skill requirements for agents. Be sure your hiring and training programs are structured to prepare agents for success in the multichannel environment. Inadequate agent skills can be a significant barrier to providing multichannel services that meet customer expectations.

- **Ensure consistency and customer satisfaction across all contact channels:** This requires a focused monitoring strategy that includes careful observation not only of how agents handle customer contacts, but also how the different technologies (queuing and routing tools, IVR systems, email management applications, etc.) respond during those contacts. In addition to holistic monitoring practices, a multichannel customer satisfaction measurement strategy needs to be in place. This involves surveying customers not only via phone and/or mail, but also via IVR, email and the Web.

(For a complete discussion of these operational and human resources issues, see ICMI's *Call Center People Management Handbook and Study Guide* and *Call Center Operations Management Handbook and Study Guide.*)

### Providing Top-Notch E-Support

While e-support is a part of the multichannel contact management component that has already been covered, it plays such a big part in the call center's emerging role that it warrants special attention here. Many organizations initially expected the rise of Web-enabled contact channels to reduce telephone call volume immediately. However, most organizations find that they experience an initial increase in telephone call volume when e-support channels are implemented.

The following are essential actions for providing top-notch e-support:

- **Implement key e-support technologies:**
    - **Email response management systems:** Automatically distribute customer email inquiries among agents and offer assistance in helping them respond with accuracy and efficiency. Since email is the most widely used agent-assisted Internet channel, email response management systems are being implemented by an ever-increasing number of call centers.
    - **Text-chat applications:** Enable customers visiting the organization's Web site to have real-time, text-based conversations with agents. Most of these applications provide agents with a host of features to enhance the speed and quality of chat sessions. Although still not as popular as email, text-chat is increasingly being used by organizations with a significant online presence.
    - **Web callback tools:** Enable Web visitors to contact the call center and request an agent to call them back. Once the callback is made, the transaction carries on as a normal voice conversation.
    - **Web call through applications:** Powered by voice-over IP (VoIP) technology, these tools enable Web site visitors to have live voice conversations with call center agents. Since the quality of VoIP calls in many cases does not yet meet customer expectations, most call centers today have not implemented this technology. However, most experts say that recent advances in VoIP technology will reduce these concerns. The advantages of cost savings and better integration with other technologies will make VoIP a very attractive technology in the future.
    - **Co-browsing and form-sharing tools (also called Web collaboration and page pushing):** These tools, coupled with other Web-based support applications like chat and Web call through, can dramatically enhance a center's e-support efforts. These tools enable cross-selling and upselling by allowing agents to view Web pages with customers and direct them to relevant areas or "push" specific pages to them. Form-sharing tools enable agents to move the

customer's cursor and help him or her fill in complex forms or applications.

- **Web self-service tools:** Enable customers to receive information and answers to questions, place orders and view order status directly from the organization's Web site without contacting the call center for assistance. The key components of Web self-service include FAQs, interactive search engines, online personal accounts and customized Web pages.

The reality is these capabilities require significant investments – not only in the technologies themselves, but also in the ongoing impact to the operational budget. But leading organizations are wisely asking "Can we afford not to provide these capabilities?"

- **Staff the center with qualified "Net reps:"** The skills required to effectively handle email and Web-based customer contacts are in some fundamental ways different from those needed to succeed on the phones. Therefore, you need to take care when determining the best way to organize agent groups to handle these channels. Generally, agent groups can be organized in three ways:
  - Agents that handle both phone and email at scheduled times during the day
  - Separate agent groups that handle only one contact channel, with separate agents for the phones and separate agents for e-support channels
  - Multimedia agents that handle a mix of contacts via multimedia queuing, which is enabled by technology applications that dynamically present a mix of contacts to agents depending on demand

  The right agent group structure will depend on the workload demand, size of the center and the agents' skills and preferences. You will also need to revisit and make necessary changes to existing agent recruiting, hiring and training practices to ensure that you have the right people in place to power your e-support efforts. (For a detailed discussion of agent group structure, see ICMI's *Call Center People Management Handbook and Study Guide.*)

- **Develop appropriate response time objectives:** Email, text-chat and Web callback transactions require that the center establish appropriate response time objectives. Don't treat these newer types of transactions as less important than phone calls. Customers have come to expect efficient service regardless of the contact channel chosen. When determining specific response time objectives, strive to strike a balance between what you feel customers will deem acceptable, and what your center can achieve.

- **Build workflow processes via business rules:** Business rules refer to various software (or manual) controls that manage contact routing, handling and follow-up. They essentially reflect the organization's thinking on how systems and processes handle workflow. Sound business rules are key to well-integrated multichannel environments and represent an opportunity to gain efficiencies while providing more personalized service. In order to achieve consistency of service across contact channels, the business rules for each contact type should be based on customer type, rather than media type.
- **Implement a formal "e-monitoring" program:** Considering the impact that effective e-support can have on customer retention and revenue, it's important to regularly observe agents' and systems' abilities to handle email and Web-based transactions. Fortunately, many of the tools that enable e-support include features that help to ease the quality assurance process. For example, most email response management systems archive all email activity and enable supervisors to easily monitor agent responses in terms of timeliness, accuracy and professionalism. Most text-chat applications not only archive complete transactions, but also enable supervisors to view chat sessions in real-time to see how agents and the technology interact with customers.
- **Measure online customer satisfaction:** The best way to know if your e-support efforts are hitting the mark is to ask your online customers. And the best way to do that is via email and Internet surveys. These surveys are similar to traditional phone and mail surveys in content, but their electronic format can dramatically enhance the speed of response, as well as increase the number of customers who choose to respond. Online customers have already demonstrated their preference for communication via email and the Web; it only makes sense to survey them via those same channels.

(For a complete discussion of these operational, technology, and human resources issues, see ICMI's *Call Center People Management Handbook and Study Guide* and *Call Center Operations Management Handbook and Study Guide.*)

## Managing Customer Relationships

The following are essential actions for managing customer relationships:

- **Openly exchange information with other key departments:** While the call center plays a critical role in an organization's customer relationship management strategy, organizationwide interaction and information sharing is the key to success. Provide relevant departments (e.g., marketing, sales, R&D, finance) with access to customer databases in the call center, and ensure that the call center has access to information gathered by other departments.

- **Revamp training and performance measurement practices:** Customer relationship management theory emphasizes quality and personalized customer service over straight productivity metrics. Managers need to put theory into practice by ensuring that agents gain the skills they need to support such a customer-focused approach. Agents will be required to manage more customer information and must be trained and coached to do so effectively. A benefit to this increased training and empowerment can be lower rates of turnover, as long as the culture supports the changes taking place. Managers also need to be sure that the performance metrics that are in place don't send agents a mixed message (e.g., "spend time with customers building relationships, but don't increase your average handling time").

- **Align agent group design with customer segmentation strategy:** Agent group design may be impacted by customer relationship management initiatives if service to individual customer segments differs significantly. When deciding how pooled or specialized your agent groups should be, it is important to weigh the practicalities of cross-training agents to handle multiple types of contacts against the inefficiencies of small, specialized queue groups.

- **Implement enabling call center tools:** Customer relationship management in the call center is about gathering customer data and using it to deliver highly personalized sales and service. Some of the technologies that come into play include:

  - Contact management applications, i.e., call tracking and logging systems, data warehousing/mining tools, customer-focused reporting tools

  - Intelligent routing applications, i.e., workflow routing, skills-based routing, priority queuing, automated number identification (ANI), dialed number identification service (DNIS)

- Screen pops and other desktop productivity tools that enable a 360 degree view of the customer
- E-support tools (see above discussion of these tools)
- Customer interaction recording (CIR) systems

(For a complete discussion of customer relationship management issues, see ICMI's *Call Center Customer Relationship Management Handbook and Study Guide.*)



**Expanding Hours for Customer Access**

The following are essential actions for expanding hours for customer access:

- **Implement customer-focused self-service tools:** Enabling customers to find answers to questions, check balances and place orders without having to speak to an agent goes a long way in increasing the availability of services. Well-designed IVR systems and Web self-service applications make it easy for customers to get what they want, whenever they want it.
- **Expand hours at single-site call centers:** As important as self-service tools are, call centers need to give customers the option to reach agents. Managers at single-site call centers need to make a case for the required staff – as well as to develop appropriate forecasting and scheduling strategies – to ensure that they have the right people in the right places to handle customer contacts. Single-site centers may want to consider using a service bureau to boost the center's expanded access efforts. (See Identifying Outsourcing Opportunities, Section 6.)
- **Create a virtual environment:** Multi-site call center operations have an advantage over their single-site counterparts with regard to expanding operating hours. The former can pool resources to form a single virtual center that can more easily handle a high volume of customer contacts at any hour. Organizations with centers spread out over wide geographic areas can create effective "follow-the-sun" strategies that provide access to customers around the globe, while offering agents more traditional working hours.

(For a complete discussion of these operational issues, see ICMI's *Call Center Operations Management Handbook and Study Guide.*)

**Developing the Call Center's Strategic Value**

The following are essential actions for developing the call center's strategic value:

- **Communicate the value of the call center across the organization:** Building internal visibility requires relentless attention to the promotion of the center, its agents and the value it offers the organization. The communication should be focused on building relationships with key individuals within each department, not the department as a whole. Relationships with these executives will provide you with advocates throughout the organization.
- **Define the benefits the call center provides to each department:** Build a small, capable team in the call center to work with you on identifying ways the call center can create the most value for the organization. Get the input of peers in other departments. Find out what is most important to them.
- **Educate other departments on the unique call center environment:** An important prerequisite to getting good support from managers both inside and outside the call center is that you and they have a basic understanding of how call centers operate. Consider developing a two-hour seminar or small group tutorial on call center dynamics and follow up with a tour of the call center. Once other departments understand the principle of having "the right number of people in the right place at the right time," they will make better decisions that impact the call center.
- **Act as "voice of the customer" consultant:** Be active in providing the organization with customer intelligence. Let other departments know the data that is available to them and how the call center can help them determine the needs and expectations of customers. The call center is uniquely qualified to gauge the pulse of the organization's customers and must take that responsibility seriously.

(See Defining of the Call Center's Value Proposition, Section 3.)

## 5. The Impact of E-commerce on the Call Center

Ready? | 1 | 2 | 3 |

### Key Points

- **E-commerce has catapulted the call center into the limelight in most organizations. These organizations rely on their call center's e-support capabilities to enhance revenue and customer retention.**
- **The call center issues most impacted by e-commerce include:**
  - **The types of contact tools implemented**
  - **Hiring and recruiting**
  - **Training**
  - **Performance measurement**
  - **Forecasting issues**
  - **Scheduling issues**
  - **Customer satisfaction measurement**



### Explanation

Ever since organizations started to establish a Web presence in the early and mid-nineties, the call for online customer support has increased rapidly. The call center – with its history of handling high volumes of customer contacts – became the logical choice to answer that call early on, and in doing so, has been catapulted into the limelight in most organizations. Today, organizations rely on their call center's e-support capabilities to enhance revenue and create high levels of customer loyalty.

#### The Specific Impact

The impact of e-commerce has been felt throughout the call center, bringing about significant changes in:

- **The types of contact tools implemented:** E-business has brought a whole new host of customer support technologies to the call center. Organizations offering the best e-support have successfully implemented email management systems, text-chat tools, Web call through and Web callback applications, as well as numerous online self-service tools. These tools have helped call centers turn Web surfers into buyers and enable customers to easily obtain assistance and information. The impact such technologies have on revenue generation (and protection) as well as customer loyalty grows daily.

Although there are many technologies to consider when supporting e-commerce channels, the agent's desktop almost always requires a transformation in order to best handle the new access channels. The ideal desktop solution would enable agents to view all types of contacts on one screen and include easy-to-read and easy-to-use screens designed with agent workflow in mind.

- **Hiring and recruiting:** New contact channels and customer expectations mean new skill and knowledge requirements for agents. The call center industry has witnessed the emergence of the "Net rep" – the new agent with high levels of Web savvy as well as excellent writing skills. To find and obtain qualified Net reps, call centers have had to change and update their recruiting and hiring practices. Many centers have incorporated progressive "e-cruiting" strategies into the mix, using the Web both to attract Net rep applicants and evaluate their e-support skills. Online help-wanted ads, email- and chat-based interviews and e-role plays have supplemented more traditional recruiting and hiring methodologies.

- **Training:** E-commerce has placed a greater demand on the skill sets required of call center agents. Whether they are just handling telephone contacts, a mix of contact channels, or only e-support channels, call center agents must have a working knowledge of the Internet and how e-commerce is handled by the organization.

- **Performance measurement:** Call centers can no longer rely solely on service level objectives and measurements to gauge performance. The rapid growth of e-commerce requires organizations to develop – and deliver on – strategic response time objectives for email, text-chat and Web callbacks. Other real-time metrics such as talk time have been replaced by metrics that correspond more to Web-based contact types. In addition, supervisors and managers must now evaluate agents' email and chat responses in terms of accuracy, grammar and "netiquette."

- **Forecasting issues:** One of the biggest e-support challenges for call center managers is getting a handle on forecasting for new contact types. With little historical data for email and chat, managers have had to make educated guesses to ensure that they have the right resources in place to handle these contacts. The good news is that the longer the organization is handling e-support channels, the easier forecasting becomes. In addition, workforce management vendors are starting to successfully incorporate features into their offerings that should ease managers' efforts.

- **Scheduling issues:** As call centers begin handling email and text-chat, several scheduling issues come into play. E.g., should all agents be trained to handle text-based access channels as well as phone-based ones? Since email doesn't have to be handled as it arrives, can agents handle it between phone calls? As you work out these fundamental scheduling issues, there are two principles that should be kept in mind. First, not all agents highly skilled in delivering service over the phone will be as effective in written correspondence. Many of them may have the potential to do so, but require training and ongoing support. Second, email must be managed to meet customer response time expectations. Simply telling agents to handle email when they are not on a call will only work in the slowest of call centers. A center that has a busy day on the phones will have frustrated email customers if agents do not have the time to respond to email contacts.
- **Customer satisfaction measurement:** E-commerce has changed not only how call centers provide customer support, but also how they measure customers' opinions of that support. Many call centers have incorporated email and Web surveys into their customer satisfaction measurement strategy. Minutes following the completion of an online transaction, a customer may get an email containing a concise questionnaire asking them to evaluate the service and support they've just received. Or that same questionnaire may pop up on the corporate Web page following the transaction. These automated surveys have greatly enhanced the speed with which call centers can obtain and evaluate online customer feedback, and have helped centers to efficiently make the changes they need to ensure customer loyalty.

### Common Barriers to Web-Enabling the Call Center

In our studies of the market and our work with organizations planning and implementing Web-enabled solutions, we have found that a number of common barriers exist. Identifying and addressing these issues is key to getting things moving:

**Lack of Organization-wide Strategy.** Developing a solid customer access strategy is essential to effectively building an e-enabled call center. Creating strategy is not a simple process. Integrated delivery channels cause ownership boundaries to overlap, which can bring progress to a grinding halt. Those that have adequately addressed this and related issues have done so with a strong message and active involvement from the leadership ranks to bring potential factions together.

**Budgetary Priorities.** The door to the CFO's office is lined with VPs and directors vying for the big piece of the budget pie. And as you already know, or will soon find out when you start researching the technology, call center/Web integration won't happen without one of those big pieces.

But there is little value in competing with other parts of the organization that are also trying to address evolving customer service challenges. For example, initiatives such as CRM or supply change management offer a similar promise to help the organization meet customer expectations, now and in the future. Progressive organizations are working hard to avoid the trap of viewing and valuing these initiatives individually.

**Current Workload.** Technologists are stretched to the breaking point trying to maintain today's platform while at the same time designing and developing tomorrow's ideal environment. Call center managers are struggling just to maintain their support of existing channels – a recent ICMI study of 579 call center managers found that only 23 percent of the respondents regularly meet their inbound telephone service level goal.

The resources available are often barely able to meet existing challenges – heaping further responsibility on call center managers is not the answer. The development of the connected call center requires competent associates from the technical and managerial disciplines fully dedicated to the integration project to get it done right.

**Technology in a State of Flux.** Given the many alternatives, sorting through the maze of technology alternatives can be confusing. Further, call center technology is in a state of development unprecedented in the history of the industry. But many suppliers offer impressive functionality that all too often comes with fine print, e.g., features that won't be available until the next release ("…it's due for general availability 'real soon'"). Further, consultants and other experts can't seem to come to any agreement – one that we spoke with described a well-known vendor's offerings as "tightly integrated," while another described the exact same solution as "bolted together." Concerns about risk abound, and with good reason.

A big part of the solution is to turn Moore's Law on its head. Yes, tomorrow's version will be faster and cheaper, but progressive organizations recognize that the risk associated with moving forward may be far less than the risk of sitting on the sideline waiting until everything shakes out – by that time, you may already be left behind. Getting into the arena gets you moving on the learning curve. The lesson may be costly, but far less so than ignorance.

**Agent Skill Sets.** This is causing great concerns in call center management circles, and for good reason. Finding trained, effective staff just to handle the inbound telephone channel has become a major challenge. Many managers are sweating over the prospect of having to fill hundreds or thousands of positions that require not just oral communication skills, but written ones, as well. Ongoing technology – and, especially, process improvements – may diminish the skill requirements somewhat. But that's of little comfort in today's tight job market.

Here again, it's time for organizations to face the inevitable. Revamping recruiting, hiring, training and career path initiatives to encourage the creation of a more Web-enabled workforce is the only sure way forward.

**No competitive mandate – yet.** The slow adoption rate of Web-enabled call center applications has, to some extent, become a self-fulfilling prophecy. "The competition's not doing it yet, so why should we?"

*(continued, next page)*

Further, though customers are clamoring for better service, they have not clearly dictated *en masse* the integrated mix of channels that suits them best. Of course, that evokes a chicken-and-egg question: How can they "embrace" anything before it becomes more commonplace? Industry leaders will recognize and leverage this opportunity to help shape expectations by offering customers as much as possible – and relentlessly surveying them to determine what is working.

Excerpt from "Building the E-Enabled Call Center: It's Time to Get Moving (Part 2)" by Brad Cleveland and Jay Minnucci, *Call Center Management Review*, November 2000.

# 6. Principles of Conducting an Environmental Scan

Ready? | 1 | 2 | 3 |

## Key Points

- **Environmental scans survey the landscape in which an organization conducts business in order to determine the current status of a specific issue or predict future trends.**
- **The process for conducting an environmental scan includes:**
  - **Identify the issue to be examined**
  - **Identify the industry or discipline that will be reviewed**
  - **Identify the selected materials that will be analyzed**
  - **Ask the right questions**
  - **Examine the facts**
  - **Make recommendations based on the results**



## Explanation

Call center managers are inundated with information from within their organizations, but it is also important to keep in touch with and learn about the external environment in which the organization operates. A proven technique for collecting external information is the environmental scan.

Environmental scans survey the landscape in which an organization conducts business in order to determine the current status of a specific issue or predict future trends. The objective of environmental scanning is to provide management with information that will assist them in planning for the future. For call centers, environmental scans can help anticipate customer expectations and requirements, and secure a common awareness of changing trends among decision makers.

The process for conducting an environmental scan is straightforward, yet flexible enough to adapt to each organization's situation and needs. Steps include:

- **Identify the issue to be examined:** Clearly define your objective. Vague statements such as "learn about customers" are unlikely to produce useful results. Narrow the scope of your research enough so that you can focus on what is important. Conducting multiple, focused scans is more likely to produce useful results than broad, "catch-all" efforts.

- **Identify the industry or discipline that will be reviewed:** For example, if you are exploring leading practices in help desk support, you may want to narrow in on the software and computer hardware industries. Understand the state of competition in an industry, i.e., the influence of suppliers, new entrants and the market share positions of other organizations.
- **Identify the selected materials that will be analyzed:** These include newspapers, magazines, journals, newsletters, the Internet, etc. Although the vast amount of information now available online constitutes a rich and accessible resource, do not overlook more traditional materials, especially targeted ones. Professional associations, libraries (including those of universities and business schools), trade publications and governmental agencies can often be helpful in furthering research efforts.
- **Ask the right questions:**

  a. How does this issue affect your industry or discipline?

  b. Who is involved – one organization, several organizations, an entire industry?

  c. How will the issue affect/influence/change/impact the industry or discipline?

  d. How will this issue affect/influence/change/impact your organization?

  e. Does this issue affect your customer base? How do your customers perceive the issue?

  f. Is this issue a trend, a sea change or a fad?
- **Examine the facts:** Follow up with qualitative interviews with key players in the industry. Ask the right questions. Just because something is in print, or published on the Internet, don't assume it is true. Exercise your own judgment and subject questionable information to careful review.
- **Make recommendations based on the results:** Don't just file reports in a drawer! Make sure you define the objective of your environmental scan so that the results will be actionable.

Environmental scans are often confused with market research. Market research requires disciplined sampling and analysis whereas environmental scanning is the process of "keeping your antenna up" about a specific issue or trend. An environmental scan is not as scientific as market research, but is an appropriate tool for general ongoing awareness. (See Key Principles of Market Research, this section.)

## 7. Key Principles of Market Research

Ready? | 1 | 2 | 3 |

### Key Points

- Market research is the disciplined process of collecting, analyzing and interpreting information about customers in order to make better decisions about meeting customer needs and expectations.
- Key concepts to keep in mind:
  - The first step should be to determine objectives
  - Design research to produce actionable results
  - What people tell you they would do and what they actually end up doing may turn out to be very different
  - Large sample sizes yield statistical reliability, but they have limitations
  - Qualitative methods improve depth of understanding, but making generalizations from them can be risky
  - The selection of who to study affects the applicability of the findings
  - When the research is conducted affects the results
  - Where and by what channel the research is conducted affects the results



### Explanation

Market research is the disciplined process of collecting, analyzing and interpreting information about customers in order to make better decisions about meeting customer needs and expectations. The call center can both benefit from market research and assist in market research efforts.

Market research can help call center managers make decisions about servicing customers, e.g., what access channels to offer to different customer segments or how many self-service options should be provided to customers. On the other hand, the call center can contribute to market research since it has a wealth of customer intelligence at its fingertips. The call center should work with other departments in the organization to provide them with the strategic customer data they require to make sound business decisions. (See The Call Center's Contribution to Marketing, Section 3.)

**Key Concepts to Keep in Mind**

The following guidelines will assist you when interpreting market research or contributing customer data to others in the organization.

- **The first step should be to determine objectives:** Market research will be most effective when everyone involved clearly understands the objectives of the research. The objectives will drive all other aspects of the research, so unclear objectives can result in unfocused or inadequate data.
- **Design research to produce actionable results:** Bear in mind that the action taken need not be dramatic or mission-critical, but there should always be a clearly defined business reason for every research effort. Market research should begin by identifying the problem and establishing the objectives of the research initiatives.
- **What people tell you they would do and what they actually end up doing may turn out to be very different:** This is an important cautionary note to keep in mind when designing market research plans. In particular, people don't speculate very accurately about their reactions to things they have never encountered before.
- **Large sample sizes yield statistical reliability, but they have limitations:** While it is critical that you understand the statistical reliability of your sample, it's also important to realize that statistical reliability is not the only important factor in market research. Small sample size research, typically conducted through focus groups or interviewing, provides valuable qualitative information that often is too costly and cumbersome to get from larger samples.
- **Qualitative methods improve depth of understanding, but making generalizations from them can be risky:** Analyzing the results of a focus group, for example, can yield valuable insights, but care must be taken in making decisions based on these results. Qualitative information should always be viewed in the context of more reliable quantitative data.
- **The selection of who to study affects the applicability of the findings:** Depending on what you want to learn, you may want to study current customers, prospective customers, former customers or another group. Findings from one group may not apply equally well to other groups.
- **When the research is conducted affects the results:** Not only who you study is important, but when you study them, as well. External events can make a difference in how people respond, e.g., after a major election

or significant volatility in the stock market. The recent activity of the customers you survey can also affect results, e.g., after they have registered a complaint or been informed of a rate increase.

- **Where and by what channel the research is conducted affects the results:** The first concern is pre-selection: is the population you want to study going to be represented in the location or channel (at a mall, for example, or on the Internet)? Only certain people will be present in certain situations, so make sure those you want to learn about will be available for you to study.



Many organizations have market research departments or contract with consultants to design and conduct market research. Large-population studies certainly require sophisticated tools and training that are best left to these professionals. But don't overlook the value of less formal market research that can take place in the call center. Capturing customer feedback and analyzing it for trends and insights is a legitimate form of qualitative market research, as well as a cost-effective opportunity to learn about your customers.

## 8. Identifying External Factors Impacting Strategy and Operations

**Ready?** | 1 | 2 | 3 |

### Key Points

- **The environment in which organizations operate consists of external factors that can be divided into two broad categories:**
  - **The market environment**
  - **The nonmarket environment**
- **Market and nonmarket forces impact an organization's strategy and operations, and astute managers identify and consider policy implications and options.**



### Explanation

The environment in which organizations operate consists of external factors that can be divided into two broad categories:

- **The market environment:** The market environment is comprised of the factors that create what Adam Smith called the "invisible hand." Components of the market environment include revenue, profits, production, finance, market strategy, competitors – in short, those things that are part of supply and demand. These forces are regulated by competition, choice and consumer behavior and should drive the organization's competitive strategy.
- **The nonmarket environment:** The nonmarket environment is characterized by political, legal and social arrangements outside of market forces. Components of the nonmarket environment include regulation, health and safety issues, trade policy, legislation, politics, the media and public pressures. These forces are intermediated by public and private institutions, e.g., regulators, courts, legislatures and public consensus.

The nonmarket environment shapes business opportunities in the market environment. For example, regulatory policies on privacy impact customer communication strategies and how firms can compete to win and serve customers. Similarly, market issues can impact the nonmarket environment, e.g., consumers who were unable to easily obtain their own credit reports demanded regulations that stipulate minimum customer access requirements for credit reporting bureaus.

Market and nonmarket forces impact an organization's strategy and operations, and astute managers identify and consider policy implications and options. Environmental scans and market research are useful tools for assessing external issues when considering strategic and operations decisions. (See Principles of Conducting an Environmental Scan and Key Principles of Market Research, this section.)

Further, it is often necessary to draw upon the expertise of specific professionals. For example, lawyers, public affairs specialists, lobbyists and others may provide necessary assistance for tackling nonmarket issues. Likewise, managers may benefit from the expertise and input of financial analysts, market researchers and consultants when formulating market strategies.



**Competitive Strategy**

According to business professor Michael E. Porter in his book *Competitive Strategy: Techniques for Analyzing Industries and Competitors*, the intensity of competition in an industry depends on several driving forces. These include:

- Threat of new entrants
- Intensity of rivalry among existing competitors (including the market share of the firms making up the industry)
- Pressure from substitute products
- Bargaining power of buyers
- Bargaining power of suppliers

Your organization may establish several goals in relation to its competitive strategy. The organization may choose to:

- Increase market share
- Increase profits
- Defend against competitive forces
- Position for profitable growth
- Position the organization to influence competitive forces

### Intensity of Rivalry Among Existing Competitors

Rivalry among existing competitors takes the familiar form of jockeying for position – using tactics like price competition, advertising battles, product introductions and increased customer service or warranties. Rivalry occurs because one or more competitors either feels the pressure or sees the opportunity to improve position. In most industries, competitive moves by one firm have noticeable effects on its competitors and thus may incite retaliation or efforts to counter the move; that is, firms are mutually dependent. This pattern of action and reaction may or may not leave the initiating firm and the industry as a whole better off. If moves and countermoves escalate, then all firms in the industry may suffer and be worse off than before.

Some forms of competition, notably price competition, are highly unstable and quite likely to leave the entire industry worse off from the standpoint of profitability. Price cuts are quickly and easily matched by rivals, and once matched they lower revenues for all firms unless industry price elasticity of demand is high enough. Advertising battles, on the other hand, may well expand demand or enhance the level of product differentiation in the industry for the benefit of all firms.

Excerpt from *Competitive Strategy: Techniques for Analyzing Industries and Competitors* by Michael E. Porter, The Free Press, 1980.

## 9. Major Legal Requirements Impacting the Call Center – US

Ready? | 1 | 2 | 3 |

### Key Points

- Two federal laws that restrict outbound call center activities (and some incoming call activities related to privacy or sales) are:
  - Telephone Consumer Protection Act (TCPA): Requires clear identification of the calling party, limits calling hours, establishes "do not call" restrictions, and provides guidelines for facsimile and auto-dialer use.
  - Telemarketing Sales Rule (TSR): Reinforces many of the provisions of the TCPA while prohibiting false or misleading claims regarding payment, products, services and other business practices.
- Two federal laws that explicitly address monitoring and recording requirements in the call center are:
  - Omnibus Crime Control and Safe Streets Act (OCCSA): The provisions of Title II of the OCCSA, passed in 1968, provide restrictions on the monitoring and recording of telephone communications for a wide range of purposes (including federal wiretapping and allowable government surveillance).
  - Electronic Communications Privacy Act (ECPA): Adopted in 1986 to address the legal privacy issues evolving with the growing use of computers and new innovations in electronic communications, the ECPA updated the OCCSA by extending the privacy protection to apply to email, cellular phones, private communication carriers and computer transmissions.

### Explanation

Federal and state legislation governing call center operations protects the rights of consumers and provides interaction guidelines for the call center industry. These laws address fraudulent business practices and speak to consumers' mounting frustration with the activities of aggressive telemarketers. Strict compliance during every interaction is imperative; violations can cost organizations thousands of dollars per incident. For organizations inexperienced in outbound calling that are looking to these programs to increase customers and revenue, knowledge of these laws is a key component of program design.

Although federal legislation primarily affects outbound calling, it is not always the type of calling (outbound or inbound) that determines whether the law applies. Some activities (e.g., payment authorization requirements, product information disclosures) are governed by these laws, regardless of which party initiates the contact.

**Telephone Consumer Protection Act (TCPA)**

Enforced by the Federal Communications Commission (FCC), this far-reaching law primarily affects outbound telemarketing operations. The TCPA requires:

- **Proper identification:** The agent or calling party must provide his or her name, the name of the business and a telephone number or address prior to the end of the call.
- **Calling hour restrictions:** Outbound calls to residential numbers are forbidden before 8 a.m. or after 9 p.m. (recipient's local time).
- **"Do not call" policies:** Each company (with the exception of nonprofit solicitations) is responsible for maintaining a list (for 10 years) of people who have requested not to be contacted in the future. A written policy must be available on demand that details the organization's list-keeping and database requirements. Agents must be fully trained and the "do not call" list must be vigilantly maintained. The TCPA suggests that the written policies include how "do not call" requests should be captured, how quickly the information should be added to the database, and how the database's accuracy will be maintained.
- **Auto dialer and Automatic Dialing Recorded Message Players (ADRMP) regulations:** An organization is prohibited from contacting certain types of numbers including emergency phone lines (e.g., 911, hospitals, physicians, health care facilities, fire protection, poison control centers, law enforcement agencies) and lines where the recipient is charged for the call (e.g., cellular phones).
- **Facsimile regulations:** Transmission of unsolicited advertisements to telephone fax machines is banned unless the caller has an established business relationship with the intended recipient. Consent to fax is assumed because of the established business relationship, unless a "do not fax" request is received. Each fax transmission must clearly state the

originating organization's name, telephone number and date/time of the transmission. The company on whose behalf the fax was sent is the party responsible for compliance.

**Enforcement and penalties:** A suit can be filed in state court to stop unwanted calls and/or to sue for monetary loss, depending on the provision of the Act violated. The penalty is $500 for each violation or actual monetary loss, whichever is greater.

For more information on the TCPA, contact the FCC at 1-888-225-5322 or www.fcc.gov.



**Telemarketing Sales Rule (TSR)**

In 1995, the Federal Trade Commission (FTC) enacted the Telemarketing and Consumer Fraud and Abuse Prevention Act (TCFPA). The TCFPA defined abusive practices common in sales and telemarketing "schemes" and gave the FTC the authority to enforce many of the existing TCPA guidelines. The FTC's ability to fine organizations up to $10,000 per violation made a substantial impact on the attention the TCFPA received in the business community.

Under the TCFPA, the FTC adopted the Telemarketing Sales Rule (TSR) that requires:

- **Proper identification:** Outbound agents must disclose the identity of the originating caller, the purpose of the call (e.g., credit card sales) and the nature of the goods or services being offered.
- **Calling hour restrictions:** Same provisions as the TCPA.
- **Specific required information:** All agents (outbound, inbound) must provide the following information so that the consumer can make an informed purchase decision before paying for the goods or services that are the subject of the sales offer:
  - Cost and quantity
  - Material restrictions, limitations or conditions to purchase, receive or use the offered goods or services
  - Whether there is a no-exchange or no-refund policy
  - Information regarding prize promotions or other special offers
- **Authorization for payment:** Consumers must express verifiable

authorization (written or taped consent, 3rd party verification) for organizations to access account funds (e.g., phone check or demand draft) to obtain payment.

- **Honest, clear claims:** Under the Rule, false or misleading claims are prohibited. Offers must be stated clearly and honestly, including how much it will cost to obtain the goods or services and what the consumer will receive in return. Misrepresenting any material aspect of the product, service, prize promotion or investment opportunity is prohibited. The Rule prohibits threats, intimidation and profane or obscene language to pressure a consumer into accepting an offer.

There are many exceptions to the TSR. The types of calls that are exempt from the TSR include:

- 900 number interactions
- Unsolicited calls from consumers
- Business-to-business calls, except calls involving the retail sale of nondurable office or cleaning supplies
- Follow-up calls after a face-to-face sales presentation
- Calls responding to catalog advertisements, unless those calls include offers of goods or services not included in the catalog

At this time, the reach of the TCFPA/TSR is limited to telephone interactions only and does not address sales contacts received in the form of email, chat or other online contact media. The unchartered territory of the Internet will undoubtedly continue to spur legislation that addresses the needs of consumers who are sold goods and services through this medium.

**Enforcement and penalties:** The TSR, which sought to strengthen the TCPA's restrictions on telemarketing activities, streamlined the process whereby individual consumers could bring civil suits against organizations that violate the act. Violation of the provisions of the TSR may result in civil penalties of up to $10,000 per violation, nationwide injunctions prohibiting specific organizational practices or redress to injured consumers.

For more information on the TSR, contact the FTC at 202-326-2222 or www.ftc.gov.

**State Legislation**

Many states, in response to consumer complaints and grassroots organizations, have gone beyond the TCPA by enacting individual state restrictions on telemarketing activities (e.g., more specific sales disclosures, increased limitations on calling hours, monitoring practice guidelines). For example, a number of states have enacted legislation that requires the sales agents to ask the recipient's permission (and receive an affirmative reply) to continue with a telephone sales pitch. If the recipient does not want to be "sold," the agent must immediately disconnect the call. Individual state laws apply to the area where the outbound call is received by the customer or the inbound call is received by the call center.

All state laws that apply to telemarketing must be complied with in addition to federal law. While some may be redundant with federal legislation, they can add an additional $2,000 to $25,000 penalty per infraction.

The future of these regulations continues to be revisited in state capitals across the country. Some states already are taking actions and others are proposing legislation that includes state "do not call" lists, bans on predictive dialers and bans on Caller ID blocking. It is imperative for call center managers to stay up-to-date on proposed legislation and current requirements. State regulation information can be obtained for a fee from the American Teleservices Association (www.ataconnect.org), which offers a comprehensive list of proposed legislation and updates.



**Monitoring and Recording Legislation**

Call monitoring in the United States requires consent of one or both parties to the call, depending on the law of the applicable states. Federal law, in the form of the Electronic Communications Privacy Act (ECPA), permits monitoring if you establish consent from one party in the call. Agent consent fulfills this requirement.

In two-party consent states, callers should hear a monitoring and recording announcement and the agents in the call center must sign a consent form. Some state statutes include the words "overhear" or "record," whereas others use the term "intercept a communication." There are also different rules to govern interstate vs. intrastate calls. In regard to the recording of phone calls, the ECPA permits recording with the consent of one party, and also allows states to enact stricter legislation. Further, Federal Communications Commission (FCC) regulations require either:

- A beep tone audible to both parties when recording
- Prior consent of all parties to recording of the conversation, or

- Notification of the other party up front that you are recording (known as the one-party notification option previously described)

However, some states specifically require two-party consent to record.

Regardless of whether you need to satisfy one-party or two-party consent, your monitoring policy should be documented and only those people with a legitimate, business need should monitor calls. It is also advisable to provide agents with unmonitored telephone lines for personal calls during breaks.

The Direct Marketing Association (DMA) maintains a State Government Relations division whose purpose is to keep on top of state statute information. Similarly, the American Teleservices Association (ATA) has a Legislative Alert Warning Service (LAWS), to provide its members with updated information on legislation pending in any state.



### Omnibus Crime Control and Safe Streets Act (OCCSA)

The provisions of Title II of the OCCSA, passed in 1968, provide restrictions on the monitoring and recording of telephone communications for a wide range of purposes (including federal wiretapping and allowable government surveillance). The OCCSA prohibits organizations from listening in or recording telephone conversations, with two exceptions:

- **Consent:** Federal regulations concede that if one party provides consent prior to communication, monitoring and recording is allowed. In most call centers this consent is quickly obtained by requiring agents to sign monitoring consent forms at the time of hire. Legislation in many states has expanded the consent exception by requiring that both parties consent to monitoring and recording. Most call centers address this requirement by playing a recorded message (e.g., "your call may be monitored for quality assurance purposes") before the call is connected to an agent.
- **Business use:** Protecting the employer's right to supervise the quality of the work being performed, the OCCSA allows employers to monitor and record telephone conversations as long as the call is conducted on a telephone that belongs to the business and this equipment is used in the ordinary course of business. This provision permits employers to intercept business-related calls without consent.

**Electronic Communications Privacy Act (ECPA)**

Adopted in 1986 to address the legal privacy issues evolving with the growing use of computers and new innovations in electronic communications, the ECPA updated the OCCSA by extending the privacy protection to apply to email, cellular phones, private communication carriers and computer transmissions.

Under the ECPA employers cannot monitor employee telephone calls or email when employees have a reasonable expectation of privacy. However, the ECPA does allow monitoring if employees are notified in advance or if the employer has reasons to believe the organization's interests are in jeopardy. The ECPA also identified specific situations and types of transmissions that would not be protected, most notably an employer's monitoring of employee email on the employer's system.

Not addressed in the ECPA was monitoring consent (of any party) for electronic interactions (e.g., email, text chat). Since electronic communications are stored in the organization's servers without explicitly requiring a special recording device, organizations are not required to inform consumers that the interaction may be recorded. Legal precedent has established that email and other forms of electronic communication are the property of the organization, and as such, can be monitored and stored for the organization's purposes.

**Other Legislation**

As managers of diverse and often large workforces, call center managers must stay abreast of laws regarding human resources management and facility requirements. (For more information on these types of legislation, see ICMI's *Call Center People Management Handbook and Study Guide* and *Call Center Operations Management Handbook and Study Guide*.)

Notes: 1) This section is designed to provide a summary only. Please direct specific legal questions to your HR and legal departments. 2) At the time of printing, the FTC was in the process of implementing new telemarketing restrictions, and mandating a national "do not call" database. See www.ftc.org for updates.

# 10. Major Regulatory Requirements Impacting the Call Center – US

Ready? | 1 | 2 | 3 |

## Key Points

- Call centers must comply with government regulations imposed on their vertical industries.
- Most federal and state industry regulations that impact the call center are designed to protect the rights of the consumer by preventing violations of privacy and ensuring honest and clear communication between organizations and customers.
- Some major industries that are monitored by governmental regulatory agencies for industry legal compliance are:
  - Emergency services
  - Financial
  - Insurance
  - High tech
  - Telecommunications
  - Utilities
  - Travel



## Explanation

In addition to ensuring the call center is within federal and state legal guidelines for telephone activities, the center must also comply with the government regulations imposed on organizations that operate in its vertical industry. Most federal and state industry regulations that impact the call center are designed to protect the rights of the consumer by preventing violations of privacy and ensuring honest and clear communication between organizations and customers.

These regulatory guidelines must be understood and followed with the same vigilance as the laws that affect the telemarketing industry. Failure to comply with industry regulations can result in legal action, financial penalties, loss of customer confidence and a tarnished reputation.

Some of the major industries that are monitored by regulatory agencies for industry legal compliance are:

- **Emergency services:** Since most emergency services (e.g., police, fire department, poison control) call centers are either operated by or contracted from a government agency which is accountable to the citizens, there are often regulatory guidelines for service level agreements, hold time standards, and the types of services delivered.
- **Financial:** Many of the regulatory agencies which govern the financial industry (e.g., Security and Exchange Commission and the Federal Financial Institutions Examination Council) enforce regulations which affect financial call center agents as they attempt to sell products to current and prospective customers. An example of a federal regulation which is enforced by the SEC is the Securities Act of 1933, which requires that investors receive financial and other significant information concerning securities that are being offered for sale and prohibits deceit and misrepresentation in the sale of securities.
- **Insurance:** Primarily regulated by state agencies, insurance companies are required to comply with a wide range of regulations for each type of insurance (e.g., health, auto, life, property and casualty). Many of these provisions concern organizations' enrollment and coverage determinations, truth in advertising, and sales and privacy issues. Some examples of insurance regulations which impact the call center are:
  - The privacy provisions of the Federal Health Insurance Portability and Accountability Act (HIPAA) of 1996 has placed unprecedented pressure on health insurance companies to protect citizens' rights to keep their medical records confidential. This law substantially impacts health insurance call centers, since this is where requests for medical records are often processed. Organizations are required (by 2003) to implement privacy standards and procedures and provide training to ensure all employees perform their customer interaction activities in compliance with this insurance regulation.
  - Many states require that certain types of insurance (e.g., life, property and casualty) be sold only by licensed agents. Call centers may be required to restrict the activities of unlicensed agents (e.g., they may be allowed to provide general information but not gather enrollment data) or hire only licensed agents to handle prospective customer inquiries.
- **High tech:** One federal law has had substantial impact on organizations which provide online services. The Electronic Communications Privacy Act of 1986 prohibits providers of electronic communication services

from disclosing the contents of communication that has been stored electronically without the lawful consent of the person who originated the communication. Regulations relating to the anonymity and privacy of the Internet – and how much information these organizations are required to provide to government, law enforcement agencies, etc. – continue to be revisited in courtrooms across the country.

- **Telecommunications:** The telecommunications industry has been the subject of federal regulations that provide strict guidelines concerning their telemarketing sales practices. The practice of "slamming" (switching a customer's long distance carrier without the customer's knowledge or consent) prompted Congress to include a provision in the Telecommunications Act that institutes additional protection – beyond the Telemarketing Sales Rule – for victims of "slamming" and requires that the organization (usually the call center) provide the required adjustments and credits for victims.
- **Utilities:** Deregulating markets introduces new and varying compliance rules and customer information sharing requirements. Representatives must strictly comply with rules that govern the deregulation process, which includes who they can sell to and what they are allowed to offer customers.
- **Travel:** Recent problems with airline security has brought the travel industry into regulatory focus. In addition to the long-standing security requirements established by the Federal Aviation Administration (FAA), airports, travel agencies and airlines are adapting to new, more stringent regulations to ensure the safety of air travel. Call centers in the travel industry must be aware of these rules when informing and servicing their customers.

Note: This section is designed to provide a summary only. Please direct specific legal questions to your HR and legal departments.

# 11. Major Legal and Regulatory Requirements Impacting the Call Center – Canada

Ready? | 1 | 2 | 3 |

## Key Points

- **Most call centers in Canada fall under the jurisdiction of provincial legislation. Only those call centers in "federally regulated" industries are governed by federal legislation.**
- **Recent federal legislation enacted by the Canadian Radio and Television Commission (CRTC) places new national restrictions on outbound telemarketing activity.**



## Explanation

Canadian legal and regulatory requirements are either federally or provincially enforced. Federal regulations apply to designated industries. However, most Canadian organizations will fall under regional territory or provincial legislation.

Federally regulated industries include:

- Interprovincial and international services such as railways, telephone systems and shipping services
- Radio and television broadcasting, including cablevision
- Air transport, aircraft operations, and aerodromes
- Banks
- Undertakings for the protection and preservation of fisheries as a natural resource
- Other undertakings declared by Parliament to be for the general advantage of Canada

Most federal Crown corporations, such as the Canada Mortgage and Housing Corporation and Canada Post Corporation, are covered by federal legislation.

### Call Center Legislation

Telemarketing restrictions have historically been issued according to province and service provider category, resulting in a patchwork application of rules across Canada. Regional legislation regulates many issues associated with outbound and inbound contacts. Increased focus on federal call center legislation is generally concerned with issues related to the growing outbound telemarketing industry and the public's dissatisfaction with the practices of some organizations.

The federal Canadian Radio and Television Commission (CRTC) has recently standardized its rules on telemarketing and extended them to include all telephone companies in Canada – including resellers and cell phone providers.

The rules include:

- Restricted calling hours
- Guidelines for identifying information
- "Do not call" list guidelines
- Ban on sequential dialing
- Ban on contacts to emergency and healthcare facilities

Consult the CRTC's Web page http://www.crtc.gc.ca/ENG/NEWS/RELEASES/2001/I010305.htm for complete information regarding these telemarketing rules.

There is national interest in expanding this legislation to cover all outbound calling, regardless of industry. The Canadian Marketing Association has established a Code of Ethics and Standard of Practice for their members, in which members agree to maintain "do not call" lists, restrict calling hours, limit the number of contacts to an individual, and use customer opt-in lists for calling campaigns. Consult the CMA's Web page http://www.the-cma.org/consumer/ethics.cfm for more information on its Code of Ethics. The sections most applicable to call centers include E3. Telephone, G. Special Considerations in Marketing to Children and Principle #3: Enabling Consumers to Reduce the Amount of Mail They Receive.

For more information, contact the CRTC (www.crtc.gc.ca) and the Canadian Marketing Association (www.the-cma.org).

### Other Legislation

As managers of diverse and often large workforces, call center managers must stay abreast of laws regarding human resources management and facility requirements. (For more information on these types of legislation, see ICMI's *Call Center People Management Handbook and Study Guide* and *Call Center Operations Management Handbook and Study Guide.*)

Note: This section is designed to provide a summary only. Please direct specific legal questions to your HR and legal departments.

## 12. Tracking and Adhering to Legal and Regulatory Requirements

Ready? | 1 | 2 | 3 |

### Key Points

- Organizations are responsible for knowing which laws and regulations apply to their operations and for implementing employee education programs and processes that ensure compliance.
- The following steps will ensure the call center is operating within the guidelines of federal and state law:
  - Know the law
  - Respect the law
  - Obey the law
  - Monitor compliance
  - Put policies in writing
  - Address consumer complaints
  - Educate employees
  - Incorporate requirements into job tools
  - Influence legal and regulatory guidelines
- Steps to ensure compliance with agent monitoring guidelines include:
  1. Document your organization's monitoring policy
  2. Explain the organization's monitoring policy during the interview process
  3. Share the specifics of the monitoring program with employees
  4. Ensure there is a written policy that regulates personal phone calls
  5. Coordinate monitoring calibration to facilitate consistency
  6. Establish a record of each call monitored
  7. Have a policy in place to protect private customer information



### Explanation

Organizations are responsible for knowing which laws and regulations apply to their operations and for implementing employee education programs and processes that ensure compliance. It isn't enough for only those directing call center activities to understand which call center practices are illegal. It only takes one employee engaging in unlawful practices for an organization to be cited for noncompliance – an action that can result in negative publicity and substantial fines.

**Steps to Ensuring Legal Compliance**

The following steps will ensure the call center is operating within the guidelines of federal and state law:

- **Know the law:** Legal and regulatory compliance is not an issue that should be left to chance. While all employees are responsible for knowing their role in compliance and following established procedures, senior management should be tasked with staying current on federal and state legal and regulatory issues and determining if there are provisions that apply to the organization's business activities. These individuals need to determine when legal consultations are necessary, join industry groups to access regulatory and legal updates, and enforce compliance throughout the organization.
- **Respect the law:** The benefits of compliance – e.g., consumer confidence and trust, consistency in ethical business practices, positive industry reputation – should be promoted across the entire organization. All employees should be encouraged to view laws and regulations as valuable protections, rather than burdens. This will create a positive atmosphere in which compliance is valued and recognized.
- **Obey the law:** This requires an organizationwide commitment to complying with applicable laws and regulations. The organization must enforce procedures and policies and consistently punish violators for infractions. For example, when an agent misleads a consumer to close a sale, appropriate disciplinary action should be taken.
- **Monitor compliance:** Major compliance issues (e.g., required verbatim disclosures) should be included as expectations on the call center's monitoring form and measured during each interaction. Additional resources or an automated technology solution should be added for the continual monitoring and updating of "do not call" lists.
- **Put policies in writing:** Applicable laws should be documented in the context of the organization. These materials can be added to the employee handbook, referred to in training and reviewed in coaching sessions.
- **Address consumer complaints:** Complaints related to legal or regulatory

compliance issues must be resolved quickly and the customer must be reassured that the situation has been addressed. Ignoring a customer complaint can escalate the situation and prompt a dissatisfied consumer to take legal action.

- **Educate employees:** Adequate training is essential to ensure employees and management know and can apply relevant laws and regulations. Classroom training, written and verbal updates and one-on-one coaching are all effective ways of communicating legal and regulatory changes. Individual accountability and responsibilities should be clearly defined and the consequences of noncompliance communicated.
- **Incorporate requirements into job tools:** Whenever possible, use technology and existing job tools to make it easier and more convenient for employees to maintain legal compliance. For example, incorporate required disclosures into online scripts.
- **Influence legal and regulatory guidelines:** Management should participate in professional associations that are active in influencing legal and regulatory bodies, e.g., the American Teleservices Association, or the Direct Marketing Association. Members can contribute to the association's mission to work with legal and regulatory bodies to enact legislation that makes sense.



**Ethical Guidelines for Agent Monitoring**

In addition to the need to stay within the guidelines of written law, organizations must also implement ethical monitoring practices. Although organizations are not required by the letter of the law to adhere to the following guidelines, it makes good business sense to take every possible precaution to protect against legal challenges.

Steps to ensure compliance with agent monitoring guidelines include:

1. **Document your organization's monitoring policy:** Include who has authorization to monitor, how the monitoring will be conducted (e.g., side-by-side, silent, taped), how the information will be used (e.g., will it be taken into account during performance reviews? Performance-based pay plans? Can an employee be terminated for poor performance during monitoring?).

2. **Explain the organization's monitoring policy during the interview process:** You can do this by adding a statement to the job application and discussing it during the interview.

3. **Share the specifics of the monitoring program with employees:** Both new and current employees should be provided with copies of the formal monitoring policy, grievance process, monitoring forms, definition documents, and any related bonus program or performance-based criteria. Make sure you explain why monitoring is done and how and when feedback will be delivered.

4. **Ensure there is a written policy that regulates personal phone calls:** A common approach is to set up a bank of separate phones that are never monitored to allow employees to make personal calls.

5. **Coordinate monitoring calibration to facilitate consistency:** For monitoring to be fair and trusted, criteria must be clear and consistently applied.

6. **Establish a record of each call monitored:** Whether electronically, e.g., through monitoring or recording technology, or on paper, keep a record of monitoring calls to allow for review if that were to become necessary.

7. **Have a policy in place to protect private customer information:** Do not share identifiable recorded call files or tapes with individuals outside the organization and clearly delineate acceptable practice within the organization (e.g., for use in internal training courses, not for use in sales presentations).

(For a complete discussion on call center monitoring practices, see ICMI's *Call Center People Management Handbook and Study Guide.*)

# The Call Center Business Environment

## Exercises

### Understanding and Applying Call Center Terminology

1. Select the most appropriate answer to each question. Note: Definitions of these and other important terms can be found in the glossary in Section 8.

Which of the following can be defined as "the connection of multiple computers (usually within close proximity) to enable sharing information, applications and peripherals?"

a. Local Area Network (LAN)

b. Virtual Private Network (VPN)

c. Wide Area Network (WAN)

Rostered staff factor is calculated after:

a. Base staffing is determined

b. Budgets are developed

c. Schedules are organized

Most ACDs are able to do all of the following EXCEPT:

a. Determine staffing requirements

b. Provide announcements or options to callers while they are in queue

c. Provide reporting capabilities

d. Route calls based on conditional parameters or agent skills

All Trunks Busy (ATB) reports provide all of the following information EXCEPT:

a. How many callers got busy signals when all trunks were busy.

b. How many times all trunks were busy

c. How much total time all trunks were busy

Which of the following levels of ISDN service provides a greater number of bearer channels?

a. Basic Rate Interface (BRI)

b. Primary Rate Interface (PRI)

Which of the following is a characteristic of the Erlang B formula?

a. Assumes that if callers get busy signals, they never retry

b. Generally overestimates trunks required

c. Used to calculate predicted waiting times

Which of the following is a characteristic of the Erlang C formula?

a. Assumes no lost calls or busy signals

b. Generally underestimates staff required

c. Used to determine the number of trunks required to handle a known calling load

The calculation, (call volume x average handling time in seconds) / (number of agents x 1800 seconds), represents which call center metric:

a. Adherence To Schedule

b. Average Handle Time (AHT)

c. Occupancy

All of the following groups of words can be used as synonyms EXCEPT:

a. Occupancy and Adherence to Schedule

b. Queue, Split and Gate

c. Rostered Staff Factor (RSF) and Shrinkage

### Unique Operational Dynamics

2. True or false

______In call centers, workload generally arrives at a steady pace throughout each half-hour of the day.

______Service level and quality are competing objectives that must be balanced.

______When service level improves, "productivity" declines.

______You need more staff on schedule than those required to handle the workload.

______The more staff you have handling a given call load, the less the load on the telecommunications network.

______As self-service usage is increasing, the demands on call center agents are decreasing.

### Characteristics of the Call Center's Emerging Role

3. Select the most appropriate answer to the question.

All of the following are key facets of the call center's emerging role EXCEPT:

a. Customer relationship management

b. Decrease in budgetary requirements

c. Heightened strategic value contribution

d. Multichannel contact management

**Principles of Conducting an Environmental Scan**

4. Select the most appropriate answer to each question.

Environmental scanning:

a. Is the process of keeping "your antenna up" about a specific issue or trend

b. Requires disciplined sampling and analysis

When conducting environmental scans, which is more likely to produce useful results?

a. Broad, "catch-all" efforts

b. Multiple focused scans

With the vast amount of information now available online, traditional research tools (e.g., libraries, trade publications and professional associations):

a. Contribute relatively little value to environmental scans

b. Still contain valuable information and should not be overlooked

**Key Principles of Market Research**

5. Briefly answer each question.

a. What is a benefit of small sample size market research?

b. What is a disadvantage of small sample size market research?

c. Why do you need to be careful about where and by what channel you conduct market research?

**Major Legal Requirements Impacting the Call Center – US**

6. To what do the following acronyms refer?

a. TCPA: Tele comm______ Comm______ Privacy______ Act

b. TSR: ____________ ____________ Rule

c. OCCSA: ____________ ____________
____________ and ____________ ____________Act

d. ECPA: ____________ ____________ ____________ Act

7. Match the following federal laws with their definitions. You will use each definition only once.

______ ECPA

______ OCCSA

______ TCPA

______ TSR

a. Extends privacy protection to apply to email, cellular phones, private communication carriers and computer transmissions.

b. Prohibits false or misleading claims regarding payment, products, services and other business practices.

c. Provides restrictions on the monitoring and recording of telephone communications for a wide range of purposes.

d. Requires clear identification of the calling party, limits calling hours, establishes "do not call" restrictions, and provides guidelines for facsimile and auto-dialer use.

**Answers to these exercises are in Section 10.**

Note: These exercises are intended to help you retain the material learned. While not the exact questions as on the CIAC Certification assessment, the material in this handbook/study guide fully addresses the content on which you will be assessed. For a formal practice test, please contact the CIAC directly by visiting www.ciac-cert.org.

# The Call Center Business Environment Reference Bibliography

## Related Articles from *Call Center Management Review* (See Section 9)

Building the E-Enabled Call Center: It's Time to Get Moving (Two Parts)

Successful E-Support: Attributes of the 'A' List

The 12 Key Principles of Customer Relationship Management

## For Further Study

**Books/Studies**

*An Abbreviated Guide to Call Center Management Terms.* Call Center Press, 1998.

Cleveland, Brad and Julia Mayben. *Call Center Management on Fast Forward: Succeeding in Today's Dynamic Inbound Environment.* Call Center Press, 1999.

*Multichannel Call Center Study Final Report.* Call Center Press, 2001.

Porter, Michael E. *Competitive Strategy: Techniques for Analyzing Industries and Competitors.* The Free Press, 1980.

**Articles**

Cleveland, Brad. "Building the E-Enabled Call Center: It's Time to Get Moving (Part 2)." *Call Center Management Review,* November 2000.

**Web Sites**

American Teleservices Association, www.ataconnect.org

Canadian Marketing Association, www.the-cma.org

Canadian Radio and Television Commission, www.crtc.gc.ga

Federal Communications Commission, www.fcc.gov

Federal Trade Commission, www.ftc.gov

**Seminars**

*Effective Leadership and Strategy for Senior Call Center Managers* public seminar, presented by Incoming Calls Management Institute.

*Essential Skills and Knowledge for Effective Incoming Call Center Management* public seminar, presented by Incoming Calls Management Institute.

*An Introduction to the Call Center Environment* Web seminar, presented by Incoming Calls Management Institute.

Section 6

# *Business Management Principles and Practices*

# Section 6: Business Management Principles and Practices

## Contents

# 1. Definitions of Strategic Business Plan and Related Terms

Ready? | 1 | 2 | 3 |

## Key Points

- **An operational model usually refers to the organization's general structure and approach for creating value in a market.**
- **A strategic business plan usually refers to the general plan that consolidates and summarizes the various plans and strategies required to meet strategic objectives. A strategic business plan is generally more dynamic – changes more frequently – than an operational model.**
- **An annual operating plan consists of many of the same components as a strategic business plan, but focuses only on the next year.**
- **Many people use these terms interchangeably. Consequently, the meaning of these and related terms must be interpreted in the context of how they are applied.**



## Explanation

Common definitions for operational model, strategic business plan and related terms include:

- **Operational model:** Usually refers to the organization's general structure and approach for creating value in a market. Put another way, it is the general framework for how an organization will fulfill its strategic objectives. For example, Dell's strategy is to do business directly with customers through the telephone and Internet, and to offer focused products and prices targeted for specific customer segments (schools, small and large businesses, government, etc.). The operational model – including the definition of customer segments, the structure of the call center, the access channels and services made available – supports the larger strategy.
- **Strategic business plan:** A strategic business plan usually refers to the general plan that consolidates and summarizes the various plans and strategies required to meet strategic objectives. The strategic business plan usually looks several years into the future and summarizes plans and strategies related to recruiting and hiring, training, processes,

technologies, communication, budgets and investments, and so on. It includes the process of identifying opportunities and threats that drive decision making. Key to developing a strategic business plan is effective communication, a supportive culture and the commitment of senior management. Since it has a relatively long-term strategic focus, specific tactical challenges are less influential. A strategic business plan is generally more dynamic – changes more frequently – than an operational model.

- **Annual operating plan:** An annual operating plan consists of many of the same components as a strategic business plan, but focuses only on the next year. It is more detailed and tactical in nature. It describes how and when the resources needed to carry out tactics will be deployed.



### Deciphering the Differences in Terms

Some use the terms operational model and strategic business plan interchangeably. E.g., the CIAC uses strategic business plan and operational model interchangeably in their competency model. In context, both refer generally to the means by which organizations accomplish strategic objectives.

To further confuse the issue, many people commonly refer to short-term plans and objectives as "strategies." For example, "his strategy this week is to work on the budget in the mornings, and schedule all meetings into the afternoons." That tends to muddle the true meaning of strategy.

Confused? Don't worry – given inconsistent usage across the business landscape, that's to be expected. One thing is very clear: the meaning of these and related terms must be interpreted in the context of how they are applied.

Again, for the purposes of this guide (and for CIAC content), here's how these terms are used. The organization's overall strategy and objectives shape the customer access strategy, which shapes the operational model and/or strategic business plan, which shapes annual operating plans.

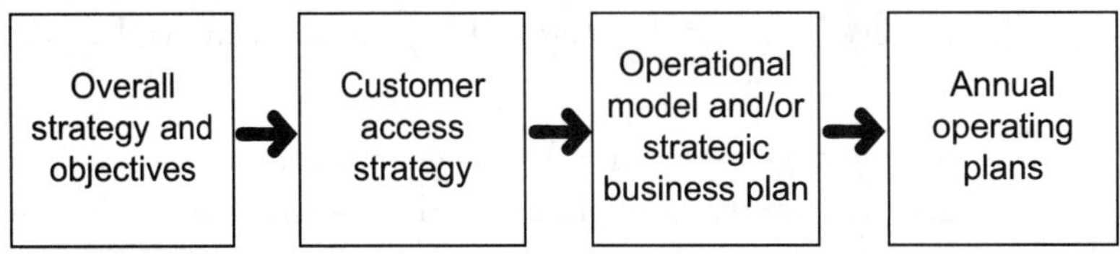

## 2. Developing an Effective Strategic Business Plan [Strategic]

Ready? | 1 | 2 | 3 |

### Key Points

- The strategic business plan is a high-level summary of the various plans and strategies required to meet strategic objectives, and usually outlines strategy for the next one to three years.
- Key components of the strategic business plan include:
  - Situational analysis
  - Performance objectives
  - Customer profile and segmentation strategies
  - Organizational design
  - Communication plans
  - Equipping people to support strategic objectives
  - Planning processes
  - Supporting technologies
  - Cross-functional teams
  - Fulfilling promises to customers
  - Budgetary requirements
- Because of the importance of the strategic business plan, it is essential to garner support for the plan from top-level management.



### Explanation

The strategic business plan is a high-level summary of the various plans and strategies required to meet strategic objectives. The plan usually outlines strategy for the next one to three years. It is updated on a fairly regular basis, e.g., annually in many organizations. It should explain where the organization is, where it wants to go and how it will get there.

Just as the organization's overall strategy and objectives should shape the customer access strategy, the customer access strategy should shape the strategic business plan. In turn, the strategic business plan must shape the annual operating plans. (See Components of an Annual Operating Plan, this section.)

**Business Plan Documents**

Documentation of the strategic business plan should include the following components:

- **Executive summary:** High-level overview of the plan.
- **Situational analysis:** Summary of where the organization is, where it wants to go and how it will get there.
- **Marketing plan:** Outline of the steps that further the organization's marketing efforts.
- **Financials:** Documents that illustrate the financial implications of the plan.
- **Control and execution:** Summary of procedures and accountabilities for accomplishing the plan's objectives.



### Sections of the Business Plan

**Executive Summary**

The executive summary briefly explains the key aspects of the plan. It describes the organization's current status, its goods or services, the benefits to customers, and the basic financial forecasts.

**Situation Analysis**

Situation analysis is the diagnostic activity of interpreting environmental conditions and changes in light of an organization's ability to capitalize on potential opportunities and ward off problems. Situation analysis requires both environmental scanning and environmental monitoring so that the organization can anticipate and deal with change. Environmental scanning is information gathering designed to detect indications of changes that may be beginning to develop. Environmental monitoring involves tracking certain phenomena, such as sales data and population statistics, to observe whether any meaningful trends are emerging.

Situation analysis also requires an inward look at the organization. An organization should evaluate its internal strengths and weaknesses in relation to the external environment. The acronym SWOT, which stands for internal Strengths and Weaknesses and external Opportunities and Threats, can serve as a reminder that the purpose of the situation analysis section of a business plan is to evaluate both the external environment and the internal environment.

A situation analysis often explains the company's microenvironment in terms of the 4Cs approach: customers, competitors, the company, and collaborators.

The section on customers identifies the markets the business intends to serve. It also defines, from the customer's perspective, the products and services that the business will be providing.

Who are the customers? What will they be buying – that is, what is the nature of your product and service? Why is it unique or otherwise appealing to consumers? Why will they buy it from your company?

A second section identifies the competition. Who are your current competitors? What are their strengths and weaknesses? For example, is the competition a large impersonal organization? A discount operation with low-quality products? What companies may become future competitors?

A third section provides a description of the business and its operating requirements, both financial and managerial.

Finance: What are the company's capital needs? How much credit will be needed? When will the money be needed? How will money needs change over the course of the company's growth?

Management: What is the background of the managers/owners? How will the company be organized? What are the responsibilities of company personnel?

If the company already exists, this section might refer readers to an appendix that includes financial statements – for example, income statements and monthly cash flow statements for the first three years of business.

A final section identifies the collaborators needed to fulfill the company's goals. What bank will be used? Who will be the suppliers? Who will be the distributors? What shipping companies will be used? Who will be the company attorney? Who will be the accountant? Who will help the company with hiring and training?

**Marketing Plan**

The marketing plan is that portion of the business plan that lays out a direction for the company's marketing strategy. A formal marketing plan is a written statement of the marketing objectives and strategies to be followed and the specific courses of action to be taken if or when certain future events occur. Although certain aspects of the plan may ultimately be scrapped or modified because of changes in society or in other portions of the market environment, the marketing plan should identify the target market, identify market position, and outline the marketing mix. The marketing plan explains who is responsible for managing the specific activities in the plan and provides a timetable indicating when those activities must be performed. A marketing plan typically has sections on strategic marketing objectives, target markets and positioning, and marketing mix.

Action-oriented objectives are a key element of any marketing plan. A marketing objective is a statement about the level of performance that the organization, SBU, or operating unit intends to achieve. Objectives are more focused than goals because they define results in measurable terms.

*(continued, next page)*

Target markets should be clearly identified. For each marketing mix variable – product, place (distribution), promotion, and price – there should be a general statement of strategies. If marketing research is to be a key element, the marketing plan should include a statement about its purpose.

**Financials**

The financial section of a business plan addresses in more detail the general questions about financial needs raised by situation analysis of the company.

**Control Procedures**

The purpose of managerial control is to ensure that planned activities are executed completely and properly. The final section of the business plan should outline acceptable performance standards. Since control requires investigation and evaluation, the plan should explain how to determine whether the activities necessary to the execution of the plan are in fact being performed.

Numerous excellent examples of business plans may be found at www.bplans.com.

Excerpt from Appendix B of *Effective Marketing: Creating and Keeping Customers in an e-commerce World*, 3e by William G. Zikmund and Michael d'Amico, located at http://zikmund.swcollege.com, published by South-Western, 2001.



## Key Components of the Strategic Business Plan

Key components of the strategic business plan include:

- **Performance objectives:** This aspect of the plan links the organization's objectives to call center goals (referred to as vertical goal setting). Call center objectives should support and further the organization's overall strategic objectives. They generally fall into five categories, including:
  - **Quality:** Call quality, first call resolution, errors and rework
  - **Accessibility:** Service level and response time, average speed of answer, abandoned and blocked calls
  - **Efficiency:** Forecasted call load versus actual, scheduled staff versus actual, adherence to schedule, average handling time
  - **Cost performance:** Cost per contact, average call value, revenue, budgeted to actual expenditures, objectives for outbound
  - **Strategic impact:** Customer satisfaction, employee satisfaction, employee turnover, overall call center ROI

  In the strategic plan, objectives are broadly defined. For example, first call resolution may be represented as, "our target is to reach a first call resolution rate of 85%, from the current 81%, by end of fourth quarter." (Performance objectives are covered in detail in ICMI's *Call Center Operations Management Handbook and Study Guide.*)

- **Customer profile and segmentation strategies:** While the marketing department generally establishes an organization's customer profile and segmentation strategy, the call center plays a significant role in supporting segmentation requirements. Agent group design, hiring and training programs, routing plans, planning processes, technology configuration – all should support and further the means to "get the right customer to the right person at the right times." (Customer segmentation and the call center's support of customer segmentation are covered in ICMI's *Call Center Customer Relationship Management Handbook and Study Guide.*)
- **Organizational design:** As with performance objectives, the strategic business plan broadly defines organizational design requirements. While there are many unique organizational structures, consistent principles behind effective design include:
  - **The organization's mission and strategy drive the structure:** Organizational structures exist to support and enable the desired way of doing business.
  - **Agent groups form the foundation of call center structure:** The call center should be built from agent groups upward. Agent groups should be designed to serve customer access requirements.
  - **Support positions are enablers:** Creating better processes, facilitating collaboration and, in general, supporting and enabling the call center's highest values are support responsibilities that will contribute to overall success.
  - **Structure facilitates branding:** Divisions, groups and responsibilities should further branding objectives.

  (Organizational design is covered in ICMI's *Call Center People Management Handbook and Study Guide.*)
- **Communication plans:** Effective communication across the organization is essential to meeting strategic objectives and leveraging the potential of the call center to create strategic value. In addition to developing effective communication within the organization, there is a need for effective communication with audiences outside the organization, including customers, investors, suppliers and vendors, outsourcers,

resellers and distributors, lawmakers and regulators. (See Creating a Communication Plan for Internal Audiences and Creating a Communication Plan for External Audiences, Section 4.)

- **Equipping people to support strategic objectives:** This part of the strategic business plan outlines recruiting, hiring, training and development initiatives for the call center's most important resource: its people. (These and related subjects are covered in ICMI's *Call Center People Management Handbook and Study Guide.*)
- **Planning processes:** Key processes involve resource planning and management, quality improvement, reporting, communication, and others. The strategic business plan identifies these processes and how they will be maintained and improved. (Processes are covered in ICMI's *Call Center Operations Management Handbook and Study Guide.*)
- **Supporting technologies:** Call centers are evolving to accommodate rapidly changing customer requirements, increased competitive pressures and business imperatives to do "more with less." Technology is a key enabler to meet these demands, and the strategic business plan broadly outlines:
    - The relative importance and impact of technologies on strategic performance
    - Summary of current capabilities
    - The vision of future capabilities
    - Timeframes and general project plans for upgrades or changes
    - Expected payback

(Technology is covered in ICMI's *Call Center Operations Management Handbook and Study Guide.*)

- **Cross-functional teams:** Cross-functional teams enable the critical organizational communication and cooperation essential for the success of strategic objectives. As the hub of customer communication, the call center is the central point for gathering customer information and disseminating that information throughout the organization to cross-functional groups, e.g., marketing, sales, finance, IT, fulfillment. The strategic business plan outlines how cross-functional teams will share information and tools, improve cross-functional education, address barriers to achieving customer satisfaction and align departmental objectives with the organization's strategic objectives. (Teams are covered in ICMI's *Call Center People Management Handbook and Study Guide.*)

- **Fulfilling promises to customers:** Most organizations make a significant investment on brand strategy designed to attract customers who resonate with the promises made through advertising, packaging, etc. The image the organization promotes helps to set customer expectations regarding the service they will receive, and the call center must deliver on its promises throughout customer interactions. Delivering on customer promises involves understanding customer needs and expectations and ensuring that people, processes, technologies and strategies align with those commitments. The strategic business plan broadly describes known deficiencies and planned developments to ensure alignment. (Fulfilling promises to customers is covered in ICMI's *Call Center Customer Relationship Management Handbook and Study Guide.*)
- **Budgetary requirements:** The strategic business plan should broadly outline current and planned expenditures in two primary categories:
    - Capital investments
    - Operational expenses

  The plan should also describe general budget allocations and how they are anticipated to evolve over the next several years. (See discussions on budgeting and financial concepts, Section 7.)

### Creating a Base of Support

Because of the importance of the strategic business plan – as well as funding requirements – it is important to garner support for plans from top-level management. Helpful steps include:

- **Get a senior management sponsor to support the plan.** Then broaden that support to include others in senior management.
- **Determine who needs to be involved in the development of the plan.** This may include managers from marketing, sales, product development, human resources and elsewhere.
- **Develop concrete strategies and tactics with timelines and designated responsibilities.** Although the strategic business plan is developed at a general level, it should consist of tangible objectives, not just goals.
- **Determine how you will measure the progress and success of the plan, and identify actions to take if you get off course.**
- **Develop methods to adjust the plan as circumstances evolve.**

## 3. Components of an Annual Operating Plan

Ready? | 1 | 2 | 3 |

### Key Points

- **An annual operating plan consists of many of the same components as a strategic business plan, but at a more detailed level.**
- **An annual operating plan is initially developed for an entire year. However, it is typically revisited and updated throughout the year based on evolving circumstances.**

### Explanation



An annual operating plan consists of many of the same components as a strategic business plan, but focuses only on the next year. It is more detailed and tactical in nature. Though operational plans vary from one organization to the next in terms of content, scope and depth, typical issues addressed include:

| Area of Focus | Typical Issues Addressed |
|---|---|
| Situational analysis | • Strengths of the organization<br>• Weaknesses of the organization<br>• Opportunities available to the organization<br>• Threats facing the organization |
| Performance objectives | • Current objectives for each role, agent group and the call center as a whole<br>• Gaps in meeting performance objectives<br>• Steps to minimize or eliminate gaps<br>• Key performance indicators |
| Customer profile and segmentation strategies | • Planned changes in profile and segmentation strategies<br>• Customer valuation plans<br>• Implications for agent group design, training, processes and system requirements |
| Organizational design | • Description of current organizational design (agent groups, divisions, reporting structure, etc.)<br>• Planned changes for organizational design<br>• Planned changes for major job roles and associated responsibilities<br>• Site selection (if applicable)<br>• Facilities projects and plans |
| Communication plans | • Target audience<br>• Media<br>• Key information to be exchanged |

| Area of Focus | Typical Issues Addressed |
|---|---|
| Equipping people to support strategic objectives | • Recruiting and hiring plans<br>• Full-time equivalent (FTE) requirements<br>• Workforce mix and scheduling alternatives<br>• Training and development plans<br>• Managing turnover<br>• Monitoring, coaching and performance review initiatives<br>• Career and skill paths<br>• Compensation |
| Planning processes | • Forecasting<br>• Staffing<br>• Scheduling<br>• Real-time management<br>• Quality improvement<br>• Service level agreements |
| Supporting technologies | • Upgrades (infrastructure and enhancements)<br>• Integration projects<br>• Acquisitions<br>• Maintenance costs and requirements<br>• Self-service system developments |
| Cross-functional teams | • Cross-functional improvement opportunities<br>• Establishing and strengthening teams<br>• Team performance objectives |
| Fulfilling promises to customers | • Customer expectations<br>• Customer satisfaction and loyalty surveys<br>• Data warehousing and data mining<br>• "Voice of the customer" analysis and communication |
| Budgetary requirements | • Current requirements<br>• Planned changes in capital investments and operational budgets<br>• Budgetary allocations<br>• Variance trends |
| Legal requirements | • Human resources<br>• Facilities<br>• Employment |
| Disaster recovery | • People<br>• Processes<br>• Technologies<br>• Facilities |
| Health, safety and security issues | • Security of building<br>• Ergonomics<br>• Workers compensation<br>• Insurance<br>• Workplace safety<br>• Health and safety training |

### Continuous Development

There are two common pitfalls in developing and using annual operating plans. On one hand, some develop the plan merely as a management exercise and never really use it. It never works its way into the decision-making process. On the other hand, some lock all decisions into the plan without considering changing circumstances that may warrant adjustments. The key to getting the most value out of the plan is to recognize it as the link between strategic objectives and day-to-day activities, and use it as a guide – a living, breathing document.

# 4. Managing and Controlling Project Plans

**Ready?** | 1 | 2 | 3 |

## Key Points

- **Key project management terms include:**
  - **Scope**
  - **Project plan, also known as work breakdown structure (WBS)**
  - **Gantt chart**
  - **Milestone**
  - **Deliverables**
  - **Owner**
  - **Sponsor/champion**
  - **Dependency**
  - **Critical path**
- **Project plans are not only management tools, but are essential for good communication among the team.**
- **When changes to projects occur, project documentation should note all the implications, including the impact on the project completion date, budget, team resources and the final project deliverable.**



## Explanation

Knowledge of project management principles and processes is essential for call center managers given the many projects with which they are involved.

Key project management terms include:

- **Scope:** The boundaries of the project, meaning a statement of what is and is not part of the project. "Scope creep" is when a project grows beyond what was originally approved, often because the scope was not clearly defined at the outset.
- **Project plan, also known as work breakdown structure (WBS):** Listing of all tasks required to complete the project showing (for each task) start date, completion date, resources required, the person responsible for each task, and a task number (numbering systems vary). The project plan also typically shows the dependencies of each task to the others.
- **Gantt chart:** Visual representation of the project plan, using bars extending to the right of each task representing the amount of time the

task requires. Sophisticated Gantt charts use arrows and symbols to indicate task dependencies, milestones, etc.

- **Milestone:** Measurable point of progress in the project plan. The milestone is listed in the project plan along with the tasks, but is present really as a marker that either has or has not been achieved – for example, "Sponsor's sign-off on Phase 2." Taken together, milestones help define the project timeline.
- **Deliverables:** Completed units of work with tangible results. For example, a report could be a deliverable, as could a software module.
- **Owner:** Person accountable for completion of a task.
- **Sponsor/champion:** Person in the organization with the authority and/or funds to make the project happen, or who advocates for the project to the organization's decision-makers.
- **Dependency:** Relationship between tasks that makes planning for one task dependent upon planning for the other. For example, "determine number of trunks needed" must be completed before "place order for trunks" can be completed.
- **Critical path:** The sequence of tasks upon which the project completion date depends. In other words, a change in the duration of any these tasks will change the project's completion date, due to dependencies among the tasks on the critical path. Tasks that are not on the critical path can be delayed without affecting the project end date.



Project management software applications are no substitute for understanding project management principles and processes. Indeed, many of the tools are so complex as to require their own training to use them effectively.

### Project Planning Practices

Project management is an entire management specialty that has its own certification processes associated with it. The Project Management Institute (PMI) is one of several organizations that offers extensive resources for learning about project management principles and best practices. At the least, call center managers should understand the basics of effective project management, including how to create and manage a project plan. Effective project planning will not only include the steps that are required to complete the project (i.e., scope), but will incorporate the time and resources required to complete these steps, e.g., funding, personnel, technology applications or even training. For large-scale projects that result in operational changes, the project plan should also include a change management plan that will help overcome resistance to change.

## Using Project Plans

Project plans are not only management tools, but are essential for good communication among the team. Listing every task, its start date, end date and the person responsible for completing it is critical to planning. Owners of tasks should be accountable for updating the status of their tasks, completing them as planned and explaining any delays or obstacles encountered. Project plans should also indicate all dependent relationships among tasks, so that the impact of delays in one task can be seen on dependent tasks.

The original planned start and finish dates are called the baseline. Any changes to the plan should be considered in relation to the baseline in order to assess the consequences. Drawing attention to progress or changes in the plan, i.e., new tasks, completed tasks and delayed tasks, is an effective way to use a project plan for communication. Team members and sponsors need to keep abreast of project progress.

Some organizations prefer text-based project plans, while others prefer graphical formats such as Gantt charts, illustrated in the following graphic. Color codes, such as green dots for on-target tasks, yellow dots for slipping tasks and red dots for overdue tasks, can aid in understanding a project plan.

**Project Development Schedule – [Gantt Chart]**

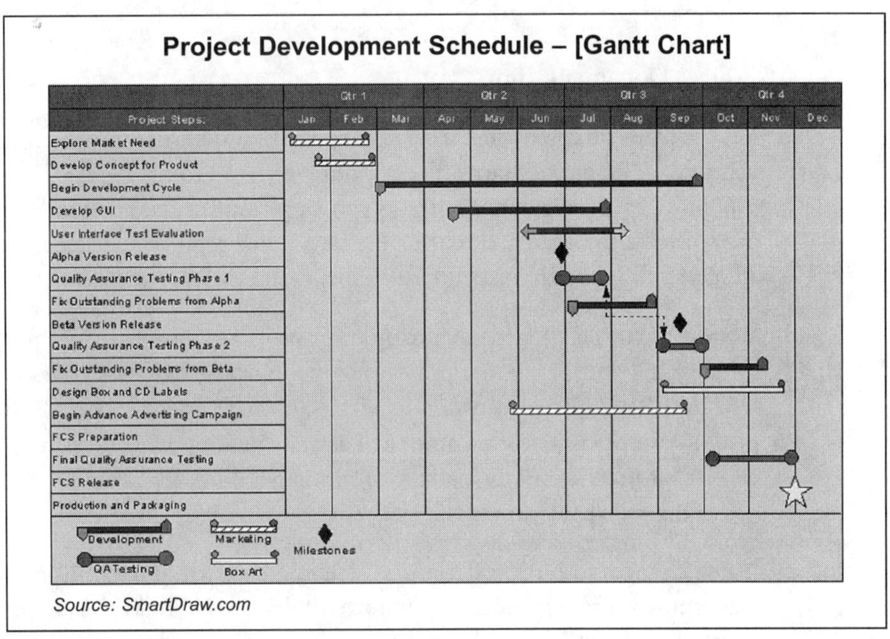


Source: SmartDraw.com

Sophisticated methods can be used to evaluate the efficiency of the project plan. For example, PERT charts, as illustrated in the following graphics, show graphically the critical path of the project, helping project managers to identify opportunities for changes, as well as the tasks that pose the greatest risk to the project's completion date.

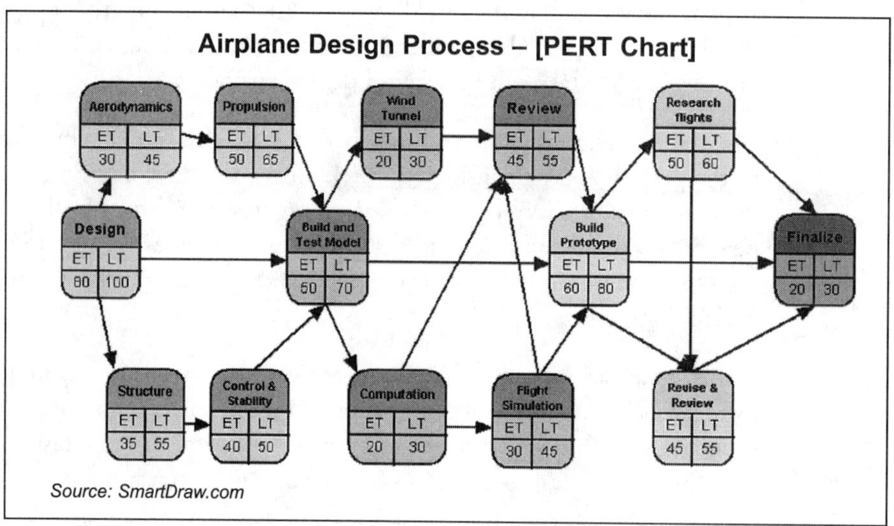

Source: SmartDraw.com

**Project Documentation**

Project plans often become long and complex so alternative communication vehicles are required. Status reports, often referred to as critical issues reports, should be issued regularly. Formats can vary from project to project and organization to organization, but the best status reports are succinct and draw attention to issues that require decisions or action.

Within the project team, documentation plays a critical role in a project's progress. Definitions of the project's scope, purpose and objectives merit close scrutiny. Down the road, when inevitable obstacles arise and tradeoffs must be made, these documents become the basis for making hard decisions. Poorly defined projects are notorious for running over budget, behind schedule and delivering unexpected results.

When changes to project definition documents are required, a formal change management process should be followed. Not only should the change itself be clearly explained, but all the implications must be spelled out, including the impact on the project completion date, budget, team resources and the final project deliverable. All team members, stakeholders and sponsors must sign off on the change document.

**Project Management vs. Operations Management**

Don't make the mistake of thinking that experience managing operations (such as a call center) is sufficient for managing projects. Although many of the fundamental management principles apply in both arenas, the differences are profound. Becoming proficient at project management requires a concentrated effort to learn the principles of this discipline.

## 5. Identifying Methods for Improving Operational Results

**Ready?** | 1 | 2 | 3 |

### Key Points

- **In the absence of good operational performance, the call center will never fulfill larger strategic objectives. Operations are where vision and strategy meet day-to-day realities.**
- **There are many resources, tools and methodologies managers can apply to improve operational results, including:**
  - **Quantitative and qualitative analysis**
  - **Quality control tools and techniques**
  - **Benchmarking**
  - **Innovation principles and methodologies**
  - **Identifying and overcoming obstacles to performance improvement**



### Explanation

In the absence of good operational performance, the call center will never fulfill larger strategic objectives. Operations are where vision and strategy meet day-to-day realities. Of all the responsibilities that call center managers handle, delivering operational results that meet or exceed objectives is fundamental to success.

There are many resources, tools and methodologies managers can apply to improve operational results. Each of the topics listed below is explained in further detail later in the study guide.

#### Quantitative and Qualitative Analysis

Effective analysis is a critical success factor in any business operation, especially operations as complex as call centers. There are almost as many different ways to analyze a problem as there are analysts, but the two primary ways to describe analytical methods are quantitative and qualitative. (See Quantitative and Qualitative Analysis, this section.)

#### Quality Control Tools and Techniques

Without the appropriate tools, identifying the root causes of quality problems in a call center is a significant challenge. If the problem is to be fixed, you need to know what to fix. Then, you can take the necessary corrective actions. The tools the quality movement has produced over the years – flow charts, cause and effect diagrams, scatter diagrams, Pareto charts, control charts and others – are necessary to understand processes and locate the root causes of problems. (See Quality Control Tools and Techniques, this section.)

### Benchmarking

Benchmarking is the process of measuring your products, services and procedures against other organizations or standards. Primarily, it is a method used to assist in improving operational results, or to assist in discovering new ideas. In the call center industry, the term is also used to describe a method for comparing call centers. (See Benchmarking, this section.)

### Innovation Principles and Methodologies

While break-through inventions may come to mind first when considering the impact of innovation, both large and small innovations are important in successful organizations. Although there is no definitive best practice that will guarantee success, there are sensible principles for unleashing innovation. (See Innovation Principles and Methodologies, this section.)

### Identifying and Overcoming Obstacles to Performance Improvement

Identifying and overcoming obstacles to performance improvement is a universal challenge. Overcoming obstacles requires clear identification of the problem and thorough analysis. While every organization faces specific challenges, common obstacles fall into four categories: human factors, organizational obstacles, management obstacles, strategic obstacles. (See Identifying and Overcoming Obstacles to Performance Improvement, this section.)

## 6. Quantitative and Qualitative Analysis

Ready? | 1 | 2 | 3 |

### Key Points

- The best analysis is holistic, using both quantitative and qualitative methods.
- Both quantitative and qualitative analysis begin with problem statements.
- Much of the quantitative analysis in the call center can be performed with a calculator or spreadsheet:
  - Variances
  - Averages
  - Ratios
  - Percentages
  - Trend analysis
- Qualitative analysis is like detective work. The basic principles are:
  - List all assumptions
  - Learn the basics
  - Observe
  - Ask questions
  - Make notes and organize them
  - Brainstorm
  - Seek patterns and anomalies



### Explanation

The best analysis is holistic. Since so many systems and factors in call centers are interrelated, it can be misleading to focus analysis efforts too narrowly. There are two primary ways to describe analytical methods:

- **Quantitative:** Focused on numerical, mathematical or statistical data.
- **Qualitative:** Interpretation of descriptive data usually expressed as text.

Before we consider either of these methods, however, it is worth dispelling a common misconception about analysis. Although analysis frequently deals with numbers and utilizes mathematical, statistical and scientific concepts, analysis is not for number crunchers alone. Equally important to effective analytical thinking are open-mindedness, perception, curiosity, creativity, subject matter expertise, powers of observation, interviewing skills and writing ability. Analysis strives to provide insight that contributes to solving problems and answering questions. Successful analysts must be able to understand context, draw meaningful conclusions from both quantitative and qualitative data, and present the results convincingly.

### Problem Definition

All analysis begins with a problem statement. What needs to be understood? What problem needs to be solved? What question needs to be answered? A well-defined problem statement establishes clear objectives for the analysis.

It is not unusual, however, for problem statements to be revised after the analysis has begun. The better you understand a problem, the better you can describe it, so as the analysis proceeds and understanding increases, it may be possible to improve the problem statement.

### Quantitative Analysis

A complete list of quantitative analysis methods, let alone an explanation of each, is beyond the scope of this handbook/study guide and is not needed by call center managers. Fundamental quantitative analysis is not rocket science, however. One can do quite a bit with a calculator or a spreadsheet and the math you learned in school. Following are the fundamental methods of quantitative analysis most applicable to call center management.

### Variances

The simplest mathematical operation is one of the most important for analyzing operational results in a call center. Calculate variance by subtracting your objective (or plan) from your actual results.

For example:

> If you planned to have 30 agents on the phone at 10 a.m. and actually had 32 agents on the phone, then your variance is: 32 – 30 = 2. Note that this is a positive variance, as you exceeded your plan.
>
> If you only had 28 agents on the phone, then your variance would be a negative variance: 28 – 30 = -2.

### Averages

Averages are both powerful and dangerous. Their power lies in the ability to summarize large amounts of data in a readily understandable way. Given a set of numbers, the average is simply the sum of the numbers in the set divided by the number (or count) of numbers in the set.

For example:

Daily call volumes can be usefully summarized by taking the average.

| Monday | 1000 |
|---|---|
| Tuesday | 800 |
| Wednesday | 500 |
| Thursday | 600 |
| Friday | 400 |
| Total | 3300 |

3300 total calls ÷ 5 days = 660 calls per day on average

However, the danger in averages is their oversimplification. Scheduling staff each day based on the average of 660 calls, for example, would produce understaffed, poor service level conditions on two days (Monday and Tuesday) and overstaffed, inefficient conditions on three days (Wednesday, Thursday and Friday).

### Ratios

Ratios have the same appeal as averages, yet they display the relationship between two sets of numbers. Ratios use division to compare two different pieces of data that have a logical relationship to each other. The ratio may be expressed as a fraction or as a percentage.

For example:

The total number of agents in a call center divided by the total number of supervisors could be expressed as

200 agents ÷ 10 supervisors = 20

which can be written as a "20:1 staff-to-supervisor ratio" and pronounced as "twenty to one staff-to-supervisor ratio."

When there is a specific balance desired between two measures, a ratio is an effective way to present it. Note, also, that since ratios can work well as objectives, variances can be measured from these objectives.

**Percentages for Estimation**

Percentages are just another form of ratios, on a normalized basis, but they can capture the relationship of more than just two numbers to each other. Percentages are the analyst's best friend, for they have many uses, including estimation.

For example:

Assume that today a call center receives 50 calls, categorized as follows:

25 Product inquiries

10 Delivery complaints

15 Billing questions

If 80 total calls are expected tomorrow, how many of each call type can be expected? Using percentages, the estimate is easy to calculate. First, calculate each category's percentage of today's total call volume.

Product inquiries: 25 calls ÷ 50 total calls = .5 or 50% of total calls

Delivery complaints: 10 calls ÷ 50 total calls = .2 or 20% of total calls

Billing questions: 15 calls ÷ 50 total calls = .3 or 30% of total calls

If it is assumed that tomorrow's distribution of calls will be similar to today's, then simply multiply each call type's percentage by the total calls forecast for tomorrow.

50% x 80 = 40 Product inquiries

20% x 80 = 16 Delivery Complaints

30% x 80 = 24 Billing questions

The danger with using percentages for estimation lies in the reliability of the underlying assumptions. How likely is it that tomorrow will mirror today? When based on enough data, percentages can be remarkably accurate. Given limited data or knowledge, percentages can offer reasonable or "better than nothing" estimates.

**Percentages for Comparing Differences**

Percentages are also valuable for comparing differences. As illustrated above, variances can compare actual results to objectives. But if an organization has multiple objectives, percentage variances provide a meaningful way to compare results and identify those most in need of attention.

For example:

Consider these two sets of performance objectives and results for a call center:

| ASA | | First Call Resolution | |
|---|---|---|---|
| Objective | 20 seconds | Objective | 80% |
| Actual | 15 seconds | Actual | 75% |
| Variance | -5 seconds | Variance | -5% |

The variance from objective for ASA is five seconds and for first call resolution is five percentage points. So does that mean that performance in both areas is comparable? You can use percentage variance to answer this question.

The percentage variance for ASA would be 5 second variance ÷ 20 second objective = -.25 or -25% percentage variance.

The percentage variance for first call resolution would be 5 percentage points ÷ 80 percent = -.0625 or -6.25% percentage variance.

Using percentage variances, it is abundantly clear that ASA performance is far different compared to plan than first call resolution performance.

### Percentages over Time Periods

Another of the many uses for percentages is comparing results in different time periods. As the previous example illustrated, percentages make it easier to compare relationships between numbers of different sizes. Similar situations frequently occur when comparing numbers from different time periods.

For example:

| Year | Annual Call Volume |
|---|---|
| 1999 | 194,872 calls |
| 2000 | 204,615 calls |
| 2001 | 214,846 calls |

It is difficult to compare the growth in call volume from 1999 to 2000 with that from 2000 to 2001 by just looking at the following annual call volumes.

By calculating the variance between each year's volume, and then the percentage variance, it's clear that call volume has increased 5% each year.

From 1999 to 2000:

204,615 calls - 194,872 calls = 9,744 call increase

9744 call increase ÷ 194,872 calls in the year before = 5% increase

From 2000 to 2001:

214,846 - 204,615 = 10,231 call increase

10,231 call increase ÷ 204,615 calls in the year before = 5% increase

**Trend Analysis**

The culmination of the above quantitative approaches for many call center managers is trend analysis, or the comparison of results over time. The most popular form of trend analysis is graphical – by plotting results on a chart or using spreadsheet software to generate a chart. In fact, visual inspection of data in chart form, e.g., line charts, bar charts, area charts, even three-dimensional charts, is often more effective than reading rows and columns of data. Our eyes tend to be better at perceiving patterns and anomalies from charts than our brains are from a list of numbers.

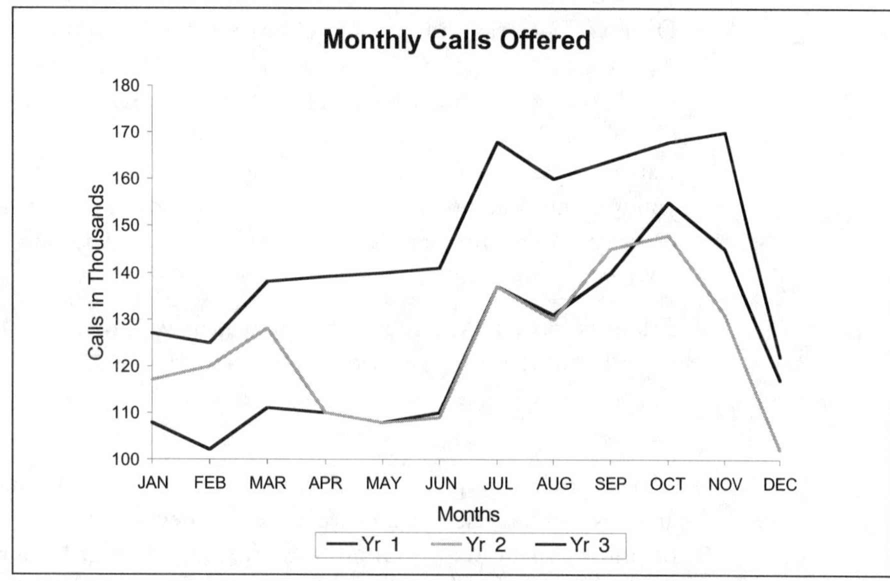


Each of the above quantitative analysis techniques can generate the data to be plotted for trend analysis: variances, averages, ratios and percentages, as well as

actual results. In addition, charts with more than one result plotted over time can be especially illuminating. Try putting your quality rate and service level percentage on the same chart over time, for example, to better understand the relationship between the two in your organization.

**Qualitative Analysis**

As opposed to quantitative analysis, qualitative analysis more closely resembles the Sherlock Holmes approach: searching for clues, interviewing everyone involved and then developing a logical construct to make sense of the information. There are many tools that have been developed for qualitative analysis, but most call center managers will find the following principles sufficient:

- **List all assumptions:** The first step is to put all of your cards on the table. What assumptions have you made? List even the most obvious, since hidden assumptions can also hide solutions.
- **Learn the basics:** It is hard to analyze what you do not understand. If a review of basic concepts is needed, get it. But experts are not always the best analysts, since they can be so committed to their own experience and expectations that they may overlook what they do not expect to see. A fresh, even naïve, perspective is valuable in qualitative analysis.
- **Observe:** One way to learn is to observe. If you are trying to understand what is going wrong with a process, for example, there is no substitute for observing the process in action. Realize, however, that the act of observation affects that which is observed. In other words, when you watch people they are likely to do things differently than they would if you were not watching. This fact does not remove the value from observation; it simply needs to be kept in mind and accounted for when interpreting the findings.
- **Ask questions:** Talk to those who know or have experience, and listen carefully to what they say. Seek clarification, details and examples. Encourage people to share what they know and whatever insight they have.
- **Make notes and organize them:** It may seem obvious, but qualitative analysis requires taking extensive notes and devising a system for organizing them. Organization pays off. Take the time to capture in writing all that you learn. In addition to preserving a record, the act of writing helps your brain to process and learn the information, as well.

- **Brainstorm:** Brainstorming can be effective at many points in the analysis process, from the start, when defining the problem statement, to the end, when looking for relationships and drawing conclusions. The key is to free your mind to consider any and all possibilities, so that you can express or uncover new ideas or spark new understanding. To work, basic brainstorming rules must be followed: no criticism, no challenging and capture every idea.
- **Seek patterns and anomalies:** At every stage in the process, look for patterns (or recurrent situations) and anomalies (or unusual situations). Although this may sound contradictory, each represents a difference from random occurrences. Patterns offer clues to cause and effect relationships. Anomalies can point to unexpected changes or errors. You can't look closely at everything, so learn to look in the places most likely to be hiding answers.

### Quantitative and Qualitative Analysis Together

This section began by noting the value of taking a holistic approach to analysis, and ends by further stressing this point. Many an analyst has gone astray by looking closely and carefully at just part of a problem. Quantitative analysis alone can produce colossal blunders due to poor understanding of the context. Qualitative analysis alone can turn into the proverbial search for a needle in a haystack, without some basis for filtering out the irrelevant information. Just remember the peanut butter and jelly sandwiches you ate as a child: quantitative and qualitative analysis belong together, and they're better that way than either one is alone.

## 7. Quality Control Tools and Techniques

Ready? | 1 | 2 | 3 |

### Key Points

- **Without the appropriate tools, identifying the root causes of quality problems in a call center is an exercise in frustration.**
- **The quality movement has produced a number of tools that are useful for call center management:**
  - **Flow chart**
  - **Cause and effect diagram**
  - **Scatter diagram**
  - **Pareto chart**
  - **Control chart**



### Explanation

Without the appropriate tools, identifying the root causes of quality problems in a call center is an exercise in frustration. Consider a recurring problem, such as providing incomplete information to callers. Maybe the cause is insufficient information in the database. Or a need for more training. Or maybe a lack of coordination with marketing. Or carelessness. Or agent stress from a chronically high occupancy rate. Or a combination of any of these factors, coupled with many other things.

If the problem is to be fixed, you need to know what to fix. Then, you can take the necessary corrective actions. The tools the quality movement has produced over the years should be applied to understand processes and locate the root causes of problems. If you've had any quality training, you are probably well versed in their use. The purpose here is to discuss how they can be applied in the call center environment.

#### Flow Chart

A flow chart is a map of a process and is used to analyze and standardize procedures, identify root causes of problems and plan new processes. Flow charts are also excellent communication tools, and can help you visualize and understand the flow of a process.

One of the most useful applications for a flow chart is to analyze the specific

types of transactions you handle. Even a simple transaction consists of many steps. To really understand a transaction, especially the more complex variety, it is necessary to chart what happens, step-by-step.

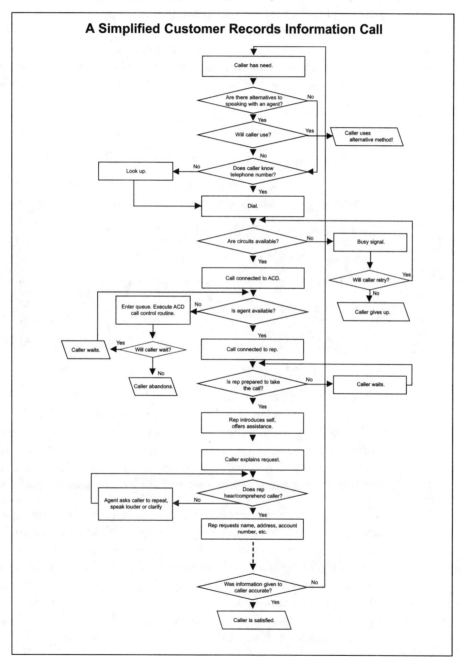

**A Simplified Customer Records Information Call**

Caller has need.
Are there alternatives to speaking with an agent?
No
Yes
Will caller use?
Yes
Caller uses alternative method!
No
Does caller know telephone number?
No
Look up.
Yes
Dial.
Are circuits available?
No
Busy signal.
Will caller retry?
Yes
No
Caller gives up.
Yes
Call connected to ACD.
Is agent available?
No
Enter queue. Execute ACD call control routine.
Will caller wait?
Yes
Caller waits.
No
Caller abandons.
Yes
Call connected to rep.
Is rep prepared to take the call?
No
Caller waits.
Yes
Rep introduces self, offers assistance.
Caller explains request.
Does rep hear/comprehend caller?
No
Agent asks caller to repeat, speak louder or clarify
Yes
Rep requests name, address, account number, etc.
Was information given to caller accurate?
No
Yes
Caller is satisfied.

If you haven't charted your transactions by type, give this task to a few of your agents. In fact, put them in a conference room for a couple of hours. Give them a stack of index cards and have them write each step in a typical transaction on individual cards, then lay the cards out in order on a large table. In a relatively short period of time, they should be able to tell you where there are procedural inconsistencies, database deficiencies and bottlenecks in the process. Post-its on a wall or PC-based flow charting software works well, too. You will eventually want to invest more than a couple of hours in this activity, but this will get you started.

Sometimes a sweeping analysis of all the activities required to process transactions is in order. With top management support and direction, representatives from the call center, billing and credit, fulfillment, marketing, information systems and other departments can map out inter-departmental and inter-organizational processes to identify areas that need overhaul.



Example applications for this tool include:

- Transactions, step-by-step
- The planning and management process
- IVR and ACD programming
- Key procedures

**Cause and Effect Diagram**

The cause and effect diagram, alternatively called a fishbone diagram after its shape, was first developed by Dr. Kaoru Ishikawa of the University of Tokyo in 1943, and has since become recognized and used worldwide. The chart illustrates the relationships between causes and a specific effect you want to study. Preparing a cause and effect diagram is an education in itself. Everyone who participates will gain new understanding of the process.

The traditional cause categories used in these diagrams have traditionally been referred to as the 4Ms: manpower, machines, methods, and materials. A variation on these categories – people, technology, methods and materials/information – works better for call centers. However, these labels are only suggestions, and you can use any that help your group focus and think through the problem. Possible causes leading to the effect are drawn as branches off the main category. The final step is to prioritize the causes and work on the most prevalent problems first.

**Cause-and-Effect Diagram**

People - Reps, Callers

Materials/Services

Methods

Technology

High Transfer Rate

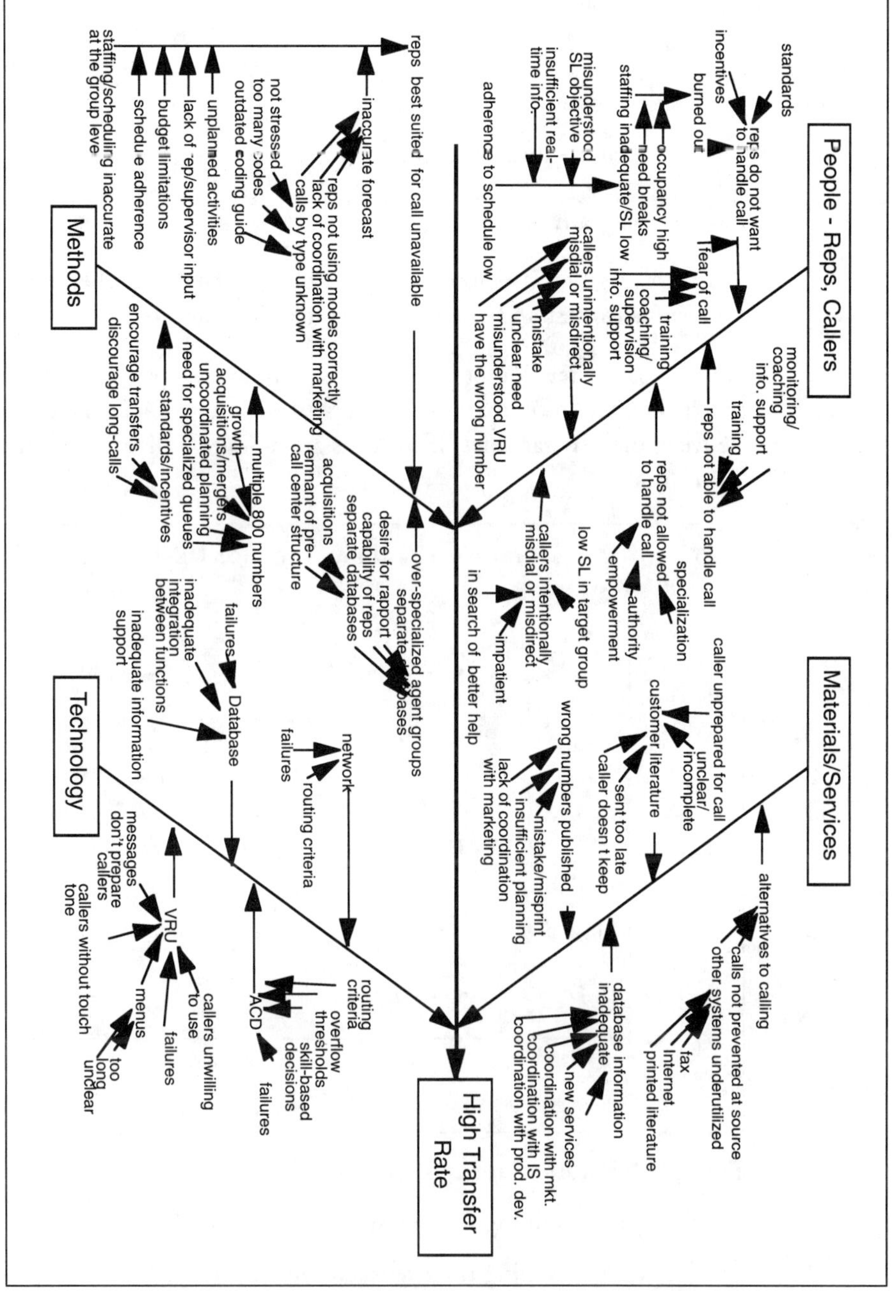

There is no one right way to make a cause and effect diagram. A good diagram is one that fits the purpose, and the shape the chart takes will depend on the group.

Example applications for this tool include:

- Long calls
- Repeat calls
- Poor adherence to schedule
- Inaccurate forecast

**Scatter Diagram**

A scatter diagram assesses the strength of the relationship between two variables and is used to test and document possible cause and effect.

If there is a correlation between the two variables, a pattern will emerge. The closer the pattern of dots is to a straight line, the stronger the correlation is between the two variables. If the dots are randomly distributed, there is no correlation.

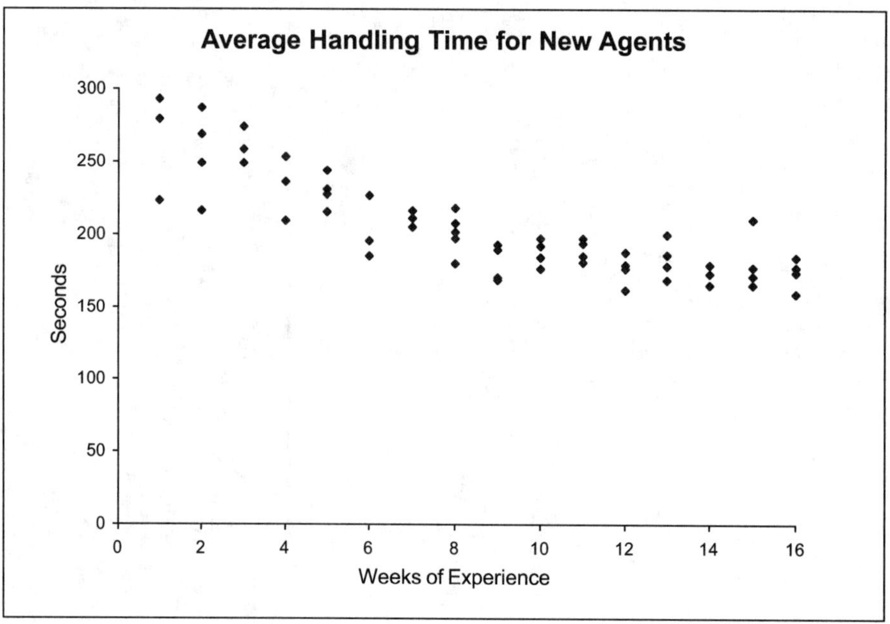


Example applications for this tool include:

- Average handling time versus experience level
- Average handling time versus revenue generated
- Service level versus error rate

- Experience level versus quality scores

**Pareto Chart**

Vilfredo Pareto (1848-1923) was an Italian economist whose theories have had widespread impact. One of better known results of his work is the Pareto chart, which is a bar chart that ranks the events you are analyzing in order of importance or frequency. The Pareto principle dictates that you should work first on the things that will yield the biggest improvements.

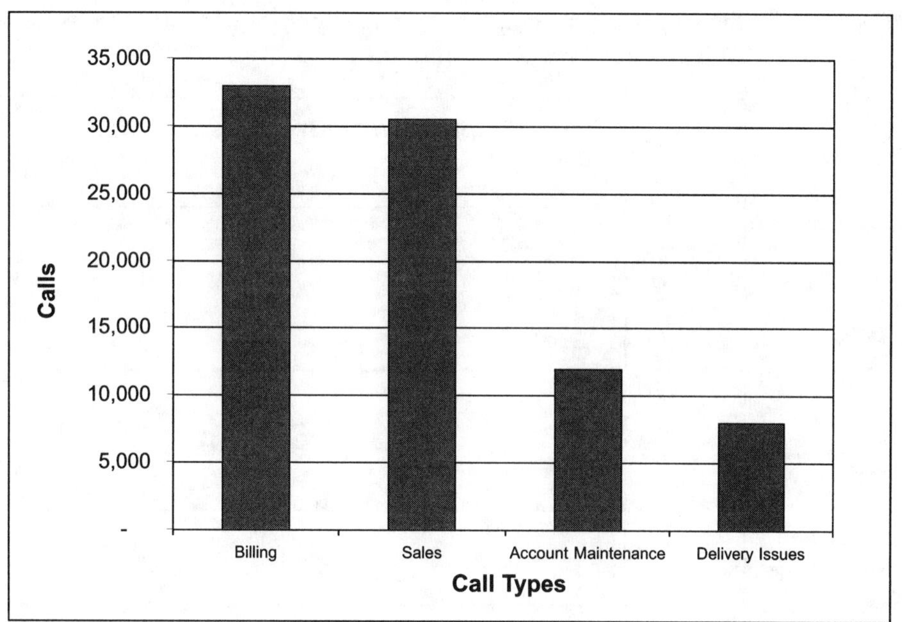


Example applications for this tool include:

- Transactions by type
- Errors by type
- Transactions by customer demographics (e.g., age, region of country and how long they've been customers)
- Responses to customer surveys

**Control Chart**

One of the reasons that quality problems in the call center are challenging and often confusing is that they are a part of a complex process, and any process has variation from the ideal. A control chart is a tool that provides information on variation. There are two major types of variation: special causes and common causes. Special causes create erratic, unpredictable variation. Examples of special causes might include an agent with degenerative hearing loss, unusual calls from unexpected publicity or a computer terminal with intermittent problems. Common causes are the rhythmic, normal variations in the system.

A control chart enables you to bring a process under statistical control by eliminating the chaos of special causes. You can then work on the common causes by improving the system and thus, the whole process. Special causes show up as points outside of the upper or lower control limits, or as points with unnatural patterns within the limits.



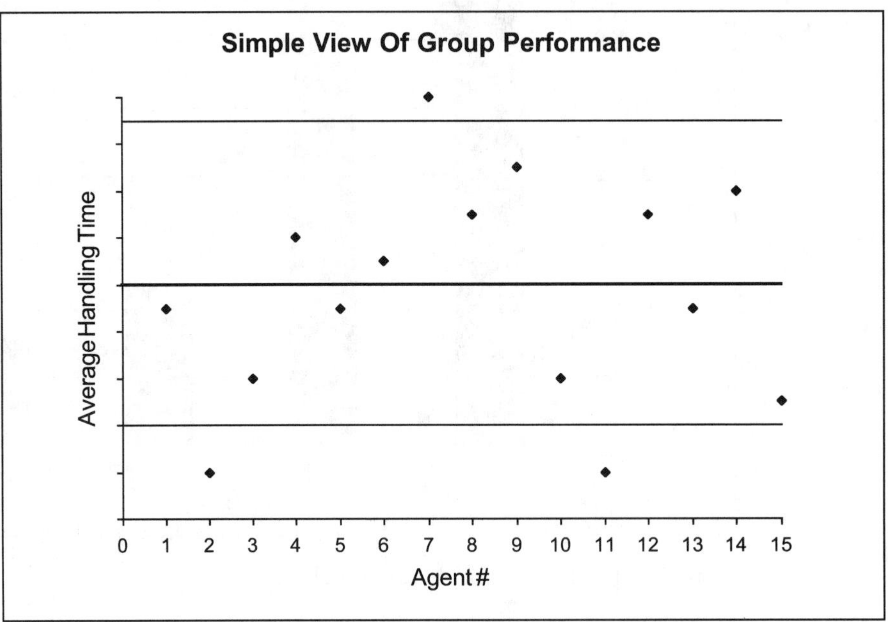


A control chart cannot reveal what the problems are. Instead, it reveals where and when special causes occur. Once special causes are eliminated, improving the system itself will have far more impact than focusing on individual causes. Improvements to the system will move the entire process in the right direction.

In short, control charts can:

- Control and reduce variation
- Prevent you from chasing the wrong problem
- Give early warning of changes in the process
- Improve predictability

- Improve planning

Example applications for this tool include:

- Average handling time
- Percent adherence
- Percent defective calls (from monitoring)
- Requests for supervisory assistance (transfers)

**Tools Are Just Tools**

With any of the tools, there is a danger of getting caught up in the tool and not moving on to problem resolution. Ensure that the tools do not become an end in themselves. Once you identify problems to tackle, you will need to assign clear responsibilities, provide necessary resources and track progress. Results are what matter!

## 8. Benchmarking

Ready? | 1 | 2 | 3 |

### Key Points

- **Benchmarking is the process of measuring your products, services and procedures against other organizations or standards.**
- **Several principles to note about standards and benchmarks include:**
  - **There is no officially sanctioned or even carefully considered consensus on what a standard for comparison of call centers would be.**
  - **Most benchmarking studies currently come from informal groups of companies, associations or government organizations, which collaborate and share information. These studies incorporate varying sample sizes and methodologies.**
  - **What is most important is knowing how the results were achieved, not just what the results are.**
- **The following is a general approach to benchmarking:**
  - **Define processes and collect performance data**
  - **Analyze collected data and identify best practices**
  - **Prepare recommendations**
  - **Apply findings**



### Explanation

The idea behind benchmarking is that new ideas often come from the outside. Benchmarking is the process of measuring your products, services and procedures against other organizations or standards. Benchmarking – or even interpreting benchmarking results – takes considerable time and energy. Merely taking a tour of a call center will be insufficient for improving methods and standards.

Benchmarking is easily misunderstood by organizations looking for an easy reference chart of performance standards by industry for things like service level, quality, abandonment, busy signals, caller satisfaction levels and the like. Organizations are different enough, even within a given industry, that universally accepted standards are usually not defensible. Variables such as labor rates, caller demographics, caller tolerances, trunk and network configurations, hours of operation and the mix of part- and full-time agents are treated differently from one organization to the next.

Further, organizations often interpret performance measures differently. For example, three different customer service centers may all have service level objectives of 80 percent answered in 20 seconds. However, one might measure service level as a daily average, another as a monthly average, while another, the number of half-hours per day that met the objective within a specified range.

Several principles to note about standards and benchmarks include:

- There is no officially sanctioned or even carefully considered consensus on what a standard for comparison of call centers would be.
- Most benchmarking studies currently come from informal groups of companies, associations or government organizations, which collaborate and share information. These studies incorporate varying sample sizes and methodologies.
- What is most important is knowing how the results were achieved, not just what the results are.

**A General Approach to Benchmarking**

With these cautions in mind, a disciplined, focused benchmarking effort can produce the information necessary to make significant improvements in areas such as forecasting, handling time, service level and customer satisfaction. The following outlines a general approach to benchmarking:

- **Define processes and collect performance data:** This involves getting agreements on processes to be compared and measurements to be used.
- **Analyze collected data and identify best practices:** This involves normalizing the raw data for differences, such as currencies, hours of operation, etc., and then identifying the best performers from each category.
- **Prepare recommendations:** This involves preparing specific recommendations in three general categories: process resources, process efficiency and customer satisfaction.
- **Apply findings:** This involves developing a plan to implement improvements.

Benchmarking, like other aspects of quality improvement, should be an ongoing effort. As the industry improves, what were once cutting-edge practices become the norm. As best practices become generally accepted, they can no longer be considered "best practices."

## 9. Innovation Principles and Methodologies

Ready? | 1 | 2 | 3 |

### Key Points

- **Innovation is essential to success in any endeavor. Both large and small innovations are important factors in successful organizations.**
- **Sensible innovation principles include:**
  - **Collect customer input to identify needs**
  - **Support risk taking**
  - **Empower people**
  - **Allocate resources**
  - **Give people work they enjoy doing**
  - **Give people training and education**
  - **Stay the course**
  - **Weave support for innovation into the organizational fabric**



### Explanation

Innovation is essential to success in any endeavor. While break-through inventions may come to mind first when considering the impact of innovation, there has likely been greater impact from the cumulative effects of small innovations made throughout history by millions of people in hundreds of thousands of organizations around the world. Both large and small innovations are important factors in successful organizations.

Naturally, many innovative methods have been developed for promoting innovation. Best-selling books, proprietary seminars, case studies of innovative companies and now an array of Web sites have put forward varied approaches to cultivate creativity and invention. The next big invention can come from you, they claim, if you follow their innovative advice.

As in so many cases where there is no definitive best practice that will guarantee success, sensible principles can still be found, including those that follow. Apply them wisely, using judgment and knowledge of your own organization.

- **Collect customer input to identify needs:** Although the processes of innovation apply across the organization, call centers have access to a rich source of information: customer input. What explicit needs are callers expressing? What needs are their calls implying that they have?

"Necessity is the mother of invention," after all. Accumulate and organize what customers consider to be necessary, and use that to spark creative solutions.

- **Support risk taking:** Innovation requires taking risks. Developing something that is new means no one knows whether it will prove successful or will fail. Organizations that foster innovation accept this and reward risk takers, rather than punish failed risks.
- **Empower people:** It is impossible to control truly creative processes. Innovation will be stifled in command-and-control organizations. Individuals and teams that embrace their own responsibility for developing unique solutions are on the path to innovation.
- **Allocate resources:** Allocating time and funds for innovation is an act of faith because there can be no guarantee that success will result. The creative process generally requires time. Trial and error, experimentation, building upon the knowledge gained from "failed" efforts all take time. Time spent on innovation, of course, is not spent on straight production work, and so incurs cost.
- **Give people work they enjoy doing:** It's unlikely every job can be filled by someone who loves performing it. To the extent that you can give people assignments that they enjoy, however, you will be enabling innovation. Intrinsic motivation is a more powerful innovative force than extrinsic motivation. Neither a carrot nor a stick is as likely to produce motivation as sheer pleasure and pride in doing one's job. People who love what they do tend to invest the energy and dedication required to innovate.
- **Give people training and education:** It does not require a college degree to be creative, but expert knowledge is a component of creativity. It's hard to come up with useful new ideas about something that you do not fully understand. An outside, naïve perspective has value in brainstorming, but developing useful solutions requires depth of understanding. Investing in people's knowledge is an investment in future innovation.
- **Stay the course:** Set a clear and consistent course for the organization. Encourage innovative approaches to achieving goals. Frequent changes in goals and objectives undermine creativity by short-circuiting long-term efforts and diverting energy into changing direction.
- **Weave support for innovation into the organizational fabric:** It is much

easier to inadvertantly discourage innovation than it is to actively encourage it. Many organizations implicitly or explicitly reward conformity and compliance, avoidance of error and constructive criticism. Organizations that value innovation have to examine all aspects of their structure and culture to root out deterrents of creativity and install support for innovation instead.

# 10. Identifying and Overcoming Obstacles to Performance Improvement

Ready? | 1 | 2 | 3 |

## Key Points

- **The process of identifying obstacles is essentially analysis, while overcoming obstacles requires the application of sound management principles.**
- **Every call center faces its own specific challenges, but many obstacles are common across organizations or industries. They fall into four general categories:**
  - **Human factors**
  - **Organizational obstacles**
  - **Management obstacles**
  - **Strategic obstacles**

## Explanation

Identifying and overcoming obstacles to performance improvement is a challenge all managers face. The process of identifying obstacles is essentially analysis, while overcoming obstacles requires the application of sound management principles. (See Quantitative and Qualitative Analysis, this section.)

Every call center faces its own specific challenges, but many obstacles are common across organizations or industries. They fall into four general categories:

- Human factors
- Organizational obstacles
- Management obstacles
- Strategic obstacles

### Human Factors

People are often cited as organizations' most valuable resources, but human nature presents obstacles that cannot be ignored.

- **Resistance to change:** For many reasons, it is common for people to prefer the status quo. Call center managers who recognize this and work to create buy-in for change will be more effective than those who dismiss its significance. One of the best ways to create buy-in is to involve those most affected by the change in the improvement process. This participation will help them understand why the change is necessary and, as a result, they will be more willing to embrace change.

- **Fear:** Fearful people may panic, act irrationally, hide information and act selfishly, just to name a few undesirable responses. Long-term performance results are much more likely to be sustained in environments where employees believe in and are committed to the organization's strategy and objectives.
- **Defense mechanisms:** Defense mechanisms are an inherent part of human activity, but failure to take personal responsibility is an insidious obstacle to performance improvement. People and groups that continue to deny they are part of a problem are not fully committed to correcting the problem. Accountability needs to be clearly established so that individuals and teams accept responsibility and are motivated to create improvements.



### Organizational Obstacles

Organizations themselves present some common obstacles to change.

- **Organizational structure and boundaries:** When roles are defined too narrowly, each person's ability to affect change is limited, "hand-offs" in processes are created and the overall understanding of entire processes suffers. Departmental boundaries tend to deter organizational change when people within departments work on improvements in a vacuum, rather than considering overall results.
- **Organizational culture:** Negative organizational culture is a notorious obstacle. Ignore the unwritten, but established, ways that things get done and you'll fail. One of the greatest challenges is to build new expectations into the culture, so that the organizational culture comes into alignment with the desired changes.

### Management Obstacles

Managers themselves are responsible for many obstacles to performance improvement.

- **Focusing on results, not processes:** A narrow focus on results encourages short-sighted corrections rather than long-lasting change. This is not to say that "results" should be ignored, of course. But results are the output of processes, so if you want different results you need to change the processes that produce them. Don't assume that demanding better results will lead people to seek out the best way to achieve them. If at all possible, people will deliver what is demanded, but how the changes are achieved is critical to long-term success.

- **Not motivating employees effectively:** Managers need a fundamental understanding of the principles of effective motivation. Many managers incorrectly assume that tying performance standards to financial compensation is always the best way to improve individual performance. Financial incentives may need to be part of overall motivation, but true motivators are not financial in nature. They include the work itself, recognition, achievement, responsibility, and the chance for growth and advancement.
- **Not understanding the root cause:** Pulling the wrong lever is more common than managers would like to believe. The best of intentions and hardest work will do little good if they do not address the cause of the problem. Unfortunately, sometimes people respond to performance improvement directives by taking action for the sake of taking action. Try not to create so much urgency that staff feel compelled to act before they have taken the time to understand what action is really called for to get the best results. For example, if your center experiences high levels of employee turnover, it is better to develop an employee satisfaction survey to uncover areas of employee dissatisfaction than to immediately put together an incentive program.
- **Lack of management focus:** Does the organization have the resources to fix all problems (at once)? It's the manager's job to prioritize and plan. Making everything the number one priority will tend to produce short-term improvements that will fade after attention has shifted to the next area to improve. Remember, there are many ways to prop up results to make them look better for a short time. If the task assigned is unrealistic, you'll set staff up to fail – or even worse, to hide the truth behind doctored reports.
- **Lack of communication:** To make sure everyone pulls in the same direction, the direction needs to be clearly and repeatedly communicated. One memo, for example, won't be enough to get buy-in throughout the organization. Dedicate skilled resources and develop an effective communication plan. (See Principles of Effective Communication, Section 4.)

- **Failing to involve employees in problem-solving:** When a problem arises that impacts frontline agents, managers need to include agents in the process of overcoming the problem. For example, if long-term call center scheduling needs change, involve agents in the process of determining what new shifts might be effective. When agents are able to give input into changes that will affect them directly, they are much more likely to be satisfied with the outcome.
- **Lip service:** Saying you want performance improvements is not enough. As the expression aptly puts it, "you have to walk the talk." Compensation and performance appraisal systems should reinforce actions that contribute to performance improvement, not undermine them. All managers need to act as a team, as well, and support the objectives in their day-to-day running of their operations.



### Strategic Obstacles

Many significant obstacles are the result of inadequate strategic planning.

- **Lack of a supporting strategy:** Without a supporting strategy, the reason for accomplishing objectives is unclear. Performance improvement plans need to be aligned with the organization's strategy so that the purpose is understood. (See Definition and Application of Strategy, Section 3.)
- **Lack of investment in building skills, knowledge and leadership:** Not investing in your people saves money in the present, but costs far more in terms of missed opportunities in the long run. This is a particularly tempting shortcut in call centers that are perceived as cost centers. Inadequate investments in people will yield inadequate performance improvements.
- **Lack of enabling technologies:** Failure to invest in appropriate technology forces people to work without the tools that could make them and the organization overall most successful. Not only will this be less productive, but it becomes demoralizing over time, especially when competing organizations have better supporting technology.
- **Lack of supporting operational plans and processes:** This might seem so obvious a problem that it would never occur. In many organizations, however, this is exactly what happens: expectations are set, and everyone gets busy trying to make changes (ready, fire, aim). Slowing down enough to plan is the best way to overcome this obstacle. (See Components of an Annual Operating Plan, this section.)

## Overcoming Obstacles

How to overcome an obstacle varies depending upon the obstacle itself. General principles of analysis and management apply, but accurate identification of the obstacle is the most important step in overcoming it. You can't very well get past what you do not understand. In many cases the solution is apparent once the problem has been discovered.

Effective reports will align performance objectives with the organization's strategy and goals. The balanced scorecard is an example of an approach that will ensure priorities and organizational focus work together. (See Aligning Tactical Activities with Values, Vision and Mission, Section 3.)

When solutions are not obvious, problem-solving systems, testing hypotheses scientifically and applying the techniques of qualitative analysis are all valuable methods for figuring out how to overcome any obstacles you face. Implementing effective solutions is the very essence of managing.

Managing operations effectively is covered in detail in ICMI's *Call Center Operations Management Handbook and Study Guide.* Managing people is explained in depth in *Call Center People Management Handbook and Study Guide.* Both of those study guides provide valuable insight for call center managers to draw upon in overcoming performance improvement obstacles.

## 11. Identifying Outsourcing Opportunities

Ready? | 1 | 2 | 3 |



### Key Points

- Call center outsourcing, technology outsourcing and contract staffing arrangements are the three primary types of contractual relationships in which call centers are commonly involved.
- Call center outsourcing relationships typically fall into one of these two types of arrangements:
  - The entire call center operation is outsourced
  - Components of the client's call center operations are outsourced, while some call center functions are handled internally
- Different types of technology outsourcing include:
  - Purchasing technology tools from an outside vendor
  - Using a vendor to develop proprietary software or customize off-the-shelf tools
  - Accessing software through an application service provider (ASP), e.g., paying per transaction, per license, etc.
  - Contracting with technology consultants and/or service providers to manage specific purchases or oversee the entire information technology operation within the organization
- There are many different contract staffing arrangements:
  - Permanent placement
  - Temporary-to-permanent placement
  - Contract workers
  - Co-sourcing arrangements

### Explanation

Call center outsourcing, technology outsourcing and contract staffing arrangements are the three primary types of contractual relationships in which call centers are commonly involved. Other contractual relationships that call center managers may be a part of include everything from capital purchase contracts to janitorial services or vending.

The growth of outsourcing call center operations, technology and human resources functions have been driven by numerous factors, including:

- Efforts to increase profits by focusing internal efforts on core business functions and outsourcing functions outside of the organization's area of expertise.
- Desire to implement customer relationship management and other initiatives that require complex technologies with minimum risk and capital investment.
- The tight labor market and high call center turnover has resulted in some organizations abandoning their internal recruiting efforts and relying on staffing services to achieve hiring goals. These issues and the significant human resources requirements of call center operations have led some organizations to outsource operations in order to happily relinquish all employee hiring and ongoing management issues.

The decision to contract strategic components of the call center to an outside vendor requires serious consideration and a strong understanding of the issues involved.



### Call Center Outsourcing

With call center outsourcing, the organization (client) contracts for an outside vendor (outsourcer) to handle some or all of their customer interactions, e.g., telephone calls, email, text-chat. The organization contracts for call center facilities, technology, and staff or selected components. Outsourcing relationships typically fall into one of these two types of arrangements:

- **The entire call center operation is outsourced.** All call center staff are employed by the outsourcer and operations are typically located at the outsourcer's facility. The client directs the program objectives and measurements, while the outsourcer handles the daily management and supervision of the program. The hardware and software used may be provided by the outsourcer or, if specialized tools are needed, by the client.
- **Components of the client's call center operations are outsourced, while some call center functions are handled internally.** Common scenarios include:
    - Routine customer inquiries are outsourced; sales and customer service escalation are handled internally.

- Peak or seasonal overflow or after-hours contacts are outsourced, while the organization maintains an internal call center.
- New multichannel communications are outsourced; telephone and fax communications are handled internally.
- Technical assistance is outsourced, while the internal call center handles sales and general customer service.

**Identifying the Need for a Call Center Outsourcing Relationship**

Organizations have as many reasons to outsource as there are types of call center operations, but there are a number of common reasons that prompt organizations to determine their call center operations would run more efficiently and effectively if they were to outsource at least some of their activities. Some of these reasons are:

- The organization is looking for a way to more effectively manage customer relationships, does not have the customer relationship management experience internally, or does not want to engage in the effort and costs to acquire it.
- The outsourcer can provide greater access to call center industry expertise.
- Expansion in multichannel communication is planned and it is outside of the organization's area of expertise.
- Physical growth is restricted and more space is required to handle existing (or growing) interaction volume within service levels.
- Effective hiring, staffing or other human resource activities require more effort and cost than the organization is willing to expend.
- Erratic call arrival patterns, peak volume, special programs or other interaction fluctuations are not being, or cannot be handled, within service levels.
- Hours of operation cannot be expanded in current location and/or with current staff.
- The call center lacks the expertise to handle new call types, e.g., technical support issues, servicing of a new product, etc.
- Redundancy is desired to provide coverage during service interruptions, e.g., inclement weather, telephone or power outages, natural disasters.
- Additional language capabilities are required that are not available in the

organization's geographic area.

- Cost savings and reductions in internal resources are achieved by sharing the cost of agents, technology and management with the outsourcer's other clients.

**Technology Outsourcing**

Some organizations choose to contract with specialized vendors to handle technology requirements such as software development, customization or integration; hardware and telecommunications equipment or support; and consulting services in the call center. The level of expertise and the time and costs associated with developing, implementing and managing sophisticated call center technology tools (e.g., contact management software, workforce management packages and customer relationship management technology) have spurred high growth in the field of call center technology outsourcing. Different types of technology outsourcing include:

- **Purchasing technology tools from an outside vendor.** This allows the organization to dive into new and complex technology (such as live Web connectivity) without the burden of costly research and development. The organization may be able to use some applications "as is" while some may require extensive and costly customization and integration. Depending on business needs, budgeting and availability of human resources, the organization may choose to handle customization, integration, updates and ongoing maintenance internally or contract these activities to an outside vendor.
- **Using a vendor to develop proprietary software or customize off-the-shelf tools.** This can be an effective way to hire the specific expertise needed for development in a tight labor market or when the organization only needs the expertise for a finite period of time, while the software is being developed and implemented. After the initial implementation, the organization must then decide if they should hire the expertise needed to maintain the application or if they prefer to contract for that function, as well.
- **Accessing software through an application service provider (ASP), e.g., paying per transaction, per license, etc.** This eliminates many IT concerns regarding capital expenditures, installation, integration and ongoing maintenance and the human resources required to handle these functions.
- **Contracting with technology consultants and/or service providers to**

**manage specific purchases or oversee the entire information technology operation within the organization.**

### Identifying the Need for Call Center Technology Outsourcing

The technology requirements of a call center are complex and demand ongoing attention and vigilance to ensure the organization's technology needs are being adequately addressed. Most organizations have vendor relationships for the wide variety of products and services they use. The best combination of internal and external resources is unique to each organization. The balance between innovative solutions and cost effectiveness is critical. Drivers of technology outsourcing include:

- The desire to minimize the risk associated with technology investments, e.g., technology requires constant maintenance, frequent costly upgrades, no one knows how to use it, the vendor goes out of business, etc.
- A lack of expertise to manage technology internally, coupled with the reluctance to spend the time or money required.
- The decision to reduce the capital expenses.
- Selection and implementation timeframes are too aggressive to be handled by the organization.
- The outsourcer can provide greater access to call center industry expertise.

### Contract Staffing

Many call centers choose to contract with staffing agencies to identify and attract qualified job candidates. Typical contract staffing arrangements include:

- **Permanent placement:** The staffing agency handles all advertising and publicity and screens candidates using basic criteria (e.g., phone screen, testing). They may also handle other administrative tasks for the contracting party (e.g., reference or background checks, security clearance process). The call center handles face-to-face interviews and hiring decisions. A one-time fee is paid to the staffing agency, either at the time of hire or after a waiting period.
- **Temporary-to-permanent placement:** Candidates are initially hired as an employee of the staffing agency and contracted on a temporary basis to the organization. This arrangement dictates that within a certain period of time the employee will be hired by the organization

permanently, provided his or her performance meets expectations. The organization may participate in the interviewing and hiring decision or they may rely on the staffing agency to handle the hiring process from start to finish.

- **Contract workers:** Contract workers may be hired on an hourly, day-to-day or week-to-week basis to handle increased interaction volume, provide technology expertise or other call center functions. This gives the call center staffing flexibility (e.g., for seasonal increases, special programs) without the commitment and cost of hiring these employees on a permanent basis. Typically contract workers are hired for a finite period of time, though an employment contract can also be open-ended.
- **Co-sourcing arrangements (also called managed staffing arrangements):** An organization may also choose to run their call center within their physical location, but outsource the human resources management – including agents, management, supervisors and trainers – to a contract staffing company. The opposite arrangement also exists in which the organization provides the management and staffing, and the call center outsourcer provides the physical location and the technology.



### Identifying the Need for Contract Staffing

Along with technology issues, human resources concerns are one of the primary challenges that call center managers face. Creative use of contract staffing may be an effective way to address staffing issues when:

- The organization needs to hire a large number of employees within a short period, e.g., staffing for a product recall program that must be implemented quickly.
- Staffing needs fluctuate according to seasonal or other variations.
- The organization decides that supervisors and managers do not the time to handle recruiting and hiring activities.
- Local labor market does not produce the applicants required, e.g., in terms of availability or education level.
- Specialized skills are required, e.g., multilingual, industry certification, specialized degrees.
- The organization prefers to try out employees before hiring them permanently to address high turnover rates during training or the orientation period.

- Special projects require additional staffing to complete work that will be finished within a finite period of time, e.g., computer upgrades, software installation, customer relationship management implementation, training design.

### Co-sourcing

If you're considering whether to build a new call center or outsource, you might want to know about another new option called "co-sourcing." Co-sourcing is based on a partnership between the call center, which can use its own management and frontline staff, and the co-sourcer that furnishes the facilities and technology. Co-sourcers can also provide training and consulting services.

According to Valerie Godin, marketing director for Brucall, based in Brussels, and John Finnegan, managing director, Call Center Solutions (CCS) in Dublin, there are several benefits to co-sourcing, especially for startup call centers, which include:

- Minimizing investment in facilities and technology
- Minimizing risk in new startup or pilot project situations
- The ability to add capacity quickly
- Access to local expertise
- Support from the co-sourcing partner, which, besides consulting and training services, can include call center expertise for companies that do not have that capability in house

Co-sourcing is not for everyone. "In terms of in-house call centers – people who want to own their own buildings and technology as well as staff – they generally are not prepared to co-source or outsource," notes Finnegan.

Co-sourcing can be an effective solution to a variety of situations. It works well for:

- Startup companies looking to establish call center operations with minimum risk and investment.
- Companies that are starting a new activity and want to focus on serving customers rather than on setting up technology and facilities.
- Organizations entering specific national or regional markets, such as establishing a pan-European organization.

Excerpt from "'Co-Sourcing' Helps Startup Centers Minimize Risk, Add Flexibility" by Leslie Hansen Harps, *Call Center Management Review,* June 2000.

## 12. Components of Effective Contractual Agreements

Ready? | 1 | 2 | 3 |

### Key Points

- **The more effort an organization puts into identifying their specific requirements, objectives and measurements prior to beginning the process of vendor selection, the more efficient and effective the selection process will be.**
- **The following steps can help you determine the ideal contractual relationship:**
  1. **Conduct internal interviews**
  2. **Create a profile**
  3. **List qualifying criteria**
- **An effective contractual agreement establishes a mutual exchange of rights among parties.**
- **Components of effective contractual agreements include:**
  - **Describe the desired partnership**
  - **Identify the "must haves" of a contract**
  - **Develop clear terms and conditions**
  - **Develop clear cost expectations**
  - **Develop valid performance expectations**



### Explanation

Many organizations jump into the vendor selection process without taking the necessary steps to arm themselves with a clear definition of the desired relationship. This haphazard approach will result in wasted time and energy, reviewing proposals and interviewing vendors that do not meet the minimum criteria.

The more effort an organization puts into identifying their specific requirements, the more efficient and effective the selection process will be. A comprehensive list of appropriate criteria allows the organization to focus their efforts on the right pool of prospective vendors.

**Determining Outsourcing Criteria**

The following steps can help you determine the ideal contractual relationship:

1. **Conduct internal interviews:** Gather input from managers who will interact with the vendor and/or be affected by the scope of the contractual relationship. Ask questions such as: Should we contract with a vendor to develop a proprietary application or customize an existing tool? Do we want to hire new employees on a permanent basis or consider temporary options?

2. **Create a profile:** Construct a generic profile of your ideal supplier based on the information gathered from internal interviews and management's consensus. The best way to ensure you identify the right vendor is to base your decision on the right criteria.

3. **List qualifying criteria:** Make a list of criteria vendors must meet to qualify as a candidate for your business. For instance, you may require that a technology vendor have experience with a certain vertical industry, that a staffing agency be able to interview candidates at your location or that an outsourcer have experience handling email contacts. This list will serve as the basis for your initial research and qualifying interviews.



**Components of Effective Contractual Agreements**

A contractual agreement establishes a mutual exchange of rights among parties. Components of effective contractual agreements include:

- **Describe the desired partnership:** Create a statement that outlines the essential details of the desired relationship. If you are planning on outsourcing your entire call center operation, for instance, the type of relationship will differ from the partnership you expect from a more limited engagement. For example, a description of a full-service arrangement could be expressed as "to engage with a full-service outsourcer to handle all aspects of our current operations." A description of a more limited arrangement may be "to find an outsourcer well versed in pharmaceutical to manage our recall program for six months while we ramp up our internal call center."

- **Identify the "must haves" of a contract:** You will save time during the selection process by quickly eliminating vendors that do not meet the organization's essential requirements. For example, if you must have a vendor that is able to visit your location on short notice, the contractual criteria should include a requirement that the vendor be located nearby. If you require a vendor that can provide you multilingual candidates, this should be included in the "must haves."

- **Develop clear terms and conditions:** Along with your "must haves," terms and conditions will serve to clearly communicate your requirements to prospective vendors. For example, if you require staffing agencies to use specific testing software for candidate selection, that should be specified.

- **Develop clear cost expectations:** It can be difficult to determine the comparative value of vendor pricing and cost structures For instance, one call center outsourcer may charge a per transaction fee and include management, training and recruiting in those costs. Another vendor may charge a per hour cost for each agent, manager, trainer and recruiter. It is important to determine your budget for the entire project and your pricing preferences prior to agreeing to a vendor's pricing structure. Consider the following fees prior to determining the structure that is most beneficial for your organization:

| Call Center Outsourcing | Technology Outsourcing | Contract Staffing |
|---|---|---|
| • Monthly base charges (per transaction, per hour)<br>• Labor<br>• Set-up programming and connectivity<br>• Ongoing programming and connectivity<br>• Long distance and other telecom fees<br>• Administrative fees (training, supervision, project management)<br>• Cost of reports, including customization<br>• Incentives and promotions | • Monthly base charges (per transaction, per hour)<br>• Software, hardware<br>• Implementation and integration<br>• Support and maintenance<br>• Upgrades | • Upfront fees<br>• Advertising costs<br>• One-time fee for permanent hire<br>• Hourly rate for contract and temp-to-perm<br>• Vacation and holiday pay<br>• Termination refunds<br>• Replacement costs |

- **Develop valid performance expectations:** While most vendors have a list of performance objectives that are commonly adopted by their clients, objectives specific to your organization's needs should be developed. Consider the following objectives in determining those appropriate for your mission:

*(continued, next page)*

| Call Center Outsourcing | Technology Outsourcing | Contract Staffing |
|---|---|---|
| • Call (or contact) quality<br>• First-call resolution<br>• Service level/response time<br>• Abandoned and blocked calls<br>• Productivity<br>• Revenue, cross-sell, upsell<br>• Customer satisfaction<br>• Conversion rates<br>• Program implementation<br>• Turnaround time | • Program implementation timelines<br>• Service level<br>• System performance and availability<br>• Support response time<br>• Turnaround time | • Fill ratio<br>• Applicant availability<br>• Candidate quality<br>• Response time, timeliness<br>• Turnover |

## 13. Legal Issues Surrounding Contractual Relationships

Ready? | 1 | 2 | 3 |

### Key Points

- **Legal issues to be considered when engaging in contractual relationships include:**
  - **The vendor selection process**
  - **Confidentiality**
  - **Accountability**
  - **Pricing agreements**
  - **Performance agreements**
  - **Provisions for termination**
- **There are two basic contract principles that will provide legal protection and allow flexibility and growth in the outsourcing relationship:**
  1. **Formulate a contract with specific requirements**
  2. **Build in flexibility to adjust these requirements as the business environment changes**



### Explanation

In today's regulated and litigious business environment it's important to take contractual relationships seriously. Legal issues to be considered when engaging in contractual relationships include:

- **The vendor selection process:** The vendor selection process should be free of bias, e.g., racial or gender discrimination. Every effort should be taken to ensure that the process is designed to consider vendors on the basis of relevant competencies. Remember that within the contractual relationship the legal document sets the mutual exchange of rights among the parties.
- **Confidentiality:** Due to the specific nature of the selection process, the organization will inevitably need to share confidential information. Binding confidentiality agreements are recommended whenever vendors are given access to sensitive information, e.g., employee and customer records, product and service information.
- **Accountability:** The contract and ongoing documentation should clearly

state who is accountable for what activities. It is imperative that all parties keep accurate records of any deviation from this agreement. In the event that any part of the work product is contested, these records may be invaluable. For instance, if a technology outsourcer fails to deliver their product within the contracted timeframe, they may counter that the client failed to provide them with the product specifications on time.

- **Pricing agreements:** The vendor's pricing agreement should be clear and comprehensive, detailing all costs associated with the project scope. The contracting organization may include a provision that allows for termination of the contract in the event that unanticipated costs are added after the agreement is signed.
- **Performance agreements:** Both parties need to negotiate appropriate incentives and penalties. For example, an organization may incorporate into the contract the option to add or subtract work from the outsourcer based on performance.
- **Provisions for termination:** The contract should clearly state the length of the agreement and requirements for termination by either party. For example, a contract between an organization and a call center outsourcer may state that the contract may be cancelled within 60 days notice with no penalty.



### Flexibility and Growth in Contractual Relationships

The internal and external business environment will likely change over the course of the contract. There are two basic contract principles that will provide legal protection and allow flexibility and growth in the outsourcing relationship:

1. **Formulate a contract with specific requirements.** Contracts should be detailed and address all relevant components of the agreement, along with responsibilities and timelines. When possible, include all collateral sales materials, correspondence, emails, promises and claims made by the vendor as part of the contract. Many organizations overlook the most obvious elements when they fail to include basic requirements, objectives and measurements.

2. **Build in flexibility to adjust these requirements as the business environment changes.** The initial contract is a set of assumptions that may not be relevant throughout the lifetime of the partnership. The contract must include the ability to change service levels, increase or decrease the

scope of the project, and retarget critical elements of the relationship on a regular basis. A termination clause should be included in the event that adjustments are not acceptable.

## 14. Qualifying Vendors and Writing the Request for Proposal

Ready? | 1 | 2 | 3 |

### Key Points

- The Request for Proposal (RFP) or Request for Information (RFI) is similar to an employment interview. The purpose is to ask questions that will uncover the prospective provider's competencies and determine if they are a fit for your organization's requirements.
- The written RFP should include the following components:
  1. Overview
  2. Vendor instructions
  3. Organization and call center information
  4. A comprehensive list of questions about the organization
  5. Pricing forms
  6. Request for client references
  7. Collateral material
- Qualifying vendors to participate in the RFP process can be the most complex component of the selection process. Casting a wide net through the careful review of multiple sources is recommended to ensure that a broad range of vendors is considered during the preliminary stages.
- To qualify vendors best-suited to be included in the selection process:
  - Research the industry
  - Draft and send a pre-RFP qualifying checklist
  - Conduct telephone interviews
  - Create a matrix to compare provider qualifications



### Explanation

Using the qualifying requirements previously gathered (e.g., ideal vendor profile, contract "must haves," terms and conditions, and costs and performance expectations), the organization can create a Request for Proposal (RFP) or Request for Information (RFI).

### Writing the RFP

The RFP is similar to an employment interview. The purpose is to ask questions that will uncover the prospective provider's competencies and determine if they are a fit for your organization's requirements. Additionally, the organization takes the opportunity to introduce itself to the prospective provider.

The RFP should include the following components:

1. **Overview:** Describe your organization, its customer contact history and the type of product or service your organization needs. Include the overall RFP project timetable including the expected dates for receipt of proposals, outsourcer selection and implementation. This information may be explained in a pre-RFP checklist and telephone interview, but should also be included in the RFP.

2. **Vendor instructions:** Directions should be given as to:

   - How you expect the vendor to respond (e.g., line by line, no references to sales collateral, all questions must be answered within the document)
   - When written responses are due
   - When vendor presentations/interviews will be held
   - When you will select the vendor
   - When you want the technology to be implemented
   - Key contact information
   - Number of copies of the proposal required

   The instructions should include a "right to reject" disclaimer, which informs the recipient that even if they meet all the requirements, the call center reserves the right to reject their response and select the vendor of their choice.

3. **Organization and call center information:** While the RFP is often viewed as an opportunity for vendors to impress prospective clients, it should also be used to showcase your desirability as a client. Proactively ask the vendor to consider a partnership with you and explain to them how they will benefit from the relationship. Include information that will help vendors better understand the organization and its needs.

4. **A comprehensive list of questions about the organization:** The heart of the RFP/RFI is the list of questions the prospective vendor will answer. Suggested questions cover:

| Call Center Outsourcing | Technology Outsourcing | Contract Staffing |
|---|---|---|
| • Vertical industry experience<br>• Horizontal application experience<br>• Recruiting and hiring practices<br>• Training and development programs<br>• Monitoring and coaching<br>• Supervision and management<br>• Technology solutions<br>• Financial viability<br>• Startup and ongoing costs<br>• Implementation timelines<br>• Call center locations | • Vertical industry experience<br>• Application experience<br>• Training services<br>• Implementation process<br>• Integration capabilities<br>• Customization capabilities<br>• Support services<br>• Financial viability<br>• Startup and ongoing costs | • Vertical industry experience<br>• Recruiting and hiring practices<br>• Testing and screening capabilities<br>• Success rates<br>• Fee structure |

5. **Pricing forms:** Create a detailed pricing form for the vendors to complete. It should include base prices as well as components or features that are optional.

6. **A request for client references:** Ask vendors for the contact information of at least three current clients to serve as references for the vendor's performance.

7. **Collateral material:** Ask vendors to include product and sales collateral material.

Requiring candidates to respond in a standard electronic format can make the responses easier for the organization to compare. Ask prospective vendors to send any additional information they wish to include separately, e.g., case studies, competency details outside the scope of what is requested, etc. Allow vendors enough time to complete their responses and keep track of all communication between the organization and the vendors.

### Qualifying Vendors

Organizations should be cautioned against relying on too few or biased sources to determine the recipients of the RFP. Casting a wide net through the careful review of multiple sources is recommended to ensure a broad range of vendors is considered during the preliminary stages. To identify the vendors to include in the selection process:

1. **Research the industry:** Search industry publications and contact client and industry professionals for service providers that may match your needs. Screen out vendors that you determine do not meet your needs.

2. **Draft and send a pre-RFP qualifying checklist:** This short document asks the vendor to complete a brief checklist that outlines your "must haves." Providers who meet all the initial criteria should be the vendors to focus on during the formal RFP processes.

3. **Conduct telephone interviews:** Contact your list of prospective suppliers with additional questions. These short interviews should focus on basic qualifying questions such as: With what types of recruiting are you most familiar? What kind of support do you offer for your products? What are your program implementation capabilities?

4. **Create a matrix to compare provider qualifications:** List your RFP questions along with each vendor's response in a matrix. Determine how many prospective vendors you will consider and formulate a short list of the top candidates who will receive the RFP.

**Vendor Selection**

A traditional method of comparing vendors is through the use of weighted criteria, or a scorecard, as illustrated in the following example. The criteria are determined and then weighted by distributing 100 points according to the importance of each item. Finally, a scale is used to evaluate each vendor's abilities to meet the criteria.

*(continued, next page)*

Scale: 1 = to a very little extent, 2 = to some extent, 3 = to a great extent, 4 = to a very great extent

**Example Vendor Evaluation**

| Criteria | Weight | X | Ratings | = | | Score |
|---|---|---|---|---|---|---|
| Product features | 10 | 1 | 2 | (3) | 4 | 30 |
| Initial costs | 5 | 1 | 2 | (3) | 4 | 15 |
| Ongoing costs | 10 | 1 | 2 | 3 | (4) | 40 |
| Usability | 10 | 1 | 2 | (3) | 4 | 30 |
| Experience with industry | 5 | 1 | (2) | 3 | 4 | 10 |
| Account team | 2 | 1 | 2 | 3 | (4) | 8 |
| Support capabilities | 10 | 1 | (2) | 3 | 4 | 20 |
| Implementation timeframe | 8 | 1 | 2 | 3 | (4) | 32 |
| Training services | 10 | 1 | 2 | 3 | (4) | 40 |
| Integration capabilities | 10 | 1 | 2 | 3 | (4) | 40 |
| Customization capabilities | 10 | 1 | 2 | 3 | (4) | 40 |
| Financial viability | 10 | 1 | 2 | 3 | (4) | 40 |
| Totals | 100 | | | | | 345 |

To determine the score of each vendor, the weighted amount is multiplied by the rating for each item. All of the scores are added together to get each vendor's total evaluation. The vendor with the highest score is typically awarded the project.

### Selection Perfection

Should you decide that outsourcing is right for your organization, consider the following steps to assist you in selecting a specific service bureau that will meet your specific budget and service requirements:

**Step 1 — Design an RFP (request for proposal).** Make sure that your RFP describes the nature of the venture and exactly what you are looking for from the service bureau, including agent skill sets, specific service level objectives, technology requirements, reporting capabilities and previous experience with your account type. Think of the RFP as a job description, but more in depth. To ensure the best match, include in the RFP such information as forecasted outsource volumes by hour of day and day of week; average call length; and even agent incentive strategies that work at your existing center.

Be sure to ask each candidate to provide you with a list of their existing call center clients, including contact information, as well as information on the bureau's fees and other additional charges. Ask specifically for information on monthly base charges, programming and connectivity costs, telephone usage costs and labor costs.

**Step 2 — Review returned RFPs and narrow down the candidates.** Select proposals that are complete, concise and meet your minimum specifications. Check out the agency's references. While it is unusual for service bureaus to give you contacts who will provide bad references, you can always read between the lines if you ask the right questions: "How productive are they now compared to when you first started doing business with them?" "If you could have the agency improve in any area, what would it be?" etc. Take careful notes during your interviews.

**Step 3 — Conduct a phone interview.** Call each service bureau that survives the initial weeding-out process. Have a list of detailed questions prepared and listen to how well the representatives of each service bureau represent themselves. Their tone of voice and the manner in which they conduct themselves is often representative of the kind of performance you can expect from their agency once it begins handling calls from your customers. Narrow your list down again to two or three finalists.

**Step 4 — Visit the service bureau and monitor its agents.** Visit the finalists' operations to get a strong feel for how they manage. Speak with their IT department, project managers and quality control supervisors to evaluate their abilities and willingness to handle your center's calls effectively and efficiently.

Ask to monitor as many agents and calls as possible to help determine the level of skill of the agency's phone staff. Some agencies may tell you that they have a privacy clause with their call center clients and thus can not allow you to monitor calls. If this occurs, ask the agency to request special permission for you to conduct your call evaluations. If the agency has a good relationship with its client, and your company is not a competitive threat to the client, this request will usually be granted. Eliminate any service bureaus that either refuse to let you monitor agents or refuse to ask clients for permission to monitor. Such agencies are likely to be hiding something. Even if they're not, you can't truly evaluate a service bureau without watching them in action.

**Step 5 — Select a service bureau and negotiate the contract.** By now you should have enough information to choose the right agency — if any — for your company based on affordability, performance and cultural compatibility.

Carefully negotiate your contract, ensuring that the agency's rates, set-up fees and terms are consistent with what was stated in the RFP. If the agency really wants your business and feels it will be a long-term venture, you will have more negotiating power.

Put all of your performance requirements in writing, and include a clause that permits you to terminate the contract without stipulations in the event that the agency doesn't perform up to your standards. Keep in mind that most service bureaus don't want such a clause in the agreement; they prefer a 30-90 day notice. If the agency is not willing to budge on these terms and if you do not have an alternative agency as a back up, try to negotiate a lower fee arrangement during the ramp-up time. If these negotiations fail, it may be back to the drawing board to find another service provider.

Excerpt from "A Concise Guide to Outsourcing Success" by Kathy Sisk, *Call Center Management Review*, October 1999.

# 15. Principles of Effective Negotiation

Ready? | 1 | 2 | 3 |



## Key Points

- **Effective negotiation skills are critical for all call center professionals because of the variety and number of groups – internal and external – with which they deal.**
- **Effective negotiators:**
  - **Understand each party's views, not just their own**
  - **Establish a framework for addressing the issues**
  - **Resolve real or perceived negative behavior**
  - **Build trust**
- **The four basic categories of negotiation tactics are:**
  - **Collaboration**
  - **Competition**
  - **Compromise**
  - **Avoidance**

## Explanation

Effective negotiation requires empathy, effort and understanding of negotiation principles. Effective negotiation skills are critical for all call center professionals because of the variety and number of groups – internal and external – with which they deal.

Effective negotiators practice the following principles:

- **Understand each party's views, not just their own:** They recognize that successful agreements must satisfy all parties' needs and that reaching agreement does not necessarily mean "compromise."
- **Establish a framework for addressing the issues:** This involves establishing a structured process that should include problem definition, timing, decision criteria, communications protocols, and so on.
- **Resolve real or perceived negative behavior:** This can include behaviors such as refusing to abandon self-serving positions, criticizing people, issuing threats or focusing too much on problems without offering alternatives.

- **Build trust:** Communicating clearly, listening actively, acknowledging problems or issues, honoring commitments and working constructively all contribute to an environment of trust.

**Negotiation Approaches**

There are four basic approaches to negotiation:

- **Collaboration (win-win):** This approach places an equal importance on all concerns, i.e., the goals, the outcome and the relationship. It seeks to satisfy all parties in the negotiation. It is most appropriate when the parties desire to maintain a lasting working relationship.
- **Compromise (lose-win):** If the relationship is more important than the short-term goal, the negotiator may adopt this approach. He or she may lose on short-term issues, but will benefit from the cooperative relationship that is developed. The compromise tactic is often used when an agreement is needed quickly or specific issues are not worth the time it would take to gain approval for the case.
- **Competition (win-lose):** If the negotiator is focused on short-term goals and places little importance on the relationship, then he or she may adopt this approach. This approach has been described as "playing hardball," and minimizes the importance of the other party's point of view. It may be appropriate when concessions are unacceptable or the other party will take advantage of other negotiation styles.
- **Avoidance:** This approach is used by parties that do not wish to come to an agreement. Specific issues are often ignored completely and stalling may be the ultimate objective. Avoidance is sometimes used when a negotiator feels he or she would make more progress at a later time, e.g., when the other party has cooled off or circumstances have changed.

**Stages of Negotiation**

The basic stages of a typical negotiation include:

- **Collect data and information:** Effectiveness in this stage will depend on factors such as the breadth and depth of thoroughness, diligence, and accuracy.
- **State your position:** Effectiveness in this stage will depend on factors such as clarity, logic, understanding and reasonableness.
- **Make concessions and take concessions:** Effectiveness in this stage will

depend on factors such as degree of knowledge of each party's views and needs, the importance each negotiator places on the outcome vs. the relationship, the communications skills of each party and the level of knowledge and experience of each party. A counter offer is the term used for requesting changes after a contract offer has been made.

- **Close and carry out:** Effectiveness in this stage will depend on factors such as clarity of common understanding, understanding of solution(s) and outcome, documentation, commitment.

**The Role of Power**

Power plays an important role in negotiation. Yet, it is often misunderstand. According to professional negotiators, true power comes from:

- Possessing accurate information
- Excellent communications skills
- Personal integrity and reputation
- Control over the agenda
- The ability to 'walk away'
- Knowledge of precedents



Effective negotiation requires both an understanding of the science of negotiation and a intuitive understanding of human nature.

**Negotiation Pointers**

If a negotiation is a test, this is the one-page cheat sheet you're allowed to bring with you. Thorough preparation and practice are the real keys to success. But a little memory jog when you're under pressure never hurt either. Below are some of the most powerful pointers we've discovered. Put them in your pocket.

1. **Your power lies in your walk-away alternatives.** Make sure that you have real, viable options that don't require an agreement:
   - You'll be empowered to support your interests.
   - Your confident attitude will compel others to listen to and meet your interests. They'll realize that they have to if they intend to obtain agreement.
2. **Do not disclose your walk-away alternatives.** When you remind others of the options you have should they not acceptably satisfy your needs, your commitment to negotiation falls into question, and the environment becomes hostile. This draws the attention away from underlying needs, and the climate becomes less conducive to the development of creative options.

**3. Figure out the walk-away alternatives of the other parties.** Knowing what options they have if no agreement is reached will help you construct options that are favorable relative to their specific negotiation. In other words, you'll be able to construct an agreement that improves on their alternatives without giving away too much.

**4. No offer is too high.** Any offer is valid provided you can present objective criteria that prove each term of the offer fills to some extent the underlying needs of all parties.

**5. Don't react emotionally.** When you encounter tactics intended to intimidate, rush, draw out discussions, or otherwise derail the focus from underlying needs and mutual gain, patiently react to the problem at hand. The discussion needs to be refocused. Draw attention back to substantive interests and options that fairly address those interests. Use personal attacks as a signal that it's time to reestablish everyone's commitment to a mutually beneficial outcome.

**6. Remember that all the needs presented are not of equal importance.** Focus time on building an understanding of which needs are most likely to influence the outcome. Strive to create options that satisfy those interests.

**7. Listen more than you talk.** As a listener, you are gathering information that can help you figure out which of the other side's needs must be met for an agreement to be considered acceptable, and to what degree those needs will have to be met. Listening gives you the advantage. The better your understanding, the more flexibility and creativity you'll have as you create options. Talking gives this advantage to the other side.

**8. Know the authority of each person in the room.** Make sure you know whether or not you are negotiating with someone empowered to make the final decision. If you aren't, make sure you present options in such a way that they meet the perceived needs of the negotiator and the other members of their organization.

**9. Analyze concessions.** Look for patterns in the types of concessions made by the other parties, and be attentive to the messages sent by your concessions:

- Small concessions give the impression that the bottom line is not far off.
- Large concessions indicate that a lot more can still be conceded before the bottom line is reached.
- Rapid or large concessions undermine the credibility of the initial offer.
- All concessions teach the lesson that more concessions will be made.

**10. Never be bludgeoned into splitting the difference.** When an apparent impasse has been reached, splitting the difference is widely regarded as the ultimate fair solution. Splitting the difference rarely results in an outcome that surpasses anyone's expectations, and it does not ensure that the interests of all parties are satisfied.

Excerpt from "Powerful Tips: A Quick Reference Guide" by Batna.com, The Negotiation Resource Center.

This item was developed with Henry Dortmans and Mike Dunne of Angus Dortmans Associates Inc.

## 16. Developing Service Level Agreements

Ready? | 1 | 2 | 3 |

### Key Points

- Traditionally, service level agreements (SLAs) have been tools that define the performance expectations between a service bureau and client company. Increasingly, however, SLAs are also used to identify and describe requirements between departments or call center groups within an organization, and establish agreements to ensure that key commitments are met.
- Typical components of a service level agreement include:
  - Products supported
  - Services provided
  - Service level and response time objectives
  - Hours of operation
  - Response time objectives for ancillary work
  - Abandoned call objectives
  - First-call resolution
  - Quality procedures and standards
  - Reporting requirements and timelines
  - Planning and management methodologies
  - Disaster recovery expectations and procedures
- To be effective, any SLA must:
  - Identify the services to be provided, along with expectations and key dependencies among parties
  - Ensure that the major resources/costs required to meet objectives are understood
  - Provide concrete objectives against which to measure performance
  - Establish an ongoing process for communicating results
  - Establish the repercussions should objectives not be met

### Explanation

As any call center manager soon learns first hand, it takes a lot of collaboration, both among parties within and outside the organization, to ensure that operations run smoothly. As services have become more complex, these interdependencies have both proliferated and become more critical. Given the time-sensitive nature of call centers, when communication breaks down or commitments are not met, ensuing problems can ripple through the organization and bring call center services to a standstill.

Understandably, effective call center managers put much focus on ensuring that the call center is getting the support it requires. Traditionally, service level agreements (SLAs) have been agreements that define the performance expectations between a service bureau and client company. Increasingly, however, SLAs are also used to identify and describe requirements between departments or call center groups within an organization, and establish agreements to ensure that key commitments are met.



### Components of a Service Level Agreement

There is often confusion surrounding the terms SLA and service level. Service level is a specific measure that refers to the objective of answering "X percent of calls in Y seconds." SLAs, on the other hand, are broader in nature and touch on all significant areas of performance. Usually, a service level objective is an important element of an SLA, but does not comprise all or even most of the agreement.

Typical components of an SLA (presented here in the context of a traditional service bureau/client relationship) include:

- **Products supported:** This section of the SLA specifies the client organization's products and services that are covered by the contract.
- **Services provided:** This section itemizes the services that will be delivered, e.g., sales and support of specified products, technical support of those products, channels provided, etc.
- **Service level and response time objectives:** Itemizes the specific service level objectives for those transactions that must be handled when they arrive and response time objectives for transactions that do not have to be handled when they arrive.
- **Hours of operation:** The days of week and times of day that operations will provide services. Whether or not operations will be open for specific holidays should also be addressed.
- **Response time objectives for ancillary work:** Specifies the timeframes in which work that is not directly related to handling contacts will be

completed, e.g., updating online resources with new information or updates to customer records.

- **Abandoned call objectives:** Specifies the target abandoned rate, often between two to four percent. (Note: Abandonment should not be used as a strict standard, because it is driven by customer behavior which cannot be directly controlled by the call center; nonetheless, abandonment is influenced by service levels and is often set as a general guideline.)
- **First-call resolution:** This is the objective for the percentage of calls that do not require any further contacts to address the caller's reason for calling (calls resolved upon initial contact ÷ total calls), e.g., 85 percent.
- **Quality procedures and standards:** This general category varies widely from one SLA to the next, but is nonetheless important to a successful relationship. It can include such things as monitoring methods and frequency, statistical methods for analyzing reports, training to be provided, etc.
- **Reporting requirements and timelines:** Identifies the reports that will be produced, e.g., on sales, service levels, first call resolution, etc., the formats required, and when and how reports will be delivered.
- **Planning and management methodologies:** Specifies such things as the methods by which forecasting data will be pulled into planning, how agent groups will be set up and managed, and minimum staff-to-supervisor and supervisor-to-manager ratios.
- **Disaster recovery expectations and procedures:** Outlines plans for preventing and recovering from service outages, and specifies the backup network services in place, staffing contingency plans (i.e., in the event of storms or system problems), power backup, etc. This should also include emergency escalation procedures.

In short, well-defined service level agreements help clarify expectations, open communication and overcome concerns about the quality of work that will be provided. The most effective SLAs will coordinate the process both contractually by establishing the rights and expectations of both parties, and procedurally by laying the ground rules for operations (e.g., the objectives, quality standards, and planning and management methodologies).

**Basic Requirements**

The components of an SLA can vary widely, especially outside the realm of a service bureau/client environment. For example, the call center may establish an SLA with an internal group tasked with providing technical support to the call center, or with departments that provide associated customer services (e.g., financing or billing services). Nonetheless, to be effective, any SLA must:

- Identify the services to be provided, along with expectations and key dependencies among parties
- Ensure that the major resources/costs required to meet objectives are understood
- Provide concrete objectives against which to measure performance
- Establish an ongoing process for communicating results
- Establish the repercussions should objectives not be met

**Preventing Problems**

While SLAs offer great potential for establishing and clarifying performance expectations, they can backfire. Problems with the SLAs are often the result of assumptions that are not well defined or a lack of understanding of call center principles. Examples include:

- **Objectives in contention:** For example, both service level and abandoned rates are often included in SLAs, but they are rarely in sync. A service level of 90% in 10 seconds is relatively aggressive, and in most environments will never be met if the organization is managing to an abandoned rate objective of 5%.
- **Not fully defining objectives:** For instance, telephone service levels can almost always be met by "busying out" enough trunks so that queue size will always remain small. To help clarify the objective, it may be best to put another objective in place – in this case, percent busy.
- **No definition around calculations:** Some managers assume that service level is service level, first-call resolution is first-call resolution and so on. But the assumptions built into calculations can vary widely. For instance, the top ACD manufacturers use four different calculations for service level, and some organizations further customize these defaults. To avoid interpretation problems, SLAs should spell out the specific calculations to be used. (Performance measures are covered in detail in ICMI's *Call Center Operations Management Handbook and Study Guide.*)
- **No "teeth" in the SLAs:** What happens if objectives are not met – or if objectives are exceeded? The SLAs should clearly spell out applicable

penalties and incentives. If the SLA is between organizations, it's also important to ensure that the requirements and implications spelled out in the SLA are legally sound, and that they are aligned with other contracts that may be in place.

- **Agreements that are one-sided:** Client organizations want outsourcers to take ownership for producing results, but it's rare that an outsourcer can take complete responsibility. What happens when a marketing program is not communicated effectively and workload is 25% over projections? Exceptions should be noted in the SLAs for those situations that nullify certain objectives.



### Education and Communication

An important prerequisite to avoiding these problems is to ensure that managers both inside and outside the call center have a basic understanding of how call centers operate. Decisions based on little more than common sense can damage the call center and the organization it supports. This involves education around several key issues, including:

- The time-sensitive nature of the call center, and unique planning and management requirements.
- The financial implications of specific objectives. An abandoned rate objective of 1/2 percent sounds impressive, but decision-makers need to understand that aggressive goals result in higher costs. The cost may be worth it, but this needs to be understood by all parties.
- The need to keep the call center abreast of changes and developments, e.g., marketing plans, new products and services, changes in policies. Forecast and staffing scenarios are effective in illustrating the need for planning accuracy.

As straightforward as these issues may seem, don't assume everyone has the same understanding of their importance. A little education upfront goes a long way. (See Unique Operational Dynamics, Section 5.)

Further, a lack of attention to details can cause a service level agreement to provide little or no value to either party. Actual results should be reported regularly and compared to objectives. Further, written reports should not be the only form of communication. The organizations or departments involved should have regular planning and review meetings to discuss performance and ensure that expectations and results are met – and to identify improvement opportunities. With the right amount of attention to detail, the SLAs will help drive performance activities that will meet program goals.

(A similar discussion on SLAs, in the traditional context of service bureau and client, can be found in ICMI's *Call Center Operations Management Handbook and Study Guide.*)

## 17. Maintaining Effective Outsourcing Partnerships

Ready? | 1 | 2 | 3 |

### Key Points

- Continuous and open communication is key to a successful outsourcing relationship.
- Each organization involved in the relationship should assign a liaison as the primary point of contact. In mission-critical partnerships, these persons should meet on a regular basis.
- Potential considerations/challenges to having service bureaus handle part or all of the organization's contacts include:
  - Quality concerns
  - Control issues
  - Cost
- An important element of an outsourcing partnership is an escalation policy. This policy defines the categories of escalation, the types of issues that fall into each category and the appropriate response.



### Explanation

Continuous and open communication is key to a successful outsourcing relationship. This communication can be both formal and informal with expectations clearly identified in the outsourcing agreement. It is important that this communication focus on the measures outlined in the agreement and be flexible enough to include the exchange of new ideas and initiatives.

Each organization involved in the relationship should assign a liaison as the primary point of contact. In mission-critical partnerships, these persons should meet on a regular basis. These liaisons are typically tasked with communicating results to others in the organization and ensuring the consistency and accuracy of the information exchanged.

When selecting an outsourcer for call center services, it is important to choose a partner with a similar organizational culture. The outsourcer will be communicating directly to your organization's customers. If the outsourcer's culture and values are different, customers may receive an undesirable image of your organization.

The outsourcer's culture will also influence the effectiveness of management communication. For example, if your organization has a more informal management structure, you may be frustrated by an outsourcer with a more bureaucratic approach.

**Considerations/Challenges**

There are a number of potential considerations/challenges to having service bureaus handle part or all of the organization's contacts, including:

- **Quality concerns:** If calls cannot be handled successfully except by expert agents or if the organization does not have solid processes and documentation in place, it will be difficult for a service bureau to match the quality of in-house staff. Similarly, organizations that have robust training processes for their own call center staff will be more likely to transfer those skills to service bureaus.
- **Control issues:** Turning your customers over to someone else inevitably reduces the amount of control you have over how those customers are treated. Service bureau contracts can provide elaborate detail specifying how the operation will be run, but in the end, you either manage the call center in-house or give up some degree of control. An important factor to consider, however, is the degree of control current call center management actually has. A competent service bureau may offer better processes and control.
- **Cost:** Depending on the variables, either solution may prove to be the most cost-effective. Setup costs, internal costs to manage the service bureau relationship, travel costs to the service bureau site, and the costs of keeping the service bureau up-to-date with the organization's plans and market must be considered.

**Managing the Venture**

Once you select your service bureau and the contract is signed, the real challenges begin! The following practices will help you effectively manage your outsourcing venture:

1. **Take control from the start.** Assign a management team from within your call center/organization to oversee the outsourcing venture and to openly communicate with the service bureau on a regular basis. This includes selecting the specific account management team at the agency that will manage your account. Some call centers opt to have one or more of their managers work onsite at the service bureau to closely supervise activity on a daily basis. Remember: the people calling the service bureau are your valued

*(continued, next page)*

customers; take whatever steps you need to ensure that the outsourcing venture remains transparent to them and that they receive the best possible service.

2. **Provide/oversee all training.** Your company is responsible for ensuring that the supervisory staff and agents at the service bureau receive all training necessary to handle your specific account. Have your management team or internal trainers educate the agency's supervisors/trainers on your products and services, upselling/cross-selling preferences, call scripts, incentives, etc. The agency's staff can then deliver the same training to its agents, under your supervision. Or you may want your own managers/trainers to provide such training to agents.

3. **Evaluate the agency's performance regularly.** Ensure that the service bureau sends your management team regular reports on call statistics, agent performance and customer feedback, and that the management team provides the bureau's managers and/or agents with any necessary feedback/additional training. In addition, have your management team visit the service bureau often and get directly involved in the monitoring process. Don't be afraid to request that a particular agent or supervisor be removed from your account if you are not satisfied with their performance.

Excerpt from "A Concise Guide to Outsourcing Success" by Kathy Sisk, *Call Center Management Review*, October 1999.



## Escalation

An important element of an outsourcing partnership is an escalation policy. This policy defines the categories of escalation, the types of issues that fall into each category and the appropriate response. This must be defined ahead of time so that you are prepared for crises when they occur.

### Example Escalation Policy from Zhone Technologies

**Escalation Policy**

Zhone escalation policies ensure that your critical issue receives attention. We measure response time, notify key management of the status of unresolved calls, and escalate problems to the right engineers to ensure customer satisfaction. The following matrix defines priority as well as the escalation guidelines that Zhone will follow when addressing technical support problems reported by the customer.

**Priority will have three possible values:**

**Network Down:** Service platform is down or not functioning. Customer is at risk of losing major business due to network impairment. Customer and Zhone are willing to commit dedicated resources around the clock until the issue is resolved or downgraded.

**Major Service Impact:** Major service interruption or loss of functionality. Customer feels this issue should be addressed as soon as possible. Possible loss of business if issue is not resolved soon

**Minor/No Service Impact:** Customer would like to see this issue resolved but the issue is not time critical, involving aesthetic changes or documentation changes.

**Escalation Matrix**

| Severity/Notification | Network Down (Critical) | Major Outage (Major) | Minor Outage (Minor) |
|---|---|---|---|
| Support Manager Notified | Immediate | 30 minutes | 4 hours |
| Support Director Notified | 15 minutes | 1 hour | Weekly |
| Account Manager/SE Notified* | 15 minutes | 1 hour | As necessary |
| VP GSS, VPGM, VP Eng, and VP Sales Notified* | 30 minutes | 4 hours | As necessary |
| CEO, CTO Notified* | 4 hours | Same day | As necessary |

*Voicemail updates as necessary for all network down and major outages

Excerpt from www.zhone.com.

# Business Management Principles and Practices

## Exercises

### Definitions of Strategic Business Plan and Related Terms

1. Complete the diagram with the following four phrases.

Annual operating plans

Customer access strategy

Operational model and/or strategic business plan

Overall strategy and objectives

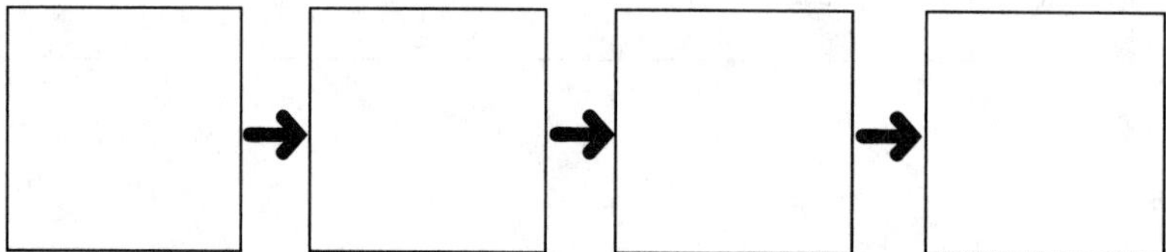

### Developing an Effective Strategic Business Plan [Strategic]

2. Select the most appropriate answer to each question.

Principles of effective organizational design include all of the following EXCEPT:

a. Agent groups form the foundation of call center structure

b. Structure facilitates branding

c. Support positions are enablers

d. The organization's structure should drive its mission and strategy

The strategic business plan broadly outlines which of the following aspects of call center technologies:

I. Expected payback

II. Summary of current capabilities

III. The vision of future capabilities

IV. Timeframes and general project plans for upgrades or changes

a. II and III only

b. II, III and IV only

c. I, II and III only

d. I, II, III and IV

**Managing and Controlling Project Plans**

3. Match the following project management terms with the most appropriate statements. You will use each statement only once.

______Critical Path

______Deliverables

______Dependency

______Gantt Chart

______Milestone

______Owner

______Project Plan

______Scope

______Sponsor/Champion

a. Completed units of work with tangible results

b. Listing of all tasks required to complete the project

c. Measurable point of progress in the project plan

d. Person accountable for completion of a task.

e. Person in the organization with the authority and/or funds to make the project happen, or who advocates for the project.

f. Relationship between tasks that makes planning for one task dependent upon planning for the other

g. The boundaries of the project

h. The sequence of tasks upon which the project completion date depends

i. Visual representation of the project plan

**Quantitative and Qualitative Analysis**

4. Calculate the variance if you planned to have 125 agents on the phone at 10 a.m. and actually had 114 agents on the phone.

5. Calculate the average daily call volume for the following week:

| | |
|---|---|
| Monday | 1430 |
| Tuesday | 1200 |
| Wednesday | 960 |
| Thursday | 1035 |
| Friday | 860 |
| Saturday | 420 |
| Total | 5905 |

6. Assume that today the call center receives 418 calls, categorized as follows:

301 Product inquiries

50 Delivery complaints

67 Billing questions

Given only this information, if 379 calls are expected tomorrow, how many of each call type can be expected?

7. Calculate the percentage variance from required staff for each agent group.

| | Agent Group 1 | Agent Group 2 |
|---|---|---|
| Required staff | 182 | 32 |
| Actual staff | 174 | 30 |
| Variance | 8 | 2 |

**Quality Control Tools and Techniques**

8. Write the name of the quality improvement tool in the blank below each one.

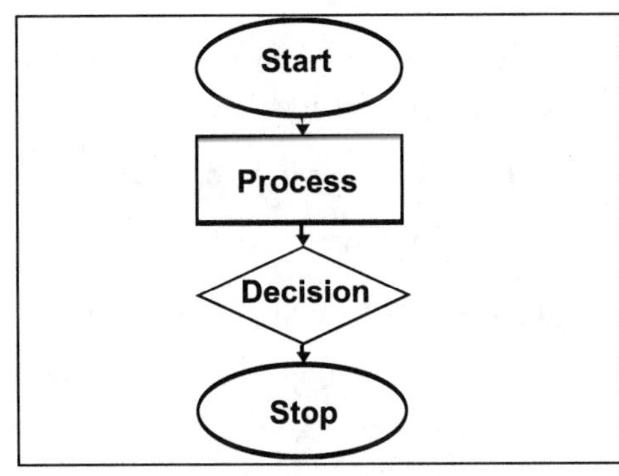


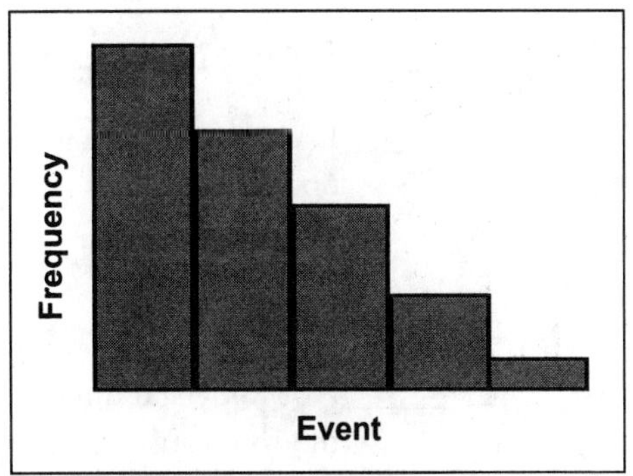


____________________ ____________________

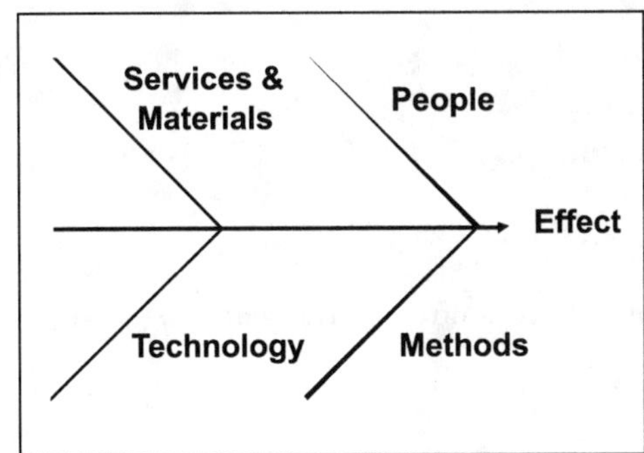


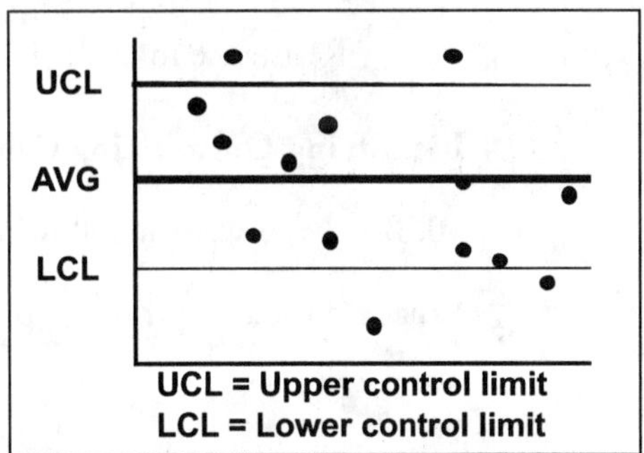


____________________ ____________________

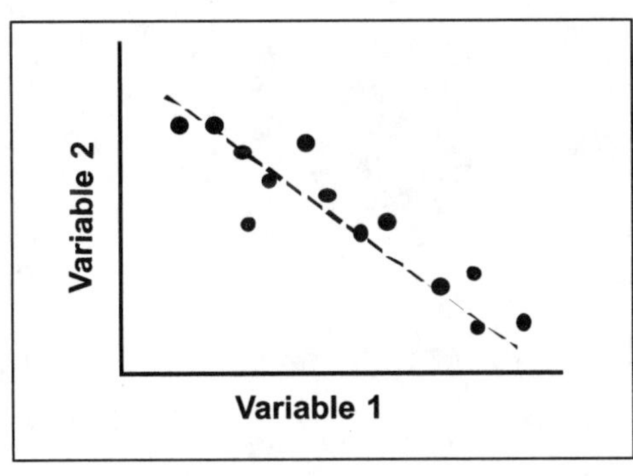


____________________

Section 6

### Identifying and Overcoming Obstacles to Performance Improvement

9. Match the following performance improvement obstacles with the most appropriate solution to overcoming it. You will use each statement only once.

| | |
|---|---|
| ______Defense mechanisms | a. Encourage staff to take the time to understand what action is really needed |
| ______Lack of supporting operational plans and processes | b. Establish clear lines of accountability |
| ______Lip service | c. Explain why improvements are needed |
| ______Not understanding the root cause | d. Slow down enough to plan |
| ______Organizational structure and boundaries | e. Support the objectives in your own actions as a manager |
| ______Resistance to change | f. Tear down departmental barriers |



### Identifying Outsourcing Opportunities

10. Briefly answer the following question.

What are the two primary options for co-sourcing arrangements?

**Principles of Effective Negotiation**

11. Select the most appropriate answer to each question.

Which of the following is the negotiation approach commonly referred to as lose-win?

a. Avoidance

b. Collaboration

c. Competition

d. Compromise

Which negotiation approach should a negotiator use if he or she feels more progress could be made at a later time?

a. Avoidance

b. Collaboration

c. Competition

d. Compromise

Which negotiation approach should a negotiator use if the relationship is more important than the short-term goal?

a. Avoidance

b. Collaboration

c. Competition

d. Compromise

Which of the following is the negotiation approach that places an equal importance on all concerns, i.e., the goals, the outcome and the relationship.

a. Avoidance

b. Collaboration

c. Competition

d. Compromise

**Developing Service Level Agreements**

12. Briefly answer the following question.

What is the difference between service level and service level agreements?

13. List 6 of the 11 typical components of service level agreements.

____________________

____________________

____________________

____________________

____________________

____________________



**Answers to these exercises are in Section 10.**

Note: These exercises are intended to help you retain the material learned. While not the exact questions as on the CIAC Certification assessment, the material in this handbook/study guide fully addresses the content on which you will be assessed. For a formal practice test, please contact the CIAC directly by visiting www.ciac-cert.org.

# Business Management Principles and Practices Reference Bibliography

## Related Articles from *Call Center Management Review* (See Section 9)

Why Benchmarking Could Be Wasted Effort

The Outsourcing Evolution: Economic Trends Make It a More Viable Option

A Four-Step Process for Landing the Ideal Outsource Provider

## For Further Study

### Books/Studies

Cleveland, Brad and Julia Mayben. *Call Center Management on Fast Forward: Succeeding in Today's Dynamic Inbound Environment.* Call Center Press, 1999.

Fisher, Roger, William Ury and Bruce Patton. *Getting to Yes: Negotiating Agreement Without Giving In.* Penguin, 1991.

Lewicki, Roy J., David M. Saunders and John W. Minton. *Essentials of Negotiation.* McGraw-Hill Higher Education, 2000.

Zikmund, William G. and Michael d'Amico. *Effective Marketing: Creating and Keeping Customers in an e-commerce World,* 3e. South-Western, 2001.

### Articles

Cleveland, Brad and Jay Minnucci. "A Primer on Service Level Agreements." *Call Center Management Review,* August 2001.

Dortmans, Henry. "Apples, Oranges and Benchmarks." *Telemanagement,* August 1999.

Dortmans, Henry. "Benchmarks: Buyer Beware." *Telemanagement,* December 1999.

Dortmans, Henry. "Managing Project Managers." *Telemanagement,* June 1999.

Dortmans, Henry. "Yes, We Have No Benchmarks!" *Telemanagement,* May 1998.

Harps, Leslie Hansen. "'Co-Sourcing' Helps Startup Centers Minimize Risk, Add Flexibility." *Call Center Management Review,* June 2000.

Jocelyn, Sandy. "The Basics of Successful Outsourcing." *Call Center Management Review,* October 1996.

Sisk, Kathy. "A Concise Guide to Outsourcing Success." *Call Center Management Review*, October 1999.

**Web Sites**

Project Management Institute, www.pmi.org

The Negotiation Resource Center, www.batna.com

**Seminars**

*Effective Leadership and Strategy for Senior Call Center Managers* public seminar, presented by Incoming Calls Management Institute.

## Section 7

# *Financial Principles and Practices*

# Section 7: Financial Principles and Practices

## Contents

## 1. Identifying Key Risk/Opportunity Tradeoffs

Ready? | 1 | 2 | 3 |

### Key Points

- **The call center's value proposition, or the set of specific benefits it provides to the organization, is the starting point for evaluating tradeoffs. Every tradeoff needs to be considered in relation to the value gained or lost by the call center with each alternative.**
- **While the specific tradeoffs that each call center faces will be unique, tradeoffs common to most centers include:**
  - **Staffing requirements vs. customer wait times**
  - **Service level vs. trunk load**
  - **Service level vs. occupancy and turnover**
  - **Pooled agent groups vs. specialized agent groups**
  - **Average handling time vs. resource requirements**
  - **First contact resolution vs. cost per contact**
  - **Capital expenditures vs. operational expenditures**
- **Many people assume there is a tradeoff between service level and quality, but these major objectives go hand-in-hand.**

### Explanation

Effective strategy decisions require making tradeoffs. At a fundamental level, this is because demands upon resources inevitably grow to exceed the resources available (remember Economics 101). At a deeper level, those who try to be all things to all people fail to distinguish themselves in any area. But how should managers evaluate the tradeoffs that they face in call centers?

Financial analysis is a sound approach for evaluating potential tradeoffs. By basing decisions on the value that they provide to the organization, it is possible to reduce risk and increase opportunities for success. The basic principle to apply is a comparison of each alternative's costs and benefits.

#### Resources Required to Fulfill the Call Center's Value Proposition

The call center's value proposition, or the set of specific benefits it provides to the organization, is the starting point for evaluating tradeoffs. (See Defining the Call Center's Value Proposition, Section 3). Fulfilling the call center's mission requires resources (human and capital) to be allocated strategically.

Every tradeoff needs to be considered in relation to the value gained or lost by the call center with each alternative. In most cases, a balance must be struck between the alternatives. To find the best balance, call center managers need to understand the dynamics underlying each tradeoff. While the specific tradeoffs that each call center faces will be unique, certain kinds of tradeoffs are common to many call centers, including those discussed below.

**Staffing Requirements vs. Customer Wait Times**

The classic tradeoff in call centers is between staffing efficiently and minimizing customer wait times. The dynamic at work in this case is between lowering costs and increasing customer satisfaction.

Skilled managers can forecast staff requirements accurately so that they know just how many agents are needed at each interval of the day to provide a targeted level of service. Reducing the number of staff will lower labor costs, but more callers will have to wait longer. Increasing the number of staff will increase labor costs (and associated facilities expenses) and improve service level performance. As illustrated in the graphic below, this relationship is not linear. Beyond a certain point, the law of diminishing returns takes effect.

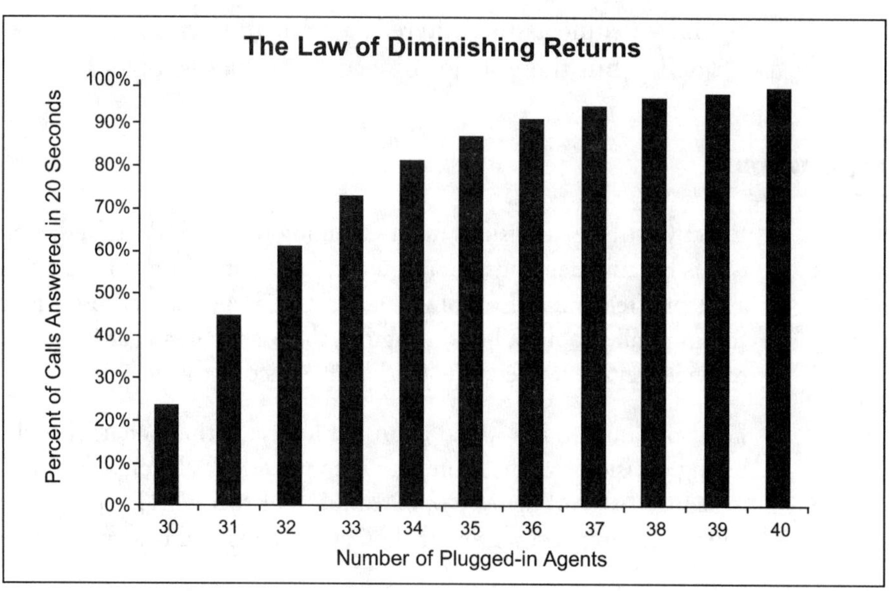


Because the dynamics in call centers are complex, other costs are also affected by this tradeoff. Although labor costs are reduced by lowering staff levels, telecom costs increase as callers wait in queue (assuming your call center provides toll-free lines for callers). The additional telecom costs must be

subtracted from labor cost savings to evaluate the net effect of staff reductions, just as the telecom cost savings should be subtracted from the increased labor cost to evaluate additions to staff.

In revenue-generating environments, this trade-off can be expanded through an incremental revenue analysis, as shown in the following table. This approach determines the potential impact of abandonment because of customer wait time on overall costs.

To use this approach, you attach a cost to abandoned calls and make assumptions around how many calls you would lose for various service levels. The theory is that you should continue to add agents and trunks as long as they produce positive incremental (marginal, additional) revenue (value) after paying for their own costs.

**Incremental Revenue Analysis (Example Only)**

Talk Time-180 sec.
After Call Work-30 sec.
Half Hour's Calls=200
Rostered Staff Factor=1.3

| Agents on Phone | Rostered Staff (Agentsx1.3) | Calls Answered in 20 Sec. | % Lost Calls (Assumed) | % Calls Lost Forever (Assumed) | Trunk Hours | Answered Calls | Gross Revenue Avg. CAll $22.25 | Labor Cost $12/hr. | Toll-free Trunk Cost 10/Min. | Net Revenue | $ Increm. Revenue |
|---|---|---|---|---|---|---|---|---|---|---|---|
| 25 | 33 | 45% | 26.0% | 7.80% | 14.6 | 184 | $4,094 | 396 | 88 | 3610 | - |
| 26 | 34 | 62% | 12.5% | 3.75% | 12.2 | 193 | $4,294 | 408 | 73 | 3813 | 203 |
| 27 | 35 | 74% | 6.5% | 1.95% | 11.2 | 196 | $4,361 | 420 | 67 | 3874 | 61 |
| 28 | 36 | 83% | 3.5% | 1.05% | 10.7 | 198 | $4,406 | 432 | 64 | 3910 | 36 |
| Optimum ▶ 29 | 38 | 89% | 2.0% | 0.60% | 10.4 | 199 | $4,428 | 456 | 62 | 3910 | 0 |
| 30 | 39 | 93% | 1.5% | 0.45% | 10.3 | 199 | $4,428 | 468 | 62 | 3898 | (12) |

This approach can be a valuable exercise, when used in conjunction with other approaches, as long as the assumptions are understood and communicated to others in the budgeting process. Nevertheless, don't let the scientific look of this approach fool you – it requires some pretty serious guesswork.

### Service Level vs. Trunk Load

Call centers require trunk capacity to accept calls, even before agents can answer them. With reasonably accurate forecasts, managers can calculate the trunk capacity required to provide a given level of service.

The trunk load includes the total time spent by callers during their contact with the call center. Since this time includes any delay the caller experiences before reaching an agent, service level directly impacts trunk load. At high service levels, customers experience little delay so fewer trunks will be needed.

At low service levels, more trunks are needed to handle the increased delay. Delivering higher service levels will result in increased staffing requirements, but decreased trunk load requirements.

**Cost of Delay**

ERLANG C FOR INCOMING CALL CENTERS BY ICMI, INC.
TALK TIME IN SECONDS = **180**
AFTER CALL WORK IN SECONDS = **30**
CALLS PER HALF HOUR = **250**
SERVICE LEVEL OBJECTIVE IN SECONDS = **20**

A: Cost per hour for TSR **$15.00**
B: Cost per hour 800 service **$ 5.00**

| Agents | COST | ASA | SL | TKLD | COST | TOTAL |
|---|---|---|---|---|---|---|
| 30 x A = | **$450** | 208.7 | 23.5% | 54.0 x B = | **$270** | **$720** |
| 31 | **$465** | 74.7 | 45.2% | 35.4 | **$177** | **$642** |
| 32 | **$480** | 37.6 | 61.3% | 30.2 | **$151** | **$631** |
| 33 | **$495** | 21.3 | 73.0% | 28.0 | **$140** | **$635** |
| 34 | **$510** | 12.7 | 81.5% | 26.8 | **$134** | **$644** |
| 35 | **$525** | 7.8 | 87.5% | 26.1 | **$131** | **$656** |
| 36 | **$540** | 4.9 | 91.7% | 25.7 | **$129** | **$669** |
| 37 | **$555** | 3.1 | 94.6% | 25.4 | **$127** | **$682** |
| 38 | **$570** | 1.9 | 96.5% | 25.3 | **$127** | **$697** |
| 39 | **$585** | 1.2 | 97.8% | 25.2 | **$126** | **$711** |
| 40 | **$600** | 0.7 | 98.6% | 25.1 | **$126** | **$726** |
| 41 | **$615** | 0.5 | 99.2% | 25.1 | **$126** | **$741** |
| 42 | **$630** | 0.3 | 99.5% | 25.0 | **$125** | **$755** |

Assume the same call load arrives two half hours in a row and use hourly staff and network costs.

Of course, when trunk load exceeds trunk capacity, callers cannot get through and hear a busy signal. Call center managers should assess the impact of busies on customer satisfaction when determining trunk capacity for their center.

**Service Level vs. Occupancy and Turnover**

Since service level is a key performance indicator for call centers, it is not surprising that it impacts so many call center tradeoffs. In this case, the dynamic involves customer satisfaction vs. lowering labor costs, but the labor costs to be considered include the cost of turnover.

As service level improves, efficiency (as measured by occupancy) decreases. In order to answer more calls faster, more agents must be idle (ready to answer the randomly arriving calls). As service level decreases, the opposite occurs, and agents have less idle time (occupancy increases).

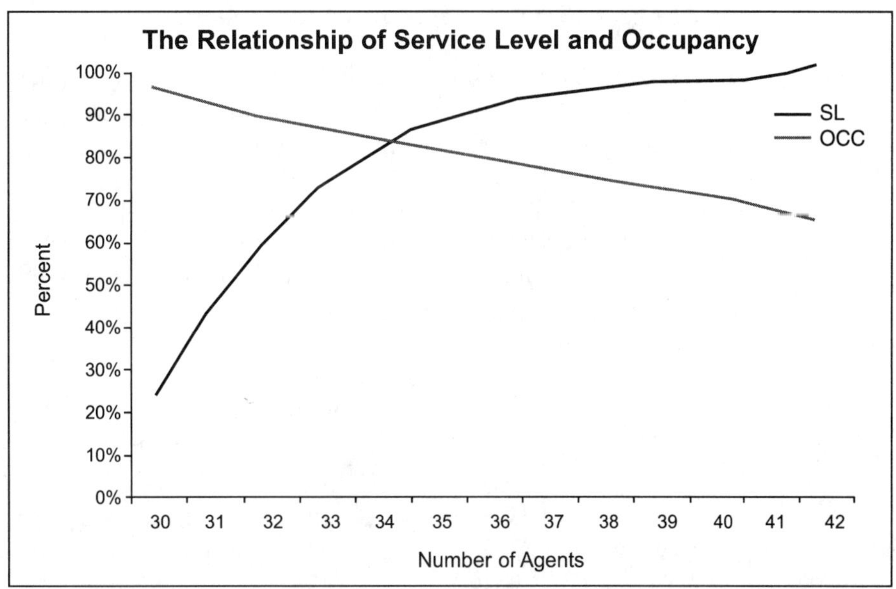

Turnover, or the rate at which agents leave their jobs, is affected by many things, and one of them is occupancy. Agents who have reasonable amounts of time to "breathe" between calls are generally more content than those who take call after call, hour after hour – as agents must when service level performance is poor. Thus service level and turnover end up as a tradeoff that call center managers must consider. Studies suggest that from 88 to 92 percent occupancy is where agents begin to burn out, if the condition lasts for an extended time, i.e., several half-hours in a row.

The danger of a self-perpetuating downward cycle must be understood, too. As service level decreases, occupancy rises, leading to increased turnover, resulting in fewer staff, and so triggering even lower service levels and a repeat of the cycle.

Turnover costs must include a number of variables. Obviously, all of the costs of hiring must be accounted for, including recruiting, interviewing, selecting and training the new staff. The loss in productivity and any extra costs incurred (e.g., overtime by remaining staff) while replacement agents are found and trained should be included, as should the lower productivity of the new-hires until they reach the proficiency levels of the staff they have replaced. Depending on the availability of suitable replacement agents, the cost of lost business opportunities resulting from extended periods of understaffed conditions may also need to be considered. (Turnover calculations and costs are covered in detailed in ICMI's *Call Center People Management Handbook and Study Guide.*)

## Pooled Agent Groups vs. Specialized Agent Groups

Agent groups share a common set of skills and knowledge, handle a specified mix of contacts and can be comprised of hundreds of agents across multiple sites. Agent groups are the building blocks of call center structure.

As the following table illustrates, mathematically, larger groups of pooled agents are more efficient than smaller groups, at the same service level. All other things equal, if you take several small, specialized agent groups, effectively crosstrain them and put them into a single group, the result will be a more efficient environment.

| Calls in 1/2 Hour | Service Level | Agents Required | Occupancy | Avg. Calls Per Agent |
|---|---|---|---|---|
| 50 | 80/20 | 9 | 65% | 5.6 |
| 100 | 80/20 | 15 | 78% | 6.7 |
| 500 | 80/20 | 65 | 90% | 7.7 |
| 1000 | 80/20 | 124 | 94% | 8.1 |

Assumption: Calls last an average 3.5 minutes.



A clear trend, though, is the recognition that different types of callers often have different needs and expectations, and that different agents with a mix of aptitudes and skills are required to provide the necessary knowledge base. Agents may be divided into more specialized groups that can better meet customer needs. These smaller groups will be mathematically less efficient (i.e., they will have lower occupancy rates), but they may have higher first contact resolution rates and higher rates of customer satisfaction.

There is a continuum between pooling and specialization, and there is no ideal formula for deciding how pooled or specialized agent groups should be. Structure must support the customer access strategy, as well as reflect the realities of agent skills and the technologies they have to work with. (See the related discussion in The Call Center's Role in Effecient Service Delivery, section 3.)

## Average Handling Time vs. Resource Requirements

There are both direct and indirect dynamics in the relationship between average handling time (AHT) and resource requirements. The direct impact AHT has upon resource requirements is straightforward: all other things equal, increases in AHT result in increases in resources required to handle calls and decreases in AHT result in decreases in resources required. As AHT changes, the total phone workload changes, so naturally the number of staff required to handle the workload changes, too. The telecom resources required also change when AHT changes.

By taking time on each call to ensure a high-quality experience for each customer, call centers increase their resource requirements. But this is not a simple tradeoff, for there are more complex dynamics involved, as well. Call centers that try to force calls to be shorter risk decreasing call quality to such a degree that customers need to call back to resolve their concerns. Thus, average handling time may decrease while total workload increases as a result of additional calls, leading to increases in resource requirements instead of the desired cost savings.

The quality of resources has an affect upon AHT, as well. Agents lacking the skills or support resources required to handle calls efficiently will take longer to handle calls. Rushing newly hired agents onto the phones before they are ready, for example, may increase AHT. Even a new online support system may increase AHT while agents learn to use it effectively.

**First Contact Resolution vs. Cost per Contact**

First contact resolution and cost per contact are both high-level measures that summarize results across multiple dimensions of performance, so the relationship between them is complex. The underlying dynamic in the trade off between first contact resolution and cost per contact is between quality and costs.

As first contact resolution rises, customer satisfaction and call quality generally rises, while the number of contacts or callbacks per customer decreases, which means that the total contact volume decreases (assuming all other factors stay the same). Conversely, decreases in first contact resolution tend to decrease satisfaction and quality while increasing call volume. But achieving higher first contact resolution usually requires longer calls, increasing average handle time. And, as explained above, forcing calls to be shorter can result in higher rates of callbacks, or lower first contact resolution.

Cost per contact is affected both by changes in volume and average handle time. Decreases in call volume may actually increase cost per contact, since the organization's fixed costs must be spread across fewer contacts. Total costs may decrease, yet on a cost per contact basis the performance picture may appear to have worsened. Furthermore, increases in average handle time raise costs per contact, also, since workload equates to cost.

An exception to this scenario can be found with truly break-through technology implementations, especially when they replace antiquated systems. If old processes were highly inefficient and the new technology provides both effectiveness and efficiency, then first contact resolution may increase while average handle time decreases. However, the cost of the new technology must be accounted for in the cost per contact as a capital expense.

### Capital Expenditures vs. Operational Expenditures

Every business faces the tradeoff between capital expenditures and operational expenditures, and call centers are no exception. The financial analysis is the same as in any other business unit, although it could be argued that call center technology is evolving so dramatically that the risks and potential benefits are extremely difficult to quantify accurately. The underlying dynamic is between short-term and long-term allocation of financial resources.

The costs of operating a call center can be computed with reasonable accuracy. Investments in capital resources such as facilities and technology need to produce benefits that exceed their costs. But estimating what benefits capital investments will bring to the call center is the hard part, especially for cutting-edge technology. Increasingly, call center technology promises benefits beyond cost savings. Call center managers must evaluate the amount of risk they can tolerate – both of jumping in too soon or of waiting too long – and account for that in their analysis.

Call centers that allocate their scarce financial resources primarily on operating expenses take care of the present. Investing in capital resources looks to the future while potentially diverting funds needed for the present. However, it's important to remember that technology investments generally account for between five and 10 percent of the total budget, while staffing accounts for 65 to 70 percent of the overall budget.

### The "Pseudo" Tradeoff, Service Level vs. Quality

Many managers assume that service level and quality must be balanced – the assumption being that they are somehow at odds. And it's true that you can achieve your service level objective regularly, and at the same time, be creating waste, extra work and low quality. However, service level and quality work together to create an environment that satisfies customers

When service level is poor, quality is also affected negatively. As agents are overworked due to constant congestion in the queue, they become less accurate and can become less "customer friendly." Callers are telling them in no uncertain terms about the tough time they had getting through. And agents make more mistakes, driving down quality.

When quality is suffering – whether due to low service level, insufficient training or other factors – service level also suffers. Mistakes made by agents contribute to repeat calls, unnecessary service calls, escalation of calls and complaints to higher management, callbacks, etc. – all of which drive service level down further. In short, service level and quality work hand in hand; they are complimentary.

## 2. Applying the Principles of the Technology Adoption Lifecycle

Ready? | 1 | 2 | 3 |

### Key Points

- The technology adoption lifecycle offers a practical perspective for call center managers to apply when evaluating new technology.
- The model forms a bell curve with five divisions that describe psychographic buying habits, including:
  - Innovators
  - Early adopters
  - Early majority
  - Late majority
  - Laggards
- Understanding where each of the following fall on the bell curve can help you to identify crucial tradeoffs and underlying assumptions:
  - You and your organization
  - Your customers
  - Your competitors
  - The technology
  - Your expectations about each of the above in the future



### Explanation

The technology adoption lifecycle, generally attributed to consultant Geoffrey Moore, offers a practical perspective for call center managers to apply when evaluating new technology. The model forms a bell curve with five divisions that describe psychographic buying habits, including:

- **Innovators:** Sometimes referred to as "technology enthusiasts," innovators buy into new technology early and often. They love trying new things, and typically will do whatever they can to help the supplier bring the product to the marketplace.
- **Early adopters:** Also called "visionaries," they are quick to understand and appreciate the benefits of new technologies, and are willing to take some risks to realize potential order-of-magnitude gains that can come from being among the first to embrace new capabilities.
- **Early majority:** Also referred to as "pragmatists," members of this large

group are driven by a strong sense of practicality. They share some of the characteristics of early adopters, but they prefer to wait until the market "shakes out" and the technology is more proven. Moore suggests that once a technology crosses the "chasm" between early adopters and early majority, it will rapidly proliferate, bringing a flood of business to suppliers and competitive pressures to end-users to get on board.

- **Late majority:** These "conservatives" want solutions that work, with little risk and few implementation hassles. Like the early majority, they have a strong sense of practicality, but would rather wait until turnkey solutions with well-defined ROIs are available.
- **Laggards:** Members of this group resist new technology and distrust conventional competitive and productivity improvement arguments. These "skeptics" are generally viewed by vendors as not worth the effort.

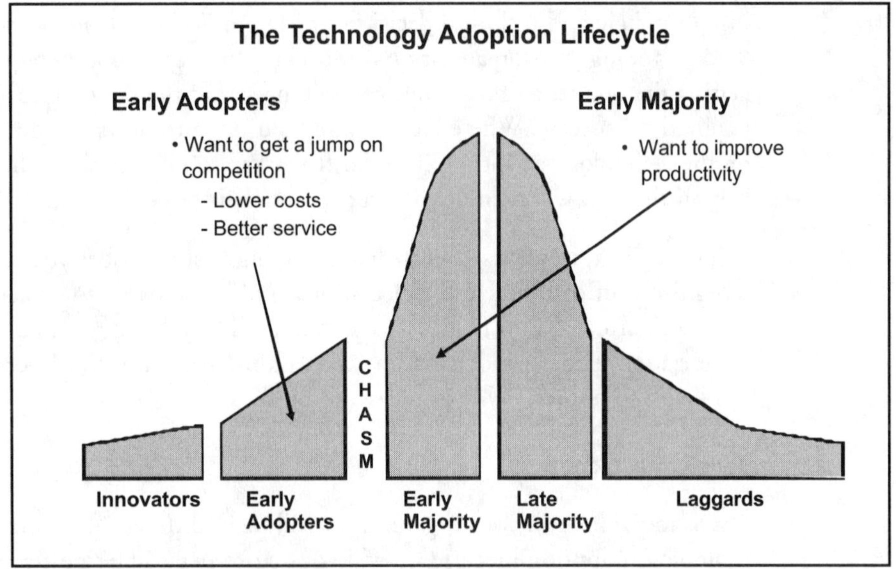


## Applications for the Model

Because call center technology is evolving so rapidly and completely, nearly all call center managers have or will be confronted with major technology decisions. Understanding the technology adoption lifecycle can help you to identify crucial tradeoffs and underlying assumptions. Although the model was developed to describe consumers of new technology, it can also be used as a prism to separate other groups into component parts.

Ask each of the following questions:

- Where is your organization on the bell curve?
- Where are your customers?
- Where are your competitors?
- Where is the technology that is being considered?
- Where do you expect all of these (your organization, customers, competitors, a specific technology) to be in the future?

**You and Your Organization**

The significant role of technology in call centers continues to grow, but call centers fall across the spectrum in terms of adopting new technology. Selecting appropriate call center technology and getting authorization to deploy it is not just a strategic and technical decision. It is a political challenge, as well. Understanding your organization's culture in this regard is a prerequisite to getting the budget authorization you will need and the ongoing support required for success. Where are you and your organization's key decision-makers on the technology adoption lifecycle? If you get too far ahead of them or too far behind them, it will be more difficult to get their buy-in.

While you're at it, ask yourself which grouping best describes you. Learn to recognize your own bias and expectations, and be prepared to explain them. Don't be surprised to find all five stages of the lifecycle represented in your organization, either. Understanding the validity of each of these perspectives can help you appreciate differences and produce better decisions.

**Your Customers**

Just as individuals in your organization will be in different positions along the technology adoption lifecycle, so will your customers. The significance of their position is one step removed, however, since only certain parts of your organization's technology will be visible to them. What are their expectations about the technology your organization uses? Providing cutting-edge customer access channels, for example, may not be appreciated by a customer base comprised mostly of laggards. In contrast, if your customers are anything but laggards and you are not offering email access or web-based tools, then your customers are farther along the curve than you.

### Your Competitors

To put both your organization and your customers in perspective, evaluate where your competitors lie on the technology adoption lifecycle. There is no "right" place to be compared to your competitors, since there are risks and benefits associated with both leading and trailing competitors in adopting technology. From a pure customer service perspective, the best place to be is where your customers want you to be, or at least closer to that ideal than your competitors are.

By studying your competitors' history of technology adoption and understanding where they tend to fall in the lifecycle, you may be able to anticipate their upcoming moves. This and other forms of competitive intelligence can help you measure your relative position on technology adoption.

### The Technology

You can also use the technology adoption lifecycle to assess the level of acceptance enjoyed by the technology in the marketplace. Determine which segments (innovators, early adopters, early majority, late majority, laggards) have purchased or implemented it. Be especially attentive to whether the technology has crossed the "chasm" between early adopters and early majority, since this may signal the start of rapid growth and create increased pressure to keep up with competitors or customer expectations. The farther to the left that the technology is on the curve, the greater the risk of obsolescence (think of Betamax VCRs). Technology farther to the right on the curve carries increased risk of competitive disadvantage for those who do not adopt it (think of touchtone phones).

### Preparing for the Future

Knowing where your organization, your customers, your competition and technologies fall on the technology adoption lifecycle curve is a useful risk/reward framework. But there is yet another dimension to consider, and it applies to all four of these views. Once you know what these positions are now, you need to anticipate how they will change.

In every way, decisions about technology require anticipating the future. In the future lies your potential ROI, your customers' assessment of how well you've met their evolving needs, and your degree of success in keeping up with your competitors. And, of course, in the future there will be even newer technology that will be compared in terms of compatibility, functionality and cost with whatever your organization has chosen to deploy. In evaluating your organization, your customers, your competition and technologies, keep your eyes on the uncertain road ahead, rather than in the rear-view mirror.

## 3. Principles of Developing an Effective Annual Operating Budget

Ready? | 1 | 2 | 3 |

### Key Points

- An appropriate level of funding is necessary for call centers to achieve success.
- Good budgets not only get approved – they also educate others on the mission and potential of the call center
- An effective budgeting process is built on seven key principles, including:
  1. Is based on solid call center valuation
  2. Is driven by the customer access strategy
  3. Is a seamless extension of resource planning
  4. Identifies both forecast and resource/results tradeoffs
  5. Maximizes cross-functional resources
  6. Builds understanding of the call center environment
  7. Is honest, responsible and visible



### Explanation

Call centers are a complex mix of people, processes and technology. The critical success factors related to these components vary greatly, but the glue that holds them together is funding. Without adequate funding, even the best plans will have little chance of success.

An annual operating budget, when developed properly, ensures that an organization will have the amount of funding necessary to meet objectives, while also ensuring that the organization does not overspend to meet these goals. It then goes beyond the goal of approval and also helps to educate key decision-makers on the value of the call center. An operating budget should only include operating expenses, not capital expenditures.

A budget is defined as a summary of proposed or agreed-upon expenditures for a given period of time, for specified purposes. It should outline how the call center will acquire and use resources, and describe how those resources will be deployed and monitored. Effective operating budgets place accountability for the budget on those individuals who have the control to influence call center expenditures. The creation of an accurate budget takes careful planning, and follows a process that:

**1. Is based on solid call center valuation:** Those who are involved in proposing and approving the budget must have a common understanding of the value the call center contributes to the organization. This agreement helps to set the direction of the center, which forms the foundation for proposed expenditures. (See Defining the Call Center's Value Proposition, Section 3.)

**2. Is driven by the customer access strategy:** An appropriate and complete access strategy defines the means by which you will identify, route, handle and track contacts, as well as how you will leverage the information that comes from them. This strategy then feeds into the assumptions that build the budget. (See The Role of the Customer Access Strategy, Section 3.)

**3. Is a seamless extension of resource planning:** In this respect, the budget is simply the final step of all the planning that happens in a call center. Budgetary work projects out over a longer horizon, and therefore may require more communication and judgment than is often used for daily operational planning. But it simply builds on the processes that should already be in place, and therefore shouldn't be viewed as an altogether separate step that requires new methodologies and effort.

**4. Identifies both forecast and resource/results tradeoffs:** The annual budgeting process provides the perfect opportunity to demonstrate to the financial decision-makers the compromises, tradeoffs and uncertainties that are inherent in running a call center. A well-prepared budget will not only display results for different potential workloads, but will also show budgetary results for different levels of service within those workload options.

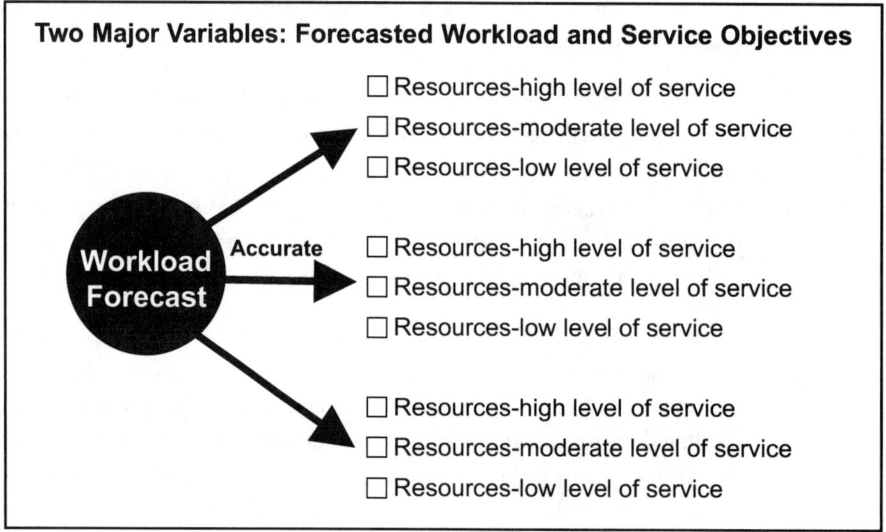

Presenting budgetary information in this format not only provides the decision-makers with options, but also allows them to see tradeoffs that occur within a call center. (See Identifying Key Risk/Opportunity Tradeoffs, this section.)

5. **Maximizes cross-functional resources:** Call centers do not exist in a vacuum. Other departments have a substantial stake in the way in which a call center operates. Sales and marketing, for instance, want to be assured that service levels will be high and that contact information is captured accurately. Legal departments want to know that email responses will minimize any risk of litigation – and may gladly provide support for the ongoing maintenance costs of an email response management system (ERMS) to help reduce this risk. A well-constructed budget identifies these relationships and ensures collaboration and agreement on budget items that impact other departments. (See The Call Center's Contribution to Unit Strategies, Section 3.)

6. **Builds understanding of the call center environment:** Those preparing the budget must realize that some of those approving the budget may not have a strong background in call center concepts. A strong budget package anticipates the questions that might arise, and provides background information to explain unusual situations. For instance, a budget that projects a 10 percent growth in workload for an organization that is assuming a flat sales curve requires explanation. Providing background on these kinds of situations, along with education on key principles like random call arrival, occupancy and schedule adherence, goes a long way toward getting a budget approved quickly. (See Unique Operational Dynamics, Section 5.)

7. **Is honest, responsible and visible:** The goal here should be getting the required funding, not getting "as much funding as possible." Funding requests need to account for past problems and must support the future mission of the organization. The budget must also be visible not only to those involved in the approval process, but also to key managers within and outside the call center.

Budgets that follow these principles not only have a greater chance of approval, but they also educate and enlighten those approving the budgets on the operation and value of the call center. Time, care and collaboration are key ingredients in producing a quality budget.

## 4. Key Steps to Developing and Obtaining Approval for an Annual Operating Budget

Ready? | 1 | 2 | 3 |

### Key Points

- The focus when creating a budget should not only be on accuracy, but also on what it will take to get the appropriate approvals.
- Communication, collaboration, education and negotiation are important elements in securing the funding necessary to meet objectives.
- The following steps outline a process for developing and obtaining approval for an annual operating budget:
  1. Analyze the environment
  2. Communicate early and often
  3. Identify and gain agreement on key assumptions
  4. Run the numbers
  5. Check and recheck for accuracy
  6. Compare the budget results to the expectations you considered in step one
  7. Identify negotiation strategies
  8. Create a communication package to explain and sell the budget
  9. Revise as required



### Explanation

As with many other call center activities, proper planning plays a central role in developing and obtaining approval for an annual operating budget. The importance of communication, collaboration, education and negotiation are especially critical to the success of the budget process. The "mechanics" of budgeting – determining staff and technology needs, pricing out the requirements, etc. – are only part of the process. Approval is also dependent on the ability to sell the vision to others.

The following steps outline a process for developing and obtaining approval for an annual operating budget:

**1. Analyze the environment:** Organizations take many different approaches to budgeting, and the methodology you choose will impact the results. Consider the following:

- Are budgets typically produced in a "bottom-up" fashion, where the call center submits the budget required to meet service? Or does the organization employ a "top-down" approach, where the dollars allocated to the department are determined from above and handed down to the call center? A "top-down" approach is harder to deal with and creates a perspective of "here's the performance we can provide for those dollars" rather than "here are the dollars we need to meet performance objectives."
- What have been the past budgeting trends? If call center budgets have increased two percent a year for the past four years and you feel that seven percent is required this year, you will need to explain why the upcoming year will be different from previous years. It is a good idea to establish a baseline budget that reflects what the call center would require if no new activities were under-taken.
- Does your organization use zero-based budgeting? Some organizations disregard prior year budgets and require managers to justify all budgeting dollars every year, not just the increases over previous years. Zero-based budgeting ensures all expenditures are reviewed and tested, not just based on precedent.
- What are the typical expectations for the call center budget? Is it tied to certain drivers, such as the client base?

**2. Communicate early and often:** The budget presentation to the senior executive team is no time for surprises. Key executives should be briefed on capital expenditures and other unexpected types of charges well in advance. Any substantial change in staffing levels and/or costs should also be discussed early on in the process. Collaboration with other departments is also critical at this step. If, for example, marketing needs better contact data, their support should be enlisted for a more robust customer relationship management package.

**3. Identify and gain agreement on key assumptions:** A lot can happen during the course of a year to impact a budget. Some of the key assumptions that require agreement include:

- The expected service level and response time objectives for the year
- Any changes to compensation plans
- Enhancements being considered for the technological environment
- Changes that may occur with regard to access channels

- Changes in the hours of operation
- Improvements required in quality and/or customer satisfaction rates
- Sales and marketing plans that will impact call volume
- What constitutes controllable and uncontrollable (fixed) expenses

4. **Run the numbers:** At this point, a first pass can be made on the numbers. Alternative scenarios should be drawn up based on changes in workload and objectives.

5. **Check and recheck for accuracy:** The presence of mathematical mistakes is one of the best ways to destroy the confidence level in a budget proposal. Take the time to ensure the numbers are accurate and make sense. If you are providing alternative scenarios (and you should), make sure the differences from one scenario to another make sense.

6. **Compare the budget results to the expectations you considered in step one:** Is your budget proposal out of line with what is going to be expected? Small differences may not be an issue, but large ones will definitely be a cause for concern. The presence of a large gap between expectations and results is an indication that you need to move back to step four and run the numbers again.



7. **Identify negotiation strategies:** It is not likely that everyone reviewing your budget will be willing to approve it without any explanation or changes. Determine what parts of the budget are critical and cannot be touched, and how you can establish benefits to others that may win your case. It is critical to understand your needs and know these areas in advance so they can be negotiated during a meeting. It is also critical to know the costs associated with any proposed cutbacks – for instance, if you are asked to reduce staff size by 10 percent, you should be able to give an indication as to the impact that will have on service levels, occupancy rates, turnover, customer satisfaction, etc. (See Principles of Effective Negotiation, Section 6.)

8. **Create a communication package to explain and sell the budget:** The whole package should include a formal written report, text, charts, illustrations and a presentation. Presentations should be constructed in a summary format, with the most important items receiving attention first. The collaboration that you began in step two should take center stage at this point in time, and your peers from other departments should be aware that their support is being counted on.

9. **Revise as required:** If and when changes have to be made, make revisions to both costs and assumptions. For instance, if the funding for a quality monitoring system is not approved, be sure to change any assumptions related to increased quality and satisfaction rates that were dependent on this technology.

Each organization is different, and therefore the focus on these steps will shift with each organization. No matter the environment, though, a strong focus on planning is critical to ensuring that a budget is not only accurate, but approved.

### Numbers or Emotions

More than ever, today's budget negotiations require you to understand thoroughly how your CEO and CFO think and what pressures they're under. Are they bottom-line driven, requiring solid return on investment right off the bat? Do they respond better to a discussion including thoughtful and creative forecasting?

Bob Whyte, formerly the CIO at DirecTV and now CIO at SAP Portals (a division of SAP AG), says speaking the CEO's language is vital. "I could get ahead with one former CEO by showing emotion and banging the table. With others, [budget success] was purely a matter of how you presented and supported your numbers."

You can learn a lot about preferences by asking successful division budgeters how they handled negotiations. Likewise, pre-meeting conversations with your CEO and others can clue you in on current CEO pressures.

The goal is to craft arguments that clearly advance your CEO's existing agenda, says Robert Bordone, a Harvard Law School lecturer and deputy director of the Harvard Negotiation Research Project in Cambridge, Mass.

Is the board of directors pressuring the CEO to slash costs, build new revenue streams or support new growth? Once you know, you can decide how to slant your project.

#### Honey or vinegar

Some negotiators think tough times require tough talk. But demanding or threatening is the wrong approach to a harmonious compromise. "Good negotiators craft choices that are good for the other side," Harvard's Bordone says.

"Negotiation is about persuading, not demanding," Bordone says. "Really good negotiators are extremely good listeners who give choices that are easy to say yes to."

Excerpt from "Power of the Purse Strings" by Stewart Deck, *Network World,* December 24, 2001.

## 5. Utilizing Variance Reports

Ready? | 1 | 2 | 3 |

### Key Points

- **Financial variance reports provide information on the expense results of a call center.**
- **To determine the reasons for the variance, the call center needs to link performance measures (inputs) to financial outputs.**
- **Output reports are important in helping call center managers assess the financial performance of their organization, but they do not typically provide any information concerning the reasons for the variance. To dig deeper into the analysis, the call center manager needs to develop and analyze input reports.**

### Explanation

Once a budget is created, controls need to be put in place. These controls provide information on the variance between actual results and the budget, and identify those areas where the variance exceeds expectations.

Financial control reports provide call center managers with output results concerning expense performance. These outputs display results for the current month along with year-to-date summaries. Besides an overall summary of department results, budget variance reports typically provide breakdowns on subcategories such as:

- Staff (agent) salary expenses
- Support staff expenses
- Telecom costs
- Technology charges (including maintenance)
- Rent and utilities
- Outside training charges
- Supplies and other office expenses

A typical budget variance report runs many pages, with the format broken down like this:

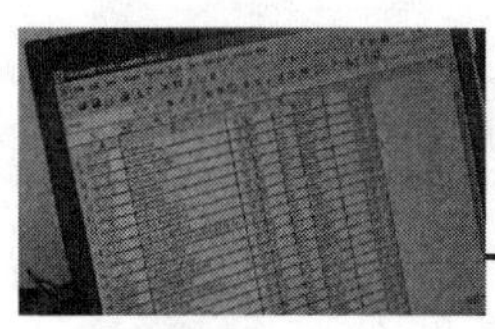

| | Month | | | | Year to Date | | | |
|---|---|---|---|---|---|---|---|---|
| | Budget | Actual | $ Variance | % Variance | Budget | Actual | $ Variance | % Variance |
| **Salary** | | | | | | | | |
| Team 1 | 36,434 | 33,079 | -3,355 | -9.21% | 101,497 | 94,331 | -7,166 | -7.06% |
| Team 2 | 39,502 | 41,441 | 1,939 | 4.91% | 116,595 | 120,037 | 3,442 | 2.95% |
| Team 3 | 31,117 | 34,508 | 3,391 | 10.90% | 95,021 | 102,595 | 7,574 | 7.97% |
| Team 4 | 34,049 | 35,089 | 1,040 | 3.05% | 101,314 | 101,010 | -304 | -0.30% |
| **Salary Subtotal** | **141,102** | **144,117** | **3,015** | **2.14%** | **414,427** | **417,973** | **3,546** | **0.86%** |
| **Building Expenses** | | | | | | | | |
| Rent | 9,000 | 9,000 | 0 | 0.00% | 27,000 | 27,000 | 0 | 0.00% |
| Utilities | 3,988 | 4,161 | 173 | 4.34% | 12,131 | 12,337 | 206 | 1.70% |
| Security | 11,150 | 13,000 | 1,850 | 16.59% | 33,450 | 37,150 | 3,700 | 11.06% |
| **Building Subtotal** | **24,138** | **26,161** | **2,023** | **8.38%** | **72,581** | **76,487** | **3,906** | **5.38%** |
| **Total** | **165,240** | **170,278** | **5,038** | **3.05%** | **487,008** | **494,460** | **7,452** | **1.53%** |

These output reports are important in helping call center managers assess the financial performance of their organization. However, they do not typically provide any information concerning the reasons for the variance. To dig deeper into the analysis, the call center manager needs to develop and analyze input reports.

An input report provides the manager with key information regarding the drivers of financial performance. An obvious input in a call center is contact workload. Minor fluctuations in projected workload vs. actual typically have little to no impact on staffing expenses. However, larger fluctuations can create a substantial gap between expectations and results. The following numbers are typical input drivers in a call center:

- Volume
- Average handle time – ideally broken down between talk and after-call work
- Service level
- Average salary
- Adherence
- Turnover
- Support staff size
- Minutes of phone usage

Some of the above numbers have further subcategories that can form the basis for variance reports. One example is volume, which in many call centers is a function of the size of the customer base and the calling rate per customer. Average handling time (AHT) is another key example since volume and AHT forecast accuracy impact staffing levels about the same. Generating variance reports at this level provides further information on the cause of differences between actual and projected results. An example of an operational input variance report for a few key indicators is as follows:

| | Month | | | | Year to Date | | | |
|---|---|---|---|---|---|---|---|---|
| | Budget | Actual | $ Variance | % Variance | Budget | Actual | $ Variance | % Variance |
| **Call Volume** | 63,087 | 66,509 | 3,422 | 5.42% | 194,507 | 208,429 | 13,922 | 7.16% |
| Membership | 2,417,509 | 2,341,997 | -75,512 | -3.12% | 2,357,914 | 2,302,816 | -55,098 | -2.34% |
| Calling Rate | 2.61% | 2.84% | 0.23% | 8.82% | 8.25% | 9.05% | 0.80% | 9.72% |
| **AHT** | 326 | 337 | 11 | 3.37% | 322 | 333 | 11 | 3.42% |
| Talk Time | 287 | 292 | 5 | 1.74% | 283 | 290 | 7 | 2.47% |
| After-Call Work | 39 | 45 | 6 | 15.38% | 39 | 43 | 4 | 10.26% |
| **Average Salary** | | | | | | | | |
| CSR | 12.48 | 12.63 | 0.15 | 1.20% | 12.43 | 12.51 | 0.08 | 0.64% |
| Team Leader | 14.27 | 14.42 | 0.15 | 1.05% | 14.27 | 14.42 | 0.15 | 1.05% |
| Asst Sup | 17.89 | 17.53 | -0.36 | -2.01% | 17.61 | 17.48 | -0.13 | -0.74% |
| Supervisor | 21.12 | 21.56 | 0.44 | 2.08% | 20.97 | 21.11 | 0.14 | 0.67% |
| **Staff Counts** | | | | | | | | |
| CSR | 61 | 60 | -1 | -1.64% | 62 | 61 | -1 | -1.61% |
| Team Leader | 8 | 7 | -1 | -12.50% | 8 | 8 | 0 | 0.00% |
| Asst Sup | 4 | 4 | 0 | 0.00% | 4 | 3 | -1 | -25.00% |
| Supervisor | 4 | 4 | 0 | 0.00% | 4 | 4 | 0 | 0.00% |

Once the key input drivers are identified, reports should be created that provide information on driver results in comparison to expectations. Use these reports as the basis to create explanations of variances in financial results. They also provide the foundation for creating action plans to address performance problems.

## 6. Definitions of Key Financial Concepts

Ready? | 1 | 2 | 3 |

### Key Points

- **As with call center management itself, the discipline of the finance profession has its own terminology and principles.**
- **An understanding of key financial concepts ensures that projects will be evaluated appropriately and that the organization will spend an appropriate percentage of available funds on call center projects.**

### Explanation

Most call centers invest significant sums of money in people and technology. Adequate funding levels are often the key difference between projects that succeed and those that fall short of expectations. Because funding is so vital to call center success, it is imperative that leaders within the call center have a firm understanding of basic financial concepts. This ensures that projects will be evaluated appropriately and that the organization will spend an appropriate percentage of available funds on call center projects.

The terms below represent key financial concepts that should be understood by call center leaders:

- **Amortization:** The gradual, planned reduction in value of capital expenditures. (*Barron's*)
- **Asset:** Anything that an organization owns that has economic value, e.g., cash, real estate, inventory, technology.
- **Capital budgeting:** A method for evaluating, comparing and selecting projects to achieve the best long-term financial gain. (*Barron's*)
- **Capital expenditures:** Long-term expenditures that are amortized over a period of time determined by IRS regulations. (*Barron's*)
- **Cost/benefit analysis:** A term used to describe the process of comparing the value of a potential project with the cost associated with it. While different calculations can be used for a cost/benefit analysis, the general concept is to determine if benefits outweigh costs enough to justify implementation.
- **Depreciation:** The allocation of an asset's cost, for tax or management

purposes, based on its age. (*Barron's*)

- **Discount rate:** The required rate of return that a firm must achieve to justify its investments. (*Barron's*)
- **Equity:** The value of the funds contributed by the stockholders plus the retained earnings (or losses).
- **Internal rate of return (IRR):** The discount rate that makes the net present value of a project equal to zero. (*Barron's*)
- **Lease:** A legal contract under which the owner of an asset gives another party the right to use an asset for a certain period of time in return for specified periodic payments. (*Barron's*)
- **Liability:** A legal debt or obligation of the organization, e.g., loans, accounts payable, mortgages.
- **Net present value (NPV):** The present value of a project's future cash flow less the initial investment in the project. (*Barron's*)
- **Opportunity cost:** The rate of return on the best alternative investment that is not selected. (Barron's)
- **Payback period:** The amount of time required to recover the initial investment in a project. (*Barron's*)
- **Replacement cost:** The current purchase price of an asset used to replace an existing asset. (*Barron's*)
- **Return on assets (ROA):** A ratio that divides net income (or earnings) by average total assets. The resulting percentage indicates how much income has been generated from each dollar of the organization's assets.
- **Return on investment (ROI):** Strictly speaking, this is the net income divided by total assets. In call center usage, it is a general term used to define one of a number of capital budgeting calculation methods that determines the value of an investment.
- **Return on sales (ROS):** A calculation that divides net income by sales to indicate if the return on sales is high enough. A low return on sales could indicate insufficient price mark-up to cover expenses.
- **Risk:** The degree of uncertainty associated with the outcome of an investment. (*Barron's*)

Note: Some definitions are taken from *Barron's Finance* by A.A. Groppelli and Ehsan Nikbakht, fourth edition, Barron's Educational Series, 2000.

# 7. Using Capital Budgeting Methods

**Ready?** | 1 | 2 | 3 |

## Key Points

- **Different capital budgeting methods are available to determine the value of a proposed investment.**
- **In typical call center use, the term return on investments (ROI) is used to define a generic method of calculating value.**
- **Three of the methods most often used to assess investment returns are:**
  - **Payback period**
  - **Net present value (NPV)**
  - **Internal rate of return (IRR)**

## Explanation

Different calculation methods are available to determine the value of capital investments, e.g., technology, buildings, furniture. Typically, an organization selects one of these methods and uses it to evaluate the expected return and risk of all investments being proposed throughout the corporation. This gives each proposal equal footing, even though they may be for completely different purposes.

A key element concerning capital budgeting methods is the treatment of the time value of money. Methods that take this value into account are generally regarded as being more valid, since they recognize that (in most cases) today's dollar is worth more than tomorrow's. However, it is important to know all of the typical valuation methods to understand how they can impact the valuation of a project.

Perhaps the most common valuation method that is discussed by call center vendors is return on investment (ROI). It is important to note that ROI in the strictest terms is not a capital budgeting method, but is instead a method of evaluating financial statements that generates a ratio of net income after taxes to total assets.

In call center use, however, ROI has come to define a generic method of calculating the value of an investment. In this manner, the ROI of a project is typically calculated as the percentage return over the first year of the investment. For example, a workforce management system vendor may claim that the system will generate a reduction in staffing expenses of $15,000 a month for the first year, or $180,000 in total for the year. This number will be compared to the initial outlay of $60,000, leading to an ROI claim of 300% ($180,000 ÷ $60,000). Such claims typically do not account for all project costs, or the time value of money, and therefore do not present an accurate representation of the value of the project.

There are three types of capital budgeting methods that are typically used to determine the value of an investment in call center technology:

- Payback period
- Net present value (NPV)
- Internal rate of return (IRR)

**Payback Period**

The payback period calculates the length of time required to recover an initial investment. By working in units of time, this valuation method has the advantage of being easy to understand by all involved. An example of a payback period calculation is provided below:

| **Initial Investment** | **-115,000** | |
|---|---|---|
| Year | Cash Flow | Running Total |
| 1 | 40,000 | 40,000 |
| 2 | 41,000 | 81,000 |
| 3 | 42,000 | 123,000 |
| 4 | 43,000 | 166,000 |
| **Payback Point** | **2.81 years** | |

In this example, the investment is recovered sometime between the end of year two (when $81,000 is recovered) and the end of year three (when $123,000 is recovered). To determine the exact payback point, the remaining investment of $34,000 that has not been recovered by the end of year two is divided by the total cash flow in year three ($42,000). The resulting number (.81) is added to the first two years to come up with the payback point of 2.81 years. In other words, this investment will be recovered in approximately two years and 10 months.

While this provides a simple and clear way to define value, it is not without flaws. First, it does not account for the time value of money. Second, and perhaps even more importantly, it does not serve as a measure of profitability, since the cash flows after the payback period are ignored. To highlight that last point, keep in mind that the payback period would be exactly the same if the forth-year cash flow was zero – though the value of the investment would clearly not be equal.

**Net Present Value**

Net present value (NPV) is the present value of a project's future cash flow less the initial investment in the project. *(Barron's)* Since the NPV accounts for the time value of money, it is important to understand the concept of the discount rate. The discount rate is the required rate of return that a firm must receive to justify its investments. Every large corporation, and most smaller ones, has a stated discount rate. It is easy to think of this as the competition you face for the funding you seek. If the corporation can already get, for example, a 10 percent return, why would they fund a proposed investment that would deliver less?

The NPV uses this discount rate to calculate the value of an investment in today's monetary terms. This is accomplished by applying a present value interest factor (PVIF) to the cash flow of a project. An example is provided below:

| **Initial Investment** | **-115,000** | | |
|---|---|---|---|
| Year | Cash Flow | PVIF (at 10%) | PV for Each Year |
| 1 | 40,000 | 0.909 | 36,360 |
| 2 | 41,000 | 0.826 | 33,866 |
| 3 | 42,000 | 0.751 | 31,542 |
| 4 | 43,000 | 0.683 | 29,369 |
| **NPV** | | | **131,137** |

The PVIF is obtained from a table that provides the values based on the discount rate and the time period involved. Fortunately, there are ways to determine the NPV without having to resort to tables. Financial calculators can provide the information, as can spreadsheet programs.

In this example, the final step is to take the NPV of the cash flows and subtract out the initial investment. When the result is a positive number, as it is in this example, the project meets the financial criteria for approval.

To use NPV to evaluate proposals, it can be converted into a profitability index (PI). The PI is the present value of cash flows divided by the initial investment outlay. A PI greater than one indicates that the project is profitable. In our example the PI would be 131,137 ÷ 115,000 = 1.14.

**Internal Rate of Return**

The internal rate of return (IRR) is similar to the NPV. Where the NPV uses a fixed discount rate to compare cash flows to the initial investment, the IRR calculates the rate of return of the cash flow. This value can then be compared to the discount rate to determine if the project is viable.

As with the NPV, the IRR can be calculated using tables. However, it is much easier and much more effective to calculate the IRR using a spreadsheet program. The following is an example of IRR:

| **Initial Investment** | **-115,000** |
|---|---|
| Year | Cash Flow |
| 1 | 40,000 |
| 2 | 41,000 |
| 3 | 42,000 |
| 4 | 43,000 |
| **IRR** | **16%** |

If the firm's discount rate is 10 percent, the project can be approved since the IRR (16 percent) is higher than the discount rate.

The payback period, NPV and IRR all provide managers with different ways of determining the value of an investment. An understanding of all three methods provides the call center manager with the ability to fully comprehend the financial implications of capital investments.

## 8. Buy vs. Lease Considerations

Ready? | 1 | 2 | 3 |

### Key Points

- **Many call center vendors offer their equipment for purchase or lease.**
- **Leasing, compared to purchasing, has both advantages and disadvantages.**
- **Deciding whether to purchase or lease is facilitated by determining the net present value (NPV) of the two options and choosing the least expensive alternative.**

### Explanation

"A lease is a legal contract under which the owner of an asset (lessor) gives another party (lessee) the right to use an asset for a certain period of time in return for specified periodic payments." (*Barron's*) Many call center vendors offer leases as an alternative to buying equipment.

In some cases, leasing can provide an attractive option compared to a purchase. Some of the advantages of leasing include the following:

- Leasing does not require a large initial investment
- Leasing can sometimes be cheaper than a purchase, since the lessor enjoys some tax advantages on the leased equipment
- In a lease arrangement, the lessee passes the risk of obsolescence to the lessor
- Applications for leases are usually approved faster, and with more relaxed credit standards, than those for borrowing

There are also disadvantages of leasing:

- The lessee has to return the equipment after a set time period, and the lessor has no obligation to renew the lease (though leasing with an option to buy is a way to avoid this problem)
- A lessee, unlike a buyer, cannot depreciate the assets, and therefore cannot enjoy the tax benefit associated with depreciation
- Any major modifications to improve the efficiency of the equipment

need the approval of the lessor

- A lease does not offer the lessee any salvage value at the end of its last year

The decision whether to purchase equipment or lease it often comes down to the advantages and disadvantages listed above, and how they impact the organization involved. For example, a larger company with a substantial tax burden may find purchasing more attractive than a small startup firm with little cash on hand. Leasing is also attractive for those organizations short on capital, or in instances where the technology being considered may soon be obsolete.

In deciding whether to purchase or lease, the manager needs to determine the least expensive alternative, generally identified by net present value. (See Using Capital Budgeting Methods, this section.) The alternative with the lowest (not highest) NPV would be the best alternative in this case. The calculation must also take into account tax implications, depreciation schedules and salvage values where appropriate.

Note: Definitions taken from *Barron's Finance* by A.A. Groppelli and Ehsan Nikbakht, fourth edition, Barron's Educational Series, 2000.

# 9. Understanding and Using Depreciation Schedules

Ready? | 1 | 2 | 3 |

## Key Points

- **Depreciation is the allocation of an asset's cost, for tax or management purposes, based on its age.**
- **IRS regulations govern the method used for tax purposes, but organizations are free to use any method available for internal evaluation purposes.**
- **Four major methods of depreciation include:**
  - **Modified Accelerated Cost Recovery System (MACRS)**
  - **Straight-line method**
  - **Sum-of-the-years'-digits method**
  - **Double-declining balance method**



## Explanation

"Depreciation is the allocation of an asset's cost, for tax or management purposes, based on its age." (*Barron's*) IRS regulations stipulate a certain method (based on the item being purchased) for tax purposes. However, management can choose from several different methods for internal evaluation. The method chosen can have a substantial impact on the purchase decision.

Four major methods of depreciation include:

- Modified Accelerated Cost Recovery System (MACRS)
- Straight-line method
- Sum-of-the-years'-digits method
- Double-declining balance method

### Modified Accelerated Cost Recovery System (MACRS)

For tax purposes, the IRS requires organizations to depreciate property placed in service after 1986 using a method called Modified Accelerated Cost Recovery System (MACRS), pronounced "makers." This method classifies most business properties into groups. Each group of assets can be written off over a different time period. For example, the following table illustrates the three-, five- and seven-year asset groups as determined by the IRS for most general business. The IRS also provides depreciation schedules for assets related to specific industries.

| 3-Year Asset | | 5-Year Asset | | 7-Year Asset | |
|---|---|---|---|---|---|
| • Tractor units for use over the road. | | • Information systems (including computers and their peripheral equipment used in administering normal business transactions and the maintenance of business records, their retrieval and analysis).<br>• Data handling equipment (including only typewriters, calculators, adding and accounting machines, copiers and duplicating equipment).<br>• Some transportation vehicles (including airplanes, automobiles, taxis, buses, general purpose trucks, trailers and trailer-mounted containers). | | • Office furniture, fixtures and equipment (includes furniture and fixtures that are not a structural component of a building. Does not include communications equipment that is included in other classes).<br>• Railroad cars and locomotives (except those owned by railroad transportation companies). | |
| Year | Depreciation rate* | Year | Depreciation rate* | Year | Depreciation rate* |
| 1 | 33% | 1 | 20% | 1 | 14% |
| 2 | 44% | 2 | 32% | 2 | 24% |
| 3 | 15% | 3 | 19% | 3 | 17% |
| 4** | 8% | 4 | 12% | 4 | 12% |
| | | 5 | 12% | 5 | 9% |
| | | 6** | 5% | 6 | 9% |
| | | | | 7 | 9% |
| | | | | 8** | 6% |

*Depreciation rates based on half-year convention.
**Note that a small portion of the asset carries beyond the final year.

Note: This information is provided for summary purposes only. Please consult your financial department for more detailed information on MACRS depreciation.

### Straight-Line Method

The straight-line method takes into account the purchase price of the asset, the life of the asset, and salvage value (the estimated selling price of an asset once it has been fully depreciated). As the name suggests, this is a simple method as indicated by the calculation below:

Annual depreciation = (purchasing costs – salvage value) ÷ (number of years the asset will be used)

The straight-line method assumes that an asset is used at a constant rate over its useful life. Though simple and easy to understand, the disadvantage to this method is that there is no acceleration of depreciation. Without the acceleration, the tax advantages of this method are not as great as with other depreciation schedules.

### Sum-of-the-Years'-Digits Method

This method is used most often when it is believed that the asset will be more useful in the earlier part of its life. The three-step procedure to figuring out the annual depreciation charges follows (example taken from *Barron's*):

1. Add all the digits of the years of depreciation together to determine the denominator (for example, a three-year depreciation would be 3+2+1 = 6).

2. Make annual fractions of the sum so that the first year's numerator is the highest digit, the second year's numerator is the next highest digit, and so on (in our example, year one would be 3/6, year two would be 2/6, and year three would be 1/6).

3. Multiply the fraction for each year by the value of the asset to get the depreciation charges for that particular year.

For example, the following table illustrates this depreciation method for an asset valued at $25,000 that is depreciated over 5 years.

| | Asset value | Multiplier | Depreciation charges |
|---|---|---|---|
| Year 1 | $25,000 | 5/15 | $8,333 |
| Year 2 | $25,000 | 4/15 | $6,666 |
| Year 3 | $25,000 | 3/15 | $5,000 |
| Year 4 | $25,000 | 2/15 | $3,333 |
| Year 5 | $25,000 | 1/15 | $1,666 |

### Double-Declining Balance Method

"The double-declining balance method uses an annual depreciation ratio equal to double the straight-line ratio. This is then multiplied by the undepreciated balance of the asset to get the depreciation charges for that particular year." (*Barron's*) The example below is based on the purchase of an asset worth $100,000, with a useful life of five years. The straight-line ratio is 1/5, or 20 percent, with twice that amount being 40 percent:

| Year | Depreciation Ratio | Undepreciated Balance | Annual Depreciation Charge |
|---|---|---|---|
| 1 | 40% | $100,000 | $40,000 |
| 2 | 40% | $60,000 | $24,000 |
| 3 | 40% | $36,000 | $14,400 |
| 4 | 40% | $21,600 | $8,640 |
| 5 | 40% | $12,960 | $5,184 |

Note that the annual depreciation charges are less than the purchase cost of the asset (in this example, the annual depreciation charges over the five years equals $92,224). The difference between the purchase cost and the total depreciation charge is the salvage value of the asset.

The double-declining balance method was popular before MACRS became mandatory, but is not used as much today.

The depreciation schedule used can have a substantial impact on the valuation of a project. For this reason, it is useful to have a basic understanding of the different options available.

Note: Some definitions and examples taken from *Barron's Finance* by A.A. Groppelli and Ehsan Nikbakht, fourth edition, Barron's Educational Series, 2000.

## 10. Definitions of Profit and Cost Centers

Ready? | 1 | 2 | 3 |

### Key Points

- **Call centers perceived as cost centers are viewed only as transaction processing environments for the organization.**
- **Call centers perceived as profit centers are seen as generating or protecting revenue and other value for the organization, over and above the total operating cost of the department.**
- **The difference in viewpoints leads to different HR policies, processes and technology decisions.**

### Explanation

Organizations differ in the way they attach value to the call center. In some organizations, there is little value placed on call center activities. From a financial perspective, these are viewed as cost centers – in other words, they are simply providing transaction processing support for the organization. When viewed as a cost center, the focus is on getting the transactions done at the least total cost to the organization. This focus drives the people management philosophy, the processes that are developed and the technology that is purchased in the center.

Other organizations take a different view of call center activities. Rather than just processing transactions, the call center is viewed as an area where revenue is generated or protected, where relationships are established and where an understanding of customer needs is developed. These call centers are viewed as profit centers, meaning that the revenue (or other value) that they generate is greater than total operating cost.

While profit centers keep an eye on expenses, they also track value activities in the call center. The attention placed on value drives different activities than those in a cost center. For example, cost centers are often focused on average handle time and doing whatever it takes to keep this as low as possible. In a profit center, the organization will look for ways to increase value during the call. This often leads to extra scripting to promote cross-sell opportunities or gather important customer data. The extra scripting increases talk time and staffing requirements, but is considered to be a worthwhile investment because the value generated by these extra steps covers the investment. (See Defining the Call Center's Value Proposition, Section 3.)

# 11. Interpreting and Using Key Financial Statements

Ready? | 1 | 2 | 3 |

## Key Points

- **Financial statements are used to determine and display the financial position of an organization. Key financial statements include:**
  - **Income statement**
  - **Balance sheet**
  - **Cash-flow statement**
  - **Statement of retained earnings**
- **Key ratios use data from these statements to provide insight regarding performance of different facets of the operation.**

## Explanation

There are numerous financial statements and performance ratios used by organizations to help explain financial performance. Covering these different forms thoroughly would take literally hundreds of pages, so no attempt will be made here to do so. Instead, the following is an overview of the some of the key financial statements and ratios with brief explanations on what they are and the information they provide.

### Income Statement

The income statement (also called the profit-and-loss or P&L statement) is popular because it cuts to the heart of what matters most to investors. It summarizes the earnings generated by an organization during a specific period of time. It generally follows a very simple formula: revenue – expenses = net profit. To get to that point, the P&L statement follows the format listed below:

Revenues
- Operating (variable expenses)
Gross profit (operating) margin
- Overhead (fixed expenses)

Operating Income
+/- Other income or expense

Pre-tax income
- Income taxes

Net Income (after taxes)

An example of a P&L statement follows:

| Years Ended December 31 | 1997 | 1998 | 1999 |
|---|---|---|---|
| **Operating Revenue** | | | |
| Freight revenue | $6,750,000 | $7,250,000 | $7,423,500 |
| Contract carrier | 645,000 | 675,000 | 698,000 |
| Mileage lease charges | 127,500 | 145,000 | 154,300 |
| Sales of fuel, parts, and labor | 48,500 | 75,300 | 87,500 |
| Vehicle rental income | 15,800 | 17,900 | 19,700 |
| Total Operating Revenue | 7,586,800 | 8,163,200 | 8,383,500 |
| **Operating Expenses** | **7,227,500** | **7,675,300** | **7,823,500** |
| **Operating Income** | **359,300** | **487,900** | **559,500** |
| **Other Income (Expenses):** | | | |
| Other income | 65,000 | 45,000 | 59,800 |
| Interest Expense | (49,000) | (53,000) | (74,000) |
| Total Other Income (Expenses)-net | 16,000 | (8,000) | (14,200) |
| **Earnings Before Income Taxes** | **375,300** | **479,900** | **545,300** |
| Income Taxes | (150,120) | (191,960) | (218,120) |
| **Net Earnings** | **$225,180** | **$287,940** | **$327,180** |

Source: www.smallcarrieruniversity.com

**Balance Sheet**

The balance sheet displays the assets of an organization, its liabilities, capital and equity. It shows the difference between assets and liabilities, which is the organization's equity, or net worth. This provides six types of information regarding the organization:

- Information on how capital is invested and how the capital structure is divided between senior issues and common stock
- Strength or weakness of the working-capital position
- Reconciliation of the earnings reported in the income account
- Data to test the true success or prosperity of the business, the amount earned on invested capital
- The basis for analyzing the sources of income
- The basis for a long-term study of the relationship between earning power and asset values and of the development of the financial structure

An example balance sheet follows:

| Years Ended December 31 | 1997 | 1998 | 1999 |
|---|---|---|---|
| **Assets** | | | |
| **Current Assets** | | | |
| Cash and cash equivalents | $245,000 | $210,000 | $263,500 |
| Trade accounts receivables, net of allowance for doubtful accounts of $-0- | 925,000 | 885,300 | 967,000 |
| Receivables from related parties | 25,000 | 22,000 | 65,000 |
| Inventories | 6,000 | 18,000 | 25,000 |
| Prepaid expenses and other | 25,000 | 27,000 | 35,000 |
| Total Current Assets | 1,226,000 | 1,162,300 | 1,355,500 |
| **Property and Equipment (Fixed Assets)** | | | |
| Transportation vehicles | 1,145,000 | 1,367,000 | 1,475,000 |
| Transportation vehicles - capital leases | 275,000 | 275,000 | 475,000 |
| Other vehicles and equipment | 235,000 | 235,000 | 235,000 |
| Leasehold improvements | 215,000 | 215,000 | 215,000 |
| | 1,870,000 | 275,000 | 475,000 |
| Less: Accumulated depreciation and amortization | (675,000) | (875,000) | (1,025,000) |
| Total Property and Equipment | 1,195,000 | 1,217,000 | 1,375,000 |
| **Other Assets** | | | |
| Cash value of life insurance | 25,000 | 38,000 | 47,000 |
| Deposits | 12,000 | 12,000 | 45,000 |
| Other | 7,500 | 7,500 | 7,500 |
| Total Other Assets | 44,500 | 57,500 | 99,500 |
| **Total Assets** | **2,465,500** | **2,436,800** | **2,830,000** |
| **Liabilities** | | | |
| **Current Liabilities** | | | |
| Trade accounts payable | 189,5000 | 227,000 | 245,000 |
| Accrued expenses and other liabilities | 95,000 | 86,000 | 103,000 |
| Current portion of long-term debt | 125,000 | 132,000 | 175,000 |
| Total Current Liabilities | 409,500 | 445,000 | 523,000 |
| **Long-Term Debt, Net of Current Portion** | 625,000 | 617,000 | 725,000 |
| **Total Liabilities** | **1,034,500** | **1,062,000** | **1,248,000** |
| **Stockholders' Equity** | | | |
| Common Stock | 125,000 | 125,000 | 200,000 |
| Retained Earnings | 1,306,000 | 1,249,800 | 1,382,000 |
| Total Stockholders' Equity | 1,431,000 | 1,374,800 | 1,582,000 |
| **Total Liabilities and Stockholders' Equity** | **2,465,500** | **2,436,800** | **2,830,000** |

*Source: www.smallcarrieruniversity.com*

Section 7

Information on the balance sheets comes from the book *Graham and Dodd's Security Analysis*, Fifth edition, by Sidney Cottle, Roger F. Murray, and Frank E. Block. McGraw-Hill Book Publishing Company, 1988.

### Cash-Flow Statement

The cash-flow statement details the sources of cash coming into and flowing out of an organization. This statement provides information on the health of an organization's earnings and how they are using cash. An income statement and balance sheet are needed to prepare a cash-flow statement.

The activity is divided into three different categories – operating activities, investing activities and financing activities. Below these different categories is a summary for the time period. An example of a cash-flow statement is provided below:

| Years Ended December 31 | 1997 | 1998 | 1999 |
|---|---|---|---|
| Cash Flows from Operating Activities: | | | |
| Net Earnings | $225,180 | $287,940 | $327,180 |
| Adjustments to reconcile net earnings to net cash provided by operating activities: | | | |
| Depreciation and amortization | 200,000 | 200,000 | 150,000 |
| Gain on sale of property and equipment | - | - | - |
| (Increase) decrease in: | | | |
| Trade accounts receivable | (25,000) | 39,700 | (81,700) |
| Receivables from related parties | (5,000) | 3,000 | (43,000) |
| Inventories | (10,000) | (12,000) | (7,000) |
| Prepaid expenses and other | (5,000) | (2,000) | (8,000) |
| Other assets | - | - | - |
| Increase (decrease) in: | | | |
| Trade accounts payable | 25,000 | 37,500 | 18,000 |
| Accrued expenses and other | 2,000 | (9,000) | 17,000 |
| **Net Cash Provided by Operating Activities** | **407,180** | **545,140** | **372,480** |
| Cash Flows from Investing Activities: | | | |
| Proceeds from sale of property and equipment | - | - | - |
| Purchase of property and equipment | (125,000) | - | - |
| Proceeds (payments) of deposits | - | - | (33,000) |
| Payments for increase in cash value of life insurance | (5,000) | (13,000) | (9,000) |
| **Net Cash Used by Investing Activities** | **(130,000)** | **(13,000)** | **(42,000)** |
| Cash Flows from Financing Activities: | | | |
| Proceeds from long-term debt | - | - | - |
| Principal payments on long-term debt | (178,000) | (27,000) | (157,000) |
| Dividends Paid | (29,180) | (540,140) | (194,980) |
| Purchase of treasury stock | - | - | - |
| Proceeds from issuance of common stock | - | - | 75,000 |
| **Net Cash Used by Financing Activities** | (207,180) | (567,140) | (276,980) |

| Years Ended December 31 | 1997 | 1998 | 1999 |
|---|---|---|---|
| Net Increase in Cash | 70,000 | 35,000 | 53,5000 |
| Cash and Cash Equivalents, Beginning of Year | 175,000 | 245,000 | 210,000 |
| **Cash and Cash Equivalents, End of Year** | **$245,000** | **$210,000** | **$263,500** |
| Supplemental Schedule of Noncash Investing and Financial Activities: Issuance of Debt to Acquire Property and Equipment | $ - | $222,000 | $ - |

Source: www.smallcarrieruniversity.com

### Statement of Retained Earnings

The statement of retained earnings is typically presented at the bottom of the P&L, in the equity section of the balance sheet or as a separate sheet in the annual report. "Retained earnings for a firm equals total earnings to date less total dividends to date, adjusted by other transactions in some cases." (*Barron's*) A sample statement is provided below (example taken from *Barron's*):

| **Retained Earnings Statement** | |
|---|---|
| For the Year Ended December 31, 2001 | |
| Retained earnings, January 1, 2001, as previously reported | $400,000 |
| Prior period adjustment | 20,000 |
| Retroactive accounting principle change | (30,000) |
| Retained earnings, January 1, 2001 as adjusted | 390,000 |
| Net income, 2001 | 70,000 |
| Cash dividends declared | (30,000) |
| Stock dividends declared | (15,000) |
| Retained earnings, December 31, 2001 | $415,000 |

### Key Ratios

The data that in various financial reports is also used to produce different ratios that help to describe the organization's financial condition.

Key ratios fall into five categories and include:

- **Liquidity**
  - **Net working capital** = current assets – current liabilities
  - **Current ratio** = current assets ÷ current liabilities

Section 7

- Activity
  - **Accounts receivable turnover** = net credit sales ÷ average accounts receivable
  - **Inventory turnover** = cost of goods sold ÷ average inventory
  - **Total asset turnover** = net sales ÷ average total assets
- Leverage (also categorized as Debt)
  - **Debt ratio** = total debt ÷ total assets
  - **Debt/equity ratio** = total liabilities ÷ stockholders' equity
- Profitability
  - **Gross profit margin** = gross profit ÷ net sales
  - **Profit margin** = net income ÷ net sales
  - **Return on total assets** = net income ÷ average total assets
- Market value
  - **Earnings per share** = (net income – preferred dividends) ÷ common stock outstanding
  - **Price/earnings ratio** = market price per share ÷ earnings per share

Note: Some definitions and examples taken from *Barron's Finance* by A.A. Groppelli and Ehsan Nikbakht, fourth edition, Barron's Educational Series, 2000.

# Financial Principles and Practices

## Exercises

### Identifying Key Risk/Opportunity Tradeoffs [Strategic]

1. Select the most appropriate answer to each question.

All other things equal, what happens to customer wait times as the number of staff available to service them increases?

a. Customer wait times decrease

b. Customer wait times increase

c. Customer wait times stay the same

All other things equal, more trunks are needed at:

a. High service levels

b. Low service levels

c. There is no direct relationship between service level and trunks required

What happens to agent occupancy when service level increases?

a. Occupancy decreases

b. Occupancy increases

c. Occupancy stays the same

2. Briefly answer each of the following questions.

Although in most cases resource requirements decrease as average handling times decrease, what scenario would produce an increase in resource requirements when average handling times are lower?

When might an increase in cost per contact be a good thing?

**Applying the Principles of the Technology Adoption Lifecycle**

3. Select the most appropriate answer to each question.

Put the following divisions of the technology adoption lifecycle bell curve in order from first adopters to last adopters.

I. Early adopters

II. Early majority

III. Innovators

IV. Laggards

V. Late majority

a. II, III, I, V, IV

b. III, I, II, V, IV

c. II, III, I, IV, V

d. III, II, I, V, IV

Between which two consecutive divisions of the technology adoption lifecycle does the "chasm" fall?

a. Between Early adopters and Late majority

b. Between Early majority and Late majority

c. Between Early adopters and Early majority

d. Between Innovators and Early majority

**Principles of Developing an Effective Annual Operating Budget**

4. Select the most appropriate answer to the following question.

All of the following statements regarding an effective annual operating budget are true EXCEPT:

a. Drives the customer access strategy

b. Identifies both forecast and resource/results tradeoffs

c. Is an extension of resource planning

d. Is based on solid call center valuation

**Key Steps to Developing an Annual Operating Budget**

5. Select the most appropriate answer to the following question.

What is zero-based budgeting?

a. A budgeting technique that bases the current year budget on those from previous years.

b. A budgeting technique that disregards prior year budgets and requires managers to justify all budgeting dollars every year.

c. A budgeting technique that requires that expenditures equal budgeted amounts.

**Utilizing Variance Reports**

6. True or false

______Analyzing output variance reports is a good way to identify the reasons for variance.

## Definitions of Key Financial Concepts

7. Match the following financial terms with their definitions. You will use each statement only once.

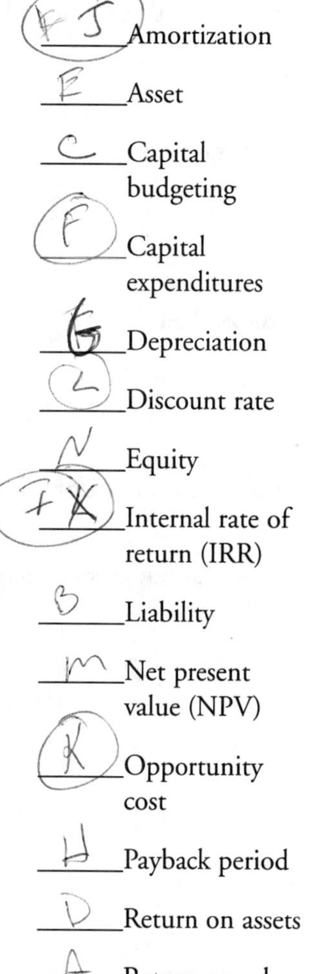

____ Amortization

____ Asset

____ Capital budgeting

____ Capital expenditures

____ Depreciation

____ Discount rate

____ Equity

____ Internal rate of return (IRR)

____ Liability

____ Net present value (NPV)

____ Opportunity cost

____ Payback period

____ Return on assets

____ Return on sales

a. A calculation that divides net income by sales to indicate if the return on sales is high enough. A low return on sales could indicate insufficient price mark-up to cover expenses.

b. A legal debt or obligation of the organization, e.g., loans, accounts payable, mortgages.

c. A method for evaluating, comparing, and selecting projects to achieve the best long-term financial gain.

d. A ratio that divides net income by average total assets. The resulting percentage indicates how much income has been generated from each dollar of the organization's assets.

e. Anything that an organization owns that has economic value, e.g., cash, real estate, inventory.

f. Long-term expenditures that are amortized over a period of time determined by IRS regulations.

g. The allocation of an asset's cost, for tax or management purposes, based on its age.

h. The amount of time required to recover the initial investment in a project.

i. The discount rate that makes the net present value of a project equal to zero.

j. The gradual, planned reduction in value of capital expenditures.

k. The rate of return on the best alternative investment that is not selected.

l. The required rate of return that a firm must achieve to justify its investments.

m. The present value of a project's future cash flow less the initial investment in the project.

n. The value of the funds contributed by the stockholders plus the retained earnings (or losses).

**Using Capital Budgeting Methods**

8. What is the payback point for the following example:

| Initial Investment | -95,000 | |
|---|---|---|
| Year | Cash Flow | Running Total |
| 1 | 45,000 | 45,000 |
| 2 | 47,000 | 92,000 |
| 3 | 49,000 | 141,000 |
| Payback Point | | |

2+, 3000/49,000
2.06 yrs

**Understanding and Using Depreciation Schedules**

9. Using the Sum-of-the-Years'-Digits Method complete the following table to determine the depreciation charges.

| | Asset value | Multiplier | Depreciation charges |
|---|---|---|---|
| Year 1 | $15,000 | | |
| Year 2 | $15,000 | | |
| Year 3 | $15,000 | | |

10. Select the most appropriate answer to the following question.

For properties placed in service after 1986, which of the four depreciation methods must be used for IRS purposes?

a. Double-declining balance

b. Modified Accelerated Cost Recovery System

c. Straight-line

d. Sum-of-the-years'-digits

Section 7

### Interpreting and Using Key Financial Statements

11. Fill in the blanks with the appropriate financial statement.

    a. Cash Flow Statement details the sources of cash coming into and flowing out of an organization. This statement provides information on the health of an organization's earnings and how they are using cash.

    b. Balance Sheet displays the assets of an organization balanced against its liabilities, capital, and surplus.

    c. P&L generally follows a very simple formula: revenue – expenses = net profit.

    d. Statement of Retained Earnings shows total earnings to date less total dividends to date, adjusted by other transactions in some cases.

**Answers to these exercises are in Section 10.**

Note: These exercises are intended to help you retain the material learned. While not the exact questions as on the CIAC Certification assessment, the material in this handbook/study guide fully addresses the content on which you will be assessed. For a formal practice test, please contact the CIAC directly by visiting www.ciac-cert.org.

# Financial Principles and Practices Reference Bibliography

## Related Articles from *Call Center Management Review* (See Section 9)

Avoiding Conflicting Objectives

The Technology Adoption Life Cycle: A Strategic Tool That Matters (Still)

The Principles Behind Effective Budgeting

Why Staff Shrinkage Perplexes Your CFO – and Shrinks Your Budget (First article in a series on calculating FTEs)

The Science and Judgement behind FTE Budgets (Second article in a trilogy on calculating FTEs)

Troubleshooting FTE Requirements (The final article in a trilogy on calculating FTEs)

Make Informed Technology Investment Decisions with Operational Cost Modeling



## For Further Study

**Books/Studies**

Cleveland, Brad and Julia Mayben. *Call Center Management on Fast Forward: Succeeding in Today's Dynamic Inbound Environment.* Call Center Press, 1999.

Cottle, Sidney, Roger F. Murray and Frank E. Block. *Graham and Dodd's Security Analysis,* Fifth edition. McGraw-Hill Book Publishing Company, 1988.

Groppelli, A.A. and Ehsan Nikbakht. *Barron's Finance,* Fourth edition. Barron's Educational Series, 2000.

**Articles**

Deck, Stewart. "Power of the Purse Strings." *Network World,* December 24, 2001.

## Seminars

*Essential Skills and Knowledge for Effective Incoming Call Center Management* public seminar, presented by Incoming Calls Management Institute.

*Effective Leadership and Strategy for Senior Call Center Managers* public seminar, presented by Incoming Calls Management Institute.

## Section 8

# *Glossary*

## Acronyms

**This list of acronyms is a combination of definitions provided by ICMI, Inc., and Vanguard Communications Corp.**


| | |
|---|---|
| ACD | Automatic Call Distributor |
| ACS | Automatic Call Sequencer |
| ACW | After Call Work |
| AHT | Average Handling Time |
| AHT | Average Holding Time on Trunks |
| ANI | Automatic Number Identification |
| ASA | Average Speed of Answer |
| ASP | Application Service Provider |
| ATA | Average Time to Abandonment |
| ATB | All Trunks Busy |
| BIC | Best In Class |
| BRI | Basic Rate Interface |
| CCR | Customer Controlled Routing |
| CED | Caller Entered Digits |
| CIS | Customer Information System (also Customer Interaction Software) |
| CLI | Calling Line Identity |
| CO | Central Office |
| CRM | Customer Relationship Management |
| CTI | Computer Telephony Integration |
| DID | Direct Inward Dialing |
| DN | Dialed Number |
| DNIS | Dialed Number Identification Service |
| DTMF | Dual-tone Multifrequency |
| ERP | Enterprise Resource Planning |

| | |
|---|---|
| EWT | Expected Wait Time |
| FX | Foreign Exchange Line |
| GUI | Graphical User Interface |
| HTML | Hyper Text Markup Language |
| IP | Internet Protocol |
| IS | Information Systems |
| ISDN | Integrated Services Digital Network |
| ISP | Internet Service Provider |
| IT | Information Technology |
| IVR | Interactive Voice Response |
| IWR | Interactive Web Response |
| IXC | Inter Exchange Carrier |
| LAN | Local Area Network |
| LEC | Local Exchange Carrier |
| LED | Light Emitting Diode |
| MIS | Management Information System |
| NCC | Network Control Center |
| OCR | Optical Character Recognition |
| ODBC | Open Database Connectivity |
| PABX | Private Automatic Branch Exchange |
| PBX | Private Branch Exchange |
| PRI | Primary Rate Interface |
| PSN | Public Switched Network |
| PSTN | Public Switched Telephone Network |
| PUC | Public Utility Commission |
| RFI | Request for Information |
| RFP | Request for Proposal |
| RFQ | Request for Quote |
| RSF | Rostered Staff Factor |

| | |
|---|---|
| SFA | Salesforce Automation |
| SMDI | Simplified Message Desk Interface |
| SMTP | Simple Mail Transfer Protocol |
| SQL | Structured Query Language |
| SS7 | Signaling System 7 |
| TCP/IP | Transmission Control Protocol/Internet Protocol |
| TSF | Telephone Service Factor |
| TSR | Telephone Sales or Service Representative |
| UCD | Uniform Call Distributor |
| VOIP/VoIP | Voice Over Internet Protocol |
| VPN | Virtual Private Network |
| VRU | Voice Response Unit |
| WAN | Wide Area Network |
| WATS | Wide Area Telecommunications Service |
| WFMS | Workforce Management System |
| WWW | World Wide Web |

# Glossary



**Abandoned Call.** Also called a Lost Call. The caller hangs up before reaching an agent.

**Adherence To Schedule.** A general term that refers to how well agents adhere to their schedules. Can include both: a) how much time they were available to take calls during their shifts, including the time spent handling calls and the time spent waiting for calls to arrive (also called Availability); and b) when they were available to take calls (also called Compliance or Adherence). See Real-Time Adherence Software and Occupancy.

**After-Call Work (ACW).** Also called Wrapup and Post-Call Processing (PCP). Work that is necessitated by and immediately follows an inbound transaction. Often includes entering data, filling out forms and making outbound calls necessary to complete the transaction. The agent is unavailable to receive another inbound call while in this mode.

**Agent.** The person who handles incoming or outgoing calls. Also referred to as customer service representative (CSR), telephone sales or service representative (TSR), rep, associate, consultant, engineer, operator, technician, account executive, team member, customer service professional, staff member, attendant and specialist.

**Agent Features.** Features on the switch specific to the needs of a call center agent. Typically include login/logout, changes to work states (available, not available/not ready, after-call work/wrapup), transaction codes, supervisor assistance request, audio trouble indication, call trace indicator (for malicious calls) and queue status.

**Agent Group.** Also called Split, Gate, Queue or Skills Group. A collection of agents who share a common set of skills, such as being able to handle customer complaints.

**Agent Out Call.** An outbound call placed by an agent.

**Agent Status.** The mode an agent is in (Talk Time, After-Call Work, Unavailable, etc.).

**All Trunks Busy (ATB).** When all trunks are busy in a specified trunk group. Generally, reports indicate how many times all trunks were busy, and how much total time all trunks were busy. What they don't reveal is how many callers got busy signals when all trunks were busy.

**Analog.** Telephone transmission or switching that is not digital. Signals are analogous to the original signal.

**Announcement.** A recorded verbal message played to callers.

**Answer Supervision.** The signal sent by the ACD or other device to the local or long-distance carrier to accept a call. This is when billing for either the caller or the call center will begin, if long-distance charges apply.

**Answered Call.** When referring to an agent group, a call counted as answered when it reaches an agent.

**Application Service Provider (ASP).** An outsourcing business that hosts software applications at its own facilities. Customers "rent" the applications, usually for a monthly

**Automated Attendant.** A voice-processing capability that automates the operator/receptionist function. Callers are prompted to respond to menu choices by entering digits on their telephone, and their call is routed based upon the selected menu choices. This function can reside in an onsite system (e.g., switch, voicemail or IVR) or in the network.

**Automatic Call Distribution/Distributor (ACD).** A software application that routes incoming telephone calls. At its most basic, the ACD usually routes calls based on the trunk group of the call or the number the caller dialed (see Dialed Number Identification Service) to the longest available agent in a group; it "queues" calls when there is no agent available – usually on a first-in/first-out basis. ACDs can also provide announcements or options to callers while they are in queue, route based on conditional parameters (see Conditional Routing), and route based on agent skills (see Skills-Based Routing). Some provide basic prompting capabilities as well. Most ACDs provide reporting capabilities either as a part of the ACD software or an add-on package. May be a stand-alone system, or ACD capability built into a Central Office, network, LAN or PBX.

**Automatic Call Sequencer (ACS).** A simple system that is less sophisticated than an ACD, but provides some ACD-like functionality.

**Automatic Number Identification (ANI).** An enhanced network service offering that provides the calling party's telephone billing number. Often used for caller identification in applications such as IVR, screen pops and intelligent routing.

**Auxiliary Work State.** An agent work state that is typically not associated with handling telephone calls. When agents are in an auxiliary mode, they will not receive inbound calls.

**Availability.** See Adherence to Schedule.

**Available State.** Agents who are signed on to the ACD and waiting for calls to arrive.

**Available Time.** The total time that an agent or agent group waited for calls to arrive, for a given time period.

**Average Delay.** See Average Speed of Answer.

**Average Delay of Delayed Calls.** The average delay of calls that are delayed. It is the total Delay for all calls divided by the number of calls that had to wait in queue. See Average Speed of Answer.

**Average Handle Time (AHT).** The sum of Average Talk Time and Average After-Call Work for a specified time period.

**Average Holding Time on Trunks (AHT).** The average time inbound transactions occupy the trunks. It is: (Talk Time + Delay Time)/Calls Received. AHT is also an acronym for Average Handling Time, which has a different meaning.

**Average Number of Agents.** The average number of agents logged into a group for a specified time period.

**Average Speed of Answer (ASA).** Also called Average Delay. The average delay of all calls. It is total Delay divided by total number of calls. See Average Delay of Delayed Calls.

**Average Time to Abandonment.** The average time that callers wait in queue before abandoning. The calculation considers only the calls that abandon.

**Base Staff.** Also called Seated Agents. The minimum number of agents required to achieve service level and response time objectives for given period of time. Seated agent calculations assume that agents will be "in their seats" for the entire period of time. Therefore, schedules need to add in extra people to accommodate breaks, absenteeism and other factors that will keep agents from the phones. See Rostered Staff Factor.

**Basic Rate Interface (BRI).** One of the two levels of ISDN service. A BRI line provides two voice-grade channels, known as "bearer" channels, which can be used for voice and/or data (data on BRI bearer channels is limited to speeds of 56 kbps) and one data channel for signaling. This configuration is commonly referred to as 2B+D. See Integrated Services Digital Network.

**Beep Tone.** An audible notification that a call has arrived (also called Zip Tone). Beep tone can also refer to the audible notification that a call is being monitored.

**Benchmark.** Historically, a term referred to as a standardized task to test the capabilities of devices against each other. In quality terms, benchmarking is comparing products, services and processes with those of other organizations, to identify new ideas and improvement opportunities.

**Best-in-Class.** A term to identify organizations that outperform all others in a specified category.

**Blockage.** Callers blocked from entering a queue. See Blocked Call.

**Blocked Call.** A call that cannot be connected immediately because: a) No circuit is available at the time the call arrives, or b) the ACD is programmed to block calls from entering the queue when the queue backs up beyond a defined threshold.

**Business Rules.** A phrase used to refer to various software controls that manage contact routing, handling or follow up. Often used interchangeably with workflow.

**Busy Hour.** A telephone traffic engineering term, referring to the hour of time in which a trunk group carries the most traffic during the day. The average busy hour reflects the average over a period of days, such as two weeks. Busy Hour has little use for incoming call centers, which require more specific resource calculation methodologies.

**Calibration.** The process in which variations in the way performance criteria (especially monitoring criteria) are interpreted from person to person are minimized.

**Call.** Also called Transaction and Customer Contact. A term referring to telephone calls, video calls, Web calls and other types of contacts.

**Call Blending.** Traditionally, the ability to dynamically allocate call center agents to both inbound and outbound calling, based on conditions in the call center and programmed parameters. This enables a single agent to handle both inbound and outbound calls from the same position, without manually monitoring call activity and reassigning the position. The outbound dialing application monitors inbound calling activity and assigns outbound agents to handle inbound calls as inbound volume increases, and assigns inbound agents to outbound calling when the inbound volume drops off. Note: Call blending has evolved to also refer to blending calls with nonphone work, or handling contacts from different channels (e.g., email and phone).

**Call-By-Call Routing.** The process of routing each call to the optimum destination according to real-time conditions. See Percent Allocation and Network Inter-flow.

**Call Center.** An umbrella term that generally refers to groups of agents handling reservations, help desks, catalog order functions, information lines or customer service, regardless of how they are organized or what types of transactions they handle. Characteristics of a call center generally include:

- Calls go to a group of people, not a specific person. In other words, agents are cross-trained to handle a variety of transactions.
- An ACD system is used to distribute calls among agents, put calls in queue when all agents are occupied, and play messages while callers are in queue.
- Call centers use advanced network services (e.g., 800 and 888 services) and most use voice-processing capabilities.
- Agents have quick access to current information via specialized database programs (status of customer accounts, products, services and other information).
- Management challenges include forecasting calls, calculating staffing requirements, organizing sensible schedules, managing the environment in real time and getting the right people in the right places at the right times.

ICMI has defined call center as "A coordinated system of people, processes, technologies, and strategies that provide access to organizational resources through appropriate channels of communication to enable interactions that create value for the customer and organization."

**Call Load.** Also referred to as Workload. Call Load is the product of (Average Talk Time + Average After-Call Work) x call volume, for a given period.

**Caller ID.** See Automatic Number Identification.

**Caller Entered Digits** (CED). The digits that a caller enters on their telephone keypad. Primarily used in auto attendant, voice response and CTI applications.

**Calling Line Identity** (CLI). See Automatic Number Identification.

**Calls In Queue.** A real-time report that refers to the number of calls received by the ACD system but not yet connected to an agent.

**Career Path.** A set of structured career advancement opportunities within the call center and/or organization. See Skill Path.

**Carrier.** A company that provides telecommunications circuits. Carriers include both local telephone companies (or Local Exchange Carriers – LECs) and long-distance providers (or Inter-Exchange Carriers – IXCs).

**Cause-and-Effect Diagram.** A tool to assist in root-cause identification, developed by Dr. Kaoru Ishikawa.

**Central Office (CO).** Can refer to either a telephone company switching center or the type of telephone switch used in a telephone company switching center. The local central office receives calls from within the local area and either routes them locally or passes them to an inter-exchange carrier (IXC). On the receiving end, the local central office receives calls that originated in other areas, from the IXC.

**Centrex.** A central office telephone switch service that serves a defined geographic area. Similar to a PBX, except that it is owned by the local telephone company and is used by multiple business and/or residential customers.

**Circuit.** A transmission path between two points in a network.

**Circuit Switching.** A method of transferring information across a network by establishing an available path ("circuit") and using that path for the entire period of connection. Typically used to transmit voice (e.g., over the Public Switched Telephone Network - PSTN).

**Client/Server Architecture.** A networking scheme in which a client application requests information from a server application. The server application processes the request and delivers the requested information back to the client application. See Server.

**Coaching.** Feedback given during ongoing meetings (formal and/or informal) between an individual and his/her manager to discuss performance, development, career, etc. Coaching can be thought of as one-on-one interactive training.

**Collateral Duties.** Nonphone tasks (e.g., data entry) that are flexible, and can be scheduled for periods when call load is slow.

**Common Causes.** Causes of variation that are inherent to a process over time. They cause the rhythmic, common variations in the system of causes, and they affect every outcome of the process and everyone working in the process. See Special Causes.

**Communications Server.** An alternative to the PBX that manages and routes voice, fax, Web and video communications within a single server. Typically based on a Windows NT platform. Communications Servers are generally seen in small to medium (five to 75 agents) size contact centers that can benefit from an integrated solution that otherwise would be cost-prohibitive as separate point solutions (e.g., IVR, ACD, CTI).

**Compensation.** Base pay, incentives and benefits given to an employee in return for services rendered. Skills-based compensation pays agents on the basis of the skills they can perform, regardless of their job title. Job-based compensation ties pay to the value of the job function, not the skills of individuals.

**Compliance.** See Adherence to Schedule.

**Computer Simulation.** A computer technique to predict the outcome of various events in the future, given many variables. When there are many variables, simulation is often the only way to reasonably predict the outcome.

**Computer Telephony Integration (CTI).** The functional integration of various computer and telephone system elements that enables voice and data networks to work together and share information. CTI enables a number of useful call center applications, including screen pops, intelligent routing, cradle-to-grave reporting and voice/data transfer.

**Conditional Routing.** Intelligently routing calls to the right groups(s), position or treatment (e.g., announcements, music, options) based on current call center conditions, defined time/day parameters, information on the call or caller type, or other parameters. Implemented through routing tables and decision trees.

**Contact Management.** Business application that creates a record of and tracks each contact made with the customer. Also provides contact history information. Creates a database that enables informed communications with customers, database marketing and proactive communications. Includes functions such as contact history database and triggers for follow-up contacts.

**Continuous Improvement.** The ongoing improvement of processes.

**Control Chart.** A control chart sifts out (identifies) two types of variation in a process, common causes and special causes. See Common Causes and Special Causes.

**Controlled Busies.** The capability of the ACD to generate busy signals when the queue backs up beyond a programmable threshold.

**Core Values.** Describe the principles the organization turns to when making its most critical decisions.

**Cost Center.** An accounting term that refers to a department or function in the organization that does not generate profit. See Profit Center.

**Cost of Delay.** The money you pay to queue callers, assuming you have toll-free service.

**Cost Per Call.** Total costs (fixed and variable) divided by total calls for a given period of time.

**Cross-Sell.** Offering additional products or services to current customers, usually based on relationships established between the customer's profile and the attributes of customers who have already purchased the products or services being cross-sold.

**Customer.** Includes individuals, households and/or organizations that have in the past, or may in the future, interact with your organization. Customers may be external (i.e., not a part of your organization) or internal (i.e., members of your organization to which you provide service).

**Customer Contact.** See Call.

**Customer Information System (CIS).** An application and database or series of linked databases that enables users to view and interact with all the available information about a customer's relationship with the company, including their transactions with each department in the enterprise. See Customer Relationship Management.

**Customer Interaction Software.** Another name for Customer Information System (see above).

**Customer Lifetime Value.** Expresses the value of a customer to the organization over the entire probable time period that the customer will interact with the organization.

**Customer Loyalty.** Typically defined in terms of the customer's repurchase behavior, intent to purchase again or intent to recommend the organization.

**Customer Profiling.** Process of collecting and maintaining information about customers and their relationship to your organization. The information is most often used for customer segmentation and building customer relationships. Customer Profiling determines what information about a customer is important to the organization. See Customer Segmentation.

**Customer Relationship Management (CRM).** The process of holistically managing a customer's relationship with a company. It takes into account their history as a customer, the depth and breadth of their business with the company, as well as other factors. CRM generally uses a sophisticated applications and database system that includes elements of Data Mining, Contact Management and Enterprise Resource Planning, allowing agents and analysts to know and anticipate customer behavior better. (There are many terms being used for CRM. It is also referred to as eCRM, eRM, ERM, EIM and BRM, and other combinations, where the small "e" refers to electronic, the large "E" refers to enterprise, the "I" refers to Interaction, and the "B" refers to Business.)

**Customer Retention Rate.** The percentage of a prior period's customers that are still customers in the current period (excluding new customers acquired).

**Customer Satisfaction.** Measures the percentage of all customers who felt satisfied. The most common way of measuring Customer Satisfaction is through customer surveys. Studies have linked Customer Satisfaction to customer loyalty, repeat purchase behavior and word-of-mouth advertising. See Customer Loyalty.

**Customer Segmentation.** Process of grouping customers based on what you know about them (see Customer Profiling), in order to apply differentiated marketing, relationship and contact treatment strategies.

**Data-Directed Routing.** Call (or other media type) routing which is controlled by information in a database. For example, a caller will be automatically routed to a collections group if his account is past due.

**Data Mining.** The use of sophisticated analysis tools, such as OLAP, to identify patterns within one or more databases (usually data from a Data Warehouse). For example, data mining can be used to identify that customers who purchase superwidgets, generally live in Minnesota. This may provide a sales opportunity to be "flagged" if a caller from Minnesota contacts the company. Data Mining helps companies learn more about their customers and leverage that information to provide customized service and expand relationships.

**Data Warehousing.** A large database that stores data generated by an organization's multiple business systems. Data can be extracted using report generators, sophisticated decision support systems or other analytical tools (see Data Mining).

**Day-of-Week Routing.** A network service that routes calls to alternate locations, based on the day of week. There are also options for day-of-year and time-of-day routing.

**Delay Announcements.** Recorded announcements that encourage callers to wait for an agent to become available, remind them to have their account number ready, and provide information on access alternatives.

**Delay.** Also called Queue Time. The time a caller spends in queue waiting for an agent to become available. Average Delay is the same thing as Average Speed of Answer. Also see Average Delay of Delayed Calls.

**Delayed Call.** A call that cannot be answered immediately and is placed in queue.

**Dialed Number (DN).** The number that the caller dialed to initiate the call.

**Dialed Number Identification Service (DNIS).** A string of digits that the telephone network passes to the ACD, VRU or other device, to indicate which number the caller dialed. The ACD can then process and report on that type of call according to user-defined criteria. One trunk group can have many DNIS numbers.

**Digital.** The use of a binary code – 1s and 0s – to represent information.

**Direct Inward Dialing (DID).** A network service offering – generally associated with local service – where a unique set of identifying digits is passed to the customer premises equipment. By mapping each set of digits to an internal extension, the switch can provide direct dialing to a particular extension. See Dialed Number Identification Services.

**Dual-Tone Multifrequency (DTMF).** A signaling system, used by the standard telephone, that sends pairs of audio frequencies to represent each digit on a telephone keypad. A related term, Touchtone, is a trademark of AT&T.

**Empowerment.** A business strategy that gives ownership and responsibility to the individuals who have direct contact with the product, service, and customer. Empowerment shifts the direction and control from the supervisor (an external force) to the individual (with an internal force or desire to perform).

**Enterprise Resource Planning (ERP).** A large-scale business application or set of applications that encompass some or all aspects of a business, such as finance, production, order processing, fulfillment, billing and HR. These are typically referred to as "back-office" functions. There is an evolution within the ERP industry to either provide add-on modules or integrate with third party applications for "front office" functions such as sales, marketing and service. Applications that combine these "front office" functions are generally referred to as Customer Relationship Management applications (See Customer Relationship Management).

**Envelope Strategy.** A strategy whereby enough agents are scheduled for the day or week to handle both the inbound call load and other types of work. Priorities are based on the inbound call load. When call load is heavy, all agents handle calls, but when it is light, some agents are reassigned to work that is not as time-sensitive.

**Environmental Scan.** Technique to survey the landscape in which an organization conducts business in order to determine the current status of a specific issue or predict future trends.

**Erlang.** One hour of telephone traffic in an hour of time. For example, if circuits carry 120 minutes of traffic in an hour, that's two Erlangs.

**Erlang, A.K.** A Danish engineer who worked for the Copenhagen Telephone Company in the early 1900s and developed Erlang B, Erlang C and other telephone traffic engineering formulas.

**Erlang B.** A formula developed by A.K. Erlang, widely used to determine the number of trunks required to handle a known calling load during a one-hour period. The formula assumes that if callers get busy signals, they go away forever, never to retry ("lost calls cleared"). Since some callers retry, Erlang B can underestimate trunks required. However, Erlang B is generally accurate in situations with few busy signals.

**Erlang C.** Mathematical tool used to calculate predicted waiting times (delay) based on three things: the number of servers (agents); the number of people waiting to be served (callers); and the average amount of time it takes to serve each person. It can also predict the resources required to keep waiting times within targeted limits. Erlang C assumes no lost calls or busy signals, so it has a tendency to overestimate staff required.

**Error Rate.** Either the number of defective transactions or the number of defective steps in a transaction.

**Expected Wait Time (EWT).** A formula that uses real-time and historical queue data to approximate how long a caller will have to wait for an agent. Depending on the wait time, callers may be offered options of staying on hold, hanging up, leaving a callback request or transferring to an IVR.

**Expert System.** Business application that aids the user in analyzing and resolving problems based on logic trees and known solutions to identified problems. (Also known as Knowledge Based System.) Includes functions such as problem analysis and problem resolution.

**Extranet.** Networks, typically connected via the Internet, providing for direct and secure business-to-business access between suppliers and vendors or other partners.

**Fast Clear Down.** A caller who hangs up immediately when they hear a delay announcement.

**Fax on Demand.** Allows callers to select (generally through a voice response system bu can also be through a Web site) and receive a fax document providing information about a particular subject, account details, or other information. Once the document is selected, it is sent to a fax machine of their choice either immediately or within a specified period of time. Fax on Demand can be part of a voice-processing application or stand-alone.

**Flow Chart.** A step-by-step diagram of a process.

**Flushing out the Queue.** Changing system thresholds so that calls waiting for an agent group are redirected to another group with a shorter queue or available agents.

**Forecasting.** In a call center, the process of predicting call (and other types of contact) volumes and workload in order to staff appropriately to meet desired service level and response time goals.

**Full-Time Equivalent (FTE).** A term used in scheduling and budgeting, whereby the number of scheduled hours is divided by the hours in a full work week. The hours of several part-time agents may add up to one FTE.

**Gate.** See Agent Group.

**Graphical User Interface (GUI).** An interface that uses icons, menus and a mouse to manage interaction with the system, instead of complex programming languages.

**Handled Calls.** The number of calls received and handled by agents or peripheral equipment. Handled calls does not include calls that abandon or receive busy signals.

**Handling Time.** The time an agent spends in Talk Time and After-Call Work handling a transaction. Handling Time can also refer to the time it takes for a machine to process a transaction.

**Help Desk.** A term that generally refers to a call center set up to handle queries about product installation, usage or problems. The term is most often used in the context of computer software and hardware support centers.

**Holding Time.** See Average Holding Time on Trunks.

**Home Agent.** See Remote Agents.

**HyperText Markup Language (HTML).** A language derived from the Standard Generalized Markup Language (SGML), primarily used to create Web pages.

**Immutable Law.** A law of nature that is fundamental and not changeable (e.g., the law of gravity). In an inbound call center, the fact that occupancy goes up when service level goes down is an immutable law.

**Incoming Call Center Management.** The art of having the right number of skilled people and supporting resources in place at the right times to handle an accurately forecasted workload, at service level and with quality.

**Integrated Services Digital Network (ISDN).** A set of international standards for telephone transmission. ISDN provides an end-to-end digital network, out-of-band signaling and greater bandwidth than older telephone services. The two standard levels are Basic Rate Interface (BRI) and Primary Rater Interface (PRI). Often used in call centers to deliver signaling information quickly for use of ANI and DNIS, and for faster call setup and tear down.

**Inter-Exchange Carriers.** Telephone companies responsible for providing long-distance services. See Carrier.

**Interface (BRI) and Primary Rater Interface (PRI).** Often used in call centers to deliver signaling information quickly for use of ANI and DNIS, and for faster call setup and tear down.

**Intelligent Routing.** The use of information about the caller, current conditions or other parameters to route calls to the appropriate group, individual, automated system, etc. DNIS, ANI, customer-entered digits and database information all can be used as routing parameters. Can augment or replace conditional and skills-based routing performed on the switch. Generally enabled via CTI.

**Interactive Voice Response (IVR).** Systems that enable callers to use their telephone keypad (or spoken commands if speech recognition is used) to access a company's computer system for the purpose of retrieving or updating information, conducting a business transaction or routing their calls.

**Interactive Web Response (IWR).** Systems that enable customers to use their PC and an Internet connection to access a company's computer system for the purpose of retrieving or updating information or conducting a business transaction.

**Interflow.** See Overflow.

**Internal Help Desk.** A group that supports other internal agent groups, e.g., for complex or escalated calls.

**Internal Response Time.** The time it takes an agent group that supports other internal groups (e.g., for complex or escalated tasks) to respond to transactions that do not have to be handled when they arrive (e.g., correspondence or email). See Response Time and Service Level.

**Internet.** A worldwide, expanding network of linked computers, founded by the U.S. government and several universities in 1969, originally call Arpanet and based on TCP/IP protocol. Made available for commercial use in 1992.

**Internet Protocol (IP).** The set of communication standards that control communications activity on the Internet. An IP address is assigned to every computer on the Internet.

**Intraflow.** See Overflow.

**Intranet.** A company's private data network that is accessed using browser-based technology and TCP/IP protocol.

**IP Telephony.** Technology that enables voice telephone calls to be carried over a data network (a private intranet or the public Internet) using the Internet protocol. Voice is transmitted in data packets. Generally used today to obtain lower costs for long-distance (often international) calls. Quality of service (latency, delays, lost packets) is the greatest challenge to widespread use for call centers (does not match circuit-switched voice over the public network today), and is being addressed. Also referred to as Internet Telephony.

**Internet Service Provider (ISP).** A company that provides Internet access to customers, either through a modem or direct connection.

**Invisible Queue.** When callers do not know how long the queue is or how fast it is moving. See Visible Queue.

**Judgmental Forecasting.** Goes beyond purely statistical techniques and encompasses what people believe is going to happen. It is in the realm of intuition, interdepartmental committees, market research and executive opinion.

**Knowledge-Based System.** See Expert System.

**Knowledge Management.** A method of organizing a company's internal and external processes, product, and service documentation, information about customers, prospects, competitors, partners, etc. It searches through company databases to enable access to collective knowledge.

**Law of Diminishing Returns.** The declining marginal improvements in service level that can be attributed to each additional agent, as successive agents are added.

**Legacy Systems.** Information systems or databases that house core business information such as customer records. May be based on older technologies (e.g., mainframes, mini-computers) but are still used for day-to-day operations.

**Load Balancing.** Balancing traffic between two or more destinations.

**Local Area Network (LAN).** The connection of multiple computers (usually within close proximity) to enable sharing information, applications and peripherals.

**Local Exchange Carrier (LEC).** Telephone companies responsible for providing local connections and services.

**Logged On.** A state in which agents have signed on to a system (made their presence known), but may or may not be ready to receive calls.

**Long Call.** For staffing calculations and traffic engineering purposes, calls that approach or exceed 30 minutes.

**Longest Available Agent.** A method of distributing calls to the agent who has been sitting idle the longest. With a queue, Longest Available Agent becomes "Next Available Agent."

**Longest Delay (Oldest Call).** The longest time a caller has waited in queue, before abandoning or reaching an agent.

**Lost Call.** See Abandoned Call.

**Management Information System (MIS).** A system that facilitates the capture and reporting of activity within the telephony and computing infrastructure.

**Market Research.** The disciplined process of collecting, analyzing and interpreting information about customers in order to make better decisions about meeting customer needs and expectations.

**Middleware.** Software that provides the means to access and integrate different types of hardware and software within a network. Typically uses open interfaces and applications programming interfaces (APIs) to access and move information.

**Mission.** Clarifies the organization's purpose. The mission statement declares why the organization exists, and therefore what it strives to do in every transaction and decision it makes.

**Modem.** A contraction of the terms Modulator/Demodulator. A Modem converts analog signals to digital and vice versa.

**Monitoring.** Also called Position Monitoring, Quality Monitoring or Service Observing. The process of listening to agents' telephone calls for the purpose of maintaining quality. Monitoring can be: a) silent, in which agents don't know when they are being monitored, b) side by side, in which the person monitoring sits next to the agent and observes calls, or c) record and review, in which calls are recorded and later played back and assessed.

**Multimedia.** Combining multiple forms of media in the communication of information. (For instance, a traditional phone call is "monomedia," and a video call is "multimedia.")

**Multimedia Queuing.** Handling customer contacts through different channels (inbound calls, outbound calls, voice messages, email, Web calls, text-chat, fax, video, etc.) in a common queue. Allows customers to choose the method of contact and ensures all contacts are handled according to business rules in a timely way. Requires advanced technology to integrate media, and route and report on it.

**Net Rep.** A call center agent trained to handle Internet transactions such as email, text chat, web callbacks, co-browsing, etc.

**Network Computer.** Sometimes referred to as a "thin" client. A computer, usually a PC, with limited or no disk storage, designed solely for connection to servers within a network. Applications reside on and are run within the server rather than the client. See Thin Client.



**Network Control Center.** Also called Traffic Control Center. In a networked call center environment, in which people and equipment monitor real-time conditions across sites, change routing thresholds as necessary and coordinate events that will impact base staffing levels.

**Network Inter-flow.** A technology used in multisite call center environments to create a more efficient distribution of calls between sites. Through integration of sites using network circuits (such as T1 circuits) and ACD software, calls routed to one site may be queued simultaneously for agent groups in remote sites. See Call-by-Call Routing and Percent Allocation.

**Network Routing.** The ability to make routing decisions in the network before selecting a location to route the call. Network routing can be based on factors such as the time of day, day of week, percentage of calls to be handled at each site, area code of the calling party, DNIS or information gathered from databases via CTI.

**Next Available Agent.** A call distribution method that sends calls to the next agent who becomes available. The method seeks to maintain an equal load across skill groups or services. When there is no queue, Next Available Agent reverts to Longest Available Agent.

**Occupancy.** Also referred to as agent utilization. The percentage of time agents handle calls vs. wait for calls to arrive. For a half-hour, the calculation is: (call volume x average handling time in seconds) / (number of agents x 1800 seconds). See Adherence to Schedule.

**Offered Calls.** All of the attempts callers make to reach the call center. There are three possibilities for offered calls: 1) They can get busy signals; 2) they can be answered by the system, but hang up before reaching a rep; or 3) they can be answered by a rep. Offered call reports in ACDs usually refer only to the calls that the system receives.

**Open Database Connectivity (ODBC).** A standard method of accessing databases on a variety of platforms. Defined by the SQL (Structured Query Language) Access Group.

**Outsourcing.** Contracting some or all call center services to an outside company.

**Overflow.** Calls that flow from one group or site to another. More specifically, Intraflow happens when calls flow between agent groups and Interflow is when calls flow out of the ACD to another site.

**Overlay.** See Rostered Staff Factor.

**Pareto Chart.** A bar chart that arranges events in order of frequency. Named after 19th century economist Vilfredo Pareto.

**PBX/ACD.** A PBX that is equipped with ACD functionality.

**Peaked Call Arrival.** A surge of traffic beyond random variation. It is a spike within a short period of time.

**Percent Allocation.** A call-routing strategy sometimes used in multisite call center environments. Calls received in the network are allocated across sites based on user-defined percentages. See Call-by-Call Routing and Network Inter-flow.

**Percent Utilization.** See Occupancy.

**Pooling Principle.** The Pooling Principle states: Any movement in the direction of consolidation of resources will result in improved traffic-carrying efficiency. Conversely, any movement away from consolidation of resources will result in reduced traffic-carrying efficiency.

**Post-Call Processing.** See After-Call Work.

**Predictive Dialing.** An application that instructs the switch to dial multiple simultaneous calls based upon a preloaded list of phone numbers. A mathematical algorithm is used to predict the correct number of calls to launch and when agents will become available. Then it seeks to match the number of live connected calls with the number of available agents. The system determines when a called party has answered and transfers only live calls (and answering machines, if desired) to agents. Agents also receive a data screen about the call. The system classifies all calls launched (e.g., connect, busy, no answer, answering machine, network tones) and updates the database accordingly.

**Preview Dialing.** An application that instructs the switch to outdial a specific phone number under control of an agent or a timer. The agent previews a screen containing information about the person to be called, monitors the call for connection (or other classification), and updates the database accordingly. Used for callbacks or other contacts where the agent needs to review information before placing the call.

**Primary Rate Interface (PRI).** One of the two levels of ISDN service. In North America, PRI provides 23 bearer channels for voice and data and one channel for signaling information (commonly expressed as 23B+D). In Europe, PRI provides 30 bearer lines (30B+D). See Integrated Services Digital Network.

**Private Automatic Branch Exchange (PABX).** See Private Branch Exchange.

**Private Branch Exchange (PBX) or Private Automated Branch Exchange (PABX).** A telephone system located at a user's premise that handles incoming and outgoing calls and provides many features for call routing and management. By adding ACD software, a PBX can provide ACD functionality, such as queuing calls.

**Private Network.** A network made up of circuits for the exclusive use of an organization or group of affiliated organizations. Can be regional, national or international in scope and are common in large organizations.

**Process.** A system of causes.

**Profit Center.** An accounting term that refers to a department or function in the organization that does not generate profit. See Cost Center.

**Progressive Dialing.** The term is either used as a variation on preview dialing or predictive dialing. Some use progressive dialing to describe preview dialing where the preview is timed before automatically launching. Some use progressive dialing to describe a form of controlled predictive dialing where multiple calls are launched only when an agent becomes available. It is still predictive in that it is predicting how many calls will connect. However, it reduces the chance of a live answer by a customer when no agent is available.



**Public Switched Telephone Network (PSTN).** The network that interconnects telephones (the good old telephone network we all use every day!).

**Qualitative Analysis.** Analysis that interprets descriptive data usually expressed as text.

**Quality Monitoring Tools.** Tools used to assess agent contact-handling skills, allowing specific or random selection of positions, trunks, queues, or other entities to monitor. Monitoring can be real-time or recorded and may include data as well as voice. Quality monitoring tools now monitor email and Web contacts as well.

**Quantitative Analysis.** Analysis that focuses on numerical, mathematical or statistical data.

**Quantitative Forecasting.** Using statistical techniques to forecast future events. The major categories of quantitative forecasting include Time Series and Explanatory approaches. Time Series techniques use past trends to forecast future events. Explanatory techniques attempt to reveal linkages between two or more variables. See Judgmental Forecasting.

**Queue.** Holds callers until an agent becomes available. Queue can also refer to a line or list of items in a system waiting to be processed (e.g., email messages).

**Queue Display.** See Readerboard.

**Queue Time.** See Delay.

**Random Call Arrival.** The normal random variation in how incoming calls arrive. See Peaked Call Arrival.

**Readerboard.** Also called Display Board or Wallboard or Electronic Display. A visual display, usually mounted on the wall or ceiling of a call center, which provides real-time and historical information on queue conditions, agent status and call center performance. It can also display user-entered messages.

**Real-Time Adherence Software.** Software that tracks how closely agents conform to their schedules. See Adherence to Schedule.

**Real-Time Data.** Information on current conditions. Some "real-time" information is real-time in the strictest sense (e.g., calls in queue and current longest wait). Some real-time reports require some history (e.g., the last x calls or x minutes) in order to make a calculation (e.g. service level and average speed of answer). See Screen Refresh.

**Real-Time Management.** Making adjustments to staffing and thresholds in the systems and network, in response to current queue conditions.

**Received Calls.** A call detected and seized by a trunk. Received calls will either abandon or be answered by an agent.

**Remote Agents.** Fully integrated call center agents residing at home or other remote location. It is transparent to callers that they are remote. Requires both telephony and data connectivity from a main site to the agent's location, and the same features and functions available to agents on site.

**Response Time.** The time it takes the call center to respond to transactions that do not have to be handled when they arrive (e.g., correspondence or email). See Service Level.

**Retention.** The continued employment of staff. Retention is the opposite of turnover. See Turnover.

**Retrial Tables.** Sometimes used to calculate trunks and other system resources required. They assume that some callers will make additional attempts to reach the call center if they get busy signals. See Erlang B and Poisson.

**Retrial.** A caller who "retries" when he or she gets a busy signal.

**Rostered Staff Factor (RSF).** Alternatively called an Overlay, Shrink Factor or Shrinkage. RSF is a numerical factor that leads to the minimum staff needed on schedule over and above base staff required to achieve your service level and response time objectives. It is calculated after base staffing is determined and before schedules are organized, and accounts for things like breaks, absenteeism and ongoing training.

**Round-Robin Distribution.** A method of distributing calls to agents according to a predetermined list. See Next Available Agent and Longest Waiting Agent.

**Sales Force Automation (SFA).** A class of business applications designed to automate the marketing and sales process. Historically, they were limited to such areas as "opportunity management" and "interactive selling." Today, the term usually refers to any technology-enabled sales tools and often includes contact and customer relationship management. See Customer Relationship Management.

**Satellite Office.** A call center location that operates using a cabinet or carrier of a switch from a main location. Used to extend one switch to another site to operate virtually without purchasing a second switch.

**Scatter Diagram.** A chart that graphically depicts the relationship between two variables.

**Schedule Compliance.** See Adherence to Schedule.

**Scheduling.** Allocating call center agents and other resources in a way that will meet service level and other goals for specific days and times. Scheduling is generally based on historical call center activity, agent skills and performance, and knowledge of planned events.

**Scheduling Exception.** When an agent is involved in an activity outside of the normal, planned schedule.

**Screen Monitoring.** A system capability that enables a supervisor or manager to remotely monitor the activity on agents' computer terminals..Call Center Operations Management Study Guide: CIAC Module Two o Version 1 o Copyrighted to ICMI, Inc., 2001

**Screen Pop.** A CTI application. See Coordinated Voice/Data Delivery.

**Screen Refresh.** The rate at which real-time information is updated on a display (e.g., every five to 15 seconds). Note, screen refresh does not correlate with the timeframe used for real-time calculations. See Real-Time Data.

**Scripting.** Sometimes referred to as "dialog manager." An application that provides scripts to agents to aid in call handling (e.g., product description, promotional offer, wrap-up information). Can generally be controlled and modified to accommodate various situations and individuals (e.g., different levels of experience, full scripts vs. reminder lists, generic or customized).

**Seated Agents.** See Base Staff.

**Server.** A computer that shares its resources with other computers on a network. For example, file servers share disk storage with other computers. Database servers respond to requests from other computers on the network (clients).

**Service Bureau.** A company that handles inbound or outbound calls for another organization.

**Service Level Agreement.** Performance objectives reached by consensus between the user and the provider of a service, or between an outsourcer and an organization. A service level agreement specifies a variety of performance standards that may or may not include "service level." See Service Level.

**Service Level.** Also called Telephone Service Factor or TSF. The percentage of incoming calls that are answered within a specified threshold: "X percent of calls answered in Y seconds." See Response Time.

**Service Observing.** See Monitoring.

**Shrink Factor.** See Rostered Staff Factor.

**Signaling System** 7 (SS7). A method of signaling within the voice network that uses a separate packet-switched data network ("common channel signaling") to communicate information about calls. In a multisite virtual call center environment, SS7 can be used to pass information in order to decide which site is "best" to route the call.

**Silent Monitoring.** See Monitoring.

**Simulation Tools.** Tools used to replicate call activity in order to test applications and resulting impact on call center performance.

**Skill Group.** See Agent Group.

**Skill Path.** Skill paths focus on the development of specific skills rather than the progression of positions through the center and/or organization. See Career Path.

**Skills-Based Routing.** A specific form of intelligent routing that matches the skills of each agent with information about the caller to route a call to an appropriate agent. When an agent logs in, the database associates a defined skill set with that position and the application routes call types that match the skills to that position. An agent can have multiple skills, preferred skills and unique combinations of skills.

**Smooth Call Arrival.** Calls that arrive evenly across a period of time. Virtually non-existent in incoming environments.

**Special Causes.** Variation in a process caused by special circumstances. See Common Causes.

**Split.** See Agent Group.

**Stakeholders.** Individuals or organizations with a share or interest in the organization, including employees, customers, investors, suppliers and vendors, resellers and distributors, and lawmakers.

**Stand-alone ACD.** A switch with software specifically designed to perform ACD routing and other call center functions. Stand-alone ACDs typically exclude many PBX capabilities, such as least-cost routing, camp-on or other functions targeted toward general business use, and may co-reside with a PBX in many office environments.

**Strategy.** The overall approach for accomplishing the organization's objectives.

**Supervisor Monitor.** Computer monitors that enable supervisors to monitor the call-handling statistics of their supervisory groups or teams.

**Supervisor.** The person who has frontline responsibility for a group of agents. Typical ratios are one supervisor to every 10 to 15 agents. However, help desks can have one supervisor for every five people, and some reservations centers have one supervisor for every 30 or 40 agents. Generally, supervisors are equipped with special telephones and computer terminals that enable them to monitor agent activities.

**T1 Circuit.** A high-speed digital circuit used for voice, data or video, with a bandwidth of 1.544 megabits per second. T1 circuits offer the equivalent of 24 analog voice trunks.

**Talk Time.** The time an agent spends with a caller during a transaction. Includes everything from "hello" to "goodbye."

**Telecommuting.** See Remote Agent.

**Telephone Service Factor.** See Service Level.

**Text Chat.** Allows agents and customers to have a "conversation" over the Internet by typing on their computers. Generally enabled through a "click-to-chat" button on a Web site, and then a separate window opens for chatting.

**Text-to-Speech.** Enables a voice-processing system to read the words in a text field aloud using synthesized – not recorded – speech. Sometimes used for large, dynamic database applications in which it is impractical to record all speech phrases. Also used to "read" email or other text-based information over the telephone.

**Thick Client.** A workstation in a client-server environment that performs much or most of the application processing. It requires programs and data to be installed on it and a significant part of the application processing takes place on the workstation. The client is "thick" in that much of the overall application is running on it.

**Thin Client.** A workstation in a client-server environment that performs little or no application processing. Often used to describe browser-based desktops. The client is "thin" in that the applications reside on and are run within the server rather than the client.

**Threshold.** The point at which an action, change or process takes place.

**Toll-Free Service.** Enables callers to reach a call center out of the local calling area without incurring charges. 800 and 888 service is toll-free. In some countries, there are also other variations of toll-free service. For example, with 0345 or 0645 services in the United Kingdom, callers are charged local rates and the call center pays for the long-distance charges.

**Touchtone.** A trademark of AT&T. See Dual-Tone Multifrequency.

**Traffic Control Center.** See Network Control Center

**Transaction.** See Call.

**Transmission Control Protocol/Internet Protocol (TCP/IP).** Protocols that support internetworking. TCP/IP specifies how information that travels over the Internet should be divided and reassembled.

**True Calls Per Hour.** Actual calls an individual or group handled divided by occupancy for that period of time.

**Trunk.** Also called a Line, Exchange Line or Circuit. A telephone circuit linking two switching systems.

**Trunk Group.** A collection of trunks associated with a single peripheral and usually used for a common purpose.

**Trunk Load.** The load that trunks carry. Includes both Delay and Talk Time.

**Trunks Idle.** The number of trunks in a trunk group that are non-busy.

**Trunks in Service.** The number of trunks in the trunk group that are functional.

**Turnover.** When a person leaves the call center. Turnover is typically calculated at an annualized rate. Turnover can be categorized as controllable or uncontrollable and voluntary or involuntary.

**Unavailable Work State.** An agent work state used to identify a mode not associated with handling telephone calls.

**Uniform Call Distributor (UCD).** A simple system that distributes calls to a group of agents and provides some reports. A UCD is not as sophisticated as an ACD.

**Universal Agent.** Refers to either: a) An agent who can handle all types of incoming calls, b) an agent who can handle both inbound and outbound calls, or c) an agent who can handle both voice contacts and electronic contacts.

**Upsell.** A sales technique of offering more expensive products or services to current customers during the sales decision. The offer usually is based on relationships established between the customer's profile and the attributes of customers who have already purchased the products or services being upsold. See Customer Profiling.

**Virtual Call Center.** Multiple Networked ACD systems that operate as a single logical system even though they are physically separated and geographically dispersed. A resource at one site can handle a call from any of the other sites. This permits economies of scale in call handling, as well as supporting disaster recovery, call overflow and extended hours coverage. Ability and degree of networking varies with system type, similarity of systems and approach to integration. Can be enabled to varying degrees using network features, switch features or CTI.

**Virtual Private Network (VPN).** Provides privacy to communications over Internet Protocol (IP) facilities, including the Internet or private IP infrastructures. Similar to a Wide Area Network (WAN).

**Visible Queue.** When callers know how long the queue is that they just entered, and how fast it is moving (e.g., they hear a system announcement that relays the expected wait time). See Invisible Queue.

**Vision.** Describes a future state of the organization in vivid, compelling terms. The organization's vision is a snapshot of the future.

**Voice Over Internet Protocol (VoIP).** Transmitting voice signals as packets of data from one computer to another over a TCP/IP network. See IP Telephony.

**Voice Processing.** A blanket term that refers to any combination of voice-processing technologies, including Voicemail, Automated Attendant, Audiotex, Voice Response Unit (VRU) and Faxback.

**Voice Response Unit (VRU).** See Interactive Voice Response. Note: VRU is sometimes used to refer to the piece of equipment, while IVR is used to refer to the capability.

**Web Call Through.** A VoIP transaction that is initiated by a customer from a company's Web site.

**Web Callback.** Transaction in which the customer clicks a button on a company's Web site, which initiates an automatic callback from an agent.

**Web Integration.** Incorporating Web contact into the call center by providing access to a live agent over the Internet when needed. Provides the customer with additional support, information and guidance during a self-service transaction. Can be enabled through text chat, Web callback or a Web call. Email is sometimes included offered as part of this integration. Often includes "co-browsing" or "pushing" Web pages to the customer.

**Wide Area Network (WAN).** A data and/or voice network that covers a large geographic area.

**Work Flow Management.** Business application that enables work tasks to be created and assigned, both manually and through automation. Because Work Flow Management is driven by business rules, it ensures that transactions are accomplished through proper and consistent steps. The movement of each task can be tracked throughout the duration of the process providing both current status and historical activity. Work Flow Management can be used to track contact handling at specific stages or for the life of a contact.

**Workforce Management System (WFMS).** Forecasting, scheduling, tracking and adherence monitoring tool used in a call center. Enables the manager to project work volume and corresponding resource needs based on historical information and other parameters (e.g., growth). Workforce management can be performed for a single site or for networked sites. In a multisite environment, forecasting and scheduling may be performed at a central site or in a decentralized fashion at each site. Tracking and adherence monitoring is generally a local function.

**Workload.** Often used interchangeably with Call Load. Workload can also refer to non-call activities.

**World Wide Web (WWW).** The capability that enables users to access information on the Internet in a graphical environment.

**Wrap-up.** See After-Call Work.

**Wrap-Up Codes.** Codes that agents enter on their phones to identify the types of calls they are handling. Generally entered at the completion of each contact. The ACD can then generate reports on call types, by handling time, time of day, etc.

**Zip Tone.** See Beep Tone.

## Section 9

# *Articles*

Leadership and Business Management

## Reference Articles

The following articles are from the pages of *Call Center Management Review* (formerly *Service Level Newsletter*), ICMI's journal for members. They were selected to provide you with further information on some of the key areas of leadership and business management.

# A Primer on Developing Effective Call Center Strategy: Part 1

*"Making strategy, once an event, is now a continuous process."*

– Thomas Petzinger Jr.
*The Wall Street Journal*

What differentiates truly great organizations – and by extension, truly great call centers – from those that are just "okay"? How can an organization create tangible advantages that make the whole greater than the sum of the parts? How do you adapt and thrive in a fast-evolving networked economy? While there are many possible answers to these questions, an effective strategy clearly plays a key role.

Unfortunately, mention strategy, and many managers justifiably conjure up images of an overused business buzzword, the latest management trends or the last conference session they sat through with too much fluff and not enough substance. All the while, many organizations struggle to create viable, sustainable strategies. Many are currently working on their approach to customer relationship management or on redefining core businesses. Some are focusing on individual components of strategy, such as organization, resources or processes. And others are taking stock of what comes after mergers, industry restructurings or shifting budgets and priorities.

Developing effective strategy is not only possible, it's a pervasive characteristic of organizations that create sustainable customer loyalty and marketplace value. Still, many organizations are grappling with fast-changing markets and technologies, and struggle to leverage the "pieces and parts" into a sustainable business advantage. Somewhere between strategy and tactics, the vision too often gets lost – or at least diluted -- in operational realities. That seems to be especially true in developing cohesive, customer contact solutions.

What's needed is a mechanism for extending corporate strategy into tangible, realistic applications. In the call center realm, strategy is embodied in what is often termed a "customer access strategy," which is ***a framework – a set of standards, guidelines and processes – defining the means by which customers are connected with resources capable of delivering the desired information and services.*** The customer access strategy is an extension of corporate strategy and often, in turn, also helps to shape corporate strategy. When approached with the right commitment and buy-in, a customer access strategy is a powerful tool for unleashing the potential of the call center.

The need for a cohesive customer access strategy is clear.

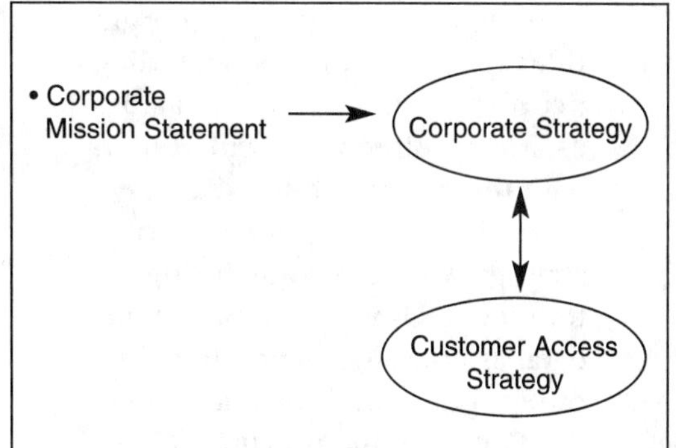


Multiple access methods are evolving. As services evolve, they become far more complicated from both the customer's and organization's perspectives, and as multiple technology "owners" exist, telling customers the same story is an important concern. Caller tolerance is evolving rapidly, and customers are growing increasingly more savvy and well informed. And being "easy to do business with" is of paramount importance.

Developing a customer access strategy has broader implications than may first meet the eye. By nature, it positions the call center as the communications hub of the organization, and customer loyalty as the primary objective. It is an effort that will touch virtually every business unit, so it must be supported by top-level management. In fact, top management must be actively involved, along with any organization accessible to customers, all technology and process owners responsible for customer services and customers (ask them how they want to be served!).

As with corporate strategy, a customer access strategy can take many different forms. And, as with corporate strategy, there is a lot of confusing and conflicting advice on how to best approach the process of developing a customer access strategy and the form it should take. But the most sus-

### A Customer Access Strategy Addresses These Business Processes:

- **Customer profiles**
- **Customer communications**
- **Contact types**
- **Access channels**
- **Routing and distribution**
- **Service level objectives**
- **Required resources**
- **Organization and processes**
- **Capturing customer data**
- **Technology architecture**
- **Investment guidelines**
- **Framework for deploying new services**

tainable strategies cover, in one form or another, 12 key business processes:

Developing ***customer profiles*** is, by necessity, a first step. Who are your customers and prospective customers; what do they want and need; and how can you best service those needs? While a strategy document generally doesn't go into individual detail, it should define specific customer types and their evolving expectations (see the discussion of customer expectations, Service Level Notes, January 2000).

***Customer communications*** broadly describes how the organization plans to communicate with customers and establishes guidelines for developing those messages and ensuring that the organization is in sync (e.g., that the call center is properly informed of marketing campaigns). Defining ***contact types*** anticipates the types of interactions with customers. General categories include such things as placing orders, changing orders, checking account status, problem resolution, etc., but most organizations wisely break these categories into more detail.

Identifying ***access channels*** is where strategy really begins to hit home for call centers. All channels of contact should be itemized: telephone, Web, fax, e-mail, IVR, kiosk, handhelds, face-to-face service, postal mail and anything else that comes along, plus corresponding telephone numbers, Web URLs, e-mail addresses, fax numbers, postal addresses, etc.

***Routing and distribution*** plans naturally follow. How – by customer, type of contact and access channel – is each contact going to be routed and distributed? (While these terms have inbound connotations this also applies to outbound; e.g., when the organization originates the contacts, through which agent group or system will the contact be made?). Next, ***service level objectives***, which in application includes both service level and response time objectives, are agreed to and specified.

Defining ***required resources*** takes strategy from the realm of "getting the customer's contact to the right place at the right time" into the realm of "doing the right thing." What resources, including people, technologies and databases, are required to provide callers with the information and assistance they need? This aspect of strategy will help guide hiring, training, technology deployment, database development and many other operational considerations.

Outlining the ***organization and processes*** necessary to support customer access requirements runs the gamut, from specifying how many call centers you will have to defining agent groups, responsibilities and planning requirements. ***Capturing customer data*** identifies the methods used for capturing information on each customer interaction, and defining how that data will, in turn, be used to strengthen customer profiles, identify trends and improve products and services.

Finally, the strategy document should establish an agreed-upon ***technology architecture***, (corporate standards and technology migration plans), ***investment guidelines*** (priorities and plans for operational and capital expenditures) and a ***framework for deploying new services*** (timeframes and approaches for expanding customer contact services).

Clearly, developing a sound customer access strategy is not something you throw together during a weekend retreat. It takes leadership, persistence, participation from across the organization, and a lot of collaboration and cooperation.

Each of the 12 processes addressed by the customer access strategy are interrelated, and when you focus on one, you will inherently be impacting and shaping others. And it's not something that happens in a vacuum; call center strategy cannot develop independent of broader corporate strategy.

But the payoffs of developing a cohesive strategy are compelling. From a customer's perspective, a good strategy will result in simplified access, consistent services, ease of use and a high degree of convenience and satisfaction. From the organization's perspective, the benefits translate into lower overall costs, increased capacity, higher customer retention and a workable framework that guides ongoing developments.

Next month, I'll focus on the process of putting these pieces together into a cohesive whole. In the meantime, I would encourage you to take stock of where your customer access strategy (whatever you may call it) stands.

CCMReview

# A Primer on Developing Effective Call Center Strategy: Part 2

As discussed in Part 1 of this two-part series, a thoughtful customer access strategy is an essential aspect of developing a cohesive, effective customer contact environment. Broadly defined as "the standards, guidelines and processes defining the means by which customers are connected with resources capable of delivering the desired information and services," a customer access strategy generally considers these business processes:

- Customer profiles
- Customer communications
- Contact types
- Access channels
- Routing and distribution
- Service level objectives
- Required resources
- Organization and processes
- Capturing customer data
- Technology architecture
- Investment guidelines
- Framework for deploying new services

Thoughtfully addressing these issues, as discussed in Part 1, is essential to making the link between corporate strategy and the call center's ongoing activities and direction.

But developing an effective customer access strategy is no easy task. Because it touches virtually every traditional business unit, it requires an immense amount of collaboration, cooperation and leadership. And, as each of the processes are interrelated, changes to one will impact all others. In short, developing strategy is not a once-and-done event; it's an ongoing process. Without a system or approach for ongoing development, strategy quickly becomes out of date and ineffectual.

Figure 1, on the facing page, illustrates "The Strategic Development Process" as taught by Incoming Calls Management Institute. Despite its somewhat lofty (stuffy?) title, it is an approach that is simple, effective and enduring. (If you are familiar with this process, you'll notice that although we have retooled some of the labels, the steps in the process remain the same). It will provide focus to your efforts to keep strategy current, along with an approach for tying the pieces together. Here's how it works:

### 1. Create a Connected Vision

Vision comes first. Vision is the creative ability to see past current circumstances to "what could be." As much as the concept of vision has been overused by some in business circles and consequently pooh-poohed by others, vision remains the undisputed motivation behind any human change or action.

*Developing strategy is not a once-and-done event... Without a system or approach for ongoing development, strategy quickly becomes out of date and ineffectual.*

We refer to a "connected" vision because it must be appropriate for today's fast-changing, networked economy. Key questions often serve as a useful catalyst in this effort. For instance, how do your customers define great service? What sort of organizational structure best supports

the integration of e-commerce and traditional telephony services? How else can the call center help the organization understand customers better? How can the call center's vision and purpose be better communicated? What is a call center?

### 2. Shape the Supporting Strategy

It is within this context that the customer access strategy is created and/or refined. The customer access strategy is a mechanism for turning vision into operational reality, and will serve as a framework for developing the steps that follow. (For a more complete discussion, please see Part 1 of this series, *CCMReview*, Feb. 2000.)

### 3. Build Skills, Knowledge and Leaders

This first involves developing a "map" of resident vs. required competencies for every key requirement (position) in the call center and identifying areas where you may be vulnerable (i.e., areas in which only a few key people possess important management or technical know-how). Other important aspects of this step involve developing appropriate hiring and training plans; imple-

Section 9

menting a systematic process for recognizing and cultivating management and leadership competencies; instilling an understanding of queuing dynamics and unique call center planning and management implications into the culture; establishing appropriate performance standards; and defining and developing attractive career- and skill-path alternatives.

### 4. Implement Connected Plans and Processes

This refers specifically to putting the planning and management processes in place which are necessary to support the customer access strategy. In today's environment, this usually involves forecasting, scheduling and real-time management across all channels of contact; simulating "what-if" scenarios given increasingly complex routing and distribution requirements; redefining agent group structure to move toward a true multimedia queuing environment; and improving collaboration and planning across the organization.

### 5. Apply Enabling Technologies

The obvious focus of this step is to specify the technology infrastructure required to turn vision into reality. However, a less-stated but equally important aspect of this process is to address the "technology conundrum," consisting of three important questions:

• *Should we buy now or buy later?* If we buy now, we begin conquering the learning curve now and will enjoy the benefits sooner. However, if we buy later, the technology will be cheaper, faster and better, and more organizations will have worked out the kinks.

• *Is the capability a sea change or diversion?* For instance, widespread video capabilities in call centers have, thus far, proved to be illusive while e-commerce services are quickly and fundamentally changing the customer service environment.

• *Who's in charge of specification and implementation decisions, the technology people or the marketing people?* (Note: There are questions within these generalized categories as well – e.g., should the data people or telecom people generally dictate direction?)

The point here is not to answer these questions, but to ensure they are addressed as a part of the process.

**Figure 1**
**The Strategic Development Process**

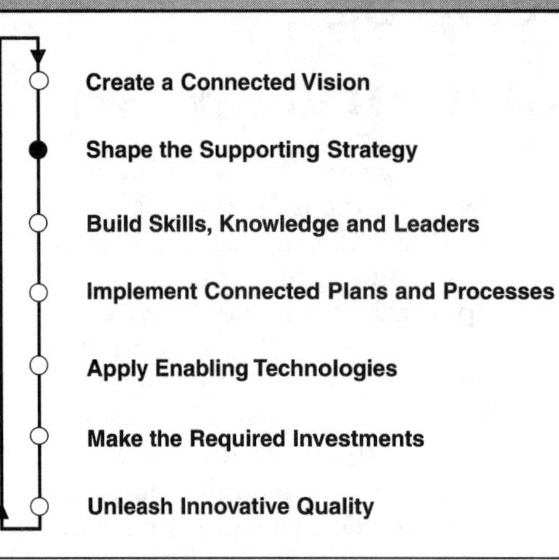
Create a Connected Vision
Shape the Supporting Strategy
Build Skills, Knowledge and Leaders
Implement Connected Plans and Processes
Apply Enabling Technologies
Make the Required Investments
Unleash Innovative Quality

### 6. Make the Required Investments

Money, money, money. Here's where vision, strategy and all of our lofty ambitions and plans can run into cold reality. For that reason, some say, this step should occur much sooner in the process. But I respectfully disagree. Why have a call center -- or, for that matter, why have an organization, if budgetary allocations predetermine possibilities? No one in his or her right mind would choose to spend money in any of these areas unless there is a reasonable return for both customers and the organization. Therein is the point: We don't even know what the possibilities are without going through the previous steps.

Yes, return on investment (ROI) analysis, FTE staff budgeting and capital planning play an important role in good management. And in the end, it's all semantics anyway because no step, including budgeting, is inseparable from any other. But as a matter of principle, the budget should not short-circuit vision and strategy before new possibilities get a chance to make their case.

### 7. Unleash Innovative Quality

When it comes to quality, three prevailing questions continue to surface:

- What are customer expectations?
- Are we meeting them?
- Are we using the fewest possible resources to do so?

Quality has never consisted only of the attributes of a product or service; it must always be defined within the context of the customers' needs, wants and expectations. The invention and application of toll-free services, ACD capabilities, Internet-based services, speech recognition – the list can go on and on – all have raised expectations to new levels (see "Customer Expectations in 2000," *CCMReview*, Jan. 2000). And that takes us back to the beginning: What's our vision?

### A Continuum

Business analyst and former *Wall Street Journal* Editor Thomas Petzinger Jr. was right when he proclaimed that: "Making strategy, once an event, is now a continuous process." Webster's New World Dictionary defines *continuum* as: "A continuous whole, quantity, or series; thing whose parts cannot be separated or separately discerned."

The key to effective strategy development is to see each step as part of a continuum. Developing good strategy is hard work. But, given the fundamental changes taking place in how organizations serve their customers, it has never been more important.

CCMReview

Section 9

# In the Center
### with Monica Kosiorek

# Mission, Vision and Values in the Call Center

*Monica Kosiorek, vice president of Bank One Services Corp. in Dallas, Texas, joined Bank One in 1992 as department head of Texas Telebanking. She currently serves as the retail call center program manager for Project One, where she directs a national effort to integrate 23 call centers into two sites.*

Deciding to embark on an adventure with an unknown destination may sound exciting for a vacation or Sunday afternoon drive, but not knowing where you want to go is a difficult way to drive for results at work. Life in a call center is hectic to say the least. Without a road map, chaos is a sure result.

Some say "I have a plan. Everyday I show up, pray to manage through the unmanageable and survive the continuous demands of the unexpected." This is less than a mediocre way to inspire your staff — you know, that critical group that represents your company to thousands of callers each day. Do you think a "survival of the fittest" demeanor goes unnoticed by those around you? Leading by example is a concept that will surely backfire for those who do not self-inspect on occasion.

What will help keep the focus? A well defined vision, mission and set of values.

Vision is an image of a desired future. Having a stated vision for your call center will help to create a future that represents your highest expectations. If you don't control your destiny, someone else will — your boss, your competitors, your stakeholders.

Mission is what you are about everyday, what you do today. Having a shared vision and mission is a vehicle for building shared meaning.

Values are the behaviors that will guide and form the culture as you journey toward the future by fulfilling your daily mission, commitment. Sound like double talk? This may help; a popular saying by internationally-known motivational speaker Zig Ziglar challenges the order of achievement. "You have to BE before you can DO and DO before you can HAVE," says Ziglar. Simply put, in this context, values define what we must BE, mission provides our daily DO, and both drive toward what we can HAVE in the future, i.e., vision. Values are deeply held views of what you as a call center find worthwhile. They are behaviors to live by and to apply to decision making.

These concepts are not new.

*Life in a call center is hectic to say the least. Without a road map, chaos is a sure result.*

They have always been the foundation for establishing a desired outcome and creating a common culture. Keep in mind that you cannot impose a set of rules that will magically produce the results you want in your call center. A change in behavior is most likely to occur

*Monica Kosiorek*

when actions speak louder than words. Collaboration is the key. Put people in control of their jobs. The long term payoff will be loyalty, pride, personal effectiveness and teamwork!

## An Effective Approach

An approach that has worked well for me in the past is to schedule a series of workshop focus groups so all employees can share their thoughts on streamlining the mission statement and values to align with the stated vision. Of course, this assumes that the written call center vision is in place. If it is not, here are some suggestions:

- Spend time contemplating the future of your call center. As its leader you have as much a right as an obligation to those you lead to come forth with a vision.
- Do your homework around your company. Talk with your boss and others in senior management, as well as your strategic business partners to get a "world view" of the call center.

- Don't rush. Creating a vision takes incubation.
- Share your vision and build the rest with the group.

  Once the call center vision is in place, ask the employee focus groups to comment on the behaviors that need to be practiced each day to ensure success. Allow time for long and serious debate to ensure that words are chosen carefully.

Here are the actual results of such an exercise that I helped conduct:

**Vision:** To become the primary service provider with 24/7/365 service delivery that outshines those recognized by the marketplace as excellent.

**Mission:** Quality is our prime directive. To this end as customer service professionals we will strive to: 1.) own every call (ownership and follow-up); 2.) make the organization work for the customer (empowerment); and 3.) delight each customer (beyond satisfaction).

**Values:** The seeds of true service start with our basic beliefs. Each employee is a vital contributor and the reason for our unified success. We believe our on-going success is dependent on the following:

- *Interdependence (teamwork):* We will cooperate with one another to achieve win-win situations that are in harmony with our shared vision and brought about through enjoyment in our work.
- *Work Ethic:* We will practice dependability, confidentially, consistency, trustworthiness, honesty and respect.
- *Responsibility:* We will demonstrate commitment to continuous learning, thereby empowering ourselves to resolve problems effectively and efficiently.
- *Empathy:* We will care for everyone in a sensitive manner — listening without bias and showing concern, understanding and patience.
- *Positive attitude:* We will be cooperative, optimistic and supportive of team goals.

These values support the daily mission and vision of the future. They serve as guiding principles for all actions and decisions.

### Inspiring Action and Change

Creating and deciding to publish your call center commitment is only the beginning, tough task that it is. The next step needs to be a rally, an event, a gathering. Something designed to inspire your staff to achieve the greatness they described in the above exercise. Everyone needs to understand what exactly their role is in the shared mission, vision and value statements. During the rally, use powerful, well-chosen language.

*Creating and deciding to publish your call center commitment is only the beginning, tough task that it is.*

Fundamental changes may have to take place to ensure your ability to "walk the talk." It's not enough to merely define how you regard your customers, how you want to treat each other and how you want to treat co-workers within your organization. You have to ensure that action follows.

Continuous dialogue is important. Look for ways to incorporate mission/vision/values into day-to-day conversations. Remember, you get what you expect.

Try to temper your skepticism — lighten up and don't be too critical as employees begin to strive to achieve the prescribed goals. Nobody should be expected to be perfect, but everyone should be expected to try. This means you, the manager, too. Look yourself in the mirror daily and ask, "Am I making an effort? Am I giving 100 percent?

Once you answer consistently, you earn the right to expectations. Find ways to make this commitment stay alive in the midst of daily activity. Provide positive reinforcement to and encourage those employees who are demonstrating the call center's values. Challenge, in a positive way, employees who aren't.

### Shared Principles Provide Long-Term Payoff

The need for mission/vision/values comes from our most basic need to have a sense of belonging. These principles promote energy among the workforce. All for one, one for all. Having shared principles that are documented is the critical first step. Actually, believing you need them is just as critical. You then need to breath life into the principles by testing each of your decision-making and risk-taking activities. When faced with a choice, always evaluate the potential outcome as something that will or will not bring you closer to the vision. Decide if it is an action that will visibly demonstrate the call center values to everyone. You are not imposing your goals, but challenging others to strive for the common good. You must enlist others to understand, accept and commit.

Through it all, stay close to your employees. Stay visible and ask for feedback regularly. Remember the long- term payoff: loyalty, pride, personal effectiveness and teamwork that will benefit all — internal/ external customers, employees and you!

SLN

# From The Field with Rose Polchin

# Navigating the Future: A Mission Statement Can Guide Centers through Turbulent Times

**A well-crafted mission statement can help your center to navigate through rough seas.**

Much like a compass guides sailors on ocean journeys, a mission statement can give direction to those of us who must navigate our way through the day-to-day business of running a call center.

The compass helps sailors to make decisions about how to steer the ship, what course to take, and when to "stay the course" or make adjustments. A concise, clear mission statement can serve similar purposes for call centers, helping to guide your business decisions. For instance, you may be considering whether to buy new technology that will speed up or reduce handle time and/or automate transactions. But first, check your compass — if your mission is to get closer to your customers by providing a human touch, this technology may not be right for your center.

Stormy seas are ahead… or, in the business world, stock prices are falling and you need to take action. True, you may be able to cut costs in the short term by reducing headcount. But to stay the course and achieve a mission focused on getting closer to the customer by providing a human touch, that action is clearly not the best alternative. Instead, you might first consider other cost-saving alternatives, such as process improvement initiatives, upsell/cross-sell programs or customer retention strategies. Having a well-defined, clearly communicated mission also will make it easier to gain the support and commitment you need to deploy these alternative strategies.

## Benefits of a Written Mission Statement

Writing a mission statement is not an easy task, but it is an important one. Besides acting as your decision-making compass, a formal mission statement serves several purposes:

■ It helps to attract and retain employees and customers. Overall, your mission is your purpose or reason for being. A company's "identity" is a function of how faithfully it pursues its mission. Consider, for example, a financial institution whose mission is "to service and satisfy the financial needs of our clients." If that same organization rarely lends money, its staff is unfriendly and apathetic, and it charges its customers for every ATM withdrawal, then clearly there is a "disconnect" between the mission and the organization's identity. Ultimately, this will lead to confusion among customers and employees, which will negatively impact satisfaction and retention.

■ It helps to unite your team. Consider the crew of a sailboat: Each member has a distinct set of goals, actions and tasks he or she must perform; however, all are working toward a common goal. So while each may operate individually, it's only through a collective effort that they can achieve the mission. But first they all must know the mission — that will allow each member to use the mission statement as a guide to making the right independent decisions.

■ It helps you to get the support and funding you need through higher visibility. The mission statement allows you to communicate what the center is, what it does and how it contributes to the overall mission of the organization.

## More Than Mere Words

The power of a mission statement isn't in the words themselves, but rather in the focus, guidance and commitment those words inspire through their repetition and the passion expressed each time they are communicated. Happy sailing! CCMReview

### Criteria for Effective Mission Statements

The following information can help you get started writing a clear, concise and effective mission statement for your call center.

THE MISSION STATEMENT:

1. Must be linked to the mission of the overall organization.
2. Should be developed collaboratively by representatives from the key groups of stakeholders.
3. Should inspire you and others to take action.
4. Should be easily understood by those outside the call center and/or the organization.
5. Should be succinct. In general, it should be no more than a sentence long. Consider Abraham Lincoln's mission "to preserve the Union." Or Franklin D Roosevelt's mission "to end the Depression." Or Mother Teresa's mission "to show mercy and compassion to the dying."
6. Should express why you and your call center team do what you do. What is the value of the service you provide to both internal and external customers?

**Rose Polchin**

*Rose Polchin is a Certified Associate of Incoming Calls Management Institute (ICMI) and president of Rose Polchin Consulting and Training, a training and consulting firm focused on call center management. She can be reached at 201-652-0443 or rpolchin@worldnet.att.net.*

Section 9

In The Center with Michael Hepworth

# The Impact of the Contact Center on Corporate Profits

**How do you move from cost center to profit center? The latest research reveals the impact of managing the customer's experience.**

Discussions with CEOs highlight customer retention as a key strategic issue for many global companies in the next year. Driving this phenomenon is the emphasis that today's financial markets highly value predictable cash flows — and a steady stream of long-term customer relationships delivers that value.

Naturally, almost all businesses need a steady stream of new business; however, many organizations rightly believe they don't really need more customers — rather more sales from the customers they already have.

It's clear that when customers who already know your company and like doing business with you are persuaded to buy more from you, the total cost of sales is reduced and more of the profit flows directly to the bottom line. What is also clear is that many companies cannot focus on increased "wallet share" for each customer while their customers are experiencing negative service interactions and ineffective handling of their service complaints.

Despite the attention and high levels of investment in measurement, technology and training, some contact centers seem to do a better job of driving customers away than retaining them. Most contact centers believe they are customer-focused. They try to build positive experiences for customers but, in doing, so they often overlook customer expectations.

When customers contact an organization for help, they expect to be able to quickly get through to a live person who can solve their problems. However, many contact centers create negative experiences for customers by introducing poorly designed technology to deliver service or by not understanding the impact of their current processes on customers.

## The Cost Center Issue

Unfortunately, most contact centers are seen as cost centers. While the *stated focus* is on improved customer satisfaction, the *reality* shows a heavy emphasis on measured cost reduction. Certainly, cost reduction is always important, but it needs to be weighed against its impact on customer loyalty.

When making changes in the cal center, consider the following issues:

- Will the change improve or damage ease of access?
- Will the change increase the likelihood that the customer will feel cared for by the organization?
- Will the change ensure better quality answers for the customer?
- Will the change ensure better follow through for the customer?
- Will the change improve the ability to resolve issues on first contact?

If the answers show that performance/customer satisfaction in any of these areas will be diminished, additional planning and analysis may be in order.

FIGURE 1

**Revenue At Risk**

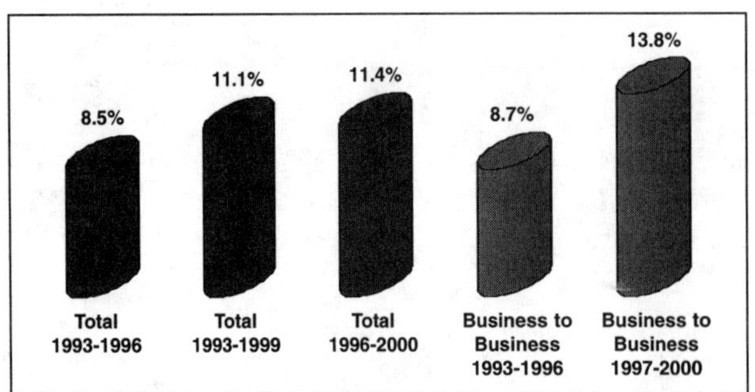


## The Latest Customer Research from Leading Businesses

Hepworth + Co. Ltd. developed a process, called the Customer Pulse System, to help organizations calculate the bottomline impact of customer service. The Customer Pulse Database contains more than 80,000 responses gathered from customers in more than 95 studies with North America's most successful businesses. The following information is culled from an updated analysis of this database in early 2001.

Over the past five years, revenue at risk has increased steadily (Figure 1). Revenue at risk is the amount of revenue put at risk as a result of negative experiences customers have with a company's products or services, and the way their complaints are handled. Our results show that, between 1996 and 2000, the amount of revenue at risk has grown by about 30 percent in total, and by almost 60 percent for the business-to-business sector.

In almost every case, we find that customers who experience problems are less likely to do business with an organization unless that problem is resolved to their complete satisfaction.

It is important to note that *complete* satisfaction is the key to customer retention. When a problem or inquiry is handled poorly, loyalty drops and puts future revenue at risk. Figure 2, on page 10, shows the importance of a response that is completely satisfactory to the customer. When the customer finds the response merely acceptable, loyalty is almost 20 percentage points lower than when the customer is completely satis-

Section 9

fied; a less than acceptable response produces over 30 points less loyalty than one that completely satisfies the customer.

Few executives make the necessary effort to understand this specific data for their own organizations and, thus, allow customers to remain victims of erratic processes and leave complaint handling to chance at the front line.

## Differences Between Top- and Bottom-Quartile Companies

The Customer Pulse Database shows that those companies which are best at managing the customer experience are also much better at achieving the desired levels of customer retention than are those who are the worst at handling customer contacts.

To distinguish the best from the worst, we examined those companies whose customers were most and least likely to be "completely satisfied" with their contact experience.

The Customer Pulse Database is divided into quartiles based on the responses to questions about the caller's level of satisfaction with the response they received to a problem or question. "Top-quartile" companies are those whose customers were most likely to be completely satisfied with the response they received, while "bottom-quartile" companies are those whose customers were least likely to be completely satisfied.

The research shows that customers of the top-quartile companies are far more likely to say they will definitely do business again with those companies than customers of bottom-quartile companies (48 percent vs. 29 percent). And though the figures are of a much smaller magnitude, it is worth noting that the customers of the bottom-quartile companies are somewhat more likely to say they probably or definitely would *not* repurchase from them (9 percent compared to 6 percent). Also, the bottom-quartile companies have twice as much revenue at risk as the top-quartile companies (17.4 percent compared to 8.6 percent).

FIGURE 2

**Percentage of Customers Who "Definitely Would Repurchase"**

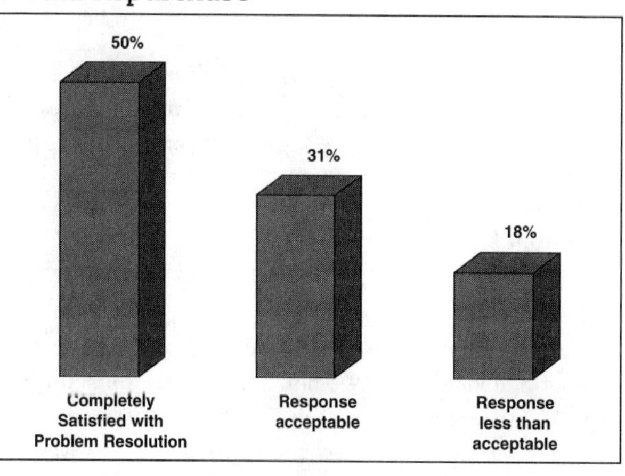


## Customer Experiences with the Best and Worst Companies

The following factors can negatively impact corporate profits:

■ **Call transfers.** On average, a customer is transferred 1.2 times before reaching someone who can assist in resolving the issue he or she is calling about. At first glance, this does not seem to be an onerous burden for the caller to bear. But it is important to note that callers to top-quartile companies report an average of 1.0 transfers, while callers to bottom-quartile companies report 1.4 transfers each — that is a performance deterioration of 40 percent.

*Implication:* Transfers are a nuisance and an inconvenience for customers who would like their questions or problems resolved quickly and smoothly, without having to repeat the story to every person to whom they are transferred. Unless you have a process in place to prevent this, ask yourself how many customers your business is putting at risk each day.

■ **Number of contacts required.** The ideal situation is for each customer inquiry to be resolved during the first call. Not only is the customer happier, but it is much less costly. However, our statistics show that, on average, it takes almost three calls to have problems resolved. Top-quartile companies averaged 2.1 contacts each, while bottom-quartile customers reported 3.4 contacts each.

*Implication:* Every additional contact to your organization costs money and reduces customer satisfaction and, thus, also reduces customer retention and loyalty. Many companies have no process to monitor or prevent this irritating chain of events. However some best-in-class companies now set goals for single-call resolution.

■ **Customer contact personnel.** The Customer Pulse Database rates customer contact personnel based on a number of attributes: professionalism, willingness to help, courtesy, concern or interest in the caller's issue, having the knowledge to resolve the problem, having the authority to resolve the problem, and followup (doing what was promised).

In regard to these attributes, customers who contacted the top-quartile companies were much more likely to say they were "very satisfied" with the representative to whom they spoke (Figure 3). This would indicate that agents at these com-

FIGURE 3

**Customer Satisfaction with CSR Attributes**

| Personnel Attribute | Top Quartile Percent "Very Satisfied" | Bottom Quartile Percent "Very Satisfied" |
|---|---|---|
| Professionalism | 68 | 52 |
| Willingness to help | 55 | 39 |
| Courtesy | 67 | 52 |
| Concern/interest in your issue | 47 | 36 |
| Knowledge to resolve your problem | 52 | 30 |
| Authority to resolve your problem | 51 | 21 |
| Follow-up | 54 | 27 |

Section 9

FIGURE 4

**Customer Satisfaction with Resolution Time**

| | Average Number of Days to Resolution | Time to Resolution was: | | | | |
|---|---|---|---|---|---|---|
| | | Less Than Expected | As Expected | More Than Expected | Acceptable | Unacceptable |
| Top Quartile | 5.6 | 21 | 53 | 17 | 86 | 12 |
| Bottom Quartile | 12.7 | 8 | 49 | 42 | 12 | 42 |

panies are generally well-selected and trained in people skills. We note that the biggest differences between top- and bottom-quartile companies in the ratings are found in knowledge, authority and followup; therefore, these attributes must be critical to producing satisfied callers.

What is the difference between these last three attributes and the others? While professionalism, courtesy and other characteristics show good intentions on the part of the representative, they are probably basic customer expectations, and should be considered "table stakes" for playing in the game. But knowledge, authority and followup stand apart in that they are directly related to having the problem resolved. Good intentions alone will not go very far toward resolving customer issues. Furthermore, these three characteristics improve the probability that the problem will be resolved on the first contact without the need for escalation to other parts of the organization.

*Implication:* The frontline customer contact representative is the translation point for your customer strategy. Typically, organizations treat these positions as entry-level and pay accordingly. In addition, frontline customer contact staff are often under-trained and under-equipped to do the job the customer expects. As a result, through no fault of their own, frontline people continue to be a weak link in the customer relationship. This inability creates negative experiences for customers every day at a time when customers are expecting the most from an organization.

■ **Time required to resolve problems.** Over the last five years, the average time required for resolving problems was reported to be 8.5 days. (Note: Average times for problem-resolution exclude results for two companies that reported extremely long resolution times.) However, the difference between the best and worst companies was considerable: top-quartile companies averaged 5.6 days, whereas those in the bottom quartile reported an average of 12.7 days for problem-resolution — more than twice as long. Also, the best companies were far more likely than the worst to meet or exceed customer expectations (Figure 4).

We also know from individual studies that the time taken to resolve problems has a major impact on satisfaction with resolution, which, in turn, affects retention.

*Implication:* As problems erode loyalty, customers who have an unresolved problem are vulnerable to defecting. While companies need to manage expectations regarding the time it will take to resolve problems, it is imperative that resolution be timely. Customer contact personnel with the training, information and empowerment to quickly and efficiently resolve problems are key in achieving this.

■ **Negative Word of Mouth.** Today, fewer customers believe marketing and advertising claims, but they do believe their friends and business associates. Customers talk about the problems they have with businesses, as well as the efforts companies make to have those problems resolved. Unfortunately, word-of-mouth tends to accentuate the negative news rather than the positive. And in the Internet age, word-of-mouth spreads faster than ever to more people than ever.

The Customer Pulse Database reveals that customers of bottom-quartile companies tell twice as many people about their negative experiences as do the customers of top-quartile companies (3.7 people told vs. two people told).

Although there is nothing in the database to confirm that word-of-mouth is spreading faster, it seems likely that the Internet has sped up the process (e.g. some Web sites are specifically set up to bash particular companies). Information from the database also indicates that the average number of people hearing negative word-of-mouth has remained quite stable over time, at about 2.8.

■ **Revenue at risk.** The average annual revenue at risk for companies, due to problem experience and contact handling, stands at 11.4 percent — in other words, more than one in every 10 customers is at risk of defecting. Over time, even as companies have been working hard to improve customer satisfaction, retention and loyalty, this figure has increased from 8.5.

## From Cost Center to Profit Center

A poor customer contact experience puts a significant amount of business at risk. A contact center that consistently satisfies callers with easy access and first-contact resolution can stem customer defection and increase the share-of-wallet with its existing customer base. The result? The contact center becomes a profit center — and an important strategic tool that CEOs can use to demonstrate predictable and growing cash flow to the company's stakeholders. CCMReview

**Michael Hepworth**

*Michael Hepworth is Managing Director of Seurat Co., a consulting firm dedicated to helping clients build Relationship Capital, where he is responsible for growing and developing program opportunities. He founded customer retention consulting firm Hepworth + Co. in 1989. Michael can be reached at 905-763 1544, ext. 109, or mhepworth@customerpulse.ca.*

Section 9

# Dispel the 'Complaint Center' Image: Promote Value Through Visibility

*by Susan Hash*

The call center industry has made significant gains since the early 1990s, expanding dramatically into a multibillion-dollar industry that continues to flourish internationally, growing at a rate of 20 to 30 percent each year.

And yet, a large number of call centers are still struggling to establish a credible presence within their own companies for being more than simply a complaint center staffed by non-professional workers.

Managers who have been successful in gaining respect, support and the necessary resources to maintain service quality admit that building internal visibility requires relentless attention to the promotion of the center, the agents and the value it offers the company as the main source of customer information.

"It's a simple truth that the more value you add, the more valuable you become," says Lawrence "Chip" Horner, director of consumer affairs, Warner-Lambert Consumer Group of Pfizer Inc. "Call centers can look at customer contacts as one-time events or as the beginning of a partnership with customers who can offer tremendous sales and profit potential for the long term. That can help the internal perception that the call center is a profit center and a relationship-building organization which builds customer loyalty."

One of the biggest hurdles to overcome is the view of the call center as a cost center and a necessary evil of doing business, says Horner. "Those perceptions get very fixed in the minds of internal customers. It takes very patient, helpful, persistent consulting and delivering of value to change those thoughts over time."

In some cases, senior management doesn't have a clear picture of the impact a call center can have on customer retention, says Michael Hepworth, CEO of Hepworth and Co. Ltd., in Richmond Hill, Ontario. "Being able to show the bottomline impact is one of the tough est things to do – and you can't do it with internal statistics."

"Managers get very internally focused on the reports that the ACDs generate or the quality monitoring," agrees Anne Nickerson, president of Call Center Coach in Ellington, Conn. "They forget that their key job is the relationship with the rest of the company."

## Establish a Personal Relationship with Stakeholders

Finding ways to partner with your key internal stakeholders can help you to build internal relationships and establish your center's value to the company.

Initially, that may involve a look inward to consider where you would like to position your center in the organization.

Rachel Grenier, call center manager for Central Maine Power Co. in Lewiston, Maine, has had to work to keep her call centers where she thought they belonged in the company's reporting structure – the area in which they could have the most direct affect, which happened to be

### Focus on 'Effectiveness Metrics'

What grabs senior management's attention faster than bottomline statistics? If you want to reposition your operation as a profit center rather than resource drain, you need to collect data on the impact of contact-handling on customer loyalty.

"Call centers tend to report the traditional operational metrics – such as average speed of answer, adherence, etc. – which are productivity measures," says Michael Hepworth, CEO of Hepworth and Co. Ltd., in Richmond Hill, Ontario. "The problem is senior management usually is not terribly interested in those. And managers often try to make them appear better than they really are to make it seem as though they're doing a good job. That often prevents them from being able to position the call center as a strategic asset for the business. The move should be away from efficiency metrics to effectiveness metrics."

For instance, research by Hepworth and Co. has found that if a customer has to make a repeat call, satisfaction is reduced by about 10 percent. If a caller is transferred internally, loyalty and satisfaction, likewise, are reduced for every transfer. "So resolution on first contact becomes very critical," he says. "If customers have their problems effectively resolved, often loyalty will go up as much as 15 to 20 percent."

When reporting data to upper-level management, Hepworth recommends not focusing on the productivity statistics, rather on how many customers experienced problems and what the call center needs to do to change those results. "Managers need to show what problems customers experience, which ones they were able to resolve, which ones they weren't and, as a result, how much business is at risk from customers defecting."

For information on calculating "Revenue at Risk," see Michael Hepworth's article "Customer Risk Management," in *The Journal of Customer Loyalty* (Issue 13, Q1, 2000) published by ELoyalty, 312-228-4500.

with the utility's field offices rather than sales and marketing.

"I've been pushing very hard to ensure that our call centers fall under the same umbrella as our field offices, so that we all report to the same executive. I want to make sure the executives of the organization that we're in understand our call centers and keep us visible."

In many industries, marketing is the ideal internal partner for the call center.

"We are managing one of the most powerful points of contact with the consumers, in fact, probably the only direct human interface with the company." says Horner. "There's a lot of magic to that point of contact. There is a chance to really own the minds of the consumers. You have to figure out how can you influence consumers to prefer your product over others. How can we create a relationship? How can we keep them coming back?"

To make the partnership truly valuable for internal customers like marketing, Horner says, the call center needs to understand that area's needs, wants and business strategies, and align its processes to meet those needs.

The Warner-Lambert Consumer Group tries to build those associations as early as possible. "We invite any new marketing person who joins our organization here for a complete overview of what we do, what we can do for them, and how we can help them to be successful in the organization. We try to bring it down to the personal level," he explains.

Establishing personal relationships with management peers is also the approach used by Andrea O'Brien, consumer relations manager for Dreyer's/Edy's Grand Ice Cream in Oakland, Calif. At the start of the relationship, she favors the "drop in" visit over other forms of internal communication as a way to establish rapport.

"Unfortunately, it's very easy to skip a voicemail or e-mail message," she says. "It's much better to pop in for those initial meetings to talk about the importance of the information you have."

For the informal, face-to-face approach to be effective, brevity is key – and lots of enthusiasm about the information being offered, she says.

### Customize the Call Center's Value to the Audience

Knowing which stakeholders you want to reach and establishing a personal relationship with the managers in those areas is a good way to get your foot in the door.

But to really grab the attention of senior-level executives or other managers, it's important to understand each individual's passions and hot buttons, says Tim Nichols, call center systems manager, Eastman Kodak, Rochester, NY.

"Try to customize your presentation to the particular individual," he says. "You need to know something about your audience, such as whether they're very numbers-oriented or emotionally swayed. Some managers are extremely focused on costs, others might be more interested in customer satisfaction, some might be very concerned about whether or not their product appears profitable. So it's really a matter of understanding where this particular manager's bread is buttered, and then twisting your presentation to emphasize those points of interest."

He suggests talking with the last three or four people who have pitched ideas to particular individuals to find out what types of questions they may have asked and what types of information appealed to them.

### Make Sure Reports Hit the Mark

A picture is worth a thousand words. Even better is a picture accompanied by a story that execs can relate to, says Jean Bave-Kerwin, president of JBK Consulting in Slingerlands, N.Y., a firm specializing in call center and customer service solutions for the public and not-for-profit sectors. Customer stories can make your goals more understandable to the people who can affect your resources, she says.

"The picture might be a declining service level because you're understaffed," she explains. "You can take your statistics, make them into graphs, and then tell the story of a real customer who tried to reach you but could not get through and the impact the lack of resources made on

### Tips for Proving Value

Be constantly on the lookout for opportunities to prove your call center's value to other departments. "The value question is: 'What can they do for me?'" says Jean Bave-Kerwin of JBK Consulting. "By constantly stepping up to the plate, that question eventually gives rise to: 'What would I do without them?'"

Here are a few of Bave-Kerwin's suggestions for demonstrating the value you can offer:

- Use regular reports to show the call center's value. Talk about what call volume translates to in terms of revenue, savings, etc. (e.g., 25,000 calls last month resulted in \$500k in revenue or \$100k in savings or 20,000 office visits avoided).
- Educate the organization. Conduct lunchtime seminars on what's new at the call center, what you're hearing from customers, etc.
- Communicate your value. Make sure all of your agents know the mission of the call center and can talk about it with others.
- Celebrate milestones, breakthroughs, new beginnings, etc. and invite other organizations to share.
- Teach people what you know. Hold informational seminars on topics that enhance knowledge.

that person. That will be very powerful for executives – and stories tend to be remembered. It will help to frame their understanding of what your call center is all about."

Central Maine Power Co.'s Grenier says that distributing monthly performance indicator reports keeps her call centers visible to senior executives. She shares information on absenteeism (for productivity goals), call center service levels, operation maintenance budgets and performance against the utility's customer service guarantee.

What other kinds of information can you use to pique the interest of senior execs?

Nickerson recommends tracking the number of complaints around a certain product or issue. A few other areas that are proven attention-getters include:

- Frequent requests for a new product or a subset of a product that your company doesn't fulfill.
- First-call resolution performance.
- Performance against customer expectations.

### Give Other Managers a Chance to Feel the Pulse of Customers

No matter how relevant the information contained in your report is, charts, graphs and statistics cannot sufficiently portray the emotion associated with customer issues. The call center can help to put a human face on customer feedback information.

The most practical and effective way you can do that is by inviting other managers to spend time in the call center – either buddy-jacking with an agent or, better yet, taking a few phone calls themselves, says Jeff Feuer, president of Call Center Management, a consulting firm in Culver City, Calif.

"Nothing works better than having people walk in your moccasins. Maybe they can't walk a mile, but if they could just go a few yards, it would do wonders," he says. "It will give mid- and senior-level executives an understanding of how complicated and physically demanding the job is. When someone experiences that, it's a memory they don't lose too easily."

In fact, a call center tour program at Central Maine Power Co. has been so successful, managers there are lining up to participate.

The utility's call center operation is able to target 12 senior managers every year by having each of its three call centers schedule one visit per quarter. Visiting managers spend one-half to three-quarters of the day in the call center learning about various operations, as well as listening in on calls. In addition, the call center manager arranges a focus group for the visitor with 10 to 12 frontline CSRs.

"The focus group provides them with an opportunity to hear more information about us, and it gives our CSRs the opportunity to ask questions about other areas of the company to get a better understanding of how the whole organization works," says Grenier.

### Get Their Support Early through Career Paths

Putting in place an agent career development process that includes other parts of the organization can ensure future management support. Positive attrition can help you to steer the organizational culture to one that is customer-focused and call center friendly. When making decisions, managers who were formerly agents will likely consider their roots and and the impact on customers.

To ensure that you're not draining your own resources for the good of the company, Nickerson suggests making an appeal for support from those areas that would benefit. She points to one call center manager who asked other departments to share their hiring budgets since the call center had a 60 to 70 percent annual internal attrition rate. In the end, she persuaded the other areas to share their hiring budgets and to only solicit agents who had worked in the center for 18 months (the center had a three- to six-month learning curve for bringing agents up to speed).

Chip Horner agrees that creating an internal career path can be a tremendously valuable asset to the organization. "The people in our contact center know our products more intimately than most people in the company. And we know how our customers think about our products. We see that as an asset – having ambassadors in other areas remind-

### More Proven Ideas for Promoting Your Call Center

- Become an active participant in new-hire orientation programs to help new employees learn about the call center.
- Assign each marketing account manager a dedicated call center agent who can provide them with customer information in their area.
- When reporting customer data, strengthen the impact by flipping the attention from retention to defection. For instance, instead of reporting on a customer retention rate of 70%, focus on the 30% of defecting customers and what the call center can do to lessen the erosion.
- Supplement customer comment data with available market research data on the particular products or services involved.
- Become the "solution center." When reporting on complaint data, offer recommendations as to how the situation can be resolved.
- Suggest senior managers monitor customer calls in lieu of (or as a foundation for) surveys or customer focus groups.

ing people what a tremendously valuable asset consumer affairs is."

### Create Continual Internal Communications

To keep the value your call center provides visible, find ways to constantly publicize your successes.

Grenier's call centers publish their own eight-page newsletter, called *The Headset Gazette*. It's produced each month in the call center, with CSRs volunteering to serve as editors and reporters. The content focuses on call center events, such as fund raisers, community benefit programs, awards, customer comments, training issues and performance indicators.

While the publication's distribution began solely in the call centers, outside departments soon began requesting copies and it's now also delivered each month to the company president and parent company president.

Besides the newsletter, Grenier's management team keeps the call centers visible by participating in call center presentations at industry conferences, which she publicizes in *The Gazette* as well as the corporate communications publication.

Jeff Feuer suggests using internal contests to promote the good work going on in the call center. You can create an event around the award presentation to which senior executives are invited and make sure it's announced in the company newsletter or by circulating memos.

### Turtle vs. the Hare: Persistence Wins the Race

Keep in mind that any campaign to raise visibility is a long-term process. "There are some activities you can do to spike the awareness, but it's not a once-and-done thing," says Bave-Kerwin. "But make sure that you have firm ground on which to build. If you don't have a solid foundation of integrity and trust, then your efforts are doomed to failure. The most effective way to raise the profile of the center is slowly, gradually and based on being of value."

Horner agrees that changing an organizational culture takes time and perseverance. "Even today, with the worldwide successes of our group, there are still vestiges of that old culture," he says. "You have to be persistent. Today, people want solutions, and they want to learn ways to build the business. Providing that is the way you begin to change the mindset – and then follow up by constantly selling your center with success stories and very tangible ways you help the business." CCMReview

## In The Center with John Gregg

# The Impact of Service Delivery on Customer Satisfaction

**What is a good service encounter? Reseach shows customers' views on satisfactory experiences.**

When it comes to delivering customer service, Ray Kordupleski, director of customer satisfaction for AT&T, has a catchy way of summing it up: "Good is not good enough." His point is that customers are not moved to take favorable actions, such as buying more products or going out of their way to recommend a product or service, unless they are completely satisfied (i.e., if asked, they would offer a top-box rating on a satisfaction rating scale; see Figure 1, below).

Companies and call centers must set the bar at the top satisfaction ratings if they want to grow their businesses using their existing customer base. This is a critical point, yet it's a practice that is not widely followed. Many call centers are so caught up with handling problems and improving process efficiencies that they only occasionally focus on delivering exemplary service and achieving top-box satisfaction.

To refocus your goals, there are some logical questions you should be able to answer about your customer base. For example:

- What portion of customers are completely satisfied?
- What constitutes particularly good, memorable service experiences for customers?
- Can customers be elevated to top-box satisfaction with one outstanding service experience; e.g., by surprising them or giving them something extra?
- What is the payoff for achieving top-box satisfaction?

### Figure 1. Top-Box Customer Recommendations (Credit Cards)

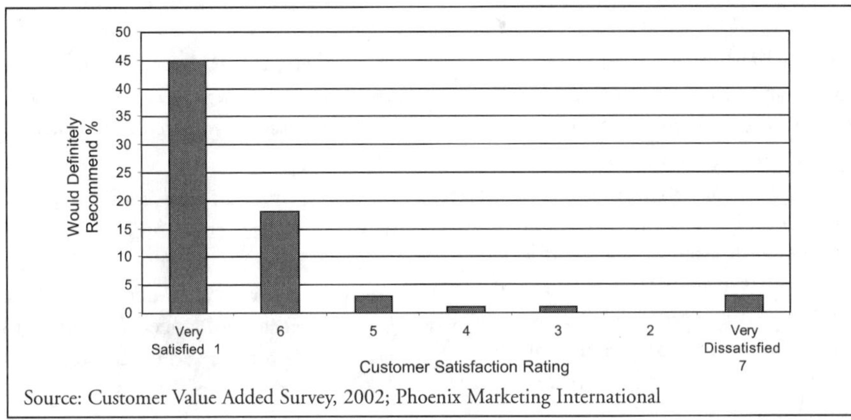


Source: Customer Value Added Survey, 2002; Phoenix Marketing International

### Figure 2. Customer Service Experience Outcomes

| | Credit Cards | Telecommunications |
|---|---|---|
| Problem Encounters | 10% | 38% |
| Satisfactory Encounters | 58% | 17% |
| Particularly Good Encounters | 32% | 45% |
| Total | 100% | 100% |

Source: ServiceSat.com, 2001; Phoenix Marketing International

### Customer Satisfaction Research Findings

Phoenix Marketing International has been tracking customer satisfaction with service delivery for more than two years through a syndicated research program called ServiceSat.com. The industries surveyed include airlines, auto insurance, banking, credit card, online shopping and telecommunications. Following are a few of the key findings:

- From a customer's point-of-view, service encounters can be divided into three classes of outcomes: 1) A problem that either began as such or evolved into a problem during the service interaction; 2) a satisfactory but unmemorable service interaction; and 3) a particularly good interaction that may have affected the customer's overall level of satisfaction and impacted the likelihood of favorable future behavior.

  Customers report that a third to one-half of all service interactions are "particularly good." Good experiences outnumber problems by 3-to-1 for credit card companies, and 1.2-to-1 for telecommunications firms. Across all categories surveyed, particularly good experiences run about 2-to-1 relative to problems (see Figure 2).

- Companies report that the financial impact of creating particularly good experiences is presently equal to or greater than avoiding problems and performing service recovery. This measure is derived from multiplying the frequency of these types of encounters by the percent of customers who say they will respectively increase or decrease their future business based on that outcome.

Of course, consumers may not do what they say or they may be less inclined to do so based on a memorable good service encounter than a problem, but the order of magnitude is still instructive: Creating particularly good service outcomes definitely is important.

■ Good experiences do drive up customer satisfaction, but slowly — about one notch at a time. However, problem experiences can deteriorate satisfaction levels in a precipitous manner. For instance, in the credit card industry, only 18 percent of customers who are more than two boxes away from top-box satisfaction move up more than one level based upon a particularly good service encounter. On the other hand, 31 percent of customers experiencing a problem will move down more than one level of satisfaction. Customers are quicker to judge than to praise, and it therefore takes far more good experiences to offset the bad ones — a case for monitoring and managing for particularly good service outcomes.

■ Customers presently judge those service encounters they deem "particularly good" as much on the friendliness and helpfulness of the employee as on the content of the interaction itself. The attitude and people skills of service employees are paramount. Frontline staff frequently carry the encounter and are considered to be of real import to customers, as well (see Figure 3).

But the factors that would contribute most — those judged to be most important — for driving up good outcomes are somewhat different. In the credit card industry, "dependable employees/good follow-through" was the strongest contributor to good service outcomes. For telecommunications companies, "being surprised with something considered to be a little extra" was key. In both industries, particularly telecommunications, "good rates and/or fees" are strong contributors to good service outcomes (see Figure 4 on page 10).

■ Being "surprised/getting something extra" does not mean that the company needs to develop expensive give-away policies and programs.

These highly impactful events are often achieved by listening to the customer and providing solutions that are basic to the company but a pleasant surprise to the customer. They have more to do with the listening and effective application of a policy or program than making a major, expensive concession to a customer. Given the importance of the outcome, they are very good trade-offs. The following consumer comments offer examples of these types of trade-offs:

*"I was having difficulty renting a car for an upcoming holiday and the Platinum Travel Service representative was able to find me the car I wanted at a very good rate."*

*"Several times merchants tried to take advantage of me by charging my credit card erroneously. Citibank and I disputed all these fraudulent charges and we won! Citibank rules!"*

*"I called to close my MasterCard account. As an alternative to having me close my account and pay the account off at my current rate, the associate offered to convert me to a gold card customer with no annual fee plus a reduction in my interest rate."*

Another type of "surprise" or "extra" involves service encounters with customers who seem to have a fairly low expectation for service quality. In these cases, just the avoidance of a problem was enough for the service to be judged favorably. For example:

*"The phone was answered in a timely manner and all my questions were answered."*

*"AARP just seemed so very honest."*

*"I wasn't talked into something I didn't want."*

*"Very polite and helpful. Did everything I could ask for."*

The third type of experience that customers consider a surprise or extra effort are those that occur when the company takes the initiative to do something and lets the customer know what they've

## Figure 3. Service Employee Impact on Customer Experiences

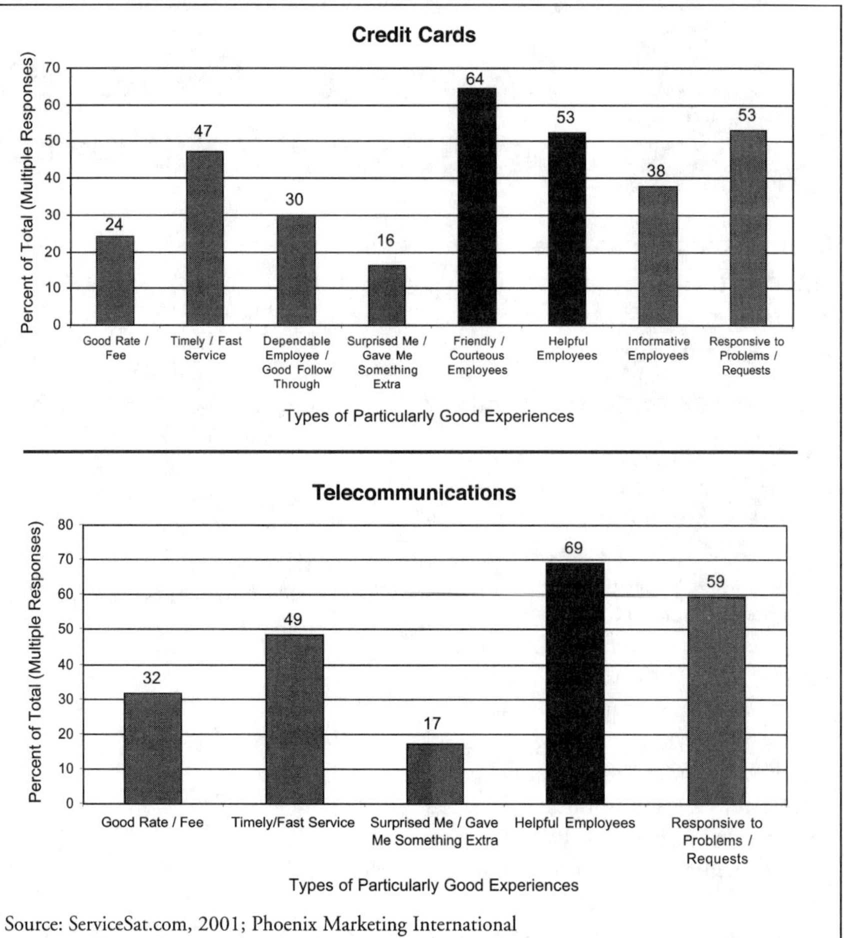


Source: ServiceSat.com, 2001; Phoenix Marketing International

Section 9

done for them. For instance:

*"I like how they contact us when we have made a lot of purchases ... just to confirm that the purchases were made by us. My husband finds it annoying, but it makes me feel comfortable that someone there is checking our account and making sure no one is misusing our card."*

*"I received an increase on my account [credit limit] without asking."*

■ Some companies have been able to distinguish themselves within, and even across, their market category. Providing "particularly good" service encounters can be a competitive advantage. While the research hasn't revealed a breakout organization in every industry, some companies have been identified by customers as impressive. Two, in particular, are USAA (auto insurance) and Amazon (online shopping). USAA customers report that 73 percent of the contacts they have with the company are "particularly good" experiences. Only 7 percent of the contacts are problems. Fifty-five percent of Amazon customer contacts are "particularly good"; only 4 percent are problematic (see Figure 6).

## Satisfaction Requires More than 'Good' Service

Creating "particularly good" service experience outcomes has an critical impact on customer satisfaction, customer behavior and long-term financial performance. However, attaining top-box customer satisfaction is not simply the result of delivering "good" service. It requires setting and managing toward lofty goals. "Particularly good" service has distinguishing characteristics that warrant monitoring and managing in addition to problem-resolution rates. Two ways to delivery "particularly good" service are providing high levels of employee friendliness and cost-effective surprises.

Consistent top-box satisfaction ratings will not come from single, magnanimous events. It takes time. But there are companies that demonstrate it is possible to deliver high levels of particularly good experiences and create a competitive advantage. CCMReview

**Figure 4. Top Factors for Driving Up Good Outcomes**

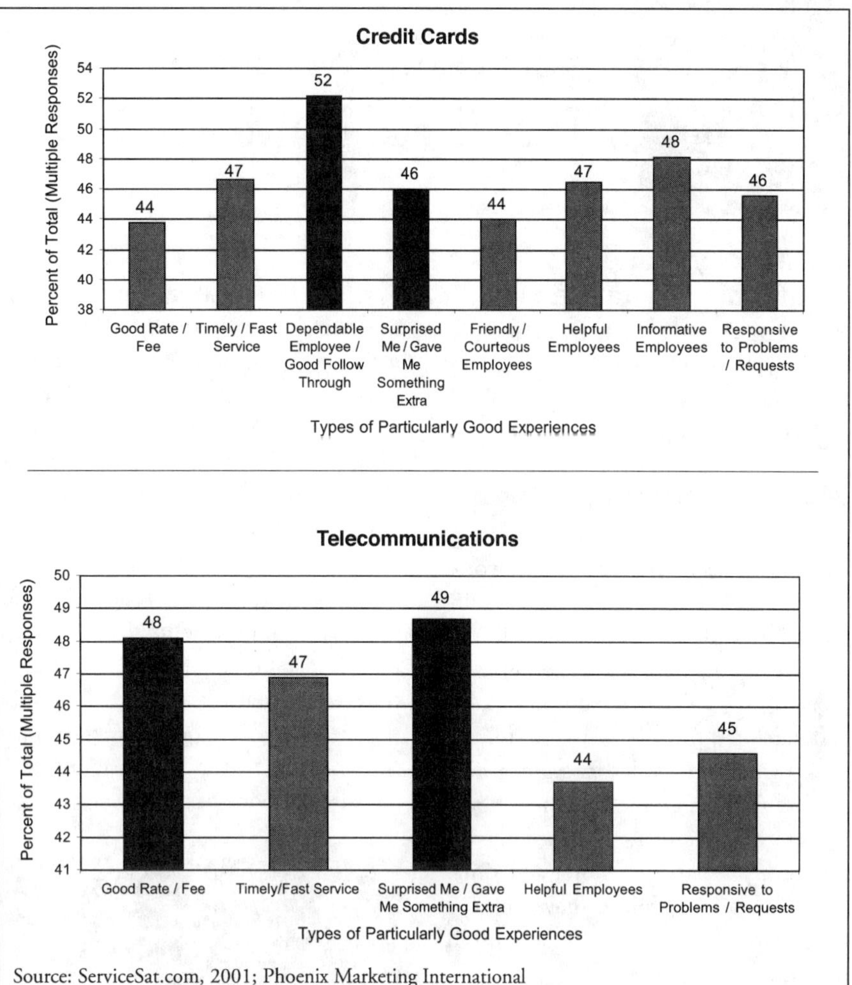


**Figure 5. Good Experience Incidences for Selected Industries and Companies**

| Industry/ Company | % of Contacts "Particular-ly Good" | Good-to-Problem Ratio | Industry/ Company | % of Contacts "Particular-ly Good" | Good-to-Problem Ratio |
|---|---|---|---|---|---|
| **Auto Insurance** | | | **Credit Cards** | | |
| Allstate | 62% | 3 to 1 | American Express | 26% | 4 to 1 |
| GEICO | 66% | 4 to 1 | Citibank | 12% | 2 to 1 |
| State Farm | 59% | 7 to 1 | Discover | 22% | 4 to 1 |
| USAA | 73% | 11 to 1 | First USA | 18% | 2 to 1 |
| **Online Shopping** | | | **Telecommunications** | | |
| Amazon | 55% | 15 to 1 | AT&T | 27% | 2 to 1 |
| eBay | 48% | 8 to 1 | Bell South | 34% | 3 to 1 |
| Priceline | 33% | 2 to 1 | MCI | 22% | 1 to 1 |
| Ticketmaster | 30% | 2 to 1 | Verizon | 30% | 3 to 1 |

Source: ServiceSat.com, 2001; Phoenix Marketing International

**John Gregg**

*John Gregg is Managing Director of Phoenix Marketing International, a marketing consulting and advanced analytical market modeling firm in Portsmouth, NH. He can be reached at 603-373-0202 or john.gregg@phoenixmi.com.*

# Successfully Leading Distributed and 24x7 Teams

**Technology alone can't break down distance and time barriers. Focus on communication and trust when building a virtual team.**

The degree to which our world has become connected has surpassed the most forward-thinking dreams of just a generation ago. Fiber optic cables crisscross the globe, and satellites provide virtually ubiquitous worldwide telecommunications service. Computer and telecommunications technologies have spawned organizations that span geography and time. And Internet capabilities have enabled people to link resources and skills in new, imaginative ways.

Many of the trends in call centers are indicative of these developments. Distributed call centers, telecommuting, cross-functional teams and 24-hour-by-seven-day-a-week operations are common examples of people working across sites and time. If you are a call center manager, chances are high that you will have the responsibility of getting results from people who work in different locations, who don't report to you or who don't work the same hours.

While technology has enabled these enormous opportunities, it hasn't eliminated the natural barriers that exist between people who work in distributed environments. For example, people who work in different places and/or at different times often have trouble seeing themselves as an integral part of a larger team. Informal opportunities that people have for getting to know each other in traditional settings (such as around the coffee pot or in the hallway) may be rare; these experiences can be tough to replicate by phone or e-mail. Further, in any organization a large amount of information is exchanged outside the formal context of memos and meetings, which, without extraordinary effort on the part of all group members, is often unevenly distributed among individuals.

Unfortunately, there is no fool-proof formula for leading a distributed group. Like leadership in general, building a cohesive virtual team defies a specific recipe. There are, however, tried-and-true principles that will significantly increase the odds of success.

**Principles of Successfully Leading 'Virtual Teams'**

1. Create a compelling vision
2. Build trust among members
3. Establish appropriate communication tools
4. Eliminate unnecessary bureaucracy
5. Develop a communications agreement
6. Consistently communicate progress
7. Listen actively and regularly
8. Celebrate accomplishments

## Create a Compelling Vision

Begin by asking key questions; e.g., Why does the distributed group exist? What is it going to collectively achieve? What's in it for the participants? Unfortunately, quite a few people have been through the process of creating "vision statements" that, for one reason or another, have had little or no impact on people's actions. Nonetheless, a clear focus that is championed by the leader is a prerequisite to pulling people in and aligning actions.

## Build Trust Among Members

In their classic work, *Leaders*, Warren Bennis and Burt Nanus contend trust is the "lubrication that makes it possible for organizations to work." (*Leaders*, Harperbusiness, 1997.) Consultant Jaclyn Kostner, who has authored several books on the subject of virtual leadership, concurs and concludes that the remote leader's No. 1 challenge is to develop trust on three levels: in the leader, in the project or organization, and among the people who are a part of the team.

How? Start by creating opportunities for the people in your distributed group to get to know each other. For example, one call center manager set up a Web page profiling the members of a multi-site team, then gave everyone a short "open book" (rather, "open Web") quiz on the interests and backgrounds of the other members. It's also important to ensure everyone gets key information at the same time and that all are kept abreast of major decisions. Remember, some expediency must be traded off for the sake of fostering a collaborative environment.

## Establish Appropriate Communication Tools

A prerequisite to a productive distributed work group is to ensure the members of the group have compatible and capable communications technologies. Telephone, e-mail, Intranet and collaboration and conferencing tools offer enormous potential, if available and compatible across the entire group (it's very important that all individuals have access to the same communications tools – no second-class members!). Further, creating a directory (paper or online) of contact numbers and addresses just for the distributed workgroup gives people the basic information they need to collaborate, and also adds to the symbolism that will help the members of the team identify with each other.

### Eliminate Unnecessary Bureaucracy

Respected management consultant Peter Drucker insists that "so much of what we call management consists of making it difficult for people to work." Distributed groups, in particular, are prone to encounter unworkable rules, policies and procedures. The result can be project gridlock.

It's important for the leader to regularly and vigilantly look for ways to scrap (or, at least, minimize) the impact of unnecessary hierarchies and cumbersome bureaucracies. That's easier said than done, but it's one of the most important steps you can take to facilitate the progress of your distributed team. Help the members of your group accomplish their tasks by eliminating stumbling blocks, such as interdepartmental barriers.

### Develop a Communications 'Agreement'

Even with all the technology bells and whistles, good communication may be lacking. For instance, have you ever received a lengthy, involved e-mail that gave no hint how or if you were to respond? Or have you ever sent a genuinely important message that warrants a timely response, but received no reply because the recipient thought the message was only an "FYI" (for your information)?

Distributed work groups need some ground rules that stipulate levels of priority and appropriate responses for: a) urgent messages requiring immediate response; b) routine messages requiring response within, say, a day; and c) non-urgent informational messages that require no response.

E-mail messages should have descriptive titles and should be written like a newspaper story with headlines first, the main points second and necessary supporting details last. Also, not using e-mail to relay negative information to someone, especially related to their performance, is wise advice; a telephone or video conference (or, of course, an in-person meeting) will allow the kind of immediate interaction that can prevent a problem from becoming even more serious and emotionally charged.

### Consistently Communicate Progress

Hazy objectives and vaguely defined tasks will destroy the productivity and morale of a distributed work group. The objectives of the group should be as concrete as possible, and projects should have clearly defined milestones, with beginning and ending points. Since projects tend to take on a life of their own as they develop, it's important to keep the group updated and on the same track.

Project tools such as Gantt charts and flow charts can be useful for identifying resources required, showing the inter-related nature of individual tasks, and tracking progress. They give a tangibility to the mission of the workgroup, and can help address questions such as: Where are we? How far have we come? What's next? They should be updated and distributed as often as something substantial changes in the ongoing direction and plans. (Unfortunately, they can also instill a rigidity that hampers necessary changes in direction as a project develops, so they shouldn't be used over-zealously.)

### Listen Actively and Regularly

There is a common myth that great leaders create compelling visions from "gifted perspectives" or "inner creativity" that others don't possess. But many studies on the subjects of leadership and strategy (e.g., from the work of Warren Bennis, Peter Senge, Michael Porter and others) have shown that the visions of some of history's greatest leaders often came from others. The leaders may have selected the best vision to focus on, shaped it and communicated it to others in a compelling way, but they rarely originated the vision. The point? Be a superb listener. Develop both formal and informal channels of communication to gain access to the ideas and insights of others. There's an added benefit of being a good listener: When people have a stake in an idea, they tend to work much harder to bring about its success.

### Celebrate Accomplishments

As your distributed group reaches critical milestones, it is important to acknowledge the accomplishments and celebrate! A shared vision is motivating. But, you have to keep the vision alive. And one of the best ways to do that is to actively recognize accomplishments along the way.

### The Challenges Are Ongoing

These principles have much personal meaning to me. As Incoming Calls Management Institute (ICMI) has grown, our team of employees, associates and joint venture partners spans an increasing number of countries, languages and backgrounds. We have learned a tremendous amount about virtual leadership by observing the habits of successful call center managers responsible for far-flung or 24x7 teams.

The challenges are real and ongoing and, I suppose, mastering these principles is a lifelong pursuit. But being part of an environment in which people surmount distance and time to succeed as individuals and as a group is one of the most rewarding professional experiences you can have! In today's world, it's also one of the most necessary. CCMReview

**Brad Cleveland**

*Brad Cleveland is president of Incoming Calls Management Institute (ICMI) and publisher of* Call Center Management Review. *He can be reached at 410-267-0700 (ext. 958), or bradc@incoming.com.*

Section 9

# Ways Call Center Managers Impede, Ways They Advance Their Careers

*Editor's Note: The following article consists of excerpts from a speech Brad gave to a gathering of call center managers in Johannesburg, South Africa on March 16, 1999.*

What a difference a decade can make! Throughout the 1980s, surveys showed that most business leaders were not aware of the meaning of "call center" or the increasingly important role call centers were playing in business strategy and development. In fact, given the lack of press and attention, many people understandably confused call centers with telemarketing organizations making outbound cold calls.

Now, fast forward to 1999. As the decade comes to a close, call centers have become widely recognized for their impact on customer retention, competitiveness and the ability for organizations to adapt to fast-changing markets. They have evolved into powerful "loyalizing" tools, the primary mechanisms for developing and maintaining relationships with customers. Senior managers are increasingly aware of that, and they are taking steps to attract capable leaders to guide their call centers through the changes ahead.

By most accounts, we are likely to see as much change and development in the next five years as we've seen in the last 10 or 15. The challenges that call center managers face – and the opportunities these challenges bring – are substantial. While some call center managers are enjoying a new level of status and influence, others are unwittingly hampering their careers. Ironically, the very things meant to help are often sabotaging opportunities...

**To impede your career, become so valuable that your call center can't function without you.** You've got the connections, the insight, the know-how. You're the hub around which the call center operates. I know of a call center once widely acclaimed that struggled considerably after their charismatic leader took another position in the company. It later became evident that many processes and decisions were hopelessly dependent on his direct involvement. There is a paradox in leadership that we all need to remember: the more valuable you are, the more vulnerable the organization is. The legacy you leave will become known, and often sooner rather than later. **To advance your career, build an organization that is strong enough to thrive without you.** That involves identifying and cultivating new leaders, building a broad base of skills and knowledge throughout the call center, and establishing well-designed processes that clip along even when key people are absent.

*To impede your career, focus on the efficiencies the call center delivers.*

**To impede your career, stay out of organizational politics.** We've all heard the words of advice: keep your nose clean, stay above the fray. But the reality is, any time you combine people, opinions and limited resources, there will be politics. Politics are an inherent part of any organization and are not inherently good or evil (unless, of course, they become corrupt or unduly unfair). **To advance your career, hit the campaign trail.** Take the message of the call center to the four corners of the organization and beyond. Have your themes of communication well thought out, and "lobby" for the visibility and collaboration the call center needs. How much time have you spent in the marketing department lately? Finance? With your upper level managers? All too often, we don't get the support we need from other areas because we haven't taken the time to understand their perspectives and pressures.

**To impede your career, focus on the efficiencies the call center delivers.** Develop a budget that stresses the cost effectiveness of the call center when compared to more expensive service delivery alternatives. Highlight how many transactions you have handled and how many customers

Section 9

you have served. Concentrate on the efficiencies you've gained in handling time and the steps you've taken to improve service level. **To advance your career, focus on the call center's effectiveness.** The problem with the efficiency approach is that it can supercede more important issues and undervalue the contribution of the call center. I am not suggesting that efficiency isn't important. But put the emphasis on the things that matter most: How is the call center supporting and furthering the organization's mission? What impact is the call center having on customer retention and loyalty? How has the call center contributed to the development of products and services? How has the call center impacted the speed of delivering service and support? Even if yours is what is generally mischaracterized as a "cost center," e.g., a governmental call center, you can – in fact must – take an effectiveness tact (for example, how has the call center improved the understanding of and subsequent compliance to regulations?)

**To impede your career, leave technology decisions to the I.S. department.** After all, they understand the bits and bites. Stick with me on this one... for those I.S. folks among us, this is not an indictment of your capabilities! In fact, most I.S. professionals are working minor miracles, along with just plain working hard, to keep today's constantly-evolving multi-vendor call centers humming along. Rather, it's a message for call center managers: **To advance your career, take responsibility for understanding technology and ensuring that it is supporting the call center's mission.** Sometimes it's easier to hide behind the banner of being a "people person" than it is to dig in, learn the stuff and take the steps to implement and manage technology in a way that it best supports your people, your customers and the organization.

**To impede your career, produce reports that put the call center in the best light possible.** While not exactly in the realm of "cooking the books," there are a lot of ways to massage reports so that they tell the right story. How you calculate service level, the routing alternatives you use, changing processes midstream, controlled busy signals.... there are lots of ways to create the numbers you want. I remember working with a call center manager in the U.K. who didn't want the reports submitted to upper level management to look any worse than those submitted by her immediate predecessor. The problem was, the information as it was presented was masking some serious resource deficiencies. **To advance your career, ensure that call center reports give the straight scoop.** Then, be prepared to explain why the results look the way they do. The manager decided to tell the story the way she knew it to be. After explaining the "drop in productivity" she was able to secure the necessary resources. She also established a level of integrity the call center didn't previously have. (Remember, there are lots of ways to creatively report activity at the supervisor and agents levels, as well. The example you set will not go unnoticed.)

*To advance your career, ensure that call center reports give the straight scoop.*

**To impede your career, assume your primary profession is with the vertical industry you are a part of,** e.g., the insurance industry, travel sector, utilities, government, financial sector, consumer products or other vertical industry. **To advance your career, recognize that you are first and foremost a call center manager.** The ties that bind us are strong. Despite the fact that very different organizations are represented here, the challenges are common and the characteristics of good call centers are unmistakable... whatever the industry. Further, caller expectations are now formed more around the experiences our customers have with other call centers than from the experiences they have with similar organizations! You probably have more in common professionally with call center managers from Stockholm to Sydney to Seattle than you do with the folks down the hall in the next department. Treat call center management for what it is: a growing global profession with a growing body of knowledge and experiences to keep up with and learn from.

**To impede your career, be sure you get the credit for call center wins and improvements.** You know, toot your own horn. After all, you brought the right players together. You provided critical direction. You had the vision. **To advance your career, give genuine credit to others.** This principle takes some faith, but if everywhere you go people are succeeding, your role will become known. More importantly, you will be enabling people to learn and develop in ways that will benefit them for the rest of their careers. As those of you who have been in this industry quite awhile would probably attest, watching other people grow and succeed is one of the best rewards in call center management.

CCMReview

## Effective Communication: A "Best Practice"

In some call centers, you can feel the energy as soon as you walk in the door. It takes many forms: pride of workmanship, enthusiasm, a feeling of community, commitment and the willingness to make the extra effort. The call center "clicks." Everybody knows what the mission is, everybody is pulling in the same direction. While there are a myriad of factors that go into creating this sort of environment, effective communication throughout the call center is essential.

Communication creates meaning and direction for people. Organizations of all types depend on the existence of what Warren Bennis, noted organizational theorist, calls "shared meanings and interpretations of reality," which facilitate coordinated action. When good communication is lacking, the symptoms are predictable: conflicting objectives, unclear values, misunderstandings, lack of coordination, confusion, low morale and people doing the bare minimum required.

So how do the best do it? How do they communicate their mission and values in a way that gets buy-in and alignment from their people? Although call centers vary dramatically from organization to organization, there are four notable similarities among leading call centers.

### Conducive Culture

First and foremost, top-notch call centers have a culture that supports effective communication (By culture, I am referring to the inveterate principles or values of the organization). Culture tends to guide behavior and can either support, or, as some have learned the hard way, ruin the best laid plans for organizational change.

Unfortunately, there's no guaranteed formula for creating a supporting culture. But many seasoned call center managers agree that shaping the culture of the organization is a primary leadership responsibility. They do not believe that culture should be left to fate. As a result, they spend an inordinate amount of time understanding the organization and the people who are part of it.

Richard Farson, author of the critically acclaimed book, Management of the Absurd (Simon and Schuster, 1996) asserts that "many programs in management training today are moving us in the wrong direction because they fail to appreciate the complexity and paradoxical nature of human organizations. Thinking loses out to how-to-do-it formulas and techniques, if not slogans and homilies, as the principle management guides."

*Creating a high-performance culture in which effective communication thrives also means driving out fear.*

Judging by their actions, the most effective call center managers seem to agree with Farson. They seem to be comfortably resigned to the fact that, as Farson puts it, "we can never quite master our relationships with each other." Consequently, they are okay with the realization that they will often be spending more of their time on "people issues" than on anything else.

Creating a high-performance culture in which effective communication thrives also means driving out fear. This was a theme the late W. Edward Deming spoke of passionately, especially in his later years, and is one of his famous "Fourteen Points." Sometimes, however, fear goes unrecognized by managers. For example, agents may be manipulating their statistics and "cheating the system." Essentially, they may be more afraid of reporting accurate statistics than of fudging the numbers. That is a symptom of what Deming would have called fear.

Of course, there are those things that we should be fearful of, such as the consequences of being dishonest or grossly irresponsible. But it's the wrong kind of fear, such as the fear of taking reasonable risks or the fear of constructive dissent, that effective call center managers work so diligently to abolish. Fear inhibits effective communication.

### Shared Information

Second, leaders of high-performance call centers are predisposed to keeping their people in the know. They actively share both good and bad news. This minimizes the rumor mill and contributes to an environment of trust (see Notes, June 1996).

Peter Senge, who popularized the notion of a learning organization in his widely read book, The Fifth Discipline (Doubleday, 1990), described a place "where people continually expand their capacity to create the results they truly desire, where new and expansive patterns of thinking are nurtured, where collective aspiration is set free, and where people are continually learning how to learn together." Futurist Don Tapscott adds that "there is no sustainable competitive advantage today other than organizational learning." Shared information is the fundamental ingredient in organizational learning.

Leading call centers cultivate both formal and informal channels of communication. The communication formats can include newsletters, meetings, visual displays, electronic mail, voice mail, posters, intranets and informal "hallway meetings." But the mission and values being communicated remain consistent. As Bennis puts it, "leadership...is based on predictability. The truth is that we trust people who are predictable, whose positions are known and who keep at it; leaders who are trusted make themselves known, make their positions clear."

One of the common formal means of communication between front-line workers and management is agent satisfaction surveys. The best call centers track results and monitor trends to ensure continuous improvement. Survey results are communicated back to the agents, and teams are often formed to address specific problems that are identified in the surveys. The progress towards resolving the problem is then tracked and communicated to agents. In short, management does a lot of active listening.

Keeping people well informed also helps them prepare for and accept change. "Today's business world is and has been about change," notes Kathleen Peterson, a recognized communication skills expert. "The concept of change becomes personal and its meaning and level of acceptance are based clearly on how the change is communicated and what people believe it to mean."

**Systematic Planning**

Third, leading call centers have cultivated a systematic, collaborative approach to call center planning. This process generally includes seven major steps:

1) Choose an appropriate service level objective
2) Collect necessary planning data
3) Forecast the calling load
4) Calculate the on-phone staff requirements
5) Calculate trunk requirements
6) Factor in roster staff factor or "shrink factor" (which reflects breaks, absenteeism, etc.)
7) Organize schedules

*...leaders of high-performance call centers recognize an interesting paradox: too much communicating inhibits effective communication.*

They have also created a flow chart that illustrates the process step by step and shows the logical sequence of events. The flow chart highlights any "disconnects" in the planing process, such as the marketing department running campaigns that the call center doesn't know about ahead of time.

Systematic planning contributes to effective communication in several ways. It creates a body of information that wouldn't otherwise be available ("here's our call load pattern and, therefore, why the schedules are structured as they are"). It also forces people to look into the future and see their work in the context of a larger framework. Perhaps most important, formal planning requires communication about values, on issues such as resource allocations, budgeting and workload priorities. As one call center manager put it, "Formal planning goes far beyond getting the right number of butts in seats." It forces the kind of communication that an active call center desperately requires.

**Optimal Communication Levels**

Finally, leaders of high-performance call centers recognize an interesting paradox: too much communicating inhibits effective communication. Farson maintains that "there seems always to be an optimal level of communication beyond which further or expanded communication becomes dysfunctional. Communication has its limits."

Too many meetings, memos, conferences, electronic mail messages and on-the-fly discussions may be symptoms of weaknesses in the process. With better tools, more focused training and appropriate levels of empowerment, the need for excessive communicating can be avoided. I once heard someone draw an analogy to a crew on a sailboat. When one of the lines breaks, nobody waits for anyone else to act and nobody needs to give orders or instructions. The members of the crew are acting in harmony and know what to do to address the problem.

**Generating Power**

Effective communication is inseparable from effective leadership. As Warren Bennis puts it, "Leaders are only as powerful as the ideas they can communicate." Effective communication results in a shared vision. And, when people are aligned behind a set of compelling values, enthusiasm and commitment — that perceptible energy — tends to follow.

SLN

# How to Get the Attention of Key Decision Makers

*by Jean Bave-Kerwin*

A frustrating fact of call center management is that, often, decisions which profoundly affect your operation's performance are made outside of the call center. Decisions to reduce staff, freeze hiring or even redesign systems are executed by decision makers who don't have a clear understanding of how a call center works, yet set the expectation that the center will be accountable for the same level of service as before.

Sound familiar? Although it may be tempting (and therapeutic) to hold the view that senior-level decision makers are simply bad managers, I don't believe that's the case. Most executives want to do a good job for their organization and its customers. Unfortunately, many times, they simply work in a part of the company that doesn't have direct contact with customers. Instead, their view is focused on solving problems, keeping costs down or reducing errors in their operation. The unintended effect on the customer care operation is rarely the main consideration.



## Getting the Word Out

The good news is, there are ways of getting your company decision makers' attention and support. Following are several approaches you can use to give them the information they'll need to make policies that benefit the call center, as well as the rest of the organization.

■ Don't be shy about giving feedback concerning the unintended consequences of any decision that adversely affects your call center operations. Convey what's happening, but be sure to back it up with data – and always suggest alternatives.

■ Do everything you can to get a seat at the decision-making table. When you're asked for input, be sure to give solid reasons for your position in terms with which decision makers are familiar. Insist on being a part of the budgeting process to better understand (and explain) how different budgets interact.

■ Use routine reporting as an opportunity to educate others on call center business drivers (i.e., random call arrival, the psychology of the queue and caller tolerance for delay). When you report your key performance indicators (KPIs), be sure to include in your comments on service level any efficiency measures that contribute to those outcomes (i.e., talk time, after call work, call demand, staffing, etc.). Make sure the relationships between these elements and the quality of service is well-understood.

■ If you're working on a process improvement project, use it as an opportunity to involve your finance managers with your operation. Ask them to help develop the cost-benefit analysis. In the process, offer information on how the call center works. Don't assume they know: They're more likely to be familiar with a straight production staff calculation than with queuing theory.

■ Request to make a presentation on call center business drivers and operations at an interdepartmental staff meeting. You can make it an overview, but be sure to give salient points about service level and the relationship of staffing to occupancy, or the importance of eliminating systemic barriers to make talk time and after call work as efficient as possible.

■ Speak their language. For instance, if you're dealing with budget people, relate your information to the bottom line – it's what they care about. Similarly, when speaking to HR people, discuss the effects of policy in human factors, such as calculating the cost of training a new employee against retaining an existing one. Use the terms and concepts to which each operating unit relates.

■ Use stories to get your point across. Stories are powerful because people tend to remember them. A success story or horror tale concerning the consequences of past decisions will make an impression – and hopefully, remind others to include you in their decision-making process.

■ Include decision makers and others who are affected by your operation in your decision-making process. They won't forget your example of asking for their opinions. At a minimum, it will improve communications.

The key to successfully educating decision makers on call center principles is to be proactive, vocal and positive. Remember, your aim is better customer service – any feedback you offer should focus on the ultimate impact on customers. Be persistent and, soon, your organization will begin to view the call center as a valuable asset in determining strategy and tactics for improving the bottom line. CCMReview

Jean Bave-Kerwin

*Jean Bave-Kerwin is president of JBK Consulting, a firm specializing in call center and customer service solutions for the public and not-for-profit sectors, founding president of the Call Center Management Association of New York and a Certified Associate of Incoming Calls Management Institute. She has managed six call centers for a large government agency, an entrepreneurial government marketing organization and served as an internal consultant to a number of agencies on call center issues. Jean has experience in organizational development, leadership, process improvement consulting, project management and human resources. She can be reached at jbaveker@nycap.rr.com.*

# A Process for Reporting Call Center Activity

Reporting call center activity to senior level management and others in the organization can seem like a daunting task. The wide variety of activities in a typical call center, the reality of senior management not having the time nor inclination to pour over detailed reports, and the fact that summary reports often gloss-over important information, all contribute to the challenge. Consequently, many diligently prepared reports either go unread or, worse, are misunderstood.

As an example of the reporting challenge, take just one facet (albeit, an important one!) of call center activity: what happens to your callers? As new channels of customer contact are invented, it becomes more difficult to measure the service that callers are receiving, and their perceptions of that service. Service level reports can tell us what percentage of transactions were handled in Y seconds for agent groups. But what about callers who used the VRU without talking to an agent? Or those handled by one of a wide variety of skills-based and/or network routing contingencies? Or those who used the Web? Or, increasingly, those transactions in which the customer utilized a variety of contact media — perhaps part Web, part VRU and part agent contact? In short, different callers have different experiences with us, which makes assessing our services that much more difficult.

Clearly, a variety of reports is necessary to paint an accurate picture of what's happening in the call center. Further, to be correctly interpreted, the reports often must be viewed in terms of how they are interrelated; any measurement by itself can be misleading.

One of the promises of Customer Relationship Management (CRM) technologies is the capability to bring disparate approaches and information together into seamless processes and reports focused on customers rather than on transactions. Thank goodness the supplier community is approaching the call center as the interrelated system of causes that it is (and always has been), and is developing tools to manage it as such. Keep your eye on the prize, but keep your expectations in check — the ability to view and manage in an integrated fashion the many systems, processes and activities that characterize the modern call center is not, thus far, a working reality to the point that it should and will be in coming years. We've got a ways to go as an industry.

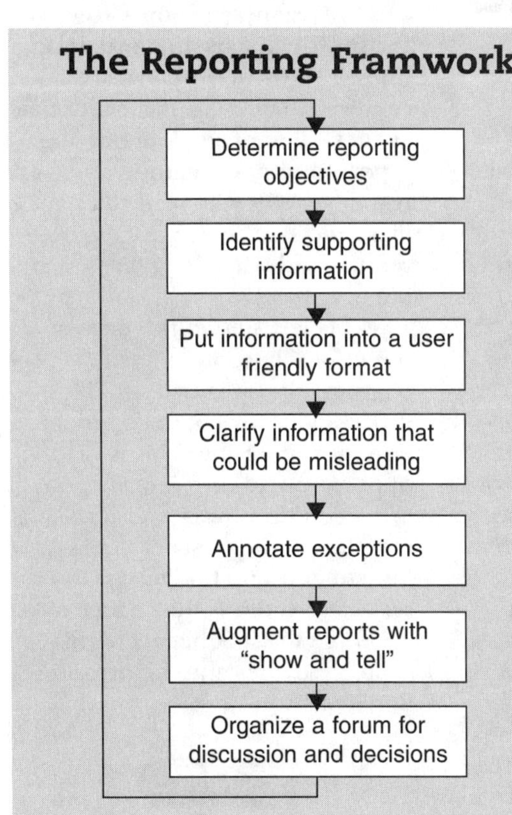
The Reporting Framwork
Determine reporting objectives
Identify supporting information
Put information into a user friendly format
Clarify information that could be misleading
Annotate exceptions
Augment reports with "show and tell"
Organize a forum for discussion and decisions

Further, the most important ingredients in effective reporting are leadership and communication, not reporting technologies. Effective call center reporting is an ongoing communication process, not an end result.

The following seven-step framework will help you establish an effective process, and prepare meaningful reports for upper-level management:

**1) Determine the objectives.** What are the objectives for the reports? If nobody knows for sure, assemble a team for an initial working discussion. A cross-section of upper management, call center managers, supervisors and agents should be involved. Topics can include:

- Workload handled and workload forecast
- Customer satisfaction and quality measurements
- Costs and revenues
- Resource utilization (staffing and scheduling needs)
- Queue reports (service level, response time, abandonment, etc.)
- Access alternatives (e-mail, Web,

telephone, VRU, video, etc.).

It's often useful to preface this exercise with a question like, "If we could simply snap our fingers, what would we know about our call center?" The objectives your team comes up with will be enlightening and will provide much needed direction for the steps that follow. And don't worry whether or not you have the reports to support the objectives you identify. Your objectives — not the reports you happen to have — should drive this process.

**2) Identify supporting information.** List the possible alternatives under each of the objectives you identified in Step 1. Include reports from customer surveys, the ACD, information databases, Internet servers, VRU servers, e-mail servers, the telecommunications network and other systems, as well as information from other areas of the organization.

The challenge now becomes one of selection. Stephanie Winston, author of the aging but popular book, The Organized Executive: A Program for Productivity: New Ways to Manage Time, Paper, People and the Electronic Office (Warner Books, 1994), advises that "a report should not simply be a compendium of facts, but a judgment tool for management; the right information presented in the right way to the right people."

To pare down the lists, Winston suggests asking a variety of questions: Is the report really necessary? What questions does it answer? Which reports would you dispense with if you were charged for them? Could several reports be combined?

**3) Put the information in a user-friendly format.** Once you have a list of desired reports, the next step is to compile them into a simple, understandable format. This often means creating graphs with the data. This may take more pages, but a 10-page or 15-page package of reports that consist primarily of graphs is often quicker to read and easier to comprehend than two pages of small, detailed numbers in rows and columns.

Often, data needs to be combined or positioned together to provide the full story. For example, service level should be interpreted with blockage and abandonment. And be sure to use the same general format for headings, periods of time covered and chart types.

*The ability to view and manage in an integrated fashion the many systems, processes and activities that characterize the modern call center is not, thus far, a working reality to the point that it should and will be.*

**4) Clarify information that could be misleading.** As any seasoned call center manager has learned, you can make many call center reports say whatever you want them to say. (Winston Churchill was right about the three kinds of lies: lies, damn lies and statistics!)

Further, summarized reports that are otherwise technically accurate can conceal important information. A manager might report that the center's average speed of answer for September was 21 seconds. What really happened is that the call center got hit hard on some days, but had idle capacity the rest of the time. This would not be evident from the cumulative report.

Similarly, some managers use weighted averages to combine the reports of multiple small and large groups into one set of numbers. In that case, small groups have less impact than larger groups on service level. But the small groups may handle important transactions, and their results should not get rolled up with other information.

The point is, are the reports telling us what we need to know or are they masking what is really happening?

**5) Annotate exceptions.** There will be points that are clearly out of the norm. Don't leave them hanging. Sometimes you need to explain what happened and why. Why did service level drop and average speed of answer go through the roof on October 6? A footnote provides the answer: VRU down.

**6) Augment reports with "show and tell."** Giving upper management a report to read on what happens on Monday mornings versus bringing them into the call center to observe what happens is the difference between night and day. You need to do both. It is virtually impossible to understand call center reports without spending at least some time in the call center.

**7) Organize an ongoing forum for discussing and acting on the information.** Many call center managers struggle with that awful feeling of sending out reports and never getting a response. You will need to establish a mechanism for discussing reports and adjusting plans on an ongoing basis.

This last step in the process sometimes becomes a casualty of busyness, but it is critical. This process is really about communication, not reporting. This is the opportunity to turn information into sound business decisions. It is the place to underscore necessary investments and budgetary requests. And it is the chance to reinforce the link between call center activities and the organization's mission.

CCMReview

## Service Level Notes with Brad Cleveland

# Building the E-Enabled Call Center: It's Time to Get Moving (Part I)

*Editor's Note: This article was co-authored by Jay Minnucci, a Senior Consultant with Incoming Calls Management Institute.*

In August 1996, our firm partnered with Angus Telemanagement Group to launch "Call Centers on the Internet" (CCOTI), the first major conference focusing on the impact of the Internet on customer services and the prospect of integrating call center and Internet-based services (CCOTI has since been acquired by Advanstar).

Planning for the event had been in the works since 1995, but forecasting attendance was difficult. Those were the days when Internet security and reliability concerns abounded and some pundits were predicting that the Internet would collapse under its own weight. The word on the street was that nobody, save the purveyors of "adult material" and some financial services firms had or would make money on the Internet. Further, some influential technology firms, e.g., Microsoft, had been slow to embrace the Internet.

All considered, we expected around 200 to 300 attendees. As it turned out, more than 700 executives crammed into the conference facility. There was an overwhelming belief among attendees that we were discussing a development destined to forever change the delivery of customer services.

### Vision Vs. Reality

What's happened in the four years since – a long, long time given the pace of development? If *bona fide* cases of integrated call center/ Internet applications are the measure of progress, then the answer is, *not much.* There are cases, but they are few and far between. Meanwhile, there has been literally thousands of articles published on call center/ Internet integration, dozens of conferences every month dedicated to the subject and billions of dollars poured into the development of products and services.

CASE STUDIES OF INTEGRATED CALL CENTER/INTERNET SERVICES

Nobody in their right mind would argue with the proposition that the Internet has pervaded our lives, and changed our economy and organizations to an extent few predicted in the mid 1990s. But Internet-enabled call center applications have largely been stuck at the starting gate.

Few doubt the eventual proliferation of fully connected call centers, which, ironically, stands in stark contrast to many significant call center developments of days gone by. For example, quite a few customer-service directors initially questioned the value of ACDs, VRUs, desktop productivity tools and other call center capabilities as they were introduced to the market. But acceptance of the *vision* of call center/Internet integration has been rapid and widespread.

So, if the collective spirit is willing – end users, suppliers, consultants and customers all want to see these channels come together – what's the holdup? And where are things... *really*?

### Slow Goes It... So Far

We have used the technology adoption lifecycle as a lens through which to assess the progress of developments (for more on the technology adoption lifecycle, see Service Level Notes, *CCMReview*, Sept. 1999). There are few statistically valid studies estimating the current penetration of these capabilities, which leaves the true state of progress to debate. But judging by the information that is available, we would describe and place general capabilities as follows (see figure 1):

**Information-only** and basic transaction-capable **Web sites** not integrated with the call center are referenced here to provide context. Information-only Web sites, often described as online, glossy brochures with only static information, represent the first level of Web development.

**Basic transaction-capable Web sites** represent a legitimate service-delivery channel, and enable customers to place orders, retrieve some user-specific information (e.g., account status, shipping progress and purchase history) and review basic FAQs. While more advanced applications such as Amazon.com's "One Click" ordering capability or Dell's Ask Dudley technical assistance feature (an enhanced FAQ powered by Ask Jeeves technology that allows natural language input to search for answers) are clearly in the early phases of development and adoption, basic capabilities are in the late majority category.

Section 9

While the majority of call centers handle customer e-mail, far fewer have implemented **e-mail response management systems**, that provide "ACD-like" capabilities: identifying, routing, queuing, tracking and reporting. However, these systems are rapidly penetrating the market and soon will cross into the early majority category.

**Text-chat** enables customers to exchange real-time text messages with agents while visiting an organization's Web site. While few applications exist, the enabling technology is feasible and available. Given the enormous popularity of instant messaging and chat groups, this channel will likely grow rapidly as customers come to expect and demand it.

Although many organizations enable customers to request a follow-up contact, **Web call-me** capability connotes integration with call center systems; the agent and customer can both converse and share a view of the Web site – services still at the innovator-stage of adoption. Generally, the customer must have an Internet connection and a separate telephone line available.

**Web call-through** enables a customer to click a button while viewing a Web site and establish a voice connection. The caller and agent can then converse and share Web pages. But bandwidth remains a barrier: Voice-over-IP quality remains erratic, and not all customers are equipped with the necessary hardware to make this feasible.

**Web collaboration** broadly refers to capabilities that enable the agent and caller to share web content by pushing pages back and forth, and/or doing some whiteboarding and page markup. It's used in conjunction with other communication channels – text-chat, Web call-me and Web call-through – and enhances the interaction by adding a shared visual element.

Given the development of the multichannel call center, the **multimedia queue** – all transactions being routed and handled based on business rules, regardless of channel – is compelling. Service level and response time can be managed from a single source, and a truly integrated view of the organization's workload can be achieved. This may be held up more by organizational and agent capability issues than technology.

**Unified reporting**, unfortunately, remains an innovator-only application. Few deny the importance of good data, but reporting all too often falls victim to the "let's-just-get-the-thing-up-and-running-and-we'll-worry-about-reporting-later" line of thinking that has become commonplace in the ever-changing call-center environment. Clearly, this is one of the reasons to choose an "all-in-one" solution from a single vendor, since that reduces the likelihood of integration problems on the reporting end.

There also are a variety of future capabilities envisioned. **Video over the Internet** would bring full multimedia capabilities to these transactions. Video is constrained by bandwidth issues and the need for the proper equipment at the customer's end. If and when these issues can be resolved, this represents an ultimate means of customer service interaction – and introduces the element of visual imagery into the agent selection process.

And as cultural acceptance grows, **call center-initiated assistance** could become more common. But the cultural hurdle may prove to be too formidable – especially since the un-requested appearance of a cyber-salesperson works against the vision of the anonymous surfing that helps differentiate web shopping from phone-based and bricks-and-mortar retailing.

**Figure 1**

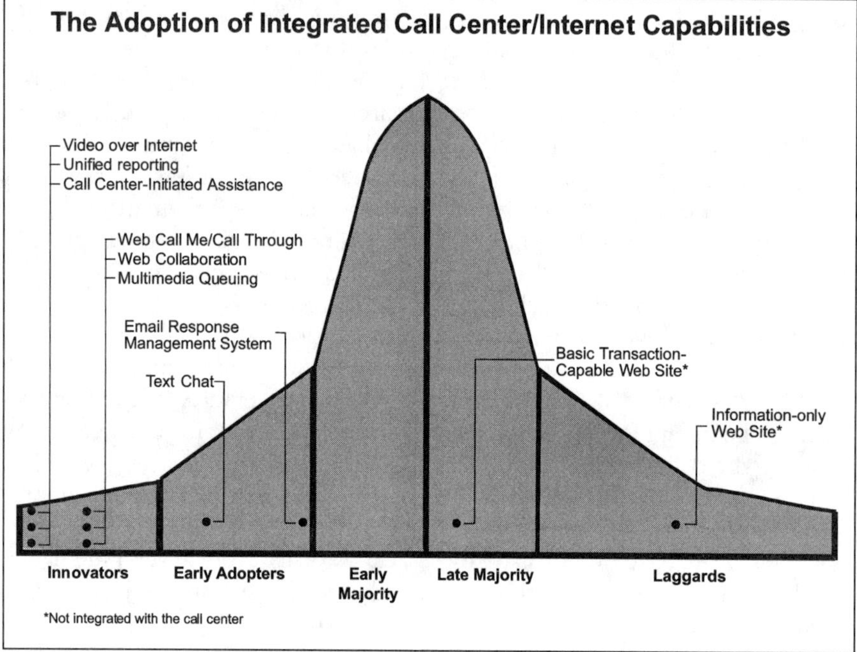


## Conclusion

Given the current state of flux, many organizations seem resigned to just let things happen as they will. As one call-center director told us, "We've got plenty to do in the meantime."

However, considering the widespread state of customer dissatisfaction with their e-contact experiences, and the impending changes in the competitive environment that e-enabled services will bring, waiting too long can be dangerous. In Part 2, we will identify common barriers to developing e-enabled call center services, and how they can – and must – be surmounted. There's been enough hype and talk. It's time to get things moving. CCMReview

Section 9

# Service Level Notes with Brad Cleveland

# Building the E-Enabled Call Center: It's Time to Get Moving (Part 2)

*Editor's Note: This article, along with Part 1, was co-authored by Jay Minnucci, a Senior Consultant with Incoming Calls Management Institute.*

The e-enabled call center will become a widespread reality. That is without question. But, as discussed in Part 1, even though acceptance of the vision of call center/Internet integration has been rapid and widespread, few bona fide cases of integrated call center/Internet applications exist.

Given the current state of flux, many organizations seem resigned to let things happen as they will. But waiting too long can be dangerous, for a number of reasons:

- As survey after survey bears out, overall customer satisfaction is at its lowest state in years – ironic, given the widespread emphasis on Customer Relationship Management (CRM) and customer lifetime value.

- Developments will not happen in linear fashion. Despite the slow start, new Web/call center integration possibilities will present themselves at breakneck pace. Forward-thinking companies will identify and embrace those that offer promise but organizations that don't do the necessary planning and positioning in advance will fall behind.

- A "one-channel-at-a-time" approach to the new environment is likely to produce lackluster results and a tangle of systems that have little chance of presenting a clear, integrated vision to your customers or your employees.

- Datamonitor has estimated that businesses lost $1.9 billion last year due to the failure to Web-enable their customer service operations. Whatever the actual number, these lost opportunities are becoming a bit too much to stomach, particularly for organizations that have seen their stock valuation punished by investors.

In our studies of the market and our work with organizations planning and implementing Web-enabled solutions, we have found that a number of common barriers exist. Identifying and addressing these issues is key to getting things moving:

**Lack of Organization-wide Strategy.** Developing a solid customer access strategy is essential to effectively building an e-enabled call center (for background on strategy, see "Service Level Notes," *CCMReview*, February, March and May 2000). Creating strategy is not a simple process. Integrated delivery channels cause ownership boundaries to overlap, which can bring progress to a grinding halt. Those that have adequately addressed this and related issues have done so with a strong message and active involvement from the leadership ranks to bring potential factions together.

**Budgetary Priorities.** The door to the CFO's office is lined with VPs and directors vying for the big piece of the budget pie. And as you already know, or will soon find out when you start researching the technology, call center/Web integration won't happen without one of those big pieces.

But there is little value in competing with other parts of the organization that are also trying to address evolving customer service challenges. For example, initiatives such as CRM or supply change management offer a similar promise to help the organization meet customer expectations, now and in the future. Progressive organizations are working hard to avoid the trap of viewing and valuing these initiatives individually.

**Current Workload.** Technologists are stretched to the breaking point trying to maintain today's platform while at the same time designing and developing tomorrow's ideal environment. Call center managers are struggling just to maintain their support of existing channels – a recent ICMI study of 579 call center managers found that only 23 percent of the respondents regularly meet their inbound telephone service level goal.

The resources available are often barely able to meet existing challenges – heaping further responsibility on call center managers is not the answer. The development of the connected call center requires competent associates from the technical and managerial disciplines fully dedicated to the integration project to get it done right.

**Technology in a State of Flux.** Given the many alternatives, sorting through the maze of technology alternatives can be confusing. Further, call center technology is in a state of development unprecedented in the history of the industry (see box, page 17). But many suppliers offer impressive functionality that all too often comes with fine print, e.g., features that won't be available until the next release ("...it's due for general availability 'real soon'"). Further, consultants and other experts can't seem to come to any agreement – one that we spoke with described a well-known vendor's

Section 9

offerings as "tightly integrated," while another described the exact same solution as "bolted together." Concerns about risk abound, and with good reason.

A big part of the solution is to turn Moore's Law on its head. Yes, tomorrow's version will be faster and cheaper, but progressive organizations recognize that the risk associated with moving forward may be far less than the risk of sitting on the sideline waiting until everything shakes out – by that time, you may already be left behind. Getting into the arena gets you moving on the learning curve. The lesson may be costly, but far less so than ignorance.

**Agent Skill Sets.** This is causing great concerns in call center management circles, and for good reason. Finding trained, effective staff just to handle the inbound telephone channel has become a major challenge. Many managers are sweating over the prospect of having to fill hundreds or thousands of positions that require not just oral communication skills, but written ones, as well. Ongoing technology – and, especially, process improvements – may diminish the skill requirements somewhat. But that's of little comfort in today's tight job market.

Here again, it's time for organizations to face the inevitable. Revamping recruiting, hiring, training and career path initiatives to encourage the creation of a more Web-enabled workforce is the only sure way forward.

**No competitive mandate – yet.** The slow adoption rate of Web-enabled call center applications has, to some extent, become a self-fulfilling prophecy. "The competition's not doing it yet, so why should we?"

Further, though customers are clamoring for better service, they have not clearly dictated en masse the integrated mix of channels that suits them best. Of course, that evokes a chicken-and-egg question: How can they "embrace" anything before it becomes more commonplace? Industry leaders will recognize and leverage this opportunity to help shape expectations by offering customers as much as possible – and relentlessly surveying them to determine what is working.

## Conclusion

Last year's holiday shopping season (1999) proved to be a publicity disaster for dot-com companies. Orders shipped late or never arrived, glaring incompatibilities between retail outlets and Web sites became obvious, and customers were trapped in poorly designed tangles of services when trying to reach organizations to resolve problems. A couple of months later, investors begin to punish "E-tail" stock prices.

These experiences created a positive point of demarcation for call centers: Before last Christmas, the call center's value in the networked economy was questioned; after last Christmas, the need for a prominent role for "call centers" was firmly established. Now is the time to build on that promise. CCMReview

## The Many Technology Choices

While suppliers are migrating to a similar vision of the e-enabled, multichannel call center, they are getting there from different perspectives.

- **Traditional ACD/PBX Systems**, e.g., the Lucent (Avaya) Definity, Nortel Meridian or stand-alone ACD systems from Aspect and Rockwell still dominate the call center market. These vendors are building on their presence. Web channels are being "pushed" into the inbound call-queuing system to provide the users with a unified look at the incoming workload. But critics wonder about how tightly integrated these solutions really are.

- **Communication Server Vendors** such as Interactive Intelligence and Apropos are offering server-based solutions that provide tight integration of channels and a unified view of contacts. But critics often cite the high level of reliability of traditional ACD/PBX systems, and cast doubt on the reliability of server based systems in mission-critical environments.

- **IP-Based ACDs**, e.g., those from Cisco and Cosmocom, approach the multichannel ACD environment from the IP perspective. They enjoy a high level of recognition from high-tech organizations, dot-coms and other Web-centric companies, and afford tight integration between channels. But these solutions are subjected to the same reliability questions from those favoring more traditional ACD systems.

- **CTI Vendors** such as Genesys (now part of Alcatel) and Davox are building on their experience with integration solutions to make the e-enabled call center a reality. They have a strong presence in many large call centers, but many view them as niche players, a perception they are trying to change.

- **Alternative Channel Vendors** include companies that got their start by focusing on a "non-phone" channel. E.g., E-gain and Kana entered the market by offering E-mail Response Management Systems (ERMS). Through acquisitions and/or product developments, this category of suppliers is evolving to offer complete communication solutions. As with CTI vendors, they are trying to move beyond the perception that they are niche players.

- **CRM Vendors**, often through mergers, acquisitions, and partnerships, are offering multichannel/CRM integrated solutions. Examples include Lucent/Siebel, Nortel/Clarify, Cisco/Oracle, Quintus/Nabnasset, Cosmocom/Onyx, Kana/Silknet and others. These providers offer a broad range of capabilities but face the challenge of ensuring end users that they can focus solutions and support on specific call center requirements.

# Successful E-Support: Attributes of the 'A' List

*by Greg Levin*

## When it comes to satisfying customers on line, top Web-based call centers take a similar approach.

Most discussions about call center e-support fall into one of two categories: 1) highly negative, or 2) highly hyped. The former is usually led by research firms who have a habit of frightening call center professionals with grim statistics showing how poorly companies are meeting online customer needs. The latter is usually led by vendors who aim to show how their latest release will turn ordinary call centers into Web-based customer contact giants.

Unfortunately, neither of these discussion types contain the kind of information call center managers really need: how exactly to provide effective e-support. The truth is, because e-business is still in its infancy relatively speaking, nobody has the definitive answers.

But a handful of companies have found some pretty good ones. After years of struggling – like most call centers –with email management and other e-support challenges, organizations such as 1-800-Flowers, J. Crew, Hewlett Packard and several others are starting to provide the level of Web-based service that today's customers demand. While still learning, these companies have moved a little closer to the ideal in terms of efficient and consistent response times and service levels, high levels of online customer satisfaction and retention, and continuous revenue generation/protection via their Web sites.

## A Lot in Common

Top e-support providers may vary in terms of industry, product/services offered and corporate culture, but their approach to satisfying online customers is similar. Here are some of the key attributes that they have in common:

■ **They empower online customers via a range of dynamic self-support options.** Companies leading the e-support revolution are experts at helping customers help themselves. They have implemented self-support tools that enable customers to quickly find answers and information while dramatically reducing the number of routine requests that call center agents must field.

The most effective self-support options implemented include:

- *Continually updated and information-rich FAQ lists.* To help determine the most useful FAQ content, top e-support providers closely analyze the inquiries their call centers receive everyday from customers via phone calls, email and chat.
- *Highly interactive search engines.* The best applications feature natural language processing that enable online customers to quickly find answers to often complex inquiries. After the customer types in his or her request or key words, the search engine scans a knowledge base and sorts all retrieved responses by relevance. If no relevant matches are found, the system asks for (or suggests) rewording of the query.
- *Online personal accounts.* These enable online customers – who each have a private password – to easily view their account histories, place/track orders, change shipping/billing addresses online, etc. 1-800-Flowers saves its call center hundreds of basic calls each day simply by providing customer access to such information via the corporate Web site.

■ **They use email management tools to help respond to all email inquiries efficiently and with quality.** Even with effective self-service options in place, many customers still prefer – or sometimes need – to contact an agent in the call center. This is most commonly done via email. To effectively handle such transactions, top e-support providers use specialized email management systems that automatically and evenly distribute customer email inquiries among the center's Web agents.

Call centers typically use the system's auto-reply feature to confirm that the message has been received and to let the customer know the expected turnaround time for a full response (the best e-support providers respond to each email in less than 24 hours). This dramatically reduces the number of "just wanted to be sure" messages and/or phone calls from concerned customers, says John Leslie, vice president and chief technical officer at the finance research company Wall Street on Demand in Boulder, Colo. "Just by sending them a confirmation that we've received their email, the customers relax. It assures them that their email hasn't gone into some black hole in the Internet, rather that there is a person on the other end who will take charge of their request."

To handle all email inquiries quickly and accurately, agents in the best e-support environments use – but don't abuse – response suggestions provided by the email management system. Staff are trained not to simply cut and paste canned responses, but rather to take relevant pieces and add to them to ensure that each customer receives personalized service.

■ **They make things easy for online customers seeking live agent support.** Customer demand for immediate live-agent support via the Web is increasing rapidly, and the best e-supporters are answering the call.

The majority of these companies, including iQVC, Hewlett Packard and Eddie Bauer, have brought their Web sites to life via advanced Web-chat applications. Such tools enable online customers to have text-based "conversations" with call center agents in real-time (or near real-time). As with email management tools, most chat applications provide response templates that agents can customize to provide efficient, quality responses to customer inquiries. In some call centers, such as iQVC, agents handle up to four or five chat sessions at once for substantial productivity gains.

A few companies, such as J. Crew, have started using innovative "click-to-talk" applications to provide real-time support via the Web. Such tools let online customers click on a "call me" icon on the Web site (after downloading the necessary software) and have a natural voice conversation with a call center agent via their PC.

To enhance the quality of live Web-based transactions, top e-support providers couple their chat and click-to-talk applications with dynamic "co-browsing" and "form-sharing" tools. Co-browsing tools enable agents and customers to view Web pages together and make it easy for the agent to direct the customer to relevant areas or "push" specific pages directly to them. And with form-sharing tools, agents are able to move the customer's cursor and help him or her fill in forms or applications if necessary.

***Customer demand for immediate live-agent support via the Web is increasing rapidly, and the best e-supporters are answering the call.***

■ **They have adapted their hiring and training programs to ensure that the center is perennially staffed with quality Web agents.** Leaders in e-support understand that the skills and knowledge needed to effectively handle email and web contacts differ from those needed to succeed on the phones, and their hiring and training practices reflect that.

To find candidates with the Web-savvy and writing skills they seek, top e-support providers have supplemented traditional recruiting with innovative "e-cruiting." This includes posting agent job openings on the company's Web site as well as on online recruiting sites like CallCenterCareers.com and CareerBuilders – places where people with the right Web agent profile are likely to frequent. It also includes assessing the skills of Web agent candidates via simulated email and chat transactions later on in the selection process.

Goodwill Toronto has found such e-role plays to be invaluable in identifying who is cut out for the fast-paced Web-chat environment. "I play the customer and give [applicants] a situation," explains Sharon Myatt, director of program development and innovation at Goodwill Toronto's call center. "I can test the skills they need to succeed in chat: grammar, keyboarding, critical thinking, paraphrasing and questioning."

To further ensure Web agents' success in the center, top e-support providers have added new modules to their training programs. These typically include overviews of the company's Web-based customer contact strategy, the Web agent's specific role and performance objectives, as well as the technology the center uses to carry out its e-support mission.

■ **They have mastered the art of online workforce management.** Top e-support providers work hard to ensure that the right number of agents are in the right place at the right times. These call centers have learned how to accurately forecast online customer contact volume and schedule the appropriate number of staff to meet the center's service level/response time objectives.

Successful centers carefully track how many email and Web contacts they receive every day, as well as when such transactions occur and how efficiently they are being handled, thus enabling the call center to uncover essential historic trends on which they can base solid staffing decisions. In addition, top centers keep close tabs on any special events (i.e., new marketing campaigns, etc.) that are likely to affect email, chat and other Web-based contacts, and then staff accordingly.

Effective online WFM isn't easy, especially considering the relatively short amount of time that companies have had to discover trends in contact volume. But effective forecasting can be achieved via focused analysis, says Leslie of Wall Street on Demand, and must be if companies want to compete in the world of e-support. "You can't manage what you can't measure," he says.

■ **They understand and practice the principles of eCRM.** Top e-support providers effectively use their Web sites to capture customer data and use that information to provide highly personalized service during future transactions. Details about account histories, product and service preferences, past service problems, etc., are stored in powerful databases and enable call centers to create customized Web pages for individual customers.

Amazon.com provides a prime example of effective online customer relationship management. The well-known e-tailer's Web site greets each existing customer by name and makes product and service recommendations based on past purchases and other transactions. To continually fuel the eCRM cycle, Amazon.com gathers key data from online customers via such features as "customize your preferences," "create a product wish-list," and "create/update your address book" (for sending gifts).

Top e-support providers use data gleaned online not only to enhance Web self-service, but also email, live Web-based support and traditional phone transactions. Agents in these companies' call centers receive relevant response suggestions and view other key screenpops right at their desktops to help them provide personalized service to all current customers, regardless of how the customer has chosen to contact the call center.

■ **They have formal "e-monitoring" procedures in place to ensure that agents and systems are effectively handling online customer transactions.** Supervisors and managers in top Web-based call centers regularly evaluate agent's email and chat responses for accuracy, spelling, grammar and personalization, and provide agents with the feedback and coaching they need to continually improve. In addition, they receive detailed reports that help to provide a more holistic view of online customers' experiences with the company. Such reports show how long customers had to wait to receive an email response or to resolve an issue via chat, as well as shed light on the effectiveness of self-support tools on the Web site.

■ **They continually measure online customer satisfaction and act on the findings.** Top e-support providers not only monitor how the center handles online customers, they ask those customers for their opinions. This is typically done by posting clearly marked "Feedback" or "Tell us what you think" icons on the Web site that link customers to surveys containing focused questions about their online experience.

Some e-support providers take a slightly more ambitious approach to measuring customer satisfaction – e-g., via surveys that pop up on the customer's computer screen following a self-support or chat session. A few other call centers email survey "invitations" to customers following email/chat transactions and online visits. These invitations contain the survey page's URL, which customers can click on to view and complete the questions.

Regardless of how they solicit online customer feedback, the best e-support providers carefully analyze the information and suggestions they receive and make strategic changes to improve Web-based services. These companies often use datamining tools to help identify trends and pinpoint problem areas, and usually have an individual or team in place whose primary responsibility is customer satisfaction measurement and evaluation.

## Learn from the Leaders

Customer demand for superior e-support shows no signs of dwindling. Getting a handle on the growing number of email and Web contacts has become a top priority at many centers. Those just getting into the game or in need of improvement can learn a lot from the handful of companies that have already achieved significant success in Web-based customer care.

While these companies may not have "written the book" on e-support, collectively they have helped to compile a good introduction. CCMReview

Section 9

## Service Level Notes with Brad Cleveland

# The 12 Key Principles of Customer Relationship Management

*Editor's Note: This article was co-authored by Ted Hopton, manager of research and development for Incoming Calls Management Institute. Ted can be reached at 856-727-7852 or tedh@incoming.com.*

Still trying to sort out what customer relationship management (CRM) really means? If so, you're not alone. The term has been so hyped, and so broadly interpreted, that it remains a source of confusion for many. Don't despair! In the 10 minutes it will take you to read this column, you'll review the core principles of this popular management movement.

Each of these 12 principles (listed below) is both compelling on its own and intertwined with the others. There is no question, though, that customer relationship management strategy as an integrated whole is greater than the sum of these parts.

### 1. Continuously learn about your customers.

This is the first principle of managing customer relationships because it is the most fundamental. From this everything else follows.

When you know your customers, you can make sound business decisions about how to develop your relationships with them. Collect and analyze information about your customers to get to know them well. Maintain your knowledge in customer profiles that are available to all who need them. But don't stop there. Apply everything you know to building a customer valuation model. Knowing the value of customer relationships is essential for managing them wisely.

### 2. Interact personally with your customers.

Desirable relationships are not one-way. Relationships result from interaction. Knowing your customers is just the first step. Use that knowledge to develop your relationships with your customers whenever you interact with them.

No matter how sophisticated the technology that organizations and customers use to communicate, your customers are people and people appreciate being recognized, listened to and understood. Letting your customers know that you care enough about them to get to know them is an important part of managing the customer relationship.

### 3. Handle different customers differently.

This idea has been repeated so many times that it's practically taken for granted now. But the power of this principle lies in the potential for optimizing the value of each customer relationship through differential treatment.

Based on customer segmentation, call centers can assign different toll-free numbers, provide different IVR and Web services, establish different agent groups, present different service levels and offer priority queuing assignments.

It is important, however, not to differentiate simply because technology exists that can do so. Segment customers sensibly. There are hidden costs to differentiation that must be weighed against the increased value that personalization can be expected to produce. Effective customer relationship management strategy ultimately seeks to optimize value.

### 4. Retain the right customers.

Customer knowledge and the capability for differentiated customer treatment significantly improve many organizations' capabilities to retain customers.

One of the truisms associated with customer relationship management is that it is cheaper to retain a customer than to acquire a new one, but that idea can be taken a step further. In order to maximize value, organizations should focus on retaining valuable customers, not necessarily all customers.

Be warned, however, that misapplication of this principle can be dangerous. Mistreating "low-value" customers, even if you are losing money on them, is hard to justify in the court of public opinion (which is where your future high-value customers are sitting).

### 5. Anticipate customer needs and offer to fulfill them.

Customer relationship management empowers and alters the selling process in many ways. Knowledge of your customers presents new opportunities for making the right offer to the right person at the right time.

Analysis of customer profiles, especially using powerful tools such as data mining, can provide insight about who buys what from you when. Contact management systems can detect cross-sell and upsell opportunities and act upon them by presenting scripts to agents during service calls, dynamically responding to customer input or automatically presenting customized offers in Web pages and interactive voice response (IVR) systems.

Even government and nonprofit organizations can use these principles to better fulfill their charters and anticipate the needs of their constituents.

### 6. Increase value for your customers and of your customers.

This is the bottomline reason for implementing customer relationship management. It is precisely because customer relationship management increases value both for customers and the organization that it is such a compelling strategy.

Section 9

There are many ways to deliver increased value, including being easy to do business with, creating efficiencies for your customers and making timely offers of products or services that perceptively address customer needs.

Similarly, there are many ways to increase the value of your customer relationships, and the most fundamental of these appear in this list of key principles. When executed properly, customer relationship management is a "win-win" for customers and the organization alike.

### 7. Present a single face to your customers.

Make customers' experiences with your organization seamless. One of the ways to create value for your customers is to simplify the ways that they deal with your organization. Take a holistic view of your customers and consolidate information from across the organization, regardless of geography, department, function or product line.

When you have a complete picture of each customer's relationship, you can design customer interaction processes from the customer's perspective, thus increasing value and letting customers know that you know them.

### 8. Focus on revenue and retention more than on reducing costs.

Unlike so many management initiatives, customer relationship management is not about cost savings. Customer relationship management strategy aims to increase the revenue received from current customers and increase the retention rate of valuable customers.

A renewed focus on the effective management of customer relationships can require so many organizationwide process changes that operational cost savings may well be realized, but in other ways, a customer relationship focus may raise the cost of doing business. Talk time on customer calls often increases as agents make the most of each opportunity to develop customer relationships. It takes time to service customers well, to listen to them, to collect information about them and to upsell and cross-sell to them.

In summary, the return on investment for customer relationship management initiatives should not be expected from operational cost savings.

### 9. Enable information sharing and interaction across the organization.

Customer relationship management affects all parts of an organization, not just the call center. It is both a requirement and a benefit of customer relationship management that organizations improve their internal communication processes.

The only way to develop a comprehensive view of each customer's relationship with the organization is with the full participation of every part of the organization. This requires strong support from top management and across the board. As the central point of contact with customers, the call center has a vested interest in driving the development of organizationwide interaction processes.

### 10. Create business rules to drive all CRM decisions and automation.

Business rules codify and automate processes, specifying what should happen in specific situations, thus enabling both differentiated customer treatment and automation. Developing organizationwide business rules is a monumental task, and how well it is done directly affects the success of any customer relationship management effort. Business rules define the ways that the strategy is executed.

### 11. Empower agents with information and training.

The "Empowered Agent Desktop," as described by Vanguard Communications Corporation, may be the sexiest technological feature of customer relationship management applications. Just as the cockpit of an airplane displays all the information a pilot needs to fly in any conditions, the contact management screen should pull together cleanly and clearly all that the organization knows about its relationship with that customer. Furthermore, business rules should dynamically change that screen to support and guide the agent in optimizing the customer relationship.

Empowerment is a key principle, however, because no set of business rules can or should fully anticipate every conceivable situation: Agents need training, information and support offered by business rules so that they can make good decisions that are consistent with the organization's strategy.

Even though customer relationship management can and should be used to develop self-service customer access channels, it should not be mistaken as a strategy for replacing agents. Customer relationship management can have far greater impact by empowering agents.

### 12. Remember, effective CRM is not just a technology project.

Customer relationship management is a way of doing business. A common misperception is that customer relationship management primarily consists of a database or set of technology tools. Technology is an enabler, but as these 12 key principles demonstrate, the effective management of customer relationships is much more than high-powered technology. Customer relationship management is about the way you do business, and technology empowers you with previously unheard of options for how you do business with each one of your customers.

Effective customer relationship management requires participation and hard work by people throughout the organization, and if done right, the work never ends. Results from these efforts should be fed back into the process to continuously refine business rules, marketing efforts and information systems. True optimization has a moving finish line that winners never stop trying to cross. CCMReview

**Brad Cleveland**

*Brad Cleveland is president of Incoming Calls Management Institute (ICMI) and publisher of* Call Center Management Review. *He can be reached at 410-267-0700 (ext. 958), or bradc@incoming.com.*

Section 9

# Why Benchmarking Could Be Wasted Effort

*by Gordon MacPherson*

*Editor's Note: This article, written by our founding publisher, first appeared in the November 1992 issue of* Service Level Newsletter *(our former name, for those of you new to* CCMReview*). We feel that Gordon's comments on benchmarking mania are as on target now as they were back then – maybe more so, considering the ever-increasing hype surrounding call center benchmarking.*

I am for just about everything that comes out of Total Quality Management practices. But, I have concerns about one practice I feel is going astray – benchmarking.

It's become an obsession in some incoming call centers. In theory, benchmarking is wonderful. It is supposed to make it possible for you to compare your call center with "best in class", and to show how they achieve such status. But in practice I think it is too often counterproductive. Novice enthusiasts tend to put too much emphasis on the benchmarks, and not enough on the "how they do it." Discovering who's "best in class" becomes a quest for the Holy Grail. The position taken becomes something like this: "After we get these benchmarks in hand, we'll really know what we should be shooting for. We'll know exactly what to do, because we'll see what the best in class models do. Then we'll start improving things."

*Service Level Newsletter* and Incoming Calls Management Institute receive a growing number of requests for benchmarking studies. In the past it was simply, "Could you recommend a few good call centers I could contact so I can see how we compare?" or, "so I can see what we should be doing?" Whenever possible, our response has been to provide contacts in call centers where we have spotted something good going on, or which have a good reputation for excellent customer service, or have experienced a lot of improvements lately. But, we always make the disclaimer that we are in no position to rank call centers. We explain that we are unaware of a uniform standard for valid comparison between call centers, and that, even if there was one, there is no unbiased source collecting and verifying data. We explain further that the sorts of statistically significant, organized, formatted, verifiable and published information which would give us a firm foundation of reliable data does not presently exist.

> *Novice enthusiasts tend to put too much emphasis on the benchmarks, and not enough on the "how they do it." Discovering who's "best in class" becomes a quest for the Holy Grail.*

But now callers want benchmark studies. They want to know which call centers are "best in class." They want to know what their service levels are, and their abandonment rates, and what type of automatic call distributor (ACD) they purchased. They want to know how many calls per hour their agents can handle, and what that works out to in terms of productivity.

I agree that you have to get outside of your own call center and see what others are doing. Part of this is reviewing call center trade literature regularly and looking for new techniques, equipment and services that might work for you. But, what's new about this? And why do we need benchmarks to compare ourselves to? And who really understands what is behind the apparent achievement in the benchmark?

### How Would You Compare Two Call Centers?

Big question: what explains the differences in performance benchmarks?

Recently, I saw an article in the trade press that implied an answer to the big question. The article published statistics on speed of answer, average delay, longest delay, abandonment rate, cost per call, and products/services used for call centers nominated as "the top 20 call centers." The article's implied answer to the big question is that the differences in results can be explained largely in terms of where these call centers – nominated by "the telecommunication industry's leading technology providers" – shop for equipment and software. How much more objectivity could you possibly ask for? And absolutely nothing (except what systems they have) is said about what made these call centers the "tops." But, I guess it makes the magazine, its advertisers, and the call centers who got recognized (and who may actually be deserving) happy.

Valid, direct comparisons between call centers are extremely complex. As a call center consultant, I have attempted to unravel the differences that would explain performance on numerous occasions. It can be tricky. A call center can give the appearance of success by having state-of-the-art equipment, software and furnishings, but fail to meet customer expect-ations and company objectives, or be bloated and inefficient.

You just can't compare call centers unless you spend a lot of time in the call centers whose performance secrets you're trying to understand. Simple-looking numbers turn out to be the result of a complex, interactive web of factors. Just figuring out whether the numbers really meet standards of excellence, without sacrificing something else, is hard enough. But finding out how the numbers were achieved is loaded with intangibles and gray areas.

How do you compare call centers – your and somebody else's?

## ACD Statistics

Could you compare call centers solely on their abandonment rates? No, because this could be explained in terms of differences in caller tolerances, rather than effective management. Or it could be because one call center has more people to put on the phones than the other. Or because one call center is hustling callers along, sacrificing quality to keep abandonment low. Or it could be because one call center has less turnover of reps and a higher average level of training, so it can keep abandonment low because it is more efficient at handling calls quickly and with quality.

Could you compare call centers solely on the basis of service level? No, because service level could be good even though busy signals are high, since ACD service levels are based only on what happens to calls that are received by the system. Or, again, it could be because of differences in talk time attributable to either sacrificing quality to gain speed or because better training and/or lower turnover enables higher speed with quality.

Could you compare call centers on the basis of service level *targets* alone? No, because setting a target obviously isn't always the same as hitting it. And service levels are sometimes achieved by sacrificing quality.

Could you compare call centers on the basis of productivity alone? No. You wouldn't want to look at calls per rep without looking at some sort of qualitative measurement to put it into perspective. And, given the verification perversity of queuing theory, service level erodes as number of calls per rep goes up. The larger the call answering group, the less true this is; but again, looking at productivity alone would be unwise.

## How Much Does ACD Choice Really Explain about Performance?

Could you compare call centers solely on the basis of the ACD system they purchased? No. Imagine a situation of two call centers, one better led and better "ACDed" than the other. Suppose you had an equal number of reps from each of these call centers trade places, taking their leaders with them, but swapping ACDs. Then suppose you send each group an equal number of calls. Would the less well-led group, now with the better ACD, outperform the better-led group? I'd bet not because differences in call center performance are much more likely to be the result of leadership than of the sophistication of their ACDs. I'm not saying that ACDs aren't important. I'm only saying that they contribute less than leadership does. Even the best ACD cannot, by itself, have much impact on the accuracy of information, the turnover rate, or the happiness of callers. Give different people a tennis racket, skis, ballet shoes, or a pen, and you get different results. Same with ACDs.

There's an argument there, though. Some would say that it takes leadership to know the true value of an ACD, and that it's no surprise that call centers with top-of-the-line ACDs tend to be successful. They have good leadership and they can afford a good ACD because they are already successful and want to provide every advantage necessary to stay that way. Interesting, huh?

**Is There An Answer?**

The secret of incoming call center excellence is simple. We all know it. It is adequate staffing and the ability to satisfy callers. It is accomplishing excellent results without waste and inefficiency. So, any valid means of comparing call centers would have to include some measurement for these things. Just looking at any one of these things would not ensure that you are getting the true picture.

The measurements I would propose for incoming call center benchmarking are: (1) percent of the time service level is achieved, (2) results from a standardized customer satisfaction survey, and (3) cost per call – but based on some sort of uniform criteria. These three measurements would be a check that all the right things are in balance.

But they still don't tell us how the results are achieved, and this will always be the most important piece.

CCMReview

***Gordon MacPherson**, now retired from the call center industry, founded both* CCMReview *(formerly* Service Level Newsletter*) and the Incoming Calls Management Institute (ICMI). A renowned call center pioneer, Gordon consulted to numerous companies around the globe and created some of today's most popular industry events, such as "The World Conference on Incoming Call Center Management" and "Call Centers on the Internet."*

# The Outsourcing Evolution: Economic Trends Make It a More Viable Option

*by Susan Hash*

**Ecommerce, globalization, CRM and the need for high-level technical skills are influencing a rebirth of outsourcing.**

As call centers struggle with the complex task of integrating e-channels with voice – and quickly – more companies are considering outsourcing partnerships to handle some or all of their e-service functions. In the rush to get ecommerce applications up and running, U.S. companies have increased spending on outsourcing for Internet operations. According to International Data Corp. (IDC), a global market intelligence and research firm, spending on Internet operations outsourcing increased from $350 million to $613 million in one year (1997 to 1998). And by 2002, the U.S. outsourcing market could be worth $3.6 billion.

Besides the obvious need in many organizations to quickly get up to speed with Internet services, increased globalization and the spread of customer relationship management (CRM) also have contributed to outsourcing's growth – and evolution.

In the past, many call center managers looked upon outsourcing with some degree of skepticism. It was considered primarily as a strategy to help manage inbound call volume. Generally, calls were outsourced based on specific peak times, peak seasons, special promotions, specific call types or to be able to offer extended operating hours.

However, many managers were not entirely convinced of an outsourcing agency's ability to service their customers with the same quality, expertise and zeal as inhouse agents.

James Witz, Carrier Corp.'s national account manager, looked into outsourcing options a couple of years ago to help with the continuously increasing volume of calls and email (at the time, Witz managed the customer relations call center).

However, he says, the heating and air conditioning equipment manufacturer ultimately decided that keeping calls inhouse made better sense. "Our concern with outsourcing was the lack of technical expertise," he recalls. Carrier's call center handles calls from distributors, retailers and consumers. "We would have had to find and train employees who, technically, would not have been equal to those we already had inhouse. In our industry, technical capabilities are very important. It's what our customers expect."

However, he adds, the company is still considering outsourcing some Web-related functions, such as frequently asked questions and its distributor/dealer locator.

## A New Face, New Focus

Long-term economic trends are creating an environment in which companies need to "focus on their core competencies and seek outside specialists to access world-class processes in non-core yet strategic functions," says Rebecca Scholl, senior analyst for Gartner Dataquest's IT services worldwide group. While she admits this trend is not new, "until recently, many companies were adopting a wait-and-see attitude." What's changed? New tools, such as Web-based collaborative applications and self-service technologies, are available that can add value to the outsourcing relationship and enable companies to keep control of their processes – even though they are outsourcing them – through regular reporting and Web access to information, Scholl says.

In the past year, outsourcing has undergone a renaissance, agrees Peter Bendor-Samuel, founder and CEO of Outsourcing Center (www.outsourcing-center.com), an online community and information center, and author of *Turning Lead into Gold: The Demystification of Outsourcing*.

"The growth of the dot-coms caused a lot of the new-economy companies to turn to outsourcing, particularly for their call center operations," he says. "Interestingly, at the same time, the whole CRM evolution was happening. Call centers were being asked to do more than just pick up the phone, answer questions and take orders. So now you have the administration of the loyalty component potentially being offered as a service."

## The Move Offshore

Another fast-growing outsourcing trend is the movement to take call centers offshore. IDC predicts U.S.-based companies will dramatically increase their spending on offshore outsourcing services in the next few years. A new report indicates the amount will more than triple, from under $5.5 billion in 2000 to more than $17.6 billion in 2005.

Although, historically, cost-savings have been the main driver for using offshore outsourcers, accessing IT talent is quickly becoming the primary motivator. "American companies unable to find, hire and retain skilled IT workers at home are finding a vast pool of highly educated technology-savvy, English-speaking workers available overseas. Companies are sending IT projects offshore to compensate for the limited pool of talent available in the United States," says Cynthia Doyle, research manager for IDC's IT and Offshore Outsourcing Strategies program. "In the past, offshore IT service firms were primarily utilized for their programming, coding and software development work, but they have expanded their skill sets and expertise and can now deliver enhanced e-business solutions."

Many technical support call centers are finding it cost-effective to send their first- or second-level support calls offshore, while keeping an inhouse operation for third-level support, says Kathy Sisk, president of Kathy Sisk Enterprises, a call center training, consulting and servicing firm. "Paying a tech support agent in the U.S. may cost upward of $50,000 in annual salary, whereas, overseas, they can acquire an individual with the same or higher level of education for probably less than $30,000 or $20,000 a year."

India is best-positioned to capture a large part of the offshore outsourcing opportunity, according to IDC. However, other regions have potential to develop as major sources of offshore outsourcing, including Canada, Mexico, the Caribbean, South Africa, Israel, Ireland and Eastern Europe.

"To be a successful provider of outsourcing services, a region must demonstrate fluency in English, a vast pool of IT talent, a solid infrastructure and experience doing business with Western companies. So far, only India meets all these requirements," Doyle says.

### When is Outsourcing Viable?

When should you consider an outsourcing partnership? In cases where you have technical limitations in your call center, says Pamela Barron Leach, director of Diebold Direct, a provider of integrated delivery systems and services. "Another reason for outsourcing would be in an overload situation where you're not able to keep up with customer demand within a necessary timeframe," she says. It's also common for companies to turn to an outsourcer when there's a lack of language capabilities. For example, in a situation where you need a center to handle calls in a primarily Hispanic or Chinese-speaking community.

Many companies outsource e-service functions to handle the initial overflow or to determine whether or not it's profitable to have an inhouse operation, adds Sisk.

In addition, she says, call centers that have consistently high turnover might want to consider outsourcing.

"High turnover is usually caused from a hiring mistake or lack of management support and training. There are three reasons: 1) a recruiting mistake – you hired out of desperation because you couldn't find anybody else and you hired the wrong person; 2) lack of training and management support; and 3) low unemployment – agents can go somewhere else and get paid a little more."

### Relationship Management Is Crucial

An outsourcing partnership can be effective and successful – it all depends on relationship management.

"The key is to develop a flexible contract," says Bendor-Samuel. "Build in very tight accountability and solid metrics. Be very clear in specifying how meetings will occur, how metrics will be communicated and the consequences for not meeting those or if something goes wrong."

Look for a service agency that is in the same industry or business that you're in, says Bob Cote, manager of Consumer Technical Support, Compaq Consumer. Cote manages six call centers in North America, four of which are outsourced.

Also, he says, select the agency that wants to be a partner. "I could have a lot of vendor relationships, but I really need a true partnership – someone who's going to put some skin in the game because they want to support Compaq and its customers."

Cote recommends visiting a potential service agency's call centers to evaluate the type of operation it runs. "Meet with the call center management teams to understand what the pluses and minuses have been for them in the relationship," he says. "Also, sit down with some of the agents on the phones to get an understanding of what types of tools they're using and what kinds of training they receive."

Finally, says Cote, make sure you have a solid quality process in place to ensure the service provider is meeting your expectations. While most outsourcing firms have processes or tools in place, he suggests being proactive in monitoring calls to see how your customers are being handled, and following up with evaluations and improvement processes.

On the flip side, Cote says, "for us to be successful, we have to make our partner successful, as well. You have to provide them with the right tools, training and technology to be able to deliver the support that you want them to deliver. You have to manage it on both sides of the house. If you get the mix right, it works very well." CCMReview

## Tips to Build a Successful Outsourcing Partnership

If you're looking into an outsourcing partnership for your call center, consider the following tips from Kathy Sisk of Kathy Sisk Enterprises (Web sites: www.kathysiskenterprises.com or www.outsourcingintl.com).

- Allow enough time to plan. While the timeline will ultimately depend on the type of project you're outsourcing and its complexity, make sure you allow your partner enough lead time for effective planning. In most cases, a 30- to 60-day lead time is sufficient, Sisk says.
- Assign project leaders who can head a team, who have initiative and who have background experience in the project that's being outsourced.
- Allow a decent budget for adequate setup. Currently, offshore firms are not charging setup fees but, eventually, they will, Sisk says. "In the U.S. and Canada, there is usually a hefty setup fee because there's a lot of prework taking place prior to rollout; for instance, custom work or training to tailor to the client's specific needs."
- Check to make sure the outsourcing agency you're considering has low turnover. Ask to see their HR reports.
- Hand-select the people who you want to be assigned to your account.
- Make sure the outsourcer has a proven background. Don't just rely on their referrals. Speak with a few of their current and/or past clients. Also be sure to interview the management staff who will be assigned to your account.
- Never give your outsourcer full control. Make sure the outsourcer has a method to allow you to assess the operation onsite and/or remotely
- Be sure to stay on top of the project on a daily basis. Often, "once a project is up and running successfully, the client will get comfortable and laid back, and then the outsourcer does, as well," she says. "Then you start to see productivity decline. Make sure everyone is held accountable for results and improvements, and conduct periodic spot-check assessments."
- Include a "way-out" clause in your agreement. First, make sure your expectations are reasonable. But, also ensure that you have a way out if the agency does not meet your expectations for performance.
- Don't focus on the cost to outsource as your No. 1 objective. Consider all other quality assurance factors – experience, history, results – that make the cost factors more profitable.
- Don't have high expectations at the start. Don't expect consistency up front – allow two weeks to 30 days for the outsourcer to ramp up.

Section 9

# In The Center with Marcia Hicks

## A Four-Step Process for Landing the Ideal Outsource Provider

**Are you stuck in the air circling the field of potential outsourcing providers? Four steps to help you select the right partner.**

Once you have decided to outsource, how do you go about finding the service provider that is right for you? It's not as simple as picking a name from a telephone book or association directory. You're choosing a supplier who will act as an extension of your company and, in some cases, the only contact your customers will have with your organization.

Selecting the right outsourcer is like landing an airplane — you need to circle your target and get a feel for the land as you get closer to your destination.

Although call center industry knowledge is certainly a fundamental component of supplier selection, you'll also need to examine your own company and clarify what is important to you and your business. Though this may sound like a no-brainer, it's one of the biggest mistakes many companies make: seeking out an outsourcer without really understanding what they want it to do.

There are four steps in the selection process, with each step designed to filter out outsourcing candidates that would not be a good match. In the spirit of our "airplane" analogy, we'll detail each step in distances, from 25,000 feet (getting started) to landing (making the final cut).

### 25,000 feet: Preliminary Research

The first step is to conduct interviews — not of suppliers, but of the managers in your own company. These interviews should be designed to determine your outsourcing goals and expectations. For instance, find out:

- What are your company's program needs?
- What services do you want the supplier to provide (e.g., take incoming calls, make outbound calls, handle email transactions, reply to Web inquiries in real time)?
- How much data do the agents need at their fingertips to work effectively?
- How long does your average contact take (including customer followup)?
- What kind of technology should the call center have (e.g., interactive voice response, monitoring and call logging systems, real-time scheduling systems)?

After completing the internal interviews, it's time to construct a generic profile — a description of the "perfect" supplier, built specifically to your program needs. The best way to hit your target is to know exactly what you want from an outsourcer.

The next step is to educate yourself on the outsourcing market. With your supplier profile in hand, you can begin searching call center industry reports and journals, and client and industry contacts for service providers that match your needs. The goal is not to find a perfect fit — you just want to determine which providers definitely do *not* meet your needs. One note about researching industry journals: It's easy to be swayed by the companies that have the biggest and boldest advertisements, but keep in mind, they may not be the best fit for your needs.

### 5,000 feet: Phone Interviews

After assessing your needs, building your idea of the perfect service provider and obtaining general information on the outsourcing market, you should have

### Is Outsourcing a Viable Solution for Your Center?

Outsourcing a percentage of calls based on specific times or call types can be an effective way for organizations to:

- Handle peak hours of the day, days of the week, or weeks of the year, including coverage for special promotions.
- Expand hours of operation.
- Provide coverage during service interruptions at the call center.
- Reduce overall call-handling and seasonal hiring costs.
- Free agents to perform value-added activities.

Prior to making an outsourcing decision, scrutinize your call mix and prioritize your call types by your internal opportunity to add value to the customer contact. Those calls with the highest priority, such as sales calls, should be kept in-house if at all possible.

Suggestions on what call types to outsource include:

- Routine calls
- Calls regarding special promotions
- After-hours calls
- Customer satisfaction tracking
- Crisis coverage
- Return inquiries
- Information requests

Section 9

screened out at least 50 percent of potential candidates. In this second phase, your objective is to look more closely at specific suppliers.

While you may have a number of potential candidates you're considering, it is not prudent to send out request for proposals (RFPs) at this stage. Asking suppliers to take the time to respond to an RFP when you are not sure if they meet your basic criteria is a waste of everyone's time, including yours. No one wants to spend the time (and money) to fill out an RFP if they are not in the running. And remember, every RFP response will take time on your part to review.

Instead, this stage in the search involves telephone interviews with your list of prospective suppliers. The plan is to find out if these companies are a good fit for your business. The interviews, which should take no longer than 20 minutes each, should focus on basic questions, such as:

- What industries do you cover?
- Do you handle inbound calls, outbound calls and/or other types of contact channels?

Once the interviews are completed, compare the companies to see which come the closest to matching your profile.

## 500 Feet: Request for Proposal

Now that you've narrowed the field of candidates, it's time to submit an RFP. This is when you start asking the "tough" questions. While the RFP is commonly thought of as a forum in which suppliers are expected to put their best foot forward, you also should use it to sell your business to them. In the RFP, ask companies to consider a partnership with you, and explain to them how they will benefit from the relationship.

Be as specific as possible. Provide your exact situation and ask for a solution. Require potential suppliers to detail their pricing, the locations where they might place your business and why they have chosen them. It's also a good idea to ask about the unemployment rates and general educational levels at their respective sites (low unemployment means that there is a smaller agent recruiting pool).

Finally, create an electronic, fill-in-the-blank format for your RFP. This will give you some consistency in the responses you receive, which will make it easier to compare them. Be forewarned, though: Suppliers will want to change your format to fit their standard reply.

When reviewing the RFP responses, narrow the candidate pool to two or three suppliers. Once you've done this, you're ready for the final screening process. (Note: For more information on developing RFPs, see "A Solid RFP Process Will Ease Vendor Selection and Management," *CCMReview*, December 2000.)

## 50 Feet: Site Visits

The final step before choosing a supplier is the site visit during which you and the supplier meet face-to-face to discuss working together. Representatives from your company will meet with account management and operations personnel at the candidates' call center(s). During the site visit, be sure to conduct interviews at every level — management, operations and frontline agents.

The purpose of the interviews is twofold: 1) You should review the RFP statement, and 2) you want to get a first-hand look at their employees, equipment and technology.

During the interview process, you should also consider whether or not you would be comfortable working with this company. Ask yourself:

- Will your managers get along with their account managers and operations personnel?
- Do you share the same goals for customer satisfaction?
- Are you comfortable with the level of training the agents receive?

In many ways, finding a good fit with a service provider is just as important as knowing they can handle your needs.

After each site visit, it's important to rate each provider component (e.g., training, technology, hiring practices) so you can compare the suppliers in an apples-to-apples forum when making your final choice. Many suppliers bundle common services, but everyone includes different components.

The entire selection process — from interviewing your managers to making a decision — typically takes at least two to three months (depending on the number of RFPs sent and number of sites you visit).

The process is not easy and it will not happen overnight, but with patience, the proper tools and a little assistance, your business can land a top-flight supplier to represent you. CCMReview

Marcia Hicks

*Marcia Hicks is a Senior Consultant at Kowal Associates, a contact center consulting firm in Boston, MA. She can be reached at 617-521-9000.*

# Avoiding Conflicting Objectives

"It's totally unworkable," a call center manager told me recently. "It's a catch-22." She was right. The budgetary and performance objectives her company had established were unattainable. Move towards one and, inherently, you'd have to move away from another

Popularized by Joseph Heller's war novel from the 1960s, a catch-22 is, figuratively, an arrangement that creates a double bind. Although the term appropriately describes this manager's dilemma, I don't believe most call centers have high level objectives that are diametrically opposed. However, many DO have expectations and standards that are at least partially in conflict, either with each other or with call center realities.

The following examples produce some rather unsavory symptoms: unclear priorities, misunderstandings, inconsistent results and hampered performance. Do any sound familiar?

**1. Service Level versus Service Level.**

I recently read a widely distributed report for the banking industry. One of the contributors suggested that setting a single standard for service level is "problematic" because for a service level of, say, answering 80 percent of calls in 20 seconds, you are ignoring the business impact of the 20 percent who have to wait longer than 20 seconds. The proposed solution was to have two standards: the first, to answer 80 percent of calls in 20 seconds; and the second, to answer the remaining 20 percent within 50 seconds. Only one problem: 100150 is a very different service level than 80/20! You can no more hit both than you can adjust the pull of gravity.

When you establish 80/20, 90/15 or anything else, you are inherently dictating what the longest wait will be. Choose an objective that is appropriate, then concentrate your energies on hitting it consistently.

**2. Service Level versus Average Speed of Answer.**

A similar problem stems from establishing objectives for both service level (SL) and average speed of answer (ASA), e.g., "our service level objective is to answer 90 percent of calls in 20 seconds, and our ASA objective is 15 seconds." Although SL and ASA calculations are based on the same set of data, they are very different reports (see the table on this page). Choose one or the other, but don't have objectives for both. (Of the two, SL tends

to be more stable and accurate, and less prone to misinterpretation.)

**3. Occupancy versus Everything.**

Occupancy is the percent of time during a half-hour that agents who are on the phones are in talk time and after-call work. The inverse of Occupancy is the time agents spend waiting for inbound

Table 1

**Talk Time: 240 sec; After Call Work; 30 sec; Calls: 150 1/2 hr.**

| Reps | SL % in 15 sec. | ASA (in sec.) | Occ. | Avg. Calls Per Rep. |
|---|---|---|---|---|
| 23 | 14% | 476 | 98% | 6.5 |
| 24 | 38% | 121 | 94% | 6.3 |
| 25 | 56% | 55 | 90% | 6.0 |
| 26 | 69% | 29 | 87% | 5.8 |
| 27 | 79% | 16 | 83% | 5.6 |
| 28 | 86% | 10 | 80% | 5.4 |
| 29 | 91% | 6 | 78% | 5.2 |
| 30 | 94% | 3 | 75% | 5.0 |
| 31 | 96% | 2 | 73% | 4.8 |
| 32 | 98% | 1 | 70% | 4.7 |
| 33 | 99% | 1 | 68% | 4.5 |

**Calculations based on Erlang C for 1/2 hour

calls, plugged in and available. Some industry benchmarking reports have suggested that 90 percent occupancy is an appropriate target.

The problem is, occupancy is a phenomenon of random call arrival and is heavily influenced by service level and group size. If you staff correctly to handle the call load at your service level objective, occupancy will be what it will be. It's dictated by the nature of the workload and the service level objective you establish (see table).

Consequently, setting objectives on occupancy - 90 percent or otherwise - is likely to conflict with just about everything else you want to achieve. For example, when service level goes up, occupancy goes down. And when schedule adherence (when and how much time your agents are handling or waiting for calls) improves, occupancy goes down.

Solution: Don't set occupancy targets. One caveat: ensure you have enough staff to keep occupancy below 90 to 92 percent, to avoid burning people out.

**4. Calls Handled Per Agent versus Queue Behavior.**

Many of the variables that impact calls handled per agent are out of the agent's control (e.g., call arrival rate, call types, callers' knowledge, callers' communication abilities, the accuracy of the forecast and schedule, and the adherence to schedule of other agents in the group). As with occupancy, calls handled per agent looks better when service level and schedule adherence deteriorate (see table).

Solution: Eliminate this objective and instead focus on schedule adherence and quality. Calls handled will take care of itself within the context of your processes and the nature of queues.

**5. Average Handling Time versus Quality.**

An important aspect of quality is that agents take the necessary time to handle transactions correctly. This, of course, means not rushing calls. But it also means not spending time on calls over and above what is required to satisfy callers and handle transactions completely and correctly. (Three key quality issues are: 1) identifying, then 2) meeting customer expectations, and 3) using the fewest possible resources.)

The nature of the calls, the processes you have in place, and the skills and knowledge of your agents determine how long calls are. If qualitative measurements are refined enough to ensure that agents are spending the appropriate amount of time handling calls, then average handling time objectives are redundant and potentially counterproductive.

**6. Cost Per Call versus Process Improvement.**

There are various ways to calculate cost per call, but the basic formula is to divide total costs by total calls for a given period of time. Conventional wisdom states that the lower the cost per call, the better. However, a climbing cost per call can be a good sign, depending on the variables driving it up. For example, better coordination with other departments may help reduce the number of times a customer has to contact your center. As a result, the fixed costs (in the numerator) get spread over fewer calls (in the denominator), driving cost per call up. But total costs will go down over time because eliminating waste and rework will drive down the variable costs. Similarly, cost per call usually goes down during the busy times of the year and up during the slower times of year.

The solution? Don't focus on cost per call without also looking at the specific variables at work.

**7. Resources versus Mission.**

Probably the most common and recurring case of incompatible objectives is between resources and mission. For example, be it too many or too few people, what you have and what you're asked to accomplish may be very different things. This issue goes to the heart of call center management and the ongoing challenge of matching resources to the workload. A characteristic of a well-managed call center is the ability to sort through and address any incompatibilities between available resources and desired results, on an ongoing basis.

**Focus on the Things that Matter**

Nobody purposely establishes objectives that are contradictory. But it's easy to do, given the many inter-related activities and processes, and the nature of random call arrival and the behavior of queues.

Sometimes conflicting objectives are the result of a type of insecurity. For example, you may be focusing on service level, quality and schedule adherence, but... you feel like you need an objective for occupancy just to be sure that "efficiency" is not being ignored. Hey, have some faith! If you concentrate on the things that matter, everything else tends to take care of itself. Then you'll have more time to focus on the things that matter. Kind of the diametrical opposite of a catch-22.

**SLN**

# The Technology Adoption Life Cycle: A Strategic Tool That Matters (Still)

Remember the technology adoption life cycle? Nope, it had nothing to do with that passing virtual-pet craze. It's a tool popular with suppliers and marketeers (and business school professors) for assessing opportunities and building markets for "discontinuous innovations." It has had surprising staying power over the past couple of decades and, with some modification, is as useful as ever.

In consultant lingo, discontinuous technologies are new ideas, or "new ways of getting rid of mice, not just better mouse-traps," explains business observer Charles Fleming (Wall Street Journal Europe, July 14, 1998). "Things like snowboards, digital cash or personal computers were all discontinuous technologies in their time." As were ACDs, IVRs and e-commerce services. Continuous innovations, on the other hand, are the normal upgrades to products and services that do not require significant changes in established behavior or thinking.

In its traditional form, the technology adoption life cycle forms a bell curve with five divisions that describe psychographic buying habits (see Figure 1 on next page):

**1) Innovators** — sometimes referred to as "technology enthusiasts," buy into new technology early on. They love trying new things and will typically do what they can to help the supplier bring the product to the marketplace.

**2) Early Adopters** — also called "visionaries," quickly understand and appreciate the benefits of new technologies and relate those capabilities to concerns. They see the possibilities for new strategic applications and are often motivated by order-of-magnitude gains that can come from being among the first to embrace new capabilities.

**3) Early Majority** — also referred to as "pragmatists," are driven by a strong sense of practicality. They share some of the characteristics of early adopters but emphasize real-world trade-offs and mission-critical applications. They like to wait until the market shakes out and the technology is more of a sure thing.

**4) Late Majority** — or "conservatives," want solutions that work, no hassles please. Like the early majority, they have a strong sense of practicality, but would rather wait until the technology is tried, proven and then tried again. They prefer turnkey, cost-effective solutions.

**5) Laggards** — resist new technology and distrust conventional competitive and productivity-improve- ment arguments. These "skeptics" are generally viewed by vendors as not worth the effort.

**Innovators**
- Buy into new technology early on
- Are often technologists who love trying new things.

Early Adopters
- Buy in early
- Understand the benefits of new technology
- Relate benefits to concerns
- Adopt new technology when there's a match.

**Early Majority**
- Share some of the characteristics of early adopters
- Typically driven by strong sense of practicality
- Normally wait to see how others are doing before committing.

**Late Majority**
- Driven by strong sense of practicality
- Want to wait for others
- Wait for emerging standards
- Buy from well-established companies.

**Laggards**
- Don't want anything to do with new technology
- Generally regarded by vendors as "not worth pursuing".

Geoffrey Moore, a high-profile consultant to the high-tech industry and author of Crossing the Chasm (Harperbusiness, revised edition, August 1999), Inside the Tornado (HarperCollins, reprint edition, August 1999) and other works on the subject, has in recent years given the model an update and fresh relevance (see Figure 2 on next page). Moore contends that there are important gaps between the traditional categories, the largest being a "chasm" between visionaries (early adopters) and pragmatists (early majority). He believes these two groups have less in common than previously

Figure 1

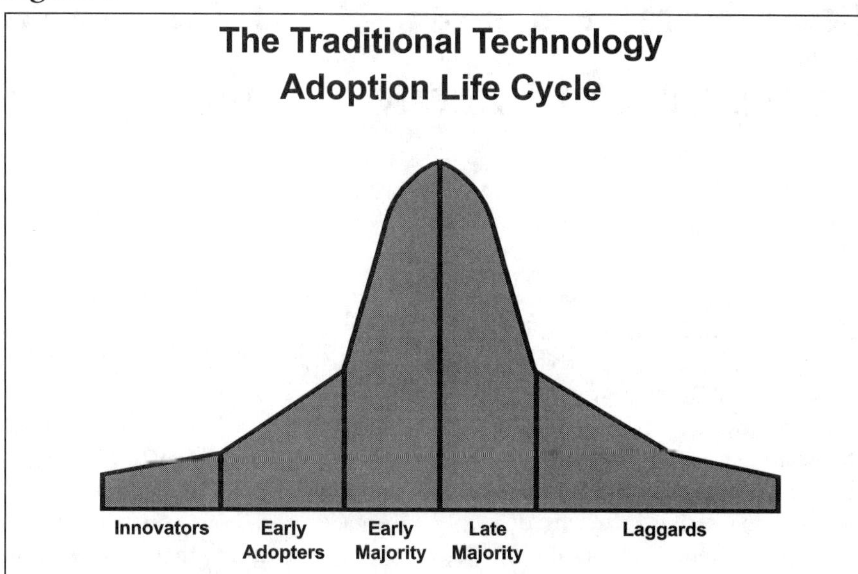


thought, e.g., pragmatist have a much greater tendency to collaborate with others and nurture buy-in when making technology decisions. For suppliers, reaching this group is the means to the mass market.

So how does this tool apply to call center management? For one thing, it is useful in project negotiations to understand how suppliers may be shaping their proposals around their perceptions of your buying habits. But there are a load of other uses:

• Any project team is likely to have individuals with differing perspectives. The pragmatists tend to view the visionaries as "dangerous," the visionaries think the pragmatists are too cautious and the conservatives are triple-checking rationale and the probability of payback. And, should you have a laggard on the team, they'll be focused on debunking the whole proposition. Understanding these perspectives can help you appre- ciate differences and produce better decisions.

• Viewing your organization, your customers, your competitors and new technologies through the lens of the model will help you identify tradeoffs between risks and rewards, and establish priorities. For example, early indications are that e-mail manage- ment systems and speech recognition capabilities have crossed or are in a position to cross the chasm, while click-to-talk services and video-equipped call center services may take longer than initially expected to reach the early majority. Assuming that is the case, what are the implications for your call center?

• The model can help you produce better budgetary proposals. Return on investment is difficult to predict until a technology crosses the chasm and solid case studies emerge. But by then, the greater opportunities of early adoption will have passed. These are considerations you need to review with your CFO. (Hint: Moore believes that technologies hit a lull before crossing the chasm. Don't buy here, he says. The early adopters have already beat you to the party, yet the mainstream group hasn't yet brought the price down or worked the pain out of early implementation challenges.)

## Not Infallible, But Insightful

The technology adoption life cycle is not an infallible forecasting tool. After all, Amazon.com has become a classic case of successfully bringing to market a discontinuous innovation, while Iridium (the world's first satellite-based phone network that can reach virtually any corner of the earth) recently filed for bankruptcy protection; both had gutsy but seemingly workable plans for reshaping their industries.

But the model can help you make better decisions and should be a working part of your strategy toolkit. Further, next time you or a friend need some real-world case studies for that B-school assignment, you'll be good to go.

CCMReview

Figure 2

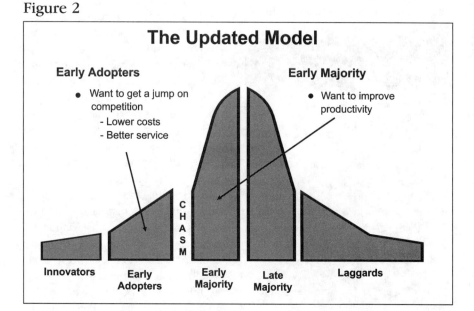

**The Updated Model**

**Early Adopters**
• Want to get a jump on competition
- Lower costs
- Better service

**Early Majority**
• Want to improve productivity

CHASM

Innovators | Early Adopters | Early Majority | Late Majority | Laggards

## Service Level Notes with Brad Cleveland

# The Principles Behind Effective Budgeting

William Gladstone, four-time prime minister of England in the mid-1800s, once said, "Budgets are not merely affairs of arithmetic but, in a thousand ways, go to the root of prosperity of individuals, the relation of classes and the strength of kingdoms." Was he stretching the point? I don't think so.

A budget is simply "a summary of proposed or agreed upon expenditures for a given period of time, for specified purposes." Sounds benign enough. But the process of putting a budget together is often seen by call center managers as tedious, time-consuming and, some say, distracting from "more important management responsibilities." We cannot forget, however, the outcome of this much-maligned process: the funding the call center has with which to accomplish its purpose.

In a thousand ways, the budget will impact the prosperity of individuals (your employees, shareholders, customers), the relation of classes (the standing of the call center in the organization and the responsibilities and influence of departments and positions) and the strength of kingdoms (the viability of your organization and to some degree the health of the economy). Gladstone was right.

Call centers that get the funding they need give budgeting the care and respect it is due. In analyzing many of these organizations, we've noticed that seven principles are at work. Building on these principles can result in a stronger process and, ultimately, the funding your call center requires.

The first principle of an effective budgeting process is that it is **based on solid "call center valuation."** Put more simply, those who are involved in proposing and approving the budget have a common understanding of the value the call center contributes to the organization. Without this basis, the budgeting process is arbitrary and contentious. But when all involved agree on the call center's contribution to customer satisfaction and loyalty, improved quality and innovation, focused marketing, efficient delivery of services and, if applicable, sales, then the requirement for funding will get the attention it deserves. (For more background on call center valuation, see "Dispel the Complaint Center Image: Promote Value Through Visibility," *CCMReview*, August 2000, pg. 1; and "Memorandum," Service Level Notes, *CCMReview*, May 2000, pg. 16).

The budgeting process must also be **driven by the customer access strategy** – the framework that defines the means by which customers access desired information and services. Just as NASA in the 1960s put backbone into the vision of going to the moon and returning safely, the customer access strategy is the tangible link between the call center's mission and the capabilities you need to put into place to live up to that mission (for an introduction to customer access strategy, see Service Level Notes, *CCMReview*, February 2000, pg. 16). By defining who your customers are, when and how they desire to reach you, the means by which you will identify, route, handle, and track those contacts, and how you will leverage the information that comes from them, the customer access strategy is the de facto blueprint for the budget.

> **An Effective Budgeting Process:**
>
> 1. Is based on solid "call center valuation"
> 2. Is driven by the customer access strategy
> 3. Is a seamless extension of resource planning
> 4. Identifies both forecast and resource/results tradeoffs
> 5. Maximizes cross-functional resources
> 6. Builds understanding of the call center environment
> 7. Is honest, responsible and visible

At a more tactical level, an effective budgeting process is a **seamless extension of resource planning**. If the call center manager spends 10 days behind closed doors, sports a long face and misses the company picnic – all on account of preparing the annual budget – something is wrong. Call centers are planning-intensive, and forecasting, staffing and scheduling activities are ongoing responsibilities. While the budget must look beyond the here and now to anticipate future staffing, technology and organizational requirements, day-to-day planning activities usually should take the process 85 percent of the way.

An effective process also **identifies both forecast and resource/results tradeoffs**. The workload forecast will over- or underestimate demand for call center services to some degree (hopefully, within just a few percentage points). And for a given workload, you can provision resources associated with high levels of service, moderate levels of service or low levels of service – with all the shades of possibility in between (see Figure 1).

Both issues raise certain inevitable questions: What happens if the forecast is high? Low? What happens if you provide a better level of service? Lower level of service? How much would you save/spend if…? Once the budget for expected workload is established, along with recommended

Section 9

resources, it is fairly straightforward to rerun scenarios of both different workload assumptions and alternative service levels. These illustrations will contribute enormously to good budgeting decisions (and will score points with the CFO).

An effective budget also **maximizes cross-functional resources**. This powerful principle brings together objectives and budgets from across the organization. For example, corporate lawyers, who are not immediately associated with their knowledge or appreciation of customer contact technologies, are increasingly going to bat for e-mail response management systems. These technologies enable the legal folks to help the call center create consistent and legally defensible scripted responses to customer inquiries, saving the legal department time, improving the call center's responsiveness and minimizing the chance of legal trouble. I/T (information technology) managers, not generally known for their interest in call center staffing levels, are underscoring the need for well-trained call center staff to ensure CRM capabilities and Web-based services are successful (e.g., to help build accurate and useful customer profiles, and to help customers identify and learn to use appropriate self-service systems). And marketing managers are increasingly willing to provide budget dollars to capture and study call center interactions for clues to consumer demands and behavior.

These possibilities become evident to the degree that relationships exist and collaboration is in place between functional areas. This takes time and organizational savvy, but the returns come in multiples.

An effective budgeting process also **builds understanding of the call center environment**. The CEO, CFO and other executives involved in the process must understand the basics of random call arrival, occupancy and schedule adherence (for an introduction to these issues, see Service Level Notes, *CCMReview*, February 1999, pg 16).

They must also appreciate the reasons that call center budgets continue to grow in most organizations (see Figure 2), e.g., more channels of access, increasing complexity, elasticity in demand and expanding services. (In a recent ICMI Web-based seminar on budgeting, 67 percent of the participants indicated they had increased funding over last year, 9 percent had the same, and only 24 percent had decreased funding. While the sample size of just under 40 respondents was too small to be considered statistically valid, it substantiates broader industry studies on these trends.) Asking for more funding is just fine, IF you are increasing customer loyalty and wallet share in the process, IF you are encouraging self-service alternatives as possible, and IF you are explaining these issues adequately to the budgeting powers that be.

Finally, the budgeting process must be **honest, responsible and visible**. It must be realistic about the recent past and whether or not the call center has been meeting its objectives. It must put that in context with customer and agent satisfaction, and with the objectives and funding being proposed. It must support the mission of the organization and dovetail with the roles and requirements of other areas. And it must be visible to those involved in the approval process as well as key managers from across the organization.

Effective budgeting requires time, care, collaboration and, yes, some arithmetic. But the investment is worth it. After all, the prosperity of individuals, relation of classes and the strength of your kingdom depends on it. CCMReview

FIGURE 1

**Two Major Variables: Forecasted Workload and Service Objectives**

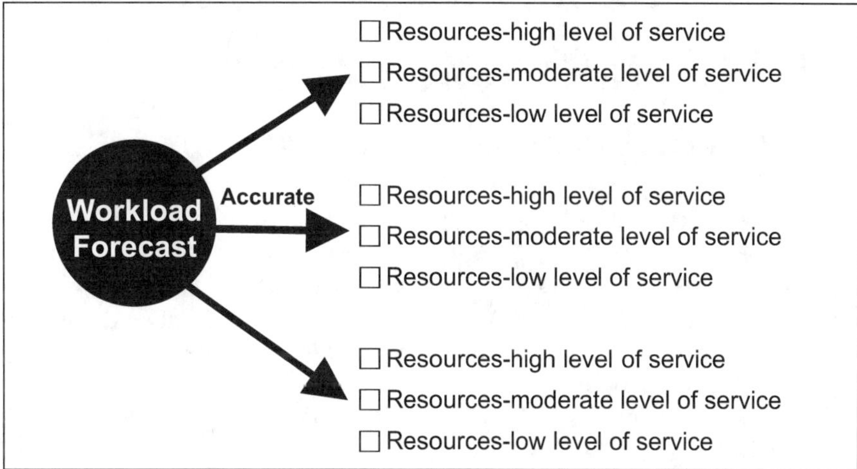


FIGURE 2

**Typical Budget Trends***

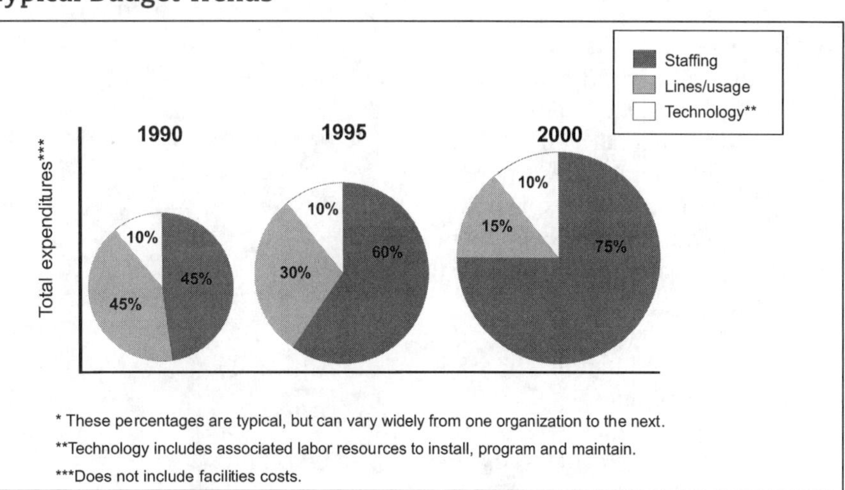

# Why Staff Shrinkage Perplexes Your CFO – and Shrinks Your Budget

*(First article in a series on calculating FTEs)*

If you're like most other call center managers on the planet, there's been a day or two when you've drifted across the floor, watching service level plummet, and wondered aloud, "Where is everybody?" It's not a comfortable feeling.

It's even less comfortable to be inadequately prepared to answer when your Chief Financial Officer (CFO) asks YOU some variation of the above question. Where are they, anyway? Just how are you call center folks spending your time?

Getting "the right number of properly skilled people and supporting resources in place at the right times to handle an accurately forecasted workload at service level and with quality" is at the heart of effective call center management. Accomplishing this objective requires accurate analysis and management at many levels, from long-term planning to intraday staffing adjustments.

But the foundation upon which your call center capacity is built is the budget. The budget process will put you squarely in front of your CFO. And he or she has a few questions...



### Call Load vs. Paid Hours

If this issue hasn't come up yet, it will. Why is the annual call load so low vis-a-vis the call center's total annual paid hours? (These kinds of tough questions help explain why CFOs get the big bucks.) Some quick pencil work proves the point:

1) 790,000 annual calls x 3.5 minutes average handle time = 2,765,000 minutes

2) 2,765,000 / 60 = 46,083 hours, annual call load

3) 55 Full Time Equivalents (FTEs) = 114,400 annual paid hours (55 x 2,080 hours)*

4) 46,083 / 114,400 = 40 percent

** Assumptions: one year = 260 work days or 2,080 hours, based on eight-hour days. The call load and FTE figures are examples only.*

**Why are you call center people spending so little time – 40 percent of aggregate paid hours – actually handling calls? Isn't that what you're here to do?**

Hmm... Why are you call center people spending so little time – 40 percent of aggregate paid hours – actually handling calls? Isn't that what you're here to do?

Of course, the first thing to ensure is that all of the responsibilities that fall under the call center's umbrella are included in the calculation. Are the loads associated with handling e-mail transactions, postal mail, outbound calls and other types of work sufficiently accounted for? Fair enough. Even so, the number is still likely to appear low, usually well under 50 percent Why? This discussion often leads to a more specific look at how individuals spend their time.

### Overall Shrinkage

If you break down an individual's paid hours across a year, it might look something like the example in the table below.

Now that looks much better. If the time agents spend away from

| | | |
|---|---|---|
| Vacation/sickness | 20 days | 7.69% |
| Breaks | two 15 minute breaks | 6.25% |
| Training | 15 days | 5.77% |
| Meetings | 30 minutes per week | 1.25% |
| Holidays | 7 days/year | 2.69% |
| Miscellaneous | 20 minutes/day | 4.17% |
| **Total** | | **27.82%** |

the workload amounts to around 28 percent, then they ought to be available to handle transactions 72 percent of the time. But why the dichotomy between this perspective and the 40 percent derived from the previous example? It is, in short, an "apples to oranges" comparison.

For one thing, those with supporting roles, who generally spend little of their time handling transactions, are omitted from the calculation. It takes a proverbial small army of trainers, technicians, analysts and supervisors to keep a call center humming along.

Another critical factor being ignored is the impact of occupancy. Occupancy is the percent of time that agents who are handling transactions are either in talk time or after-call work (wrap-up). The inverse of occupancy is the time agents spend waiting for calls, plugged in and available. Occupancy is inversely related to service level; when service level improves, agents will spend more of their time waiting for calls to arrive. This is an immutable law stemming from the phenomenon of random call arrival. Want to provide a good service level? Your "efficiency" will inherently be lower. The size of agent groups also affects occupancy; small groups are inherently less efficient than larger groups. (For a review of occupancy, see *Service Level Notes* in our May 1997 issue).

There may also be questions around schedule adherence and whether the factors included realistically reflect the activities that keep agents from the phones. The time spent on training, off-line research and miscellaneous projects has a tendency to expand over time. However, don't draw quick conclusions without a closer look; some or most of this time may necessarily reflect the growing responsibilities of today's call centers. There is also a danger in utilizing aggregate shrinkage in budget calculations, given that the things that keep agents off the phone vary by time of day, day of week and season of the year. The analysis will have to be more specific.

But perhaps the toughest issue to come to grips with revolves around scheduling accuracy and flexibility. Inbound call centers inherently operate in a "demand-chasing" mode. Much of the time, there are either more calls to be answered than resources available, or more resources than calls. Because supply and demand are rarely equal, demand must be "chased" with the supply of answering capabilities. The tough question is, what level of "insurance" do you want to build into your staffing calculations for those times when your forecasts and plans are off the mark or when schedules are not flexible enough to sufficiently respond to peaks and valleys in the workload?

> **The CFO has a right to ask tough questions and to assess how wisely we're using the budget they are entrusting to our stewardship.**

When considering this issue, remember two caveats: 1) Budget projections usually assume ideal schedules with just the right number of base staff to handle the anticipated workload, plus expected shrinkage; although it's tough to admit that your projections may not always be on the mark, you will need to build some worst-case scenarios to draw adequate attention to this question. 2) Unlike most other work environments, inbound call centers can't stockpile finished calls (work ahead) or handle unfinished calls in batch at a later time (catch up); the resources have to be in place when the work arrives, or we risk the consequences of angry callers, stressed agents and the high costs associated with long queues.

### Educate at the Executive Level

The bottom line... er, crux of the matter is that we need to be able to dialog intelligently and thoroughly on these issues. The CFO has a right to ask tough questions and to assess how wisely we're using the budget they are entrusting to our stewardship. But they are going to need at least a basic understanding of call center dynamics in order to understand the numbers. We have the responsibility of educating them on this unique environment and providing analysis that accurately reflects call center activities. If we don't, we're likely to end up with an inadequate budget.

The budget process also invariably leads to questions of strategy. For example, what is the call center's mission? How committed are we to providing good service even when the forecasts may be uncertain? What are our priorities, and how can we improve efficiency? What role will new technologies or processes serve and how will they impact the budget? Be ready for these discussions; they are opportunities for you to present thoughtful insight. This process is a healthy part of ongoing call center development.

We'll pick up with the issue of projecting required FTEs next month. In the meantime, take a few minutes to run through the call load versus paid hours and overall shrinkage exercises. How do your numbers come out? Any surprises?

CCMReview

*Brad Cleveland is president of Incoming Calls Management Institute and is publisher of* CCMReview. *He has advised organizations across five continents and has written numerous articles on the call center industry for business and trade publications. He is also co-author of* Call Center Management on Fast Forward, Succeeding in Today's Dynamic Inbound Environment.

# The Science and Judgement behind FTE Budgets

*(Second article in a trilogy on calculating FTEs)*

Few call center management responsibilities require as much insight, know-how and collaboration as does budgeting for FTEs (full-time equivalents). It is a multi-faceted process laden with both "science" and "judgement." The steps based firmly on science (formulas, principles or immutable laws that yield predictable results) tend to be the most straightforward. Those that require decisions around tradeoffs and unknowns tend to be more difficult and time-consuming.

Knowing where judgement comes in versus the analysis best left to science is a challenge, but it's an important prerequisite to developing an appropriate budget. The following summarizes this process.

**1) Analyze current results vs. stated objectives.** What is the call center's mission? What are the supporting objectives? Are we meeting them? Why or why not? Was the budget from the last cycle appropriate? Did we forecast requirements accurately? What adjustments to the budget would we have made? Could we have better predicted outcomes? What can we learn this time around? This important first step includes some scientific analysis, but is largely based on business decisions.

**2) Forecast expected workload.** The principles of time-series forecasting (based on historical data), regression analysis (e.g., calls versus new customers) and other types of quantitative forecasts are grounded in science. However, virtually all forecasts also require some judgement. E.g., how will the call mix change as Web traffic grows? How should we structure agent groups (one cross-trained group requires one forecast, while many specialized groups require many specific forecasts)? What impact will changes in marketing, competitor activities, laws, consumer behavior and other developments have on the workload?

**3) Calculate base staff and trunk requirements.** Staff calculations are relatively straight-forward and firmly based on science. Granted, all mathematical formulas or simulation models contain assumptions (e.g., what should we assume about busy signals and abandoned calls?). But the resources it will take to consistently achieve service level and response time objectives is a matter of mathematics.

**4) Add in RSF requirements and assemble model schedules.** Rostered staff factor (also called an "overlay" or "shrink factor") leads to the minimum staff needed on schedule over and above base staff required. Although planning around issues such as schedule adherence and non-phone activities requires judgement, the RSF calculations themselves are straightforward and reliable. Defining schedule alternatives and coverage rules, on the other hand, tends to be more of an iterative, creative process.

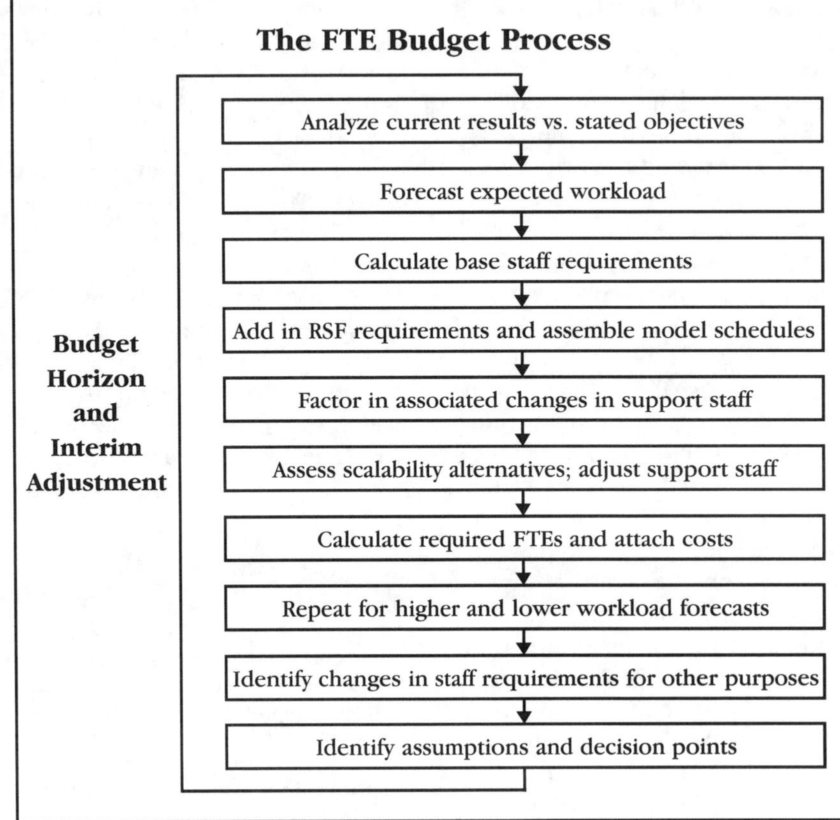
The FTE Budget Process
Analyze current results vs. stated objectives
Forecast expected workload
Calculate base staff requirements
Add in RSF requirements and assemble model schedules
Factor in associated changes in support staff
Assess scalability alternatives; adjust support staff
Calculate required FTEs and attach costs
Repeat for higher and lower workload forecasts
Identify changes in staff requirements for other purposes
Identify assumptions and decision points
Budget Horizon and Interim Adjustment

**5) Factor in associated changes in support staff.** What should your staff-to-supervisor ratio be? How should the call center be organized? What analyst roles are necessary? This step depends more on observation, experience and good business sense than on science.

**6) Assess scalability alternatives; adjust support staff.** Scalability refers to the call center's ability to expand or contract without making changes in FTEs. E.g., can other departments help handle the load when the call center is busy? What other staffing contingencies are available? How committed is the organization to consistently meeting service level and quality objectives? These are business decisions.

**7) Calculate required FTEs and attach costs.** At this point, FTE and cost calculations are relatively straightforward. They are, of course, built on all of the assumptions that have come before.

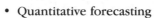

| **Leans towards "science"** ⟵ | ⟶ **Leans towards "business decisions"** |
|---|---|
| • Quantitative forecasting | • SL and RT objectives |
| • Base staff calculations | • Agent group design |
| • Impact of "immutable laws" | • Judgmental forecasting |
| • RSF coverage | • Contingencies/real-time plans |
| • Schedule requirements | • Schedule coverage rules |
| • Accounting and cost analysis | • Schedule and budget horizons |

**8) Repeat for higher and lower workload forecasts.** This step acknowledges any uncertainties in forecasts and is geared around different assumptions for workload.

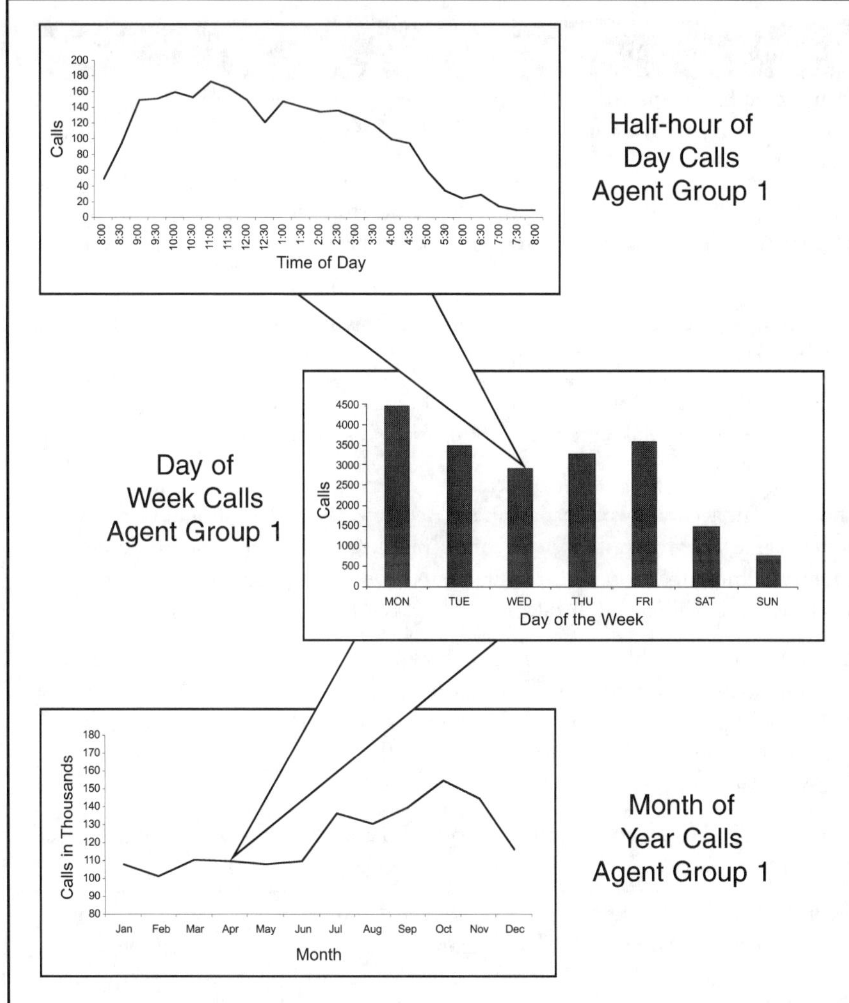


**9) Identify changes in staff requirements for other purposes.** As in step five, identifying the needs for staff not directly associated with handling the workload is largely a matter of experience and observation.

**10) Identify assumptions and decision points.** In this final, critical step, you do an inventory of the assumptions made along the way. Not only will this impress the financial folks, it will create an efficient basis for discussing key issues and coming to agreements. Most importantly, it will increase everybody's understanding of key tradeoffs and improve the overall quality of the final budget.

## No Magic Formula

New managers often ask for "the formula" to calculate future FTE requirements. Sorry, there's no such thing. Instead, this is a process built on a combination of scientific calculations, business decisions and sound judgement. It depends on good communication and a solid understanding of the tradeoffs. And it requires that every decision-maker have a good understanding of what makes call centers tick.

We will continue this topic in the third and final installment of this series next month.

CCMReview

# Troubleshooting FTE Requirements

*(The final article in a trilogy on calculating FTEs)*

Predicting and budgeting for required staff — typically represented as full-time equivalents (FTEs) — is a management responsibility that is fundamental to an effective call center. The process involves establishing the call center's mission, predicting the workload, defining agent groups, identifying required skills, determining staff and schedule requirements, and anticipating costs — in short, it spans virtually every aspect of operating a call center.

The first installment in this series (see Notes, February 1999) highlighted typical misconceptions around the principles of total paid hours and shrinkage, and emphasized the need to educate senior management on these issues. The second article (see Notes, March 1999) summarized the 10-step FTE budget process and differentiated between the steps based on science and those that require judgement (business decisions).

This final installment focuses on troubleshooting. The following guide is designed to help you think through common problematic areas and isolate the issues that need additional attention.

| Problem | Possible Causes and Solutions |
|---|---|
| **You do not know how many FTEs you need.** | You have not established specific service level and response time objectives for all types of transactions that make up the workload. Agree on appropriate targets; this is a necessary prerequisite. |
| | Staff predictions are based on ratios, e.g., number of customers per agent or number of calls per agent. You do not have a concrete connection between workload and required agents; switch to the 10-step FTE process. |
| | Funding is based on the last cycle's budget, plus or minus "x" percent. Build FTE requirements and budgets around future workload, not precedent based on past requirements. |
| | You do not have the systems necessary to track all types of transactions that the call center is handling (e.g., e-mail). Make the necessary investments to put routing and tracking capabilities in place. |
| | You do not have an accurate workload forecast. Accurate forecasting should be a high priority; to the degree your forecasts are inaccurate, build several different schedule models that demonstrate the impact on FTE requirements. Decide with senior management what levels of staff you are willing to fund if the call load is greater than expected. |
| | The call load is highly variable; you aren't sure how to staff for peaks and valleys. Build model schedules (and corresponding FTE requirements) that illustrate schedule possibilities given scheduling alternatives, union requirements, scalability, outsource options and your organization's commitment to maintain service levels; the models will highlight trade-offs and identify decision points. |
| | Some steps in the FTE budgeting process are not in place. Review each of the 10 steps; add and strengthen as necessary. |
| **You do not get sufficient budget for FTEs.** | The call center is undervalued by senior management. You are getting no more than they believe the call center is worth; explore valuation approaches, including customer satisfaction and retention, competitive differentiation, improvements and innovations the call center has contributed to, and customer and market information captured. |

Section 9

| Problem | Possible Causes and Solutions |
|---|---|
| **You do not get sufficient budget for FTEs** *(cont'd).* | Senior management believes the call center could be operated more efficiently. Illustrate, step by step, how you arrived at FTE requirements; identify ongoing process improvments. Ensure that the principles discussed in the first installment of this trilogy (Notes, Feb. 1999) are understood. |
| | You have not identified and quantified the high costs of not getting the required FTEs. E.g., what are the costs of poor service levels, high occupancy, high trunk load and associated network costs, higher abandonment rates and less satisfied customers? |
| | You have overestimated the reduction in workload that IVR, Web and other self-service alternatives were expected to deliver. New and improved services often grow new traffic without an equivalent reduction in the need for live answer; track the changing call mix carefully and be conservative in budgets until you see actual results. |
| | Off-line activities are not adequately anticipated or managed. Most call centers are spending more time on increasingly diverse workloads and associated training and research; these activities must be realistically reflected in projected FTE requirements. |
| **You do not reach the FTEs provisioned for in the budget.** | High turnover is hampering your ability to reach the full compliment of staff. Quantify the costs of turnover; identify the root causes and work on the sources. Establish a new perspective within the organization: the call center is an increasingly complex and critical environment and can no longer afford to be the defacto training grounds for other areas. |
| | The benefits you are providing are not sufficient to attract the staff you need. Quantify the costs of not having the required staff; explore options for providing more attractive career paths within the call center. |
| | Recruiting, hiring and training times significantly trail budget cycles. Produce a graph showing actual versus budgeted FTEs for each cycle and account for the necessary leadtime in FTE budgets. |
| | You are not getting the right kind of FTEs (the necessary skill sets). The FTE budget process is misinterpreted; the purpose of the process is not just to count people, but to identify required skills and supporting costs; revisit the 10 steps. |
| **You have volatile service levels, even with requested FTEs.** | FTE requirements are built around the wrong timeframes. Workload forecasts, base-staff calculations and rostered staff factors should be geared around detailed time frames (usually half hours) while schedules and budgets should piece the half hours together into overall requirements; don't circumvent these steps. |
| | Your group structure is overly specialized or complicated. Keep group design as simple as possible, within the context of getting the right calls to the right agents at the right times; utilize computer simulation to verify resource requirements in complex network and skills-based routing environments. |
| | Your ongoing planning is insufficient. The FTE process is not a substitute for planning for scheduling purposes. |
| | The budget cycle is too long. You have to anticipate specific requirements too far in advance, and changing circumstances create inaccuracies midway through the cycle; adjust the budgeting time-frames as necessary. |

**Respect the Process**

The key theme that runs throughout this series is that predicting and budgeting for FTEs is a process, and must be respected and treated as such. There is no one formula and no shortcut to calculating FTEs. But the payoff of going through the necessary steps is compelling: you will not only identify FTE requirements more accurately, you will generate the solid buy-in and support from senior management and others involved in the process.

CCMReview

# Technology Focus with Eric Miller

# Make Informed Technology Investment Decisions with Operational Cost Modeling

**Staying competitive in a difficult economy requires wise investment decisions based on fact, not wishful thinking.**

Making wise investments in the right technologies that can reduce costs while improving service quality is the challenging balancing act of today's call center management.

High customer expectations and competitors vying for a larger piece of the market have call center managers redefining strategies and building a new family of call centers to deliver thorough, cohesive and user-friendly services. Everyone agrees that "competition-ready" call centers and service levels will require the benefits of information technology. But which ones? For which processes? And what will provide the biggest benefit for your precious technology budget?

## Look Beyond Basic Metrics When Evaluating Technology

The ability to provide a realistic cost-benefit analysis (CBA) can help to stretch budget dollars further and is often the deciding factor on whether or not a call center technology project is funded.

Analyzing the call center operation and being able to confidently and accurately predict the anticipated impact of increases in call volume, process changes or technology implementation is a requirement for getting support for investments and to demonstrate the resulting return on investment. Relating call center activities to manual or automated tasks within an operational cost model (OCM) will enable you to better quantify anticipated five-year benefits within your CBA.

To develop an effective CBA, you need to look beyond the basic metrics, such as abandonment rate, average speed of answer and average call time. If you limit yourself to just these measurements, the technology evaluation will be based on its ability to automate and do more with fewer people and dollars.

While automation of repetitive tasks is a good thing, the other benefit (arguably the bigger benefit) is in refining the process and changing caller behavior in a way that makes the call center easier to do business with by delivering better service in reduced time with reduced costs.

## Consider the Caller's Technology Potential

When looking at technology investments, there are several key customer service-related considerations:

- How can callers be enticed to use self-service technology instead of choosing a live-agent option?
- What types of services can be effectively offered using technology?
- How do you strike the right balance to ensure callers can get to an agent without knowledge of "the secret handshake" to escape the IVR?

The right balance for call center excellence is a combination of operational efficiency, customer satisfaction and effective technology implementation. After all, what's the benefit of reducing operational costs and doing things faster, if customer satisfaction suffers? You're taking one step forward, two steps back. The trick is finding the key to the process changes that will improve customer satisfaction and, therefore, customer retention, while controlling costs to a manageable level.

## Gather Operational Facts

To make the technology and process decisions that support your goals, you need to arm yourself with the facts – the operational facts, that is. To predict the impact changes will have on your operation, you first must look at your call center operation's current state and history. Again, it's important to look beyond the basics like number of calls and average talk time. Ask yourself:

- What are the characteristics of each call?
- What path do calls take through the

### Putting the OCM to Work

An effective operational cost model (OCM) can help to take the guesswork out of cost-benefit analysis for technology investments. With the OCM in hand, you will be able to predict the future and make informed decisions relative to process change, staffing levels and technology implementation. For example, if 30 percent of today's calls are handled by IVR and 70 percent go to agents, what is the impact on the OCM if call distribution is shifted to 40/60?

But putting a plan in place to initiate this shift requires knowing which calls, if better handled through IVR, will remain in IVR. If call volume increases, will the 40/60 still hold or is it highly dependent upon the type of call? Knowing the characteristics of the call is critical to successfully making the shift and predicting the impact of call volume increases or decreases.

The call statistics and characteristics, combined with average pay, benefits, agent capacity, call center square footage and equipment finally provide the complete picture to model the operation. As more data is collected, the model will get better and more accurate in its representation of the present operation and predictive modeling for the future.

operation?

- Why aren't callers staying in the IVR?
- What types of calls are successfully handled through the IVR?
- Which calls are going to agents that should remain in the IVR?

These types of questions help you to gain insights into your callers' characteristics and behaviors (i.e., knowing the customer). After all, one of your goals should be to have the calls that should go to agents go to them, while others are handled effectively through self-service platforms. Without the intimate knowledge of the characteristics of the calls, this analysis is virtually impossible.

Let's be honest – how many call centers have tracked calls and service levels to this degree of detail? To say just a few might be a generous estimate. But the good news is that historical information doesn't have to be perfect, just good enough. If all of the information is not available, start with what you have and collect the rest going forward.

The process for collecting the statistics doesn't need to be sophisticated – it can be as simple as a tic-sheet on which agents can record each type of call so that wait, talk time, etc., can be tracked based on call characteristics. Calls should be tracked for every day of the week and during all shifts to identify any patterns and trends.

This might sound complicated but, in reality, the key is to *make the commitment* to operational cost modeling and stick to it. As information is collected, the operational knowledge and detail will just keep getting better and better. Call center operational knowledge is not a one-time event but, rather, an iterative process. The hardest part is getting started – learning to crawl, walk and finally run to operational excellence. You do this by beginning with whatever information is available, collecting more over time and refining the model as lessons and facts are learned (the figure, just below, illustrates this iterative process).

***By collecting the "what" and "how many" over time, you will soon find you have the operational facts and can begin making decisions based on information rather than best guesses or gut instinct.***

As your operational cost model evolves, the impact of any changes on the call center operation should be incorporated into the model, with the potential effects on metrics (such as wait time, abandonment rate, call time, percent to self-service platforms, percent to live agents, etc.) more accurately predicted.

## Learning to Walk Before You can Run

While operational cost modeling may sound like a daunting task, just remember, walking will always come before running. Start by dissecting the call center operation into discreet tasks and defining metrics for each, including cost and time. Begin with the information that is available and commit to collect operational data going forward. By collecting the "what" and "how many" over time, you will soon find you have the operational facts and can begin making decisions based on information rather than best guesses or gut instinct.

As you continue to collect data and incorporate it into the model, the accuracy of the analysis and knowledge of your operation will get better and better. Naturally, decisions based on this new "knowledge" will get better, as well.

## Informed IT Decisions for Your Call Center Needs

With the facts in hand, you can predict the impact that increased call volume will have on the call center when faced with the prospect of increases in call volume. Depending upon the types and characteristics of the increased calls, the application of technology or increase in manpower can be better analyzed, decided and defended. It's hard to argue with the facts.

Most importantly, remember that operational modeling is not a one-time event or a stagnant model. The model is constantly changing as product mix, call volumes, business levels and caller profiles change.

Having a good operational cost model in place will allow the knowledge-rich call center manager to effectively predict the future and prepare the call center for the necessary process, personnel and technology changes required to maintain a competition-ready, user-friendly operation. CCMReview

### The Operational Model Process

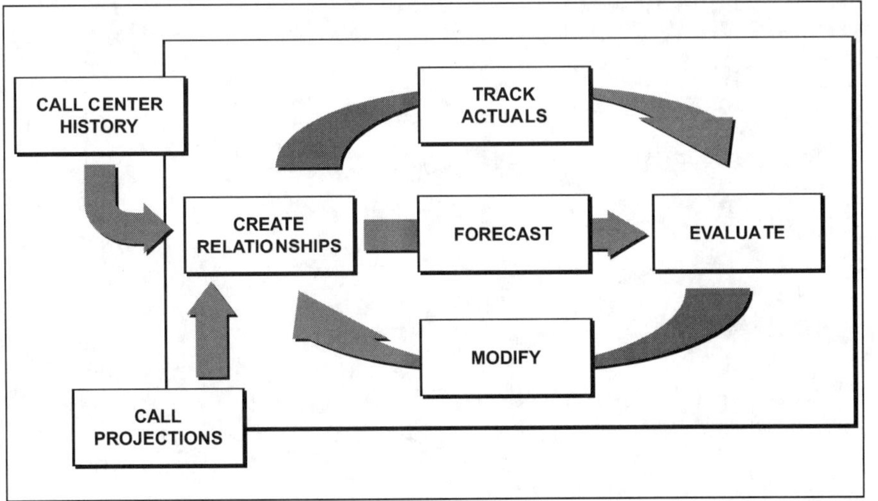


**Eric Miller**

*Eric Miller is a senior principal with Highpoint Consulting Inc. He is an operations management expert and specializes in technology-related cost benefit analysis. Eric can be reached at ericmiller@highpoint-consulting.com.*

Section 9

# Section 10

## *Answers to Exercises*

## Answers to Exercises

### Strategy and Valuation

1. c, b

2. T

3. c

4. e, b, a, d, f, c

5. Customer segmentation; Major contact types; Access channels; Service level and response time objectives; Hours of operation; Routing methodology; Person and technology resources required by contact; Knowledge bases; Tracking and integration

6. a. vision

   b. strategy

   c. skills, knowledge

   d. plans, processes

   e. technologies

   f. investments

   g. quality

7. d

8. This phenomenon is a direct result of the more personal relationship that the customer now has with the organization due to the contact experience.

9. a

10. a. $90,000

    b. $900,000

    c. $990,000

    d. 4.95%

11. T, T, T

**Leadership and Communication**

1. F, F

2. Management; Leadership

3. a. shared

   b. alignment

   c. management

   d. communicate, celebrate

   e. model

4. i, c, c, c, i, c, c, i, c, c, c, c, c

5. F

6. a. audience, information

   b. tools

   c. document

   d. liaison, cross-functional

   e. reports

   f. service level

   g. collaborative, education

7. One-of situations; Project-oriented issues; Ongoing processes

8. a. A cumulative summary report by day (e.g., service level for Monday was 82 percent in 20 seconds) would not show an accurate representation of customer experiences, since a poor service level in the morning may look fine if you have idle staff at other times.

   b. If you mask serious resource deficiencies or process problems, the call center is less likely to get the resources and support it needs.

**The Call Center Business Environment**

1. a, a, a, a, b, a, a, c, a

2. F, F, T, T, T, F

3. b

4. a, b, b

5. a. Small sample size research provides valuable qualitative information that often is too costly and cumbersome to get from larger samples.

   b. Small sample size research is not as statistically reliable as large sample size research.

   c. To ensure that the population you want to study is represented at the location or channel you use for the research.

6. a. Telephone Consumer Protection Act

   b. Telemarketing Sales Rule

   c. Omnibus Crime Control and Safe Streets Act

   d. Electronic Communications Privacy Act

7. a, c, d, b

**Business Management Principles and Practices**

1.

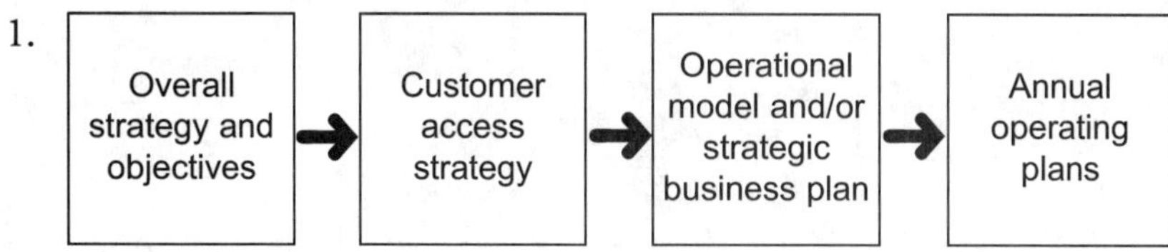


2. d, d

3. h, a, f, i, c, d, b, g, e

4. 114 – 125 = -11

5. 5905 total calls ÷ 6 days = 984 calls per day on average

6. 379 x .72 = 273 Product inquiries

379 x .12 = 45 Delivery complaints

379 x .16 = 61 Billing questions

7. Agent Group 1: 8 ÷ 182 = 4.4%

Agent Group 2: 2 ÷ 32 = 6.3%

Section 10

8. Left to right: Flow chart, Pareto chart, Cause and effect diagram (or fishbone), Control chart, Scatter diagram

9. b, d, e, a, f, c

10. The two primary options for co-sourcing arrangements are :

- An organization may choose to run their call center within their physical location, but outsource the human resources management to a contract staffing company.
- An organization may provide the management and staffing, and the call center outsourcer provides the physical location and the technology.

11. d, a, d, b

12. Service level is a specific measure that refers to the objective of answering "X percent of calls in Y seconds." Service level agreements, on the other hand, are broader in nature and touch on all significant areas of performance. Usually, a service level objective is an important element of an SLA, but does not comprise all or even most of the agreement.

13. Include any six of the following:

Products supported

Services provided

Service level and response time objectives

Hours of operation

Response time objectives for ancillary work

Abandoned call objectives

First call resolution

Quality procedures and standards

Reporting requirements and timelines

Forecasting and planning methodologies

Disaster recovery expectations and procedures

**Financial Principles and Practices**

1. a, b, a

2. a. Call centers that try to force calls to be shorter risk decreasing call quality to such a degree that customers need to call back to resolve their concerns. Thus, average handling time may decrease, while total workload increases as a result of additional calls, leading to increases in resource requirements instead of the desired cost savings.

   b. Decreases in call volume may actually increase cost per contact, since the organization's fixed costs must be spread across fewer contacts. Total costs may decrease resulting in cost savings, even though on a cost per contact basis the performance picture may seem to worsen.

3. b, c

4. a

5. b

6. F

7. j, e, c, f, g, l, n, i, b, m, k, h, d, a

8. Payback point = 2 years + (3,000 ÷ 49,000) = 2.06 years

9.

| | Asset value | Multiplier | Depreciation charges |
|---|---|---|---|
| Year 1 | $15,000 | 3/6 | $7,500 |
| Year 2 | $15,000 | 2/6 | $5,000 |
| Year 3 | $15,000 | 1/6 | $2,500 |

10. b

11. a. The cash-flow statement

   b. The balance sheet

   c. The profit-and-loss (P&L) statement

   d. The statement of retained earnings

Section 10

Section 11

# *CIAC Certification Handbook*

## Leadership and Business Management

# INFORMATION HANDBOOK

## Call Center Industry Advisory Council (CIAC)

**Setting Standards of Excellence
For The Contact Center Profession**

# CIAC CERTIFICATION

# INFORMATION HANDBOOK

This **Handbook** contains information about CIAC Certification. It explains the purposes and benefits of CIAC Certification, the CIAC Certification process, assessment requirements, and registration procedures. Adherence to the policies and procedures described in this Handbook is essential to achieve and maintain CIAC Certification. Questions about information contained in this Handbook and/or CIAC Certification should be directed to:


**Call Center Industry Advisory Council, Inc. (CIAC)**
**330 Franklin Road**
**PMB 390**
**Brentwood, Tennessee 37027 USA**

**Telephone:**
**888-859-2422**
**615-373-2376**

**Fax:**
**615-515-1879**
**Email:**
**info@ciac-cert.org**

**Web site:**
**www.ciac-cert.org**


Section 11

# TABLE OF CONTENTS

## ABOUT CIAC

CIAC is a not for profit corporation established by the contact center industry to provide standardized, competency-based professional certification for individuals who lead, manage and work in contact centers. It exists to promote the establishment of standards of competence and professionalism in the contact center industry and to recognize professionals who through successful completion of the CIAC Certification process have demonstrated mastery of industry-established, knowledge, skill, and behavioral requirements that are specific to their job role.

### CIAC Mission

The mission of CIAC is twofold: 1) to raise the stature of the contact center profession; and 2) to heighten awareness of the strategic and economic value of contact centers. The ultimate goal of CIAC is to legitimize the contact center profession in order to inspire more people to purposely choose contact center careers, thereby, increasing the number of qualified professionals available for the growing number of contact center jobs.

### CIAC Objectives

The primary objectives of CIAC are to:

- Promote advancement of the contact center profession and industry.
- Legitimize the contact center profession by establishing standards that define the knowledge, skills, and behaviors required for mastery-level job performance.
- Certify individuals based on their ability to demonstrate mastery of contact center role-specific competencies.
- Provide industry-recognized knowledge and skill requirements to help training providers more effectively prepare individuals for success in working in contact centers.
- Provide career pathing for the contact center career and specific guidelines for success and advancement.
- Promote a positive image of contact centers by educating the general public, government, and business community on the economic and strategic value of contact centers.
- Represent the profession on issues relating to contact centers and the individuals who lead, manage, and work in contact centers.

CIAC is not a professional association, membership organization, or training company. Its role is to serve as the vendor-neutral standards and certifying body for the contact center industry and profession.

# INTRODUCTION TO CIAC CERTIFICATION

## Definition of CIAC Certification

CIAC Certification is the process by which the competence of contact center professionals is assessed, validated, and formally recognized in specific areas of expertise based on the requirements of their job role as defined by the industry. It allows professionals to demonstrate an in-depth understanding of contact centers, comprehensive knowledge of the essential aspects of their job role, and to demonstrate behaviors identified as essential for success. Achievement of CIAC Certification indicates that a contact center professional (1) has demonstrated mastery of industry-established knowledge, skill, and behavioral requirements; and (2) is committed to continual learning and ongoing professional development.

CIAC Certification is an essential tool for establishing and maintaining a standard of performance excellence for contact centers. It is applicable to individuals working in all types and sizes of contact centers, across all industries. CIAC Certification is vendor-neutral and free of bias. It is focused on empowering professionals who lead, manage, and work in contact centers to enhance their job performance and advance their career through an industry-recognized credential that recognizes them to be the best in the industry. CIAC-Certified professionals enable contact center organizations to achieve and sustain best practices that exemplify performance excellence.

## Purpose of CIAC Certification

The purpose of CIAC Certification is: 1) to raise the stature of the contact center profession in order to make working in contact centers a more attractive career choice; 2) to ensure professional competence and motivate the individuals who lead, manage, and work in contact centers and contact center organizations to achieve the highest standards of performance; and 3) to promote recognition that contact centers are a critical component of an enterprise's business strategy. To fulfill this purpose, CIAC:

- Worked with the industry to establish competencies based on recognized knowledge, skills, and behaviors for contact center job roles.
- Developed certification assessments that are linked to the established competencies.
- Established a certification process designed to raise the bar in order to cultivate a workforce of superior performers.
- Works with training providers to ensure the availability of quality programs that are aligned with the competencies and other required criteria necessary to effectively prepare individuals for the CIAC Certification assessments.

## Benefits of CIAC Certification

CIAC Certification formally acknowledges a mastery-level command of the requirements of the job role and a commitment to maintaining high standards. The key benefits of CIAC Certification for individuals leading, managing and working in contact center include:

- Formal acknowledgement of specialized expertise.
- Achievement of a respected industry credential.
- Recognition as a role model and leader.
- Demonstration of ability to achieve business results.
- Increases an individual's current value and future marketability.
- Enhances career growth by providing motivational goals and a framework for professional development.
- Promotes continual learning through a commitment to ongoing professional development.
- Demonstrates a personal commitment to performance excellence.

CIAC Certification is important to contact centers because it:

- Provides credible criteria for making hiring decisions, evaluating performance, and/or determining training needs.
- Reduces turnover – helps to ensure "right fit" from the start.
- Increases productivity, employee morale, and commitment.
- Provides job mobility and increased career paths.
- Reduces training costs – learning is directly related to the job.
- Promotes a professional image throughout the enterprise and to customers.
- Demonstrates a commitment to performance excellence.

CIAC Certification also benefits the contact center profession and industry because it:

- Raises the stature of the profession by formally recognizing the requirement for specialized knowledge, skills, and abilities.
- Inspires career choices in contact centers by legitimizing the profession.
- Heightens awareness of advancement opportunities.
- Establishes industry-recognized competency requirements.
- Raises the bar and promotes performance excellence.

## Use of CIAC Certification

CIAC Certification is voluntary in nature and intended solely for the purposes and benefits stated in this Handbook.

## CIAC CERTIFICATION TRACKS

### Management Track

Because job titles and descriptions tend to be narrowly defined and vary across organizations, CIAC Certification is based on "roles" rather than job titles. Roles more effectively capture the full responsibilities of a job. Role-based certification allows professionals to pursue certification in the role that best defines what they *actually* do and their *actual* scope of authority and influence; it also allows for overlap between job functions. For example, in some centers the job title contact center manager has both operational and strategic responsibility.

CIAC's first certification track is for professionals who lead and manage contact center organizations. There are also role designations for individuals who are pursuing a career in contact center management and contact center consultants. The roles represented in the CIAC Certification Management Track are:

- Strategic
- Operational
- Apprentice
- Consultant

*CIAC Certification for other contact center roles (supervisors, team lead, and agents) will be provided in the future. Contact CIAC for availability.*

CIAC Certification can be achieved in the following Management Track role designations:

**CIAC-Certified Strategic Leader** (***CCSL***) – This certification designation is for senior executives who are responsible for setting the strategic direction and vision for customer care across all channels of the organization. This role typically has bottom line responsibility for the contact center and is responsible for aligning contact center objectives with corporate business goals. Typical job titles are vice president, director, and senior-manager. In some organizations the title manager may have strategic responsibilities. CIAC Certification as a Strategic Leader requires a minimum of one year of experience specifically in a strategic management role that touches on all of the competencies required for the CCSL designation.

**CIAC-Certified Operations Manager** (***CCOM***) – This certification designation is for management professionals who are responsible for day-to-day contact center operations. This role typically has tactical responsibility for the center including administering the contact center budget, and management of customer care staff. The typical title for this role is manager although in some organizations supervisors may have responsibilities that overlap into operational management. CIAC Certification as an Operations Manager requires a minimum of one year of experience specifically in an operational management role that touches on all of the competencies required for the CCOM designation.

**CIAC-Certified Management Apprentice** (***CCMA***) – This certification designation is intended for three distinct types of professionals:

1. Individuals who are not employed in a contact center, but wish to pursue a career in contact center management.
2. Individuals working in a contact center, not in a management role, who wish to pursue a career path into contact center management.
3. Supervisors who wish to accelerate their advancement into contact center management.

Those pursuing CIAC Certification as a Management Apprentice are required to commit to a program of education, training and professional development focused on the specific competencies for the CCMA role. After one year of job experience in a contact center management role, professionals certified in the Apprentice designation may complete their CIAC Certification in the appropriate management role designation. (Apprentice certification does not require completion of a Work Product Assignment or 360° Review).

**CIAC-Certified Management Consultant** (***CCMC***) – This certification designation is for senior level contact center consultants, ideally who have hands-on experience in contact center management. This designation certifies that a consultant has the required knowledge in contact center management; it does not certify or verify the consultant's expertise or effectiveness in other areas of consultancy. Individuals pursuing CIAC Certification in this designation are required to successfully complete the objective assessments (knowledge assessments) based on the *strategic role* contact center management competencies. (Consultant certification does not require completion of a Work Product Assignment or 360° Review).

Through the CIAC Certification process, professionals are assessed against competency criteria that link their knowledge, skills, and behaviors with the performance requirements of a specific job role. CIAC is committed to building a strong relationship between on-the-job performance and CIAC Certification.

To accomplish this, the CIAC Certification Management Track has four domains of knowledge and skill competency requirements and a set of behavioral characteristics that cross all of the domains. The Management Track competency domains are:

- People Management
- Operations Management
- Customer Relationship Management
- Leadership & Business Management

Within each domain, there are role-specific knowledge, skill, and behavioral requirements for mastery-level contact center management. The competencies were developed by CIAC and practicing contact center executives and managers over a two-plus year period and were validated through industry surveys, focus groups, expert panel review, and secondary research. Go to the CIAC Certification web site at www.ciac-cert.org to review and/or download the Contact Center Management Competencies for each certification designation.

## CIAC CERTIFICATION DESIGNATION AT-A-GLANCE ✧ SELECT YOUR DESIGNATION BELOW

| | CIAC CERTIFIED STRATEGIC LEADER CCSL | CIAC CERTIFIED OPERATIONS MANAGER CCOM | CIAC CERTIFIED MANAGEMENT APPRENTICE CCMA | CIAC CERTIFIED MANAGEMENT CONSULTANT CCMC |
|---|---|---|---|---|
| **WHO** | • Senior executive who is responsible for setting the strategic direction and vision for customer care across all channels of the organization`. Has a minimum of one year experience in a strategic management role that touches all areas of the CCSL competencies<br>• Has bottom line responsibility for the contact center<br>• Responsible for aligning contact center objectives with corporate business goals<br>• Examples of job titles are: vice president, director, and senior-manager | • Professional who is responsible for managing day-to-day contact center operations. Has a minimum of one year of experience in an operational management role that touches all areas of the CCOM competencies<br>• Responsible for managing customer care staff and the contact center operation<br>• Typically administers and manages adherence to the contact center budget<br>• Example of job title is: manager | • Individual who is pursuing a career in contact center management through training or other professional development who is presently not working in a contact center; or an<br>• Individual who is working in a contact center but not in a management role, who wishes to pursue a career in contact center management<br>• Supervisors who wish to accelerate their advancement into contact center management. Has a minimum of one year experience in a contact center operational management role that touches all areas of the competencies required for the CCMA designation<br>• Testing for CCMA certification can be applied toward certification for the CCOM designation | • Senior level contact center consultants, ideally who have hands-on experience in contact center management<br>• Certifies that a consultant has the required knowledge in contact center management; does not certify or verify the consultant's expertise or effectiveness in other areas of consultancy<br>• Required to successfully complete knowledge assessments based on competencies for the CCMC designation |
| **VALUE** | • Proves ability to achieve business results<br>• Validates mastery-level competence of full scope of strategic contact center management<br>• Helps to advance the contact center profession - serves as role model for future leaders<br>• Demonstrates a commitment to performance excellence<br>• Attainment of a prestigious industry credential | • Recognition of specialized expertise<br>• Increases value and marketability<br>• Achievement of an industry-recognized credential<br>• Facilitates continual learning<br>• Provides a framework and goals for ongoing career development<br>• Raises the bar for the contact center management profession | • Provides a framework and goals for ongoing career development and advancement<br>• Increases value and marketability<br>• Demonstrates a commitment to the contact center profession/industry<br>• Establishes a career track and accelerates advancement into a contact center management role | • Validation of specialized knowledge<br>• Enhances professional image<br>• Demonstrates a commitment to the contact center profession/industry<br>• Increases value and marketability to clients |
| **COMPETENCY DOMAIN** | • People Management<br>• Operations Management<br>• Customer Relationship Management<br>• Leadership and Business Management | • People Management<br>• Operations Management<br>• Customer Relationship Management<br>• Leadership and Business Management | • People Management<br>• Operations Management<br>• Customer Relationship Management<br>• Leadership and Business Management | • People Management<br>• Operations Management<br>• Customer Relationship Management<br>• Leadership and Business Management |
| **ASSESSMENTS** | • People Management<br>• Operations Management<br>• Customer Relationship Management<br>• Leadership and Business Management<br>• Work Product Assignment<br>• 360°Review | • People Management<br>• Operations Management<br>• Customer Relationship Management<br>• Leadership and Business Management<br>• Work Product Assignment<br>• 360°Review | • People Management<br>• Operations Management<br>• Customer Relationship Management<br>• Leadership and Business Management<br>• CCMA designation does not complete Work Product Assignment or 360° Review | • People Management<br>• Operations Management<br>• Customer Relationship Management<br>• Leadership and Business Management<br>• CCMC designation does not complete Work Product Assignment or 360° Review |
| **CRITERIA** | • Minimum of one year of experience in a contact center strategic management role that touches all areas of the competencies required for the CCSL designation<br>• A minimum score of 75 percent is required on all knowledge assessments<br>• On the 360°Review a mean score of 3.0 (on a scale of 0 - 5) is required for each competency area and a score of 3.5 is required for the overall 360°Review<br>• Must pass all knowledge assessments in order to receive the Work Product Assignment<br>• Testing must be completed within two years from the date the first assessment is taken | • Minimum of one year of experience in a contact center operational management role that touches all areas of the competencies required for the CCOM designation<br>• A minimum score of 75 percent is required on all knowledge assessments<br>• On the 360° Review a mean score of 3.0 (on a scale of 0 - 5) is required for each competency area and a score of 3.5 is required for the overall 360°Review<br>• Must pass all knowledge assessments in order to receive the Work Product Assignment<br>• Testing must be completed within two years from the date the first assessment is taken | • A minimum score of 70 percent is required for all knowledge assessments based on the competencies for the CCMA designation<br>• Testing must be completed within two years from the date the first assessment is taken | • A minimum score of 75 percent is required for all knowledge assessments based on the competencies for the CCMC designation<br>• Testing must be completed within two years from the date the first assessment is taken |
| **SELF-ASSESSMENTS** | CIAC strongly encourages candidates pursuing CIAC Certification to complete a Self-Assessment for each competency domain to assess current knowledge, skills, and experience against the required competencies. This will enable candidates to identify areas where training and/or additional job experience may be necessary before testing. | | | |

## CIAC CERTIFICATION ASSESSMENTS

**Registering for CIAC Certification** can be done the following ways:

- Online at www.ciac-cert.org via a link to www.ciaccertification.com.
- Online at www.ciaccertification.com.
- Call the CIAC Certification Operations Center at 888-859-2422 or 615-373-2376.

### General Information

Candidates complete a knowledge assessment for each of the four (4) competency domains (four knowledge assessments in total). Candidates pursuing certification for the CIAC-Certified Strategic Leader and CIAC-Certified Operations Manager designations also complete a role-specific Work Product Assignment and a 360° Review to assess behavioral characteristics. Candidates pursuing certification as a CIAC-Certified Management Apprentice (CCMA) and Management Consultant (CCMC) do not complete the Work Product Assignment or 360° Review.

CIAC does not dictate the method by which competence necessary to achieve CIAC Certification is acquired. Candidates may prepare for the certification process by on-the-job experience, formal education, training and other means of professional development.

CIAC Certification testing is Internet-based and administered online. Knowledge assessments are administered in a proctored environment. Three hours is allowed to complete each knowledge assessment. Testing is conducted at public testing centers located in major cities and select colleges and universities. A listing of CIAC-authorized test centers can be found at www.ciaccertification.com. CIAC Certification can also be employer-sponsored in which case CIAC coordinates onsite testing through an organization's human resources or training department. For information about onsite testing contact the CIAC Certification Operations Center at 888-859-2422 or 615-373-2376 or email at info@ciac-cert.org.

The Work Product Assignment is issued upon completion of the knowledge assessments. It is completed at the candidate's work place or other location of choice. Six (6) weeks or thirty (30) workdays is allowed to complete the Work Product Assignment. Upon completion, Work Products are first reviewed and approved by the candidate's manager and then submitted to CIAC for evaluation.

The 360° Review is also completed at the work place by the candidate, his/her manager, selected peers, and direct reports. Three weeks or fifteen (15) workdays is allowed for completion of the 360° Review. The completed 360° Review is sent to CIAC for statistical compilation. A report of the results and feedback is provided to the candidate for professional development purposes. The 360° Review may be completed at any time during the CIAC Certification process.

All CIAC Certification requirements must be completed within two years from the date the first assessment is taken. Failure to complete within the allotted time will require a restart of the CIAC Certification process in full. The candidate may elect to stop the certification process at any time.

## Testing Schedule

CIAC does not dictate a testing schedule. A candidate is allowed to take an assessment when ready, given that he/she has registered, received confirmation of registration, designated a testing location, and confirmed a testing date/time. It is typical that the CIAC Certification assessments are completed one at a time; however, candidates may complete the assessments one at a time or in multiples of their preference.

## Assessment Scoring

CIAC understands the importance of the certification assessment results and makes every effort to ensure accurate scoring. The knowledge assessments are computer-scored and structured to have one correct answer. CIAC-trained assessors with subject matter expertise evaluate Work Products using CIAC-provided checklists with content validity. The 360° Reviews are computer-scored, providing totals and mean values for each competency area.

## Communicating Assessment Results

CIAC sends assessment results directly to the candidate at the postal or email address provided on the Candidate Profile within four (4) hours after the assessment is completed. A "PASS/FAIL" notification is issued. Actual assessment scores may be accessed via the candidate's transcript. Assessment scores are maintained as confidential and released to other parties only with written authorization from the candidate. The candidate is responsible for communicating the results to his/her manager and, if applicable, for submitting a copy of the results to the human resources department for personnel record.

## Assessment Results and Status

- CIAC promotes that industry certification be used for professional/career development purposes. An individual's performance on the assessments should not be used to make decisions such as demotion, transfer, termination, etc.

- In situations where CIAC Certification is employer-sponsored, CIAC provides the assessment results to the candidate in order to maintain confidentiality. It is the responsibility of the candidate and his/her manager to discuss performance on the certification assessments.

CIAC maintains a database for tracking the certification progress and status of candidates and re-certification of certified professionals. The system provides automatic status and information by candidate name and flags certified individuals who are nearing time for re-certification.

## Certificates of Completion

Candidates receive a "Certificate of Completion" for each assessment that is successfully completed.

After successful completion of all certification requirements, CIAC issues the appropriate CIAC Certification credential.

## PREPARING FOR CIAC CERTIFICATION TESTING

CIAC Certification testing consists of a series of assessments that are based on competencies unique to the professional's job role. The competencies are both broad and deep in breadth that cover the *full range* of knowledge, skills, and abilities related to contact center management. They are designed to be high-end in order to cultivate a workforce of master performers. CIAC Certification testing requires in-depth comprehension of the competencies. CIAC strongly encourages candidates to thoroughly review the competencies for their role designation to determine their current level of preparedness and to complete the CIAC-provided Self-Assessments to identify knowledge and skill gaps before testing.

The CIAC Contact Center Management Competencies can be viewed and/or downloaded at www.ciac-cert.org.

The number and types of assessments are determined by the candidate's certification designation (e.g., CIAC-Certified Strategic Leader, Operations Manager, etc.). All designations complete four multiple-choice knowledge assessments consisting of 60 – 100 questions each. The questions are thought-provoking and require in-depth, conceptual knowledge of the subject matter in addition to extensive hands-on experience. Those pursuing CIAC Certification as a Strategic Leader and Operations Manager also complete a Work Product Assignment and a 360° Review.

In order to establish high value around CIAC Certification, the certification process is intentionally rigorous. The process guarantees that a person who achieves CIAC Certification has mastery-level expertise and knows how to apply it on the job. CIAC strongly encourages candidates to prepare in advance of testing. The extent of preparation required is unique to each person depending on his/her current command of the required competencies, both knowledge and application. While some candidates require only refresher training, the majority of person's pursuing CIAC Certification require more extensive training in each of the competency domains.

Preparation for CIAC Certification testing is the candidate's responsibility. CIAC strongly encourages that candidates utilize the CIAC-provided Self-Assessments to compare existing knowledge, skills, and experience against the requirements in each competency domain. This enables candidates to identify specific areas where training and/or job experience is necessary before testing for CIAC Certification. Self-Assessments are available for each domain at www.ciac-cert.org.

Candidates can view and/or download the CIAC Certification 'Preparing to Test Orientation' presentation at www.ciac-cert.org.



## RE-CERTIFICATION

Achieving CIAC Certification represents demonstrated mastery of the full range of required competencies for the job role. This first step demonstrates a commitment to continual learning and ongoing professional development. Re-certification is the mechanism by which a CIAC-Certified Professional demonstrates currency of expertise and maintains a competitive edge.

To maintain active CIAC Certification, the candidate completes a Master Knowledge Assessment based on current competency requirements every three (3) years from the first date of CIAC Certification issuance. To avoid a lapse in certification, the re-certification process should be completed prior to expiration of current CIAC Certification. Re-certification is available only in the current CIAC-Certified designation (e.g., CIAC-Certified Operations Manager re-certifies as same).

CIAC strongly encourages that certified professionals actively participate in industry/profession-specific professional development activities such as attending and speaking at conferences; authoring articles; active membership in industry associations; and completing related educational courses/programs.

## ELIGIBILITY FOR CIAC CERTIFICATION

To qualify for CIAC Certification candidates must meet all of the requirements outlined in this Handbook.

### Criteria for CIAC Certification

The criteria for CIAC Certification have been developed based on industry input as well as research of other successful certification programs.

Requirements for the Management Track designations are as follows:

- **CIAC-Certified Strategic Leader** – CIAC Certification in this designation requires a minimum of one year of experience in a contact center strategic management role. A minimum score of 75 percent is required on each of four knowledge assessments that are based on role-specific competencies; on the 360° Review a mean score of 3.0 (on a scale of 0 – 5) is required for each competency area and a 3.5 is required for the total 360° Review. Candidates must pass all knowledge assessments to receive the Work Product Assignment. All CIAC Certification testing must be completed within two years from the date the first assessment is taken.

- **CIAC-Certified Operations Manager** – CIAC Certification in this designation requires a minimum of one year of experience in a contact center operational management role. A minimum score of 75 percent is required on each of four knowledge assessments that are based on role-specific competencies; on the 360° Review a mean score of 3.0 (on a scale of 0 – 5) is required for each competency area and a 3.5 is required for the total 360° Review. Candidates must pass all knowledge assessments to receive the Work Product Assignment. All CIAC Certification testing must be completed within two years from the date the first assessment is taken.

- **CIAC-Certified Management Apprentice** – CIAC Certification in this designation requires a minimum score of 70 percent on each of four knowledge assessments that are based on role-specific competencies. This designation does not complete a Work Product Assignment or 360° Review. All CIAC Certification testing must be completed within two years from the date the first assessment is taken.

- **CIAC-Certified Management Consultant** – CIAC Certification in this designation requires a minimum score of 75 percent on each of four knowledge assessments that are based on role-specific competencies. This designation does not complete a Work Product Assignment or 360° Review. All CIAC Certification testing must be completed within two years from the date the first assessment is taken.

## CIAC Certification Process

Each candidate (person) is required to complete the following process:

1. Candidate determines his/her appropriate role designation (CIAC-Certified Strategic Leader; CIAC-Certified Operations Manager, etc.).

2. Candidate completes the Self-Assessments to identify knowledge and skill gaps and to determine training need(s) before testing. Self-Assessments for each domain are available at www.ciac-cert.org.

3. Candidate acquires any necessary training or on-the-job experience. CIAC does not dictate how competence is acquired.

4. Candidate logs onto the CIAC Certification Online Registration System to initiate the CIAC Certification process. The online registration system is accessed through the CIAC Certification web site at www.ciac-cert.org by clicking ***Register*** on the homepage. This links the candidate to the online registration system at www.ciaccertification.com. Upon entry to the registration system, the candidate first creates a Profile following the outlined procedures:

   a) The CIAC Certification screen will appear. Click ***Register***.

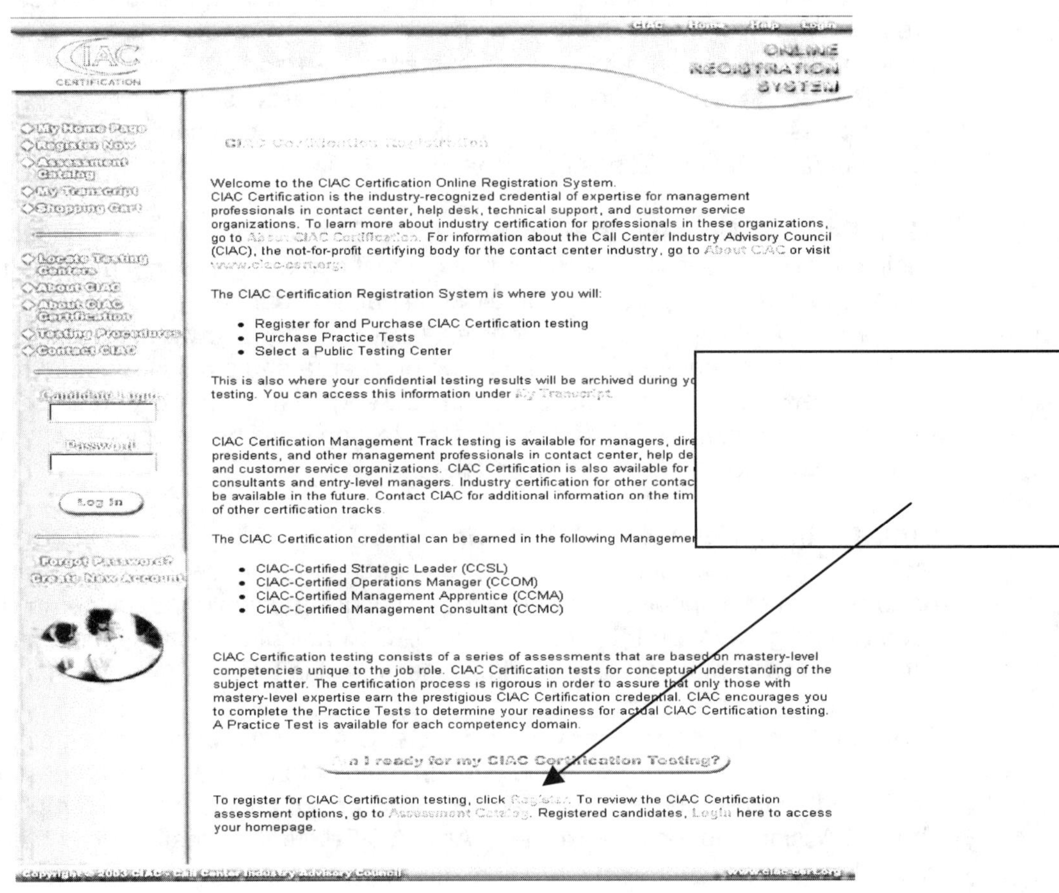

**Note:** The below screen will appear:

- Candidate Login: Created by candidate for login to registration system.
- First Name, Last Name, Email address.
- Secret Word: Created by candidate and used for ID purposes when contacting CIAC.
- Phone, Company Name, Title.
- Candidate selects his/her role designation.
- Tell us how you heard about CIAC Certification.

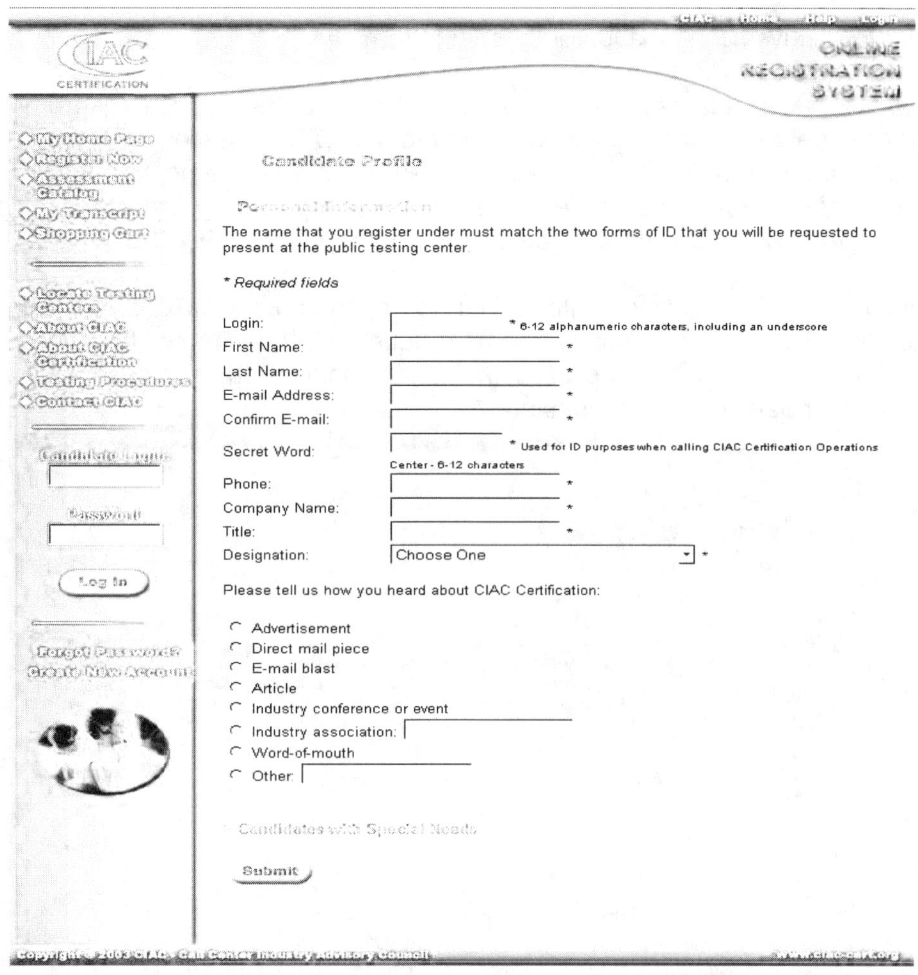

CIAC | Home | Help | Login

CIAC CERTIFICATION

ONLINE REGISTRATION SYSTEM

My Home Page
Register Now
Assessment Catalog
My Transcript
Shopping Cart

Locate Testing Centers
About CIAC
About CIAC Certification
Testing Procedures
Contact CIAC

Candidate Login

Password

Log In

Forgot Password?
Create New Account

Candidate Profile

Personal Information

The name that you register under must match the two forms of ID that you will be requested to present at the public testing center.

* Required fields

Login: * 6-12 alphanumeric characters, including an underscore
First Name: *
Last Name: *
E-mail Address: *
Confirm E-mail: *
Secret Word: * Used for ID purposes when calling CIAC Certification Operations Center - 6-12 characters
Phone: *
Company Name: *
Title: *
Designation: Choose One *

Please tell us how you heard about CIAC Certification:

- Advertisement
- Direct mail piece
- E-mail blast
- Article
- Industry conference or event
- Industry association:
- Word-of-mouth
- Other:

Candidates with Special Needs

Submit

Copyright © 2003 CIAC - Call Center Industry Advisory Council    www.ciac-cert.org

Click ***Submit*** to Continue

**Note:** A registration notification is automatically emailed to the candidate. This notification will have the candidate's login and system-generated password to be used when logging onto his/her CIAC Certification homepage at www.ciaccertification.com.

Candidates purchasing CIAC Certification testing at a price different than the Standard North American Published Price should contact the CIAC Certification Operations Center or CIAC Certification Reseller to complete the purchase transaction.

5. Candidate logs onto the Registration System using the login and password received by email to purchase certification assessment(s).

6. Candidate selects the Register-Purchase Link.

7. Candidate specifies certification track and role designation.

8. Candidate selects type of purchase. CIAC Certification can be purchased as a "package"; a single assessment; or any combination of assessments.

9. Candidate selects testing center and testing date, if applicable. If testing will be conducted at an employer site, CIAC coordinates with the appropriate contact to arrange for the required testing environment.

10. Candidate purchases CIAC Certification.

11. Candidate receives confirmation of purchase from CIAC.

    *Optional:* Candidates are encouraged to purchase the Practice Test(s) before testing in order to determine their readiness to test for CIAC Certification. A Practice Test is available for each domain and can be taken online at any time and at the candidate's choice of location. Practice Tests may be purchased at www.ciaccertification.com or by calling the CIAC Certification Operations Center at 888-859-2422 or 615-373-2376.

12. The first time a candidate logs onto his/her homepage on the CIAC Certification Online Registration System, the candidate will be requested to provide additional profile information. To do this, select ***Edit Profile***. Additional information such as work and company information will be requested.

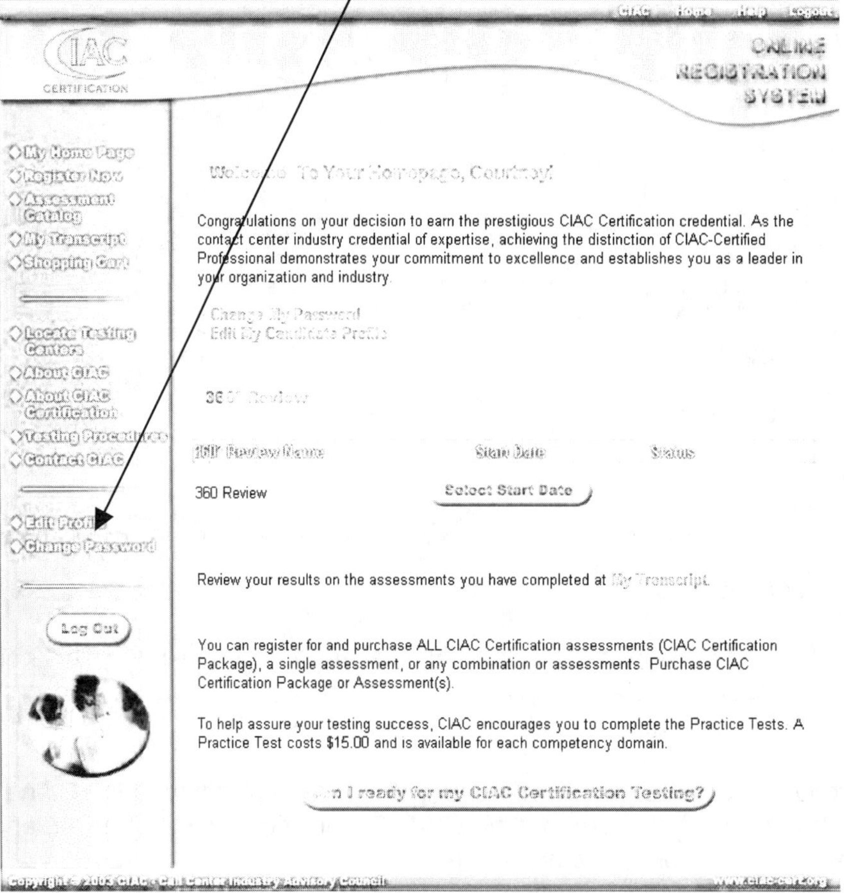


13. Candidate is responsible to contact the selected testing center to schedule date and time to take each knowledge assessment.

14. Candidate initiates 360° Review by logging onto his/her homepage and selecting a start date (the 360° Review may be completed at any time during the certification process).

15. Candidate selects 360° Review start date by clicking ***Select Start Date*** or selects a date in the future.

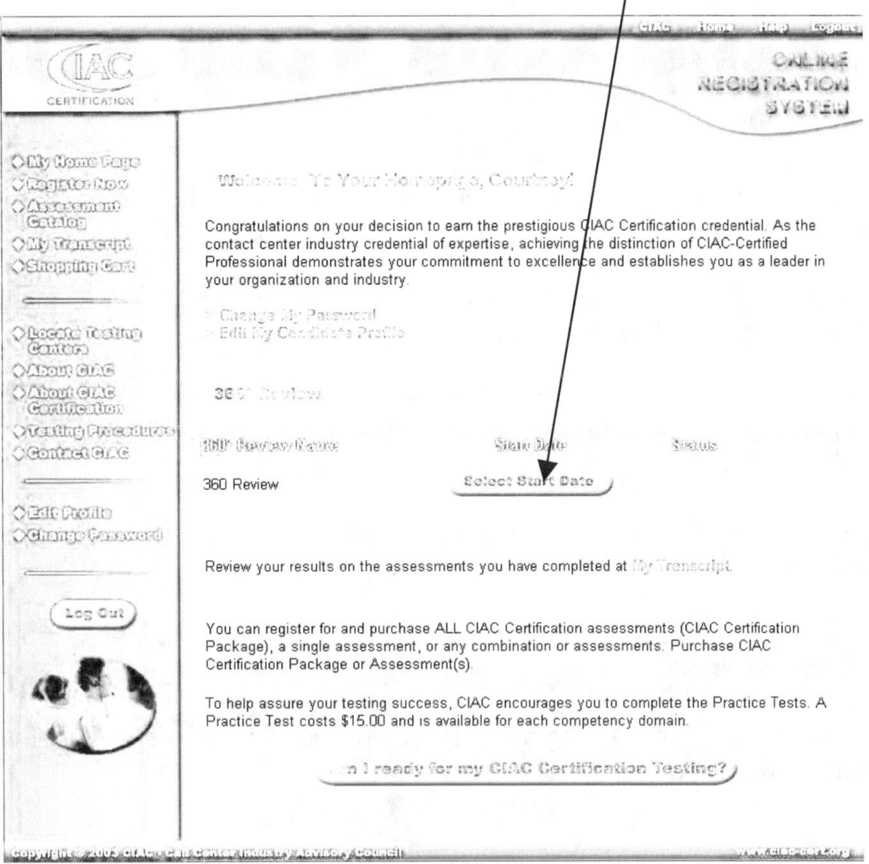


**Note:** A candidate will have the option to choose whether to start the 360° Review process now or designate a future start date.

16. Upon the specified start date, CIAC issues the 360° Review instrument to the candidate and the candidate's designated raters. Candidate and raters complete the 360° Review and submit it to CIAC. A mean value of 3.0 is required in each competency group and for the overall 360° Review a score of 3.5 is required (on a scale of 0 – 5). (Candidates for Management Apprentice and Management Consultant certification do not complete the 360° Review).

17. Candidate receives 360° Review Feedback Report from CIAC. If the required score is not achieved on the 360° Review, candidate completes a Professional Development Plan. Another 360° Review must be completed within twelve (12) months.

18. Candidate receives a PASS/FAIL score upon completion of each knowledge assessment with feedback indicating the scoring outcome per competency sub-category. Scoring notification is issued to the address provided in the candidate's Profile.

    a. If the minimum required score is not achieved on any assessment, the candidate refers to CIAC-provided feedback to determine additional training needs and acquires additional competence.
    b. Candidate registers to retest.
    c. Candidate retakes knowledge assessment(s).

19. Candidate receives "Certificate of Completion" by postal mail for each PASSED assessment and his/her official transcript is updated accordingly.

20. Candidate is issued a role-specific Work Product Assignment when all knowledge assessments are successfully completed. (Candidates for Management Apprentice and Management Consultant certification are not required to complete the Work Product Assignment).

21. Candidate completes the online Work Product Assignment and secures manager's review and sign-off. Manager approved Work Product is submitted to CIAC.

22. CIAC evaluates the Work Product and issues candidate a complete/incomplete status and feedback based on completeness and accuracy of outcome.

23. If the Work Product is incomplete or does not receive a PASS score, candidate utilizes CIAC provided feedback to complete the Work Product Assignment. Candidates are allowed fifteen (15) workdays to complete the Work Product Assignment.

24. After successful completion of all certification assessments, CIAC verifies the candidate has met full requirements.

25. Candidate is awarded the CIAC Certification credential for his/her role and Candidate's Official Transcript is updated.

26. Candidate must re-certify by passing a Master Knowledge Assessment every three (3) years to maintain an active CIAC Certification credential.

Refer to the CIAC Certification Handbook for additional information on each step of the certification process. Go to www.ciac-cert.org to view and/or download the handbook.

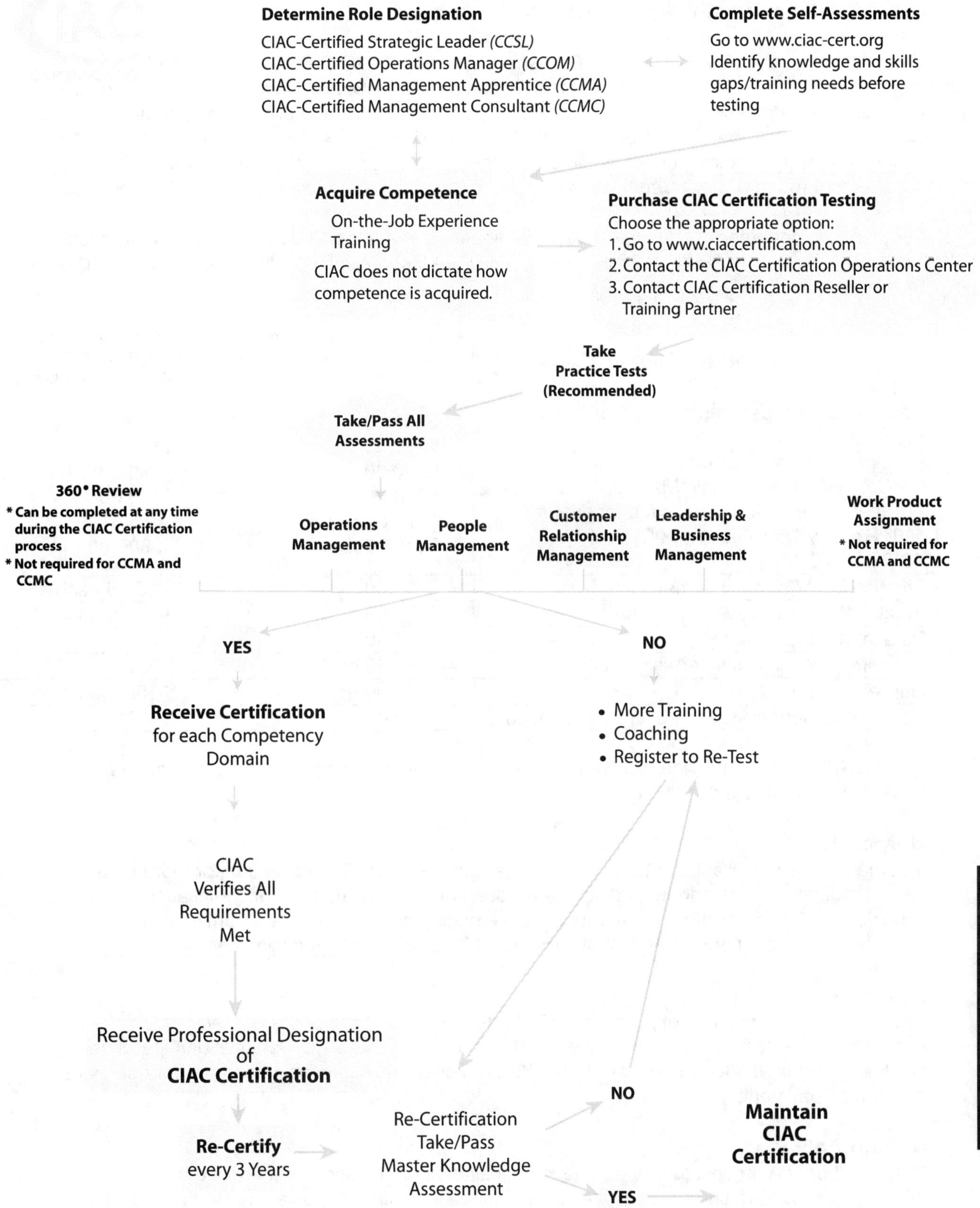

**Determine Role Designation**

CIAC-Certified Strategic Leader *(CCSL)*
CIAC-Certified Operations Manager *(CCOM)*
CIAC-Certified Management Apprentice *(CCMA)*
CIAC-Certified Management Consultant *(CCMC)*

**Complete Self-Assessments**

Go to www.ciac-cert.org
Identify knowledge and skills gaps/training needs before testing

**Acquire Competence**

On-the-Job Experience
Training

CIAC does not dictate how competence is acquired.

**Purchase CIAC Certification Testing**

Choose the appropriate option:

1. Go to www.ciaccertification.com
2. Contact the CIAC Certification Operations Center
3. Contact CIAC Certification Reseller or Training Partner

**Take Practice Tests (Recommended)**

**Take/Pass All Assessments**

**360° Review**
* **Can be completed at any time during the CIAC Certification process**
* **Not required for CCMA and CCMC**

**Operations Management**

**People Management**

**Customer Relationship Management**

**Leadership & Business Management**

**Work Product Assignment**
* **Not required for CCMA and CCMC**

**YES**

**Receive Certification** for each Competency Domain

CIAC Verifies All Requirements Met

Receive Professional Designation of **CIAC Certification**

**Re-Certify** every 3 Years

Re-Certification Take/Pass Master Knowledge Assessment

**YES**

**Maintain CIAC Certification**

**NO**

- More Training
- Coaching
- Register to Re-Test

## PRICING AND PAYMENT

### CIAC Certification Management Track Pricing

The pricing shown below is *Standard Published* pricing for CIAC Certification testing for a single purchase of CIAC Certification testing for individuals in the U.S. and Canada. Volume pricing is available for the purchase of three or more CIAC Certification testing packages. Contact the CIAC Certification Operations Center at 888-859-2422 or 615-373-2376 or by email at info@ciac-cert.org for information on volume pricing and other special offers. If testing is purchased through a CIAC Certification Reseller contact this organization for information.

For pricing in countries outside the U.S. and Canada, contact the CIAC Certification Operations Center by phone at 615-373-2376 or email at info@ciac-cert.org for the name of the local CIAC Certification Reseller.

| STANDARD PUBLISHED PRICING | *Certified Strategic Leader & Certified Operations Manager* | *Certified Apprentice & Certified Consultant (no Work Product or 360°)* |
|---|---|---|
| **Knowledge Assessments** (with Work Product): | | |
| ▪ People Management | $280.00 | $150.00 |
| ▪ Operations Management | $280.00 | $150.00 |
| ▪ Customer Relationship Management | $280.00 | $150.00 |
| ▪ Leadership and Business Management | $280.00 | $150.00 |
| **360° Review with Feedback Report** | $ 75.00 | NA |
| TOTAL | **$1195.00** | **$600.00** |
| Practice Test (for each domain) | $ 15.00 each | $ 15.00 each |
| Retake a Knowledge Assessment | $ 75.00 each | $ 75.00 each |
| Retake the 360° Review | $ 75.00 each | NA |
| Resubmit a Work Product Assignment | $ 75.00 each | NA |
| Official Transcripts | $ 15.00 each | $ 15.00 each |
| Master Knowledge Assessment (recertification) | $225.00 | $225.00 |

While CIAC strives to provide high value for the fees charged, pricing is subject to change based on marketplace conditions.

### Corporate Pricing

Volume pricing is available for organizations that purchase CIAC Certification for more than three candidates. The amount of discount is based on the total number of certification candidates. For more information about volume pricing contact the CIAC Certification Operations Center at 888-859-2422 or 615-373-2376 or email at info@ciac-cert.org.

### Payment

Payment is due at the time of purchase. Methods of Payment are check or credit card. Purchase Orders are accepted from organizations. Contact the CIAC Certification Operations Center by phone at 888-859-2422 or 615-373-2376 or email at info@ciac-cert.org for questions concerning payment.

### Refund Policy

CIAC will honor a request for refund due to cancellation of an assessment based on the following policy. A refund request must be submitted in writing by postal mail to the address provided in the front of this Handbook or by email to info@ciac-cert.org. For questions about obtaining a refund or to discuss a refund contact the CIAC Certification Operations Center at 888-859-2422 or 615-373-2376.

- CIAC's General Policy for cancellation of an assessment less than sixty-one (61) days from date of purchase:

  CIAC's first choice for a request to cancel an assessment within sixty (60) days of its original purchase is to grant full credit toward a future purchase on an open account basis. If requested, the full payment amount will be refunded. A credit or payment refund will be issued to the organization. In the event of a full refund, if payment was by check, CIAC's refund will be by check. If payment was by credit card, the card of origin will be credited.

- CIAC's General Policy for cancellation of assessments greater than sixty-one (61) days but less than one (1) year from date of purchase:

  CIAC will issue full credit toward a future purchase on an open account basis per the above crediting procedures. Requests for a payment refund will be charged a 25% processing fee per assessment.

- CIAC's General Policy for cancellations of assessments greater than one year from date of purchase:

  Outside of extenuating circumstances, CIAC will not grant credit for or issue a payment refund for cancellation of an assessment purchased more than one year ago.

- CIAC's General Policy for cancellations of an assessment purchased as part of "a package" regardless of date of purchase:

  CIAC will honor a request to cancel one or a portion of assessments purchased as "a package" by issuing a pro-rated credit on the basis that each of the assessments not cancelled will be calculated at the then prevailing full retail price of a stand-alone assessment. These stand-alone amounts will be deducted from the package price and the difference will be refunded to the originating purchaser less 25% processing fee.

### Ineligibility of Refund

In some instances, CIAC will not refund registration fees. These situations include:

- Refund requests made by telephone. Refund requests must be made in writing (email is acceptable).
- Failure to take a scheduled assessment (no show).
- For the 360° Review, after the review instrument has been distributed.
- Transcripts once processed.

## REVIEW AND NOTIFICATIONS

### Denial and Revocation of CIAC Certification

CIAC Certification will be denied or revoked for any of the following reasons:

- Failure to pass required certification assessments.
- Violation of certification assessment procedures and/or policies.
- Falsification of information.
- Not completing certification requirements within the allowed time (two years from the date the first assessment is taken).
- Failure to meet re-certification requirements.

A candidate may appeal for reconsideration by submitting a written appeal to the CIAC President stating the reason(s) for the request. CIAC will review the appeal and notify the candidate of the resulting decision.

### Address Change

All correspondence and assessment scores will be sent to the postal or email address specified in the Candidate Profile. In the event of a change in this information, the candidate can revise his/her contact information by following the instructions to "Edit Profile" in the online registration system. The candidate may also contact the CIAC Certification Operations Center at 888-859-2422 or 615-373-2376 to request a change of mailing or email address. CIAC will issue a confirmation to verify the change of information.

### Assessment Date Change (Reschedule)

To change a confirmed assessment date and time, the candidate is required to contact the test center where he/she is registered to test. To change from one test center to another, it will be necessary for the candidate to notify the CIAC Certification Operations Center.

### Accommodations for Candidates with Disabilities

CIAC complies with all laws and regulations pertaining to persons with disabilities and makes every reasonable effort to accommodate the needs of disabled or impaired candidates. In order to accommodate the special needs of disabled or impaired candidates, CIAC requests these candidates contact the CIAC Certification Operations Center at 888-859-2422 or 616-373-2376 to discuss the needed accommodations.

Below are a few examples of special needs:

- Candidate requires the services of a test reader because of vision impairment.
- Candidate needs someone to operate the keyboard due to a physical handicap.
- Candidate needs a time extension because of a learning disability.

Candidates with special needs are required to submit a form identifying the type of accommodation requested. In some cases, a physician's name may be required. When approved, CIAC will contact the test center to arrange for the necessary accommodations and/or assistance. CIAC will make every effort to expedite requirements to accommodate disabled candidates. Please note that this process can take up to thirty (30) days after notification to complete.

## CIAC Certification Testing

### Public Testing Centers

Testing for CIAC Certification is offered at authorized public testing centers. A listing of authorized public testing centers by location is available at www.ciaccertification.com or by calling the CIAC Certification Operations Center at 888-859-2422 or 615-373-2376 or local CIAC Certification Reseller.

### Onsite Testing

As an alternative to public testing centers, organizations with multiple candidates can administer CIAC Certification testing onsite. A proctor is required for onsite testing and certain other conditions must be met to ensure a high integrity-testing environment. CIAC will work with the organization's human resources or training department to arrange for onsite testing. Contact the CIAC Certification Operations Center at 888-859-2422 or 615-373-2376 for information about onsite testing.

## Testing Center Policies

### Test Area Admission - General Policies

- Only individuals actively engaged in CIAC Certification testing are permitted in the testing room. Any other persons accompanying the candidate must wait in the lobby area of the testing center. Unaccompanied children are not allowed at the Test Center.
- Personal items may not be taken into the testing room. This includes bags, purses, hats, briefcases, books, beepers, cell phones, calculators, palm pilots and watches. All personal items will be placed in a secure storage compartment provided by the test center and the candidate will retain the key during the test session. All electrical equipment must be turned off before the item is placed in the storage compartment so as not to disrupt the testing environment. Items too large to be stored in the compartment must be stored off the premises. Candidates must keep their identification with them at all times.
- Tobacco products, food, drink, and chewing gum are not allowed in the testing room.

### Before the Test Session

- A proctor will escort the candidate to the testing room.
- The candidate's assessment will be loaded at the designated workstation.
- Study materials or scratch paper cannot be brought into the testing area. The proctor can provide scratch paper if needed.
- Any papers used by the candidate while testing will be collected at the end of the test, including scrap paper.
- If needed, the proctor will provide a calculator upon request.

### During the Test Session

- Do not attempt to browse outside of the "testing window" or access the Internet. This will cause automatic submittal of the assessment for scoring.
- Do not click the 'Submit' button until the assessment is completed and ready to be submitted for scoring.
- Three hours is allowed to complete each knowledge assessment. Break time is not built into the time allotted for testing. If a break is necessary, the clock will continue to run, decreasing the amount of time remaining to complete the assessment. If a break is

taken the candidate must sign out/in using the "Sign-in/Sign-out Log". The assessment will be terminated if the candidate leaves the testing room without notifying the proctor. Personal belongings may not be accessed during a break.

### Candidate Misconduct

If a candidate engages in misconduct the proctor will request the behavior to cease. If the behavior persists, the candidate will be requested to leave the testing room and the assessment will be terminated. The following behaviors are considered misconduct:

- Giving or receiving assistance of any kind during the assessment.
- Using prohibited aids.
- Attempting to take the test for someone else.
- Attempting to remove scratch paper from the testing room.
- Talking with other candidates during testing.
- Tampering with the operation of the computer or attempting to use it for any function other than taking the test.
- Distracting any other candidate in any way from taking their assessment.

### Reasons to Notify the Proctor

- Loss of Internet connection.
- Technical problems with the testing software.
- Need to leave the testing room.
- Disruptive behavior from other test candidates.
- Uncomfortable testing environment.

*The proctor cannot answer any questions concerning the assessments.*

### After Submittal of CIAC Certification Assessment

- Candidate will be prompted to inform the proctor to end the testing session.
- Changes are not allowed once the assessment has been submitted.
- Assessment results will be emailed to candidate's registered email address. The proctor or any other employee of the test center does not have access to test results.
- Test Center computers are for assessment purposes only.

***Refer to the CIAC Certification web site www.ciac-cert.org for Frequently Asked Questions and Answers.***

Section 12

# *About ICMI*

## About Incoming Calls Management Institute

Incoming Calls Management Institute (ICMI), based in Annapolis, Maryland, offers the most comprehensive educational resources available for call center (contact center, interaction center, help desk) management professionals. ICMI's focus is helping individuals and organizations understand the dynamics of today's customer contact environment in order to improve performance and achieve superior business results. From the world's first seminar on incoming call center management, to the first conference on call center/Internet integration and subsequent research on multichannel integration, ICMI is a recognized global leader. Quality, usability and value have become trademarks of ICMI's award-winning services. ICMI is independent and is not associated with, owned or subsidized by any industry supplier; ICMI's only source of funding is from those who use its services.

**ICMI's services include:**

- Public and onsite (private) seminars
- Web seminars and e-learning courses
- Certification review seminars and study guides
- Industry studies and research papers
- Consulting services
- Software tools for scheduling and analysis
- Books (including the industry's best-selling book, *Call Center Management on Fast Forward*)
- *QueueTips*, the popular (and free) monthly e-newsletter
- Membership in Incoming Calls Management Institute
- *Call Center Management Review*, the authoritative monthly journal for ICMI members

For more information and to join a network of call center leaders, see www.incoming.com

Incoming Calls Management Institute
Post Office Box 6177
Annapolis, Maryland 21401
410-267-0700 • 800-672-6177
icmi@incoming.com
www.incoming.com

## Bring This Content to Life in Your Own Organization!

Want to instill the most important principles from this series into the culture and operational dynamics of your organization? What would it be worth to have your entire management team truly working in sync to create services that generate loyalty and create exceptional value?

ICMI's powerful educational seminars provide you with real-world solutions to help you improve performance and achieve better business results. Benefits of bringing one of ICMI's seminars into your organization include:

- Content is based on the experiences and practices of the world's leading call centers.
- Programs are delivered by the industry's top facilitators.
- Content is tailored to your specific environment.
- Courses build a common understanding throughout your organization.
- ICMI's first-hand knowledge of the call center environment eliminates misconceptions and fads from the seminar content.
- You are guaranteed an objective, educational experience, since ICMI is independent and is not associated with, owned or subsidized by any industry supplier.
- Learning occurs in a stimulating atmosphere that is both productive and fun!

Visit www.incoming.com for a current listing of Web-based, public and in-house seminars. Or contact ICMI at 410-267-0700, or icmi@incoming.com

## ICMI's Mission

Incoming Calls Management Institute (ICMI) exists solely to advance the call center profession by promoting managerial excellence. We are dedicated to fostering the development of a new breed of call center management professionals – individuals with the vision, expertise, and commitment necessary to enable their respective organizations to thrive in an era of fast-changing, networked economies, global competition and heightened customer expectations.

## Order Form

| QTY. | Item | Price | Total |
|---|---|---|---|
| | **ICMI Handbook and Study Guide Series** | | |
| | Module 1: People Management*** | $199.00 | |
| | Module 2: Operations Management*** | $199.00 | |
| | Module 3: Customer Relationship Management*** | $199.00 | |
| | Module 4: Leadership and Business Management*** | $199.00 | |
| | Call Center Management On Fast Forward: Succeeding In Today's Dynamic Inbound Environment | | |
| | Book** | $34.95 | |
| | Cassette set, 6 tapes** | $49.95 | |
| | Book and Cassette tape set bundle*** | $69.95 | |
| | Call Center Technology Demystified: The No-Nonsense Guide to Bridging Customer Contact Technology, Operations and Strategy** | $39.95 | |
| | **Topical Books: The Best of *Call Center Management Review*** | | |
| | Call Center Recruiting and New Hire Training* | $16.95 | |
| | Call Center Forecasting and Scheduling* | $16.95 | |
| | Call Center Agent Motivation and Compensation* | $16.95 | |
| | Call Center Agent Retention and Turnover* | $16.95 | |
| | **Industry Studies** | | |
| | Monitoring Study Final Report II (published 2002)* | $99.00 | |
| | Multichannel Call Center Study (published 2001)* | $99.00 | |
| | Agent Staffing and Retention Study (published 2000)* | $79.00 | |
| | **Forms Books** | | |
| | Call Center Sample Monitoring Forms* | $49.95 | |
| | Call Center Sample Customer Satisfaction Forms Book* | $49.95 | |
| | **Software** | | |
| | QueueView: A Staffing Calculator – CD ROM* | $49.00 | |
| | Easy Start™ Call Center Scheduler Software – CD-ROM* | $299.00 | |
| | Call Center Manager's Jump-Start Toolkit**** | $279.00 | |
| | Call Center Humor: The Best of *Call Center Management Review* Volume 3* | $9.95 | |
| | The Call Centertainment Book* | $8.95 | |
| | Shipping & Handling @ $5.00 per US shipment, plus .50¢ per* item, $1.00 per** item, $2.00 per*** item and $3.00 per**** item. Additional charges apply to shipments outside the US. | | |
| | Tax (5% MD residents, 7% GST Canadian residents) | | |
| | TOTAL (US dollars) | | |

Please contact us for quantity discounts

For more information on our products, please visit **www.incoming.com**

## Order Form

☐ Please send me a free issue of *Call Center Management Review* (ICMI's journal for members) and information on ICMI's publications, services and membership.

Please ship my order and/or information to:

Name ______________________________

Title ______________________________

Industry ______________________________

Company ______________________________

Address ______________________________

City ____________________ State ________ Postal Code __________

Telephone (        ) ______________________________

Fax (        ) ______________________________

Email ______________________________

Method of Payment (if applicable)

☐ Check enclosed (Make payable to ICMI Inc.; U.S. Dollars only)

☐ Charge to: ☐ American Express ☐ MasterCard ☐ Visa

Account No. ______________________________

Expiration Date ______________________________

Name on Card ______________________________

Fax order to: 410-267-0962
call us at: 800-672-6177
410-267-0700
order online at: www.incoming.com
or mail order to: ICMI Inc.
P.O. Box 6177, Annapolis, MD 21401

## About the Authors

**Brad Cleveland** is President and CEO of Annapolis, Maryland based Incoming Calls Management Institute. Recognized for his pioneering work in call center management, he has advised organizations ranging from small start-ups to national governments and multinational corporations, and has delivered keynotes and seminars in over 25 countries. Brad has appeared in a wide range of media, including *The Washington Post, Wall Street Journal*, and on PBS, CNBC and Knowledge TV. His critically-acclaimed book, *Call Center Management on Fast Forward: Succeeding in Today's Dynamic Inbound Environment*, co-authored with journalist Julia Mayben, is used by call center managers around the world.

**Debbie Harne** is Director of Educational Services for ICMI, and spearheaded the launch of ICMI Membership, a network of management professionals from over 40 countries. With a background in training and education, Debbie has been instrumental in developing ICMI's technology-based educational services, and has responsibilities for the quality and direction of ICMI's instructor-led and Web-based management seminars. She is proficient in instructional design and ensuring the transfer of training to the job, and has customized ICMI educational services for innovative, in-house study programs in a variety of companies.

### How to Contact the Authors

Do you have suggestions for future editions? Comments? Feedback? Please contact us!

Incoming Calls Management Institute
Post Office Box 6177
Annapolis, Maryland 21401
410-267-0700 • 800-672-6177
icmi@incoming.com
www.incoming.com
Brad Cleveland, direct: bradc@incoming.com
Debbie Harne, direct: debbieh@incoming.com